School Counseling Practicum and Internship

I would like to dedicate this book to my husband, Dr. Thomas Spierling, and my children, Amanda Buchanan Scott and Sean William Buchanan. My family and friends are my world.

SAGE was founded in 1965 by Sara Miller McCune to support the dissemination of usable knowledge by publishing innovative and high-quality research and teaching content. Today, we publish over 900 journals, including those of more than 400 learned societies, more than 800 new books per year, and a growing range of library products including archives, data, case studies, reports, and video. SAGE remains majority-owned by our founder, and after Sara's lifetime will become owned by a charitable trust that secures our continued independence.

Los Angeles | London | New Delhi | Singapore | Washington DC | Melbourne

School Counseling Practicum and Internship

30 Essential Lessons

Helen S. Hamlet
Kutztown University

Los Angeles | London | New Delhi
Singapore | Washington DC | Melbourne

FOR INFORMATION:

SAGE Publications, Inc.
2455 Teller Road
Thousand Oaks, California 91320
E-mail: order@sagepub.com

SAGE Publications Ltd.
1 Oliver's Yard
55 City Road
London, EC1Y 1SP
United Kingdom

SAGE Publications India Pvt. Ltd.
B 1/I 1 Mohan Cooperative Industrial Area
Mathura Road, New Delhi 110 044
India

SAGE Publications Asia-Pacific Pte. Ltd.
3 Church Street
#10-04 Samsung Hub
Singapore 049483

Acquisitions Editor: Nathan Davidson
Development Editor: Abbie Rickard
eLearning Editor: Morgan Shannon
Editorial Assistant: Carrie Montoya
Production Editor: Libby Larson
Copy Editor: Diane DiMura
Typesetter: C&M Digitals (P) Ltd.
Proofreader: Dennis W. Webb
Indexer: Molly Hall
Cover Designer: Glenn Vogel
Marketing Manager: Shari Countryman

Printed in the United States of America

Library of Congress Cataloging-in-Publication Data

ISBN 978-1-5063-0487-8

This book is printed on acid-free paper.

16 17 18 19 20 10 9 8 7 6 5 4 3 2 1

CONTENTS

PREFACE

This book is a result of collaboration, consultation, and an abiding respect for the integrity, expertise, and collegiality of my colleagues. No counselor educator works in a vacuum. Reaching out to colleagues and experts in the field is best practice. Not a day passes that I haven't touched base with a colleague—"just to make sure." My strongest recommendation as students prepare to enter the field of counseling is to network, consult, be humble, and know that none of us knows it all.

Counselors are faced with unique circumstances and situations on a daily basis. After years of experience, I can attest to "not knowing" until a student walks into my office and presents the unique situation of his or her life and worldview. With this in the forefront, the 30 lessons in *School Counseling Practicum and Internship* are grounded in the knowledge that every interaction develops within and is influenced by the individuals' context and frame of reference.

School Counseling Practicum and Internship incorporates current information and resources from experts in the field of school counseling into a collection of lessons and techniques. These lessons and strategies provide critical information needed to work in the field of school counseling. This book especially provides resources for counselors who find themselves in those "not knowing" situations. For example, what if . . .

- a 15-year-old student decides that his identity is that of a transgendered individual and is seeking your assistance in managing the day-to-day challenges of his changing identity?
- a 17-year-old student with high-functioning autism requests your support in deciding between going directly into the workforce or going to college?
- the school district has assigned the development of the PreK–12 professional school core curriculum to your team?

These situations challenge the school counselor to rely not only on his or her own knowledge, but also the input of other professionals. This book provides all of this in one resource.

School Counseling Practicum and Internship is a practical guide to the "real" world of professional school counseling.

ACKNOWLEDGMENTS

The colleagues who have contributed to this book gave of their time, provided their support, and shared their expertise. Many thanks and gratitude to the following: Patti Brenner, Theo Burnes, Tricia Walsh Coates, Susan Hansen, Stacey Havlik, Margaret Herrick, Denise Horton, Leonissa Johnson, Christy Land, Cheri Lovre, Kristin Malott, Lauren Moss, Tim Poynton, Heidi Roselle, Diane Shea, Sarah Springer, Malti Tuttle, and Brian Wlazelek.

My sincere gratitude goes to Dr. Fred Redekop. He encouraged me to write this book and provided a bridge for me to SAGE Publications.

I would like to thank the reviewers of this book for their input, guidance, and time spent. And, I would like to thank Kassie Graves, Carrie Montoya, and Abbie Rickards for shepherding me through the publication process.

INTRODUCTION

"Experience without theory is blind, but theory without experience is mere intellectual play."

—Immanuel Kant

Welcome to the field-experience phase of your graduate education in professional school counseling! The practicum and internship experiences and courses are a major component of the graduate training program in school counseling and are essential to the development of the requisite skill set. These field experiences are also a standard of practice identified by the American School Counseling Association (ASCA), Council for Accreditation of Counseling and Related Educational Professions (CACREP), and many states' Departments of Education. In light of the mandate for field experience, a comprehensive educational and field experience is essential. A guide providing structure, resources, and practical information from the field is a valuable resource. Hence, the purpose of this book is to provide you with 30 lesson plans, associated standards, and materials that you can take into the field and expand your knowledge.

Chapter 1 is the only lesson that has two sections: a practicum section and an internship section. This chapter lays the foundation and specifies the requirements for each of these individual field experiences. In addition, it addresses the professionalism required of a professional school counseling practicum and internship student.

Chapter 2 should be used for both practicum and internship experiences. This chapter focuses on getting to know the site and the site requirements, policies, and procedures. I have found that even if a counselor-in-training returns to the same site for internship, the site information they gleaned in practicum is far from comprehensive.

The other lessons address information and practical approaches with resources for situations and topics specific to the role and responsibilities of the school counselor. Each lesson in this book is present in lesson plan format. This format provides a model for use in developing curriculum and lessons. In addition to the model of lesson plan development, this book includes a plethora of resources and reproducible handouts.

Importantly, this book is based on years of experience in the field. It provides the information gained from hands-on, face-to-face interactions with students, parents, teachers, administrators, and community stakeholders. Counselors-in-training will be prepared for the challenges that occur in the daily life of a school counselor. This book addresses the "oh my goodness" moments—the practical side of school counseling.

Let's begin with a self-awareness reflection. How do you feel as you embark on the beginning of the field-experience aspect of your professional journey?

____

____

____

PART I

FOUNDATIONS

LESSON 1

GETTING STARTED

Real Life

Counselor-in-training: Prior to the first day of class, Melissa visits her faculty supervisor's office and announces she doesn't think this is the right time to do an internship. I asked her to tell me more about why she felt this way. Melissa went on to say that she had a great internship site and a wonderful supervisor who was looking forward to supervising this internship. Melissa shared that she was afraid that she would not be able to live up to all the obligations, responsibilities, and assignments required of an internship experience. She wasn't sure how she would manage standing in front of a classroom of students teaching a curriculum lesson because she was not a teacher and had never taught a lesson. Additionally, she feared that the students at her site wouldn't like her and none of them would want to work with her.

Faculty Supervisor: Listens empathically, expresses understanding and notes that every year multiple students express the same concerns and fears.

Lesson One

Getting Started

"What are the class and internship requirements?"

Essential Question: How do you get the most out of your practicum or internship and have a successful experience?

Objectives

Students will

- demonstrate an understanding of the professional behaviors required of a professional school counseling trainee.
- demonstrate an understanding of the purpose and requirements of the practicum and internship field experience.
- communicate the roles and responsibilities of the student, on-site supervisor, and faculty supervisor
- explain the assigned tasks and their purpose.
- communicate the information provided in the Practicum/Internship Handbook.
- accurately classify direct versus indirect service hours.
- collect data monitoring hours at site.

CACREP 2016 Standards (Appendix A)

- Knowledge of professional organizations, preparation standards, and credentials relevant to the practice of school counseling (5.G.2.l)

MPCAC Standards (Appendix B)

- Professional counselor identity, ethical behavior, and social-justice practices

Video Spark

https://www.youtube.com/watch?v=JAAsWDNcgtM

Thank You: School Counselors Make a Difference/2012 Fall Counselor Workshops (The College Board)

● INTRODUCTION

Professionalism

Although the school counseling practicum and internship experiences are learning experiences and coursework in your graduate education, the expectations are very high. At this point in your career, you have had multiple courses addressing ethics, orientation to the school counseling profession, counseling techniques, statistics and research, assessment, human growth and development, multicultural competencies, and career counseling to name a few. Field experience on-site supervisors are aware that you have had this coursework and know that experiences in the field should build on this large font of knowledge. The expectation is that you are not entering the field as a *tabula rasa* (blank slate) but as an engaged, well-educated and informed trainee. Now is the time to present as a professional while listening, learning, and respecting the practicum and internship growth and opportunities that these experiences provide.

First Impressions

Amy Cuddy (Cuddy, Kohut, & Neffinger, 2013), a Harvard Business School social psychologist, has studied first impressions. As a result of her studies, she found that two impressions, not one, are formed in that first impression. Cuddy's research indicates that when meeting someone new, the warmth and trustworthiness of the person is assessed in addition to assessing the strength and competence of the person. These two factors account for 80% to 90% of first impressions. Warmth, trustworthiness, and competence are the keystones to being a professional school counselor. If first impressions provide information on those qualities or characteristics to the field experience supervisors, than meticulous preparation for those first meetings are of extreme importance.

How do we make a good first impression? Nonverbal communication is essential in making a first impression. This can include everything from attire to facial expression to posture to arriving on time and respecting the schedule. When considering nonverbal communication, reflect upon your career goals. The goal is to eventually get a job as a professional school counselor. An important and well-known tenet in the business world is to dress for the position to which you aspire to not the position that you currently have, so dressing for the role of the professional school counselor makes sense. While being sensitive to local norms, dressing in a clean, neat, and professional style is recommended. Years ago, I worked in a grant program that focused on helping people transition from welfare to the workplace. I went to work every day dressed as though I was going to an interview. I wanted to "walk the walk" by modeling the behavior of what professional work attire is and demonstrating that you can be comfortable while "looking the part."

How to Demonstrate Professionalism in a School Counseling Field Experience

Present as a professional. Emily Driscoll (2013) writes that it is important for interns not to be too casual. She recommends to act naturally while dressing and acting professionally. Viewing an internship as an ***extended interview*** will help you stay focused on your role as a professional school counselor-in-training.

Dress as a professional. Dress for the job you want, not the position that you have. Dress consistent with the standards set by the professionals in the school.

Set and adhere to a schedule. Establishing a set schedule alleviates any miscommunication on when the intern is expected to arrive or leave. This also provides the opportunity for a mutual understanding of the site supervisor's expectations. E-mailing the schedule to the site supervisor is recommended.

Be respectful to all. Field experiences can be stressful. It is important to see beyond the stress and remember to treat each person with respect. As Albert Einstein said "I speak to everyone in the same way, whether he is the garbage man or the president of the university."

Be patient. As an intern, you are experiencing a new complex system. Demonstrate professionalism by exhibiting patience with the system and its requirements. For example, many schools prefer or require students to see the counselor during nonacademic periods only. Be patient and observe how the professional school counselors manage meeting students within these boundaries.

Be ethical. As a school counselor–in-training, you will experience complex varied situations for the first time. Collaborating with your site supervisor on how to proceed in an ethical manner is essential to professionalism.

Display competence. Competence is demonstrating that you can do what you say you can do. Competent individuals know the skills required in their role and demonstrate their developing mastery of those skills (JWilliams Staffing, 2016).

Be prepared. Preparation is essential to professionalism. Do the homework. For example, if you are running small groups, present your site supervisor with the overall schedule and content for each group meeting.

Seek supervision. Supervision is an essential part of the field experience. Seeking supervision demonstrates an awareness of your developing professional skills.

Demonstrate professionalism in use of technology. This area of professionalism ranges from crafting professional e-mails to turning off your mobile devices to the use of social networking. This area of professionalism is multifaceted. Information on the standards specific to the field experience site will be available through supervision or school district policy.

• PRACTICUM

CACREP Standards for Practicum

Students must complete supervised practicum experiences that total a minimum of 100 clock hours over a minimum 10-week academic term. Each student's practicum includes all of the following:

1. At least 40 clock hours of direct service with actual clients that contributes to the development of counseling skills
2. Weekly interaction that averages 1 hour per week of individual and/or triadic supervision throughout the practicum by a program faculty member, a student supervisor, or a site supervisor who is working in biweekly consultation with a program faculty member in accordance with the supervision contract
3. An average of 1½ hours per week of group supervision that is provided on a regular schedule throughout the practicum by a program faculty member or a student supervisor
4. The development of program-appropriate audio/video recordings for use in supervision or live supervision of the student's interactions with clients
5. Evaluation of the student's counseling performance throughout the practicum, including documentation of a formal evaluation after the student completes the practicum

MPCAC Standards for the Practicum/Internship experiences

At least two (2) academic terms of supervised field placement experiences that focus on issues related to the promotion of mental health, human development, wellness, cultural competence, and social justice advocacy (at least three semester hours or five quarter hours per academic term in a counseling and/or related human service setting with 300 hours of supervised field training).

The practicum/internship experience (commensurate with program goals and state licensure requirements) shall be completed under the clinical supervision of appropriately credentialed professionals (e.g., licensed professional counselor, social worker, marriage and family therapist, school counselor, psychologist, or physician with a specialty in psychiatry).

Practicum—Introduction

Beginning your practicum and internship experiences often evokes conflicting emotions—pleasure that you have reached this point in your professional development and anxiety about the requirements of these life-changing experiences. One tried and true method to reduce anxiety is to be prepared for the experience and knowledgeable about the expectations. Lesson 1 takes a step-by-step approach to introducing the course and field experience requirements for practicum and for internship.

The purpose of the **practicum** field experience is to gain a more in-depth understanding of the counseling process and what promotes effectiveness in counseling by presenting students with the latest research findings regarding best practices in the counseling field. Students will be presented with material on the following topics in order to improve their counseling and interpersonal skills: basic counseling skills, case conceptualization, assessment, treatment planning, multicultural competence, ethical applications, self-development, advocacy, and consultation. Students will spend some time in the field, and their progress will be monitored via on-site supervision and classroom interaction.

Practicum Reflection

What is your site and why did you select that site?

____

____

____

After hearing about your colleagues/classmates sites, what do you think you can learn from their experiences?

____

____

____

How do you feel starting your practicum experience?

____

____

____

If you have already been at your site, what was that experience like for you?

____

____

____

Share what you hope to get from this experience.

____

____

____

What specific skills you would like to learn more about in this practicum class?

____

____

____

Practicum Class Activities

- Review the **SKATES** form (Appendix C)
- Review the On-site Hours Logs (Appendix D)

● INTERNSHIP

CACREP Standards for Internship

The program requires completion of a supervised internship in the student's designated program area of 600 clock hours, begun after successful completion of the practicum. The internship is intended to reflect the comprehensive work experience of a professional counselor appropriate to the designated program area. Each student's internship includes all of the following:

1. At least 240 clock hours of direct service, including experience leading groups
2. Weekly interaction that averages 1 hour per week of individual and/or triadic supervision throughout the internship, usually performed by the onsite supervisor
3. An average of 1½ hours per week of group supervision provided on a regular schedule throughout the internship and performed by a program faculty member
4. The opportunity for the student to become familiar with a variety of professional activities and resources in addition to direct service (e.g., recordkeeping, assessment instruments, supervision, information and referral, in-service and staff meetings)
5. The opportunity for the student to develop program-appropriate audio/video recordings for use in supervision or to receive live supervision of his or her interactions with clients
6. Evaluation of the student's counseling performance throughout the internship, including documentation of a formal evaluation after the student completes the internship by a program faculty member in consultation with the site supervisor

MPCAC Standards for the Practicum/Internship Experiences

At least two (2) academic terms of supervised field placement experiences that focus on issues related to the promotion of mental health, human development, wellness, cultural competence, and social justice advocacy (at least three semester hours or five quarter hours per academic term in a counseling and/or related human service setting with 300 hours of supervised field training). The practicum/internship experience (commensurate with program goals and state licensure requirements) shall be completed under the clinical supervision of appropriately credentialed professionals (e.g., licensed professional counselor, social worker, marriage and family therapist, school counselor, psychologist, or physician with a specialty in psychiatry).

Internship

The purpose of the **internship** field experience is to integrate, apply, and refine the skills learned throughout the graduate program. Students will have direct experience and interaction with individuals and groups seeking counseling services. Supervision of this process takes place on-site and during a weekly seminar and experiences are reviewed through discussion, case studies/presentations, and videotape review/instruction. Students are expected to participate in the full range of counseling services working with a student population of varied background and problem areas. Students will acquire a personal knowledge of the school counseling process while developing their professional identity as a counselor. During internship, the counselors-in-training are expected to demonstrate their effectiveness as a school counselor.

Introductory Discussion

What is your site and why did you select this site?

____

____

____

How do you feel starting your internship experience?

____

____

____

What do you hope to get from this field experience?

____

____

____

Reflect upon your practicum experience. What experiences would you like to build upon? What would you like to do differently in internship vs. practicum?

____

____

____

Having completed practicum, what skills/knowledge do you feel you have learned and feel confident bringing to the internship experience?

____

____

____

What specific skills you would like to learn more about in this internship class?

____

____

____

Internship Class Activities

- Review the SKATES form (Appendix C)
- Review the On-Site Hours Logs (Appendix D)
- Review the Sample Timeline for On-Site Hours (Appendix E)

● REFERENCES

Cuddy, A., Kohut, M., & Neffinger, J. (2013). Connect, then lead. *Harvard Business Review, 91*(7–8), 54–61.

Council for Accreditation for Counseling and Related Program. (2014). *2016 Standards*. Retrieved from http://www.cacrep.org/for-programs/2016-cacrep-standards/

Driscoll, E. (2013). *Four intern mistakes to avoid*. Retrieved from http://www.foxbusiness.com/features/2013/05/28/4-intern-mistakes-to-avoid.html

JWilliams Staffing. (2013). *The core values of workplace professionalism*. Retrieved from http://www.jwilliamsstaffing.com/Blog/Blog-Detail/The-Core-Values-of-Workplace-Professionalism-4014.cfm

Masters in Psychology and Counseling Accreditation Council. (2015). *Accreditation Manual*. Retrieved from http://www.mpcacaccreditation.org/about/accreditation-manual

● APPENDIX A

Council for Accrediation of Counseling and Education 2016 Standards

Section 5: entry-level specialty areas

G. school counseling

Students who are preparing to specialize as school counselors will demonstrate the professional knowledge and skills necessary to promote the academic, career, and personal/social development of all P–12 students through data-informed school counseling programs. Counselor education programs with a specialty area in school counseling must document where each of the lettered standards listed below is covered in the curriculum.

1. FOUNDATIONS
   a. history and development of school counseling
   b. models of school counseling programs
   c. models of P–12 comprehensive career development
   d. models of school-based collaboration and consultation
   e. assessments specific to P–12 education

2. CONTEXTUAL DIMENSIONS
   a. school counselor roles as leaders, advocates, and systems change agents in P–12 schools
   b. school counselor roles in consultation with families, P–12 and postsecondary school personnel, and community agencies
   c. school counselor roles in relation to college and career readiness
   d. school counselor roles in school leadership and multidisciplinary teams
   e. school counselor roles and responsibilities in relation to the school emergency management plans, and crises, disasters, and trauma
   f. competencies to advocate for school counseling roles
   g. characteristics, risk factors, and warning signs of students at risk for mental health and behavioral disorders
   h. common medications that affect learning, behavior, and mood in children and adolescents
   i. signs and symptoms of substance abuse in children and adolescents as well as the signs and symptoms of living in a home where substance use occurs
   j. qualities and styles of effective leadership in schools
   k. community resources and referral sources
   l. professional organizations, preparation standards, and credentials relevant to the practice of school counseling
   m. legislation and government policy relevant to school counseling
   n. legal and ethical considerations specific to school counseling

3. PRACTICE
   a. development of school counseling program mission statements and objectives
   b. design and evaluation of school counseling programs
   c. core curriculum design, lesson plan development, classroom management strategies, and differentiated instructional strategies
   d. interventions to promote academic development
   e. use of developmentally appropriate career counseling interventions and assessments
   f. techniques of personal/social counseling in school settings
   g. strategies to facilitate school and postsecondary transitions
   h. skills to critically examine the connections between social, familial, emotional, and behavior problems and academic achievement
   i. approaches to increase promotion and graduation rates
   j. interventions to promote college and career readiness
   k. strategies to promote equity in student achievement and college access

l. techniques to foster collaboration and teamwork within schools
m. strategies for implementing and coordinating peer intervention programs
n. use of accountability data to inform decision making
o. use of data to advocate for programs and students

● APPENDIX B

Standards

1. Masters in Psychology and Counseling Accreditation Committee (MPCAC)

The standards for accreditation are intended as guidelines for the preparation of scientist-practitioners at the master's level in the counseling or closely related profession with an emphasis on multiculturalism and a social justice perspective. These standards should be dealt with in their entirety by a department's faculty undergoing a self-study in preparation for a site visit. The faculty should evaluate the program(s) against each standard as outlined in this manual.

1. The program should be identifiable as a counseling or closely related professional training program. This descriptor is to be defined primarily in terms of the coursework, field work, and disciplinary affiliations of those that teach in and administer the program.
2. The program should be the equivalent of at least two academic years of full-time study. This time period should include a **minimum** of 48 semester hours, or the equivalent quarter hours. Programs seeking MPCAC accreditation can include as many course credits/semester hours as appropriate that are consistent with the mission, philosophy, and purpose of the program.
3. The program must include evidence of promoting competence in the following professional domains:
    a. **Professional counselor identity, ethical behavior, and social justice practices.** Including but not limited to: assisting students to acquire knowledge related to the history of the helping profession; professional counseling roles and functions; ethical standards related to professional organizations in the field of counseling; and public policy processes including system advocacy strategies on behalf of the profession, clients, and the communities that counselors serve.
    b. **Human development and wellness across the life span**. Including but not limited to: the study of life span development; maturational and structural theories of human development; wellness counseling theories; strategies to deal with developmental processes and transitions; human behavior; disabilities; environmental, contextual, and multicultural factors that contribute to healthy human development and relevant culturally competent counseling practices; and the promotion of social justice in society.
    c. **Neuroscientific, physical, and biological foundations of human development and wellness.** Including but not limited to: facilitating students' acquisition of new knowledge related to neuroscience, health, and wellness; addictions; and the use of neuroscientific research findings for culturally competent counseling practices and social justice advocacy interventions.
    d. **Ecological, contextual, multicultural, social justice foundations of human development**. Including but not limited to: the study of culture from ecological, contextual, multicultural,

and social justice perspectives; evidence-based strategies for working with diverse groups (related to but not limited to age, race, culture, ethnicity, disability, sexual orientation, gender, class, religion/spirituality); the impact of power, privilege, and oppression and micro/macro aggressions on human development; and culturally competent counseling and social justice advocacy interventions.

e. **Counseling, consultation, and social justice advocacy theories and skills**. Including but not limited to: training in preventive counseling; consultation; individual, group, couples, marriage, family, and addictions counseling; systems change intervention strategies and skills; and social justice advocacy interventions.

f. **Group theory, practice, and social justice advocacy.** Including but not limited to: principles of group dynamics, group process, and group leadership; theories and methods of group counseling; and the application of group work theory and practice to organizational dynamics and social justice advocacy in different environmental settings (e.g., family, school, university, workplace, and community settings).

g. **Career and life development.** Including but not limited to: the study of vocational/career development theories and decision-making models; career assessment instruments and techniques; occupational and related educational systems; career development applications; career counseling processes/techniques; and the application of social justice theories to people's vocational/career development.

h. **Assessment of human behavior and organizational/community/institutional systems**. Including but not limited to: assessment and diagnosis of individual psychiatric disorders as defined by classification systems such as the Diagnostic Statistical Manual (DSM) and the International Classification of Diseases (ICD); understanding of defined diagnostic disorders relative to the helping context; knowledge of cultural biases associated with classification systems; assessment strategies designed to promote healthy human functioning; and assessment strategies that focus on organizational/community/social justice advocacy dynamics as they impact human development, wellness, and the perpetuation of psychiatric disorders as listed in various classification systems.

i. **Tests and measurements.** Including but not limited to promoting an understanding of the theoretical and historical basis for, as well as knowledge of cultural biases associated with: assessment techniques; testing methods; knowledge of various types of tests and evaluation strategies that result in knowledgeable selection, administration, and interpretation; and use of assessment/evaluation instruments and techniques that foster social justice among diverse client populations.

j. **Traditional and social justice-oriented research and evaluations.** Including but not limited to: quantitative and qualitative research design and methods; statistical analyses, principles, practices, and application of needs assessments; the design and process of program evaluation; organizational, community, and social justice advocacy evaluation strategies; and knowledge of cultural biases associated with research practices.

k. **Practicum/Internship experiences.** At least two (2) academic terms of supervised field placement experiences that focus on issues related to the promotion of mental health, human development, wellness, cultural competence, and social justice advocacy (at least three semester hours or five quarter hours per academic term in a counseling and/or related human service setting with 300 hours of supervised field training). The practicum/internship experience (commensurate with program goals and state licensure requirements) shall be completed under the clinical supervision of appropriately credentialed professionals (e.g., licensed professional counselor, social worker, marriage and family therapist, school counselor, psychologist, or physician with a specialty in psychiatry).

● APPENDIX C

SKATES FORM: Weekly Journal Summary

S=Skills, K=Knowledge, A=Attitude, T=Thoughts, E=Ethics, S=Supervision

Please provide a specific example in each category.

S	What did you learn to *DO* this week?
K	What did you learn *ABOUT* this week?
A	How has your experience this week *ADDED* to your view of being a professional counselor?
T	What is your *PLAN* for next week in terms of skills, knowledge, and attitude?
E	What *ETHICAL ISSUES* did you encounter this week and how were they handled?
S	What would you like to receive *SUPERVISION* on this week?

● APPENDIX D

Supervised Field Experience

Hours log

Date	*Direct Hours*	**Total Direct Hours*	*On-Site Hours*	*Total*** *On-Site Hours*	*On-Site Supervisor's Signature*

*Total direct hours: Keep a cumulative count of your direct service hours.

**Total on-site hours: Keep a cumulative count of your on-site hours over the semester.

APPENDIX E

Sample Internship Hours Timeline

Fall Semester				
Week	*Direct*	*Total Direct*	*On-Site*	*Total On-site*
1	0.5	0.5	16	16
2	2	2.5	16	32
3	3.5	6	16	48
4	4	10	16	64
5	5	15	16	80
6	5.5	20.5	16	96
7	6	26.5	16	112
8	6	32.5	16	128
9	6.5	39	16	144
10	7	46	16	160
11	7	53	16	176
12	7.5	60.5	16	192
13	7.5	68	16	208
14	7.5	75.5	16	224
15	8	83.5	16	240
16	8	91.5	16	256

Spring Semester				
Week	*Direct*	*Total Direct*	*On-Site*	*Total On-site*
1	8.5	100	16	272
2	8.5	108.5	16	288
3	8.5	117	16	304
4	8.5	125.5	16	320
5	9	134.5	16	336
6	9	143.5	16	352
7	9	152.5	16	368
8	9.5	162	16	384
9	9.5	171.5	16	400
10	9.5	181	16	416
11	9.5	190.5	16	432
12	9.5	200	16	448
13	10	210	16	464
14	10	220	16	480
15	10	230	16	496
16	10	240	16	512

LESSON 2

ORIENTATION TO PRACTICUM/INTERNSHIP SITES

"Counselors-in-training are guests in the site supervisor's world."

Real Life

Counselor-in-training: "It's only my third week of internship, and today a student came to me and told me that she thought she was pregnant. My site supervisor was busy at the time and I wasn't sure how to proceed in my work with this student. I didn't know what to say or how to handle this situation."

Site Supervisor: "There's a policy for that . . ." The school district in which this interaction took place had a very specific procedure/policy for this situation. School District policy had been written, reviewed, and approved. The established procedures include guidelines for who may be contacted regarding this information and who could not be contacted. Also, consultation with the site supervisor is mandatory at this point in the field experience.

Lesson Two

Orientation to Practicum/Internship Sites

"Counselors-in-training are guests in the site supervisor's world."

Essential Question: How do I acquire comprehensive knowledge of the field experience site?

Objectives

Students will

- demonstrate an understanding of the role of intern in the school setting.
- demonstrate knowledge about the policies and procedures of the district and school.
- communicate the organizational structure of the school district and school.
- explain the process for meeting with students.
- demonstrate an understanding of potential student interventions and resources available.
- communicate how supervision and training will take place at the site.
- demonstrate knowledge of roles, functions, settings, and professional identity of the school counselor in relation to the roles of other profession and support professional in the school.

CACREP 2016 Standards

- Understand ethical and legal considerations specifically related to the practice of school counseling (5.G.2.n)
- Demonstrate knowledge of community resources and referral sources (5.G.2.k)

MPCAC Standards

- Counseling, consultation, and social-justice advocacy theories and skills

Video Spark

https://www.youtube.com/watch?v=SFnMTHhKdkw

Rita Pierson: Every kid needs a champion.

INTRODUCTION

Schools are multitiered, complex systems. Each school is a unit within a larger district which is another multitiered, complex system. Within these systems are critical formal, written policies and procedures. Learning the school district's organizational structure and its policies/procedures are part of a student's field experience. On-site supervisors will provide students with an orientation to their site and school district. This orientation process will provide students with a comprehensive introduction to the systems in place. In addition to the formal and acknowledged procedural systems are unwritten policies and procedures. The unwritten processes can be as important as the written and will take time to learn.

This lesson provides a structure and format intended to assist you in acquitting knowledge of both the formal and informal school policies and procedures.

Getting to know the practicum/internship site is a fact-finding mission requiring communication skills, interpersonal skills, and a large dose of finesse. Schools, as with most systems, have policies and procedures. Schools, as with most systems, don't always clearly document or follow those policies and procedures. It is the interns' job to become acquainted with their site through their orientation with the site supervisor and by paying attention to both the spoken and the unspoken policies and procedures.

The first step in this process is to read the school district's student handbook given to the students at your site. This will provide you with information on what the school standards are for students. Handbooks include information that ranges from dress code to behavioral expectations and disciplinary procedures. Interns will proactively ask their site supervisors for a copy of the student handbook. Reading the handbook establishes a knowledge base for the intern with information that often reflects the culture of the school and the expectations of the administration. Additionally, administrators greatly appreciate it when interns are well informed and demonstrate a proactive motivated attitude.

Knowing school policy for students is also important when working directly with students. Knowledge is power—it is best not to be reliant on information that students' provide regarding policy violations. A well-informed counseling intern can provide students with a grounded perspective on whether policy has been violated and possibly why an administrator or teacher may have felt that there was a violation. In addition, reviewing the handbook can be used as a classroom lesson, which provides an opportunity to work directly with the students.

The second step in orientation to the school setting is to identify the multiple sources of established policies. For example, schools have a Crisis Management Plan. This plan provides specific procedures for how to handle an emergency, the roles of staff and faculty members, and the responsibilities of each member of the school community. Interns, with the assistance of their site supervisor, will identify just where this type of procedure or policy is housed. One school distributed this policy to all staff and faculty. Another school posted it on the school website with the expectation that all staff and faculty would access and read it. A third school district had a binder at the front desk of each school with the policies. Locating the policies will be your first task; reading them will follow. Being informed on all of the procedures or policies will be critical when unexpected situations, such as a crisis, occur. Although often overlooked, performing this comprehensive task will distinguish the intern as an asset to the system rather than a potential burden on the site supervisor.

● ACTIVITIES

Using "Orientation to School Placement: Policies and Procedures" (Appendix A), identify the information or policies/procedures of the school and/or school district. Keep a list of each as you identify the information. Sharing this information with your field experience colleagues would be well worth your time. You may find that different schools approach school life, policies, and procedures from varying perspectives.

*Appendix A is to be used throughout your practicum and internship.

● REFERENCES

Council for Accreditation for Counseling and Related Program. (2014). *2016 Standards*. Retrieved from http://www.cacrep.org/for-programs/2016-cacrep-standards/

Masters in Psychology and Counseling Accreditation Council. (2015). *Accreditation Manual*. Retrieved from http://www.mpcacaccreditation.org/about/accreditation-manual

● APPENDIX A

Orientation to School Placement: Policies and Procedures

When you first enter the school setting, you must become familiar with your new environment. In order to do this, you must spend much of your time, at least at the onset of the field experience, observing the school counselors at work. In addition, becoming familiar with the school and school district's policies and procedures is essential. Follow all procedural guidelines or policies established by the school, in conjunction with following your ethical standards. This list does not include all procedural guidelines or organizational structures within the school but rather offers suggestions regarding policies and procedures to which field experience students should become familiar. Review all materials. In addition, ask yourself the questions included in the list below.

Policies and Procedures

- Are there any board policies that impact on the functioning of the school counselor?
- Is there a discipline policy/code? Who administers discipline?
- Is there a safety or crisis plan? A drug and alcohol policy? Harassment policy?
- Does the school have procedural guidelines for school counselors to deal with crisis, suicide ideation, threat assessment, or other policies regarding confidentiality?
- Is there a student handbook?
- Is there a copy of the ethical standards from ASCA and state guidelines?
- Does the school follow any of these ethical guidelines?
- Are the special education regulations readily available? What is the school counselor's involvement with special education? 504 plans?

Building Organization

- How will I be introduced to faculty? Parents? Administration? Community?
- What is the "chain of command" in the building? In the district?
- To whom am I directly responsible?
- Do I need prior approval for work I wish to do within the field experience? From whom?
- How is the daily schedule of the counselor organized?
- How do I make up missed time (you must maintain the equivalent of two full days each week)?
- What do I do if I am unable to keep to my schedule?
- Is there teacher/team planning time? Can I meet with teachers then?
- What interaction does the counselor have with the teachers? How do I contact or notify teachers?
- Have I met with the teachers?
- Do counselors meet on a regular basis either schoolwide or districtwide?
- Am I responsible for any special education procedures? What exposure can I get to special education?
- Who is in charge of organizing building-level testing?

● STUDENT INTERACTIONS

Meeting With Students

- Is there a permission form or suggested format available for interns?
- Is there a standard procedure regarding audio or videotaping?

- How are appointments scheduled? Do students need a pass?
- How are students assigned to counselors?
- Is there a certain time allowed with each student?
- Can the counselor see students at any time? During academic subjects? Or only during study hall or flex time?
- Did I explain limits of confidentiality? Did I establish professional boundaries?
- What if the student is resistant?
- How will I determine if the student has made progress?
- Do counselors meet with every student on their caseload each year?

Student Interventions

- Is a calendar available outlining school counseling activities for the year?
- What services can the school counselor provide through the counseling office?
- What support programs are available in school? In community?
- Are there outreach workers? Truancy officers? Probation officers in the school?
- Is there a school counseling core curriculum? Is it in the daily/weekly schedule?
- Is there a student assistance program? How does it function?
- Does school offer support groups and small-group counseling?
- How is a plan of intervention devised?
- Do any outside consultants come into the school to offer services?
- Is there a policy for contact with other agencies?
- Is there a policy for contact with parents? How much family interaction is allowed?

● FORMS/DOCUMENTATION

Files

- How and where are student records kept?
- Who is responsible for keeping records up to date?
- Is there more than one file per student? If so, how are they delineated?
- What are the procedures to view files?
- Who actually files information?
- What information is kept in the file? What is documented in the file?
- Are phone logs kept?
- Is a copy of the Federal Educational Rights and Privacy Act (FERPA) available? Who monitors the application of FERPA?
- How do the counselors document their work?

Forms and Resources

- Are there any standard forms used within the school?
    - release of information
    - permission for services from the counselor (intern)
    - permission for taping
    - new entrant forms or transfer student forms
    - schedule changes

- parent contact letters
- test interpretation

- Is there clerical assistance available?
- Is there a budget for materials?
- What materials are available and where?
  - professional journals or books
  - testing material
  - diagnostic material
  - group materials
  - curriculum

● SUPERVISION AND TRAINING

- How will on-site supervision be arranged? To whom am I directly responsible?
- Can I work with all the counselors in the department?
- When will supervision take place?
- Is peer supervision possible?
- Is there opportunity to consult on a regular basis with fellow professionals?
- Are there any in-service programs or training options for counselors?
- What are the procedures for staff development?
- What arrangements can I make for professional development? Will the district support attendance in any way?

(This form was adapted from an unpublished work by Dr. Deborah Barlieb)

LESSON 3

ASSESSMENT OF FIELD EXPERIENCE STUDENT'S COUNSELING SKILL DEVELOPMENT

"How am I going to be graded in this course?"

Counselor–in-Training: "Field experiences require a lot of time and energy. We're also being graded?? How is the course graded?"

Faculty Supervisor: "The expectations for the field experience courses are on the syllabus. The grades combine the course assignments and the on-site supervisor feedback. The on-site supervisor's evaluation forms are available in the Practicum/Internship Handbook."

***NOTE: It is important to note that the evaluations in this lesson are just samples and that each counselor education program will have its own process and evaluation system. Additionally, each counselor education program will provide this information to its students in various methods and may not necessarily be included in the practicum/internship handbook. Please check with your faculty supervisor or advisor to learn more about your particular program. Thank you!**

Lesson Three

Assessment of Field Experience Student's Counseling Skill Development

"How am I going to be graded in this course?"

Essential Question: What measure is going to be used to assess counseling skill development?

Objectives

Students will demonstrate understanding of how skill development is assessed during practicum and internship.

CACREP 2016 Standards

Student will demonstrate an understanding of

- professional organizations, preparation standards, and credentials relevant to the practice of school counseling (G.5.2.l)

MPCAC Standards

- Professional counselor identity, ethical behavior, and social justice practices
- Assessment of human behavior and organizational/community/institutional systems
- Tests and measurements
- Traditional and social-justice-oriented research and evaluations

Video Spark

https://www.youtube.com/watch?v=5aH2Ppjpcho

Dan Ariely: What makes us feel good about our work?

● INTRODUCTION

Assessment of the skills necessary to become an effective professional school counselor is a construct of increasing visibility in the counseling literature (Schaefle, Smaby, Packman, & Maddux, 2007). The Council for Accreditation of Counseling and Related Educational Programs (CACREP), which provides an educational framework for counselor education programs, has set specific standards for counselor education programs. The goal of these standards is to ensure competency and mastery in identified areas of knowledge and skills, thus preparing students for careers in counseling. An essential aspect of meeting the professional responsibilities set for counselor education programs is "the assessment of student learning and performance on professional identity, professional practice, and program area standards" (Council for Accreditation of Counseling and Related Educational Programs [CACREP], 2009, p. 7). Along with the standards set by CACREP for the assessment of student knowledge and skills, the American School Counselor Association (ASCA), and the Council for the Accreditation of Educator Preparation (CAEP) have identified competencies, domains, and proficiencies to be met by students who are entering the field of professional school counseling (American School Counselor Association [ASCA], 2007; Council for the Accreditation of Educator Preparation [CAEP], 2009). Assessment of these professional standards and proficiencies help to ensure that students achieve necessary, skill-based competencies in order to act as ethical, competent professionals. The assessment of students' skills based upon these standards is paramount in determining whether students are prepared to begin their role as professional school counselors, as few other mechanisms are in place ensuring the skill development necessary for a successful transition for school counseling trainees in their move from student to professional (Steward, Neil, & Diemer, 2008).

A critical point in this developmental process is the culminating field training experience for school counseling trainees: the practicum and internship experiences. CACREP's updated standards state that these field experiences are "intended to reflect the comprehensive work experience of a professional counselor appropriate to the designated program area" (CACREP, 2009, p. 16). As gatekeepers for the profession, counselor educators are charged with the ethical responsibility (American Counseling Association [ACA], 2005, Section F.5) and curricular responsibility (CACREP, 2009) to implement standards-driven assessment. Prior to this internship, graduate counseling students complete the majority of the required coursework and an initial field training experience, or practicum, composed of 100 hours of field training, of which 40 should be comprised of direct service delivery. The required coursework addresses eight core competencies in a range of domains that prepare the trainee for these experiences (CACREP, 2009). Consistent with CACREP's standards, the CAEP (2013) identifies the domains and candidate proficiencies as: Knowledge (communication, interpersonal skills, and critical thinking), Skills (scholarly inquiry, reflective wisdom, integration of discipline, technology integration, organization, and classroom management), and Dispositions (cultural awareness) as essential competencies that school counseling trainees should exhibit during their training in order to successfully transition into their roles as professionals. As evidenced by these competency requirements, the content knowledge and skills that trainees are required to obtain before the field experiences are extensive.

This comprehensive knowledge and skill base provide counseling trainees with the foundation needed to address the multiple roles and functions of school counselors. Building on this foundation, the practicum and internship are designed to facilitate the theory-to-practice transition. The field experiences are comprised of an intense, focused field experience with 1 hour of individual and/or triadic supervision with the site supervisor weekly, as well as 1½ hours of group supervision a week with the university supervisor. In total, CACREP standards require a 100-hour practicum with 40 direct services hours and a 600-hour-internship with 240 direct service hours. The practicum and internship requires students to participate in the daily activities of the school counselor. One requirement of the practicum and internship is for the interns to experience or minimally be exposed to the multiple and complex roles and tasks of a school counselor.

ASCA's 2009 Role Statement highlights the various roles of the professional school counselor: Professional "school counselors are certified/licensed educators with a minimum of a master's degree in school counseling making them uniquely qualified to address all students' academic, personal/social and career development needs by designing, implementing, evaluating and enhancing a comprehensive school counseling program that promotes and enhances student success" (p. 1). Consistent with this role definition, the skills and knowledge that students learn during their internship experience often vary, as the role of the school counselor often varies by school, school day, and time of the academic year. For example, a day in the life of a school counselor may begin with changing a student's schedule due to academic achievement concerns and end with crisis management requiring a significant mental health intervention. Throughout that same day, the counselor may be providing college search information, providing postsecondary counseling, facilitating conflict mediation, being a student advocate, or using their knowledge of special education and various educational options to appropriately meet a student's needs. The internship is an active, developmental learning process providing students with the opportunity to integrate information learned in academic courses and the practicum while under the supervision of an experienced counselor and participating in the daily responsibilities and tasks of a school counselor.

DEVELOPMENTAL PERSPECTIVES IN SCHOOL COUNSELOR TRAINING

As with most skill acquisition, learning, maintaining, and honing counseling skills is a developmental process. However, few standardized measures have been designed to specifically address the developmental and multifaceted process of trainees' acquisition of the skills and professional identity of a school counselor. Scholars have called for the creation of measures that assess the specific requirements of the counselor's role as well as the developmental aspects of skill acquisition (Luke & Bernard, 2006). Such writings suggest that assessment of a counselor-in-training's process should be organized and structured around the developmental aspects of the student skill acquisition and be assessed at significant developmental milestones throughout the internship process.

The etiology of measuring knowledge and skill acquisition is extensive. Developmental perspectives on measuring such acquisition can be traced as far back as Plato in Western philosophy (Ivey & Rigazio-DiGilio, 2009) to Bloom's Taxonomy of Educational Objectives (Bloom, Engelhart, Furst, Hill, & Krathwohl, 1956). Recognition of the developmental approach to skill acquisition and counseling supervision gained a foothold in the counselor education field during the 1980s (Borders & Brown, 2005). More recently, Darcy Granello (2000) applied a developmental approach to counseling supervision by using Bloom's Taxonomy to inform best practice in facilitating the cognitive development of counseling interns. The systematic cognitive developmental supervision model provides a framework for providing supervision designed to meet the individual needs of the counselor-in-training. Mark D. Nelson, Patrick Johnson, and Jill M. Thorngren (2000) integrated the developmental approach to supervision with a discriminative model that addresses the stages of supervision, roles of the supervisor, and various skills and needs of trainees.

Building on the acceptance of the developmental approach to supervision and the need for an integrated developmental/multicultural supervision model, Anne M. Ober, Granello, and Malik S. Henfield (2009) presented the synergistic model of multicultural supervision (SMMS). This model integrates three important, developmental concepts: cognitive development (Bloom's Taxonomy), interpersonal development (heuristic model of nonoppressive interpersonal development [HMNID]), and multicultural awareness/competencies (multicultural awareness competencies [MCCs]). This model of developmental supervision is designed to support counselor-in-training skill development within the supervisee's developmental stage and developmental level of multicultural competence. In addition, it provides supervisors with a model to guide the supervision process with particular attention to multicultural counselor competence and to the intern's stage of skill development. Although the SMMS provides a developmental, multicultural model of supervision, this model does not include a measure designed to assess an intern's skill development, knowledge, and multicultural competency across the course of the school counseling internship experience. Such a measure is still needed and can provide further foundation for the expansion of theory, research, and practice in professional school counseling.

Although developmental theory of supervision has been accepted since the early 1980s, objective, standardized, developmental assessment of the internship experience has not been addressed. A major challenge to assessment in the field of school counseling is not only incorporating the developmental nature of the internship experience, but also operationally defining the multiple roles and functions of the school counselor. Thus, assessing the multifaceted and varied knowledge and skills required of school counselors is a complex endeavor. In light of these complexities, establishing a framework for the assessment is essential. An example of this type of framework is the school counseling supervision model (SCSM).

The SCSM (Luke & Bernard, 2006) bridges traditional supervision models with the multiple roles of the school counselors within comprehensive school counseling programs. It also provides a theoretical model for supervision and addresses the complexity of supervising school counseling interns. This model highlights that an important domain of supervising professional counseling trainees is the assessment of interns' skill development within the context of the multiple roles and responsibilities of a school counselor. Although this model highlights the need for an evaluation tool that assesses school counseling' trainees learning of the different professional roles of a school counselor, there still remains a dearth of assessment tools and corresponding literature to meet this need. Building on the recognition of the multiple roles and functions identified in the SCSM, the timing of when trainees are assessed during their internship experience is important. Assessment of the required skills should be commensurate to the intern's developmental stage (e.g., the assessment should be assessing skills critical to the specific period of the internship experience). A developmental-focused assessment would focus on the progression of skill development, knowledge acquisition, and multicultural competency.

L. DiAnne Borders and Lori L. Brown (2005) provide an overview of three developmental stages. Interns at the early stage demonstrate a basic understanding of the counseling process, tend to be constrained in their interventions, and often lack confidence. Interns at the middle stage demonstrate stronger counseling skills, are more varied in intervention use, and have greater confidence in their ability. At the later stages, interns are better able to conceptualize clients and utilize more creative and advanced interventions.

These developmental milestones of the internship experience are also identified in the three stages of developmental supervision offered by Robert Haynes, Gerald Corey, and Patrice Moulton's "Blueprint for Developmental Supervision." in *Clinical Supervision in the Helping Professions* (2003). These stages are (a) the beginning stage, in which the trainee-intern's goal is to develop the relationship, assess competencies, educate, and monitor early experiences; (b) the middle stage, in which the trainee-intern's goal is to transition from dependency to independent practice. This stage is often characterized by a struggle in the supervisory relationship, as supervisees want to move forward and supervisors tend to tread carefully; and (c) the ending stage, in which the primary goal is to foster independence and prepare supervisee for work as an independent professional. Based on developmental and stage models, the evaluation system developed in this study is a three-phase assessment process.

The evaluation or assessment for practicum is clearly identified at the top of the form. It is completed at the middle and at the end of the practicum field experience. The evaluation or assessment for internship has three forms and is identified as Counseling Internship Developmental Assessment of Counseling Skills (CIDACS-R). The evaluations take place at 1/3, 2/3, and 3/3 points of the internship experience.

Sample Practicum and Internship Evaluations Are in the Appendices

Activity: At the end of each week, review the practicum evaluation form for the practicum field experience and the internship evaluation form for internship field experiences. Reflect on your skill development for the week. Mark what skills and level you have accomplished thus far. Set goals for skill acquisition for the following week.

• REFERENCES

American Counseling Association. (2005). *ACA code of ethics*. Alexandria, VA: Author.

American School Counselor Association. (2007). *School counselor competencies*. Retrieved from http://www.schoolcounselor.org/files/SCCompetencies.pdf

American School Counselor Association. (2009). *The role of the professional school counselor*. Retrieved from http://www.schoolcounselor.org/asca/media/asca/home/RoleStatement.pdf

American School Counselor Association. (2012). *The ASCA National Model: A framework for school counseling programs* (3rd ed.). Alexandria, VA: Author.

Bloom, B. S., Engelhart, M. D., Furst, E. J., Hill, W. H., & Krathwohl, D. R. (1956). *Taxonomy of educational objectives: The classification of educational goals; Handbook I: Cognitive domain*. White Plains, NY: Longman.

Borders, L. D., & Brown, L. L. (2005). *The new handbook of counseling supervision*. New York, NY: Lawrence Erlbaum.

Council for Accreditation for Counseling and Related Program. (2014). *2016 standards*. Retrieved from http://www.cacrep.org/for-programs/2016-cacrep-standards/

Council for the Accreditation of Educator Preparation. (2013). *CAEP accreditation standards*. Washington, DC: Author. Retrieved from http://caepnet.org/standards/introduction

Granello, D. H. (2000). Encouraging the cognitive development of supervisees: Using Bloom's taxonomy in supervision. *Counselor Education and Supervision, 40*(1), 31–47.

Haynes, R., Corey, G., & Moulton, P. (2003). *Clinical supervision in the helping professions*. Pacific Grove, CA: Brooks/Cole-Thomson.

Ivey, A. E., & Rigazio-DiGilio, S. A. (2009). Developmental counseling and therapy: The basics of why it may be helpful and how to use it. *Turkish Psychological Counseling and Guidance Journal, 4*(32), 1–11.

Luke, M., & Bernard, J. M. (2006). The school counseling supervision model: An extension of the discrimination model. *Counselor Education & Supervision, 45*, 282–295.

Masters in Psychology and Counseling Accreditation Council. (2015). Accreditation manual. Retrieved from http://www.mpcacaccreditation.org/about/accreditation-manual

Nelson, M. D., Johnson, P., & Thorngren, J. M. (2000). An integrated approach for supervising mental health counseling interns. *Journal of Mental Health Counseling, 22*(1), 45–58.

Ober, A. M., Granello, D. H., & Henfield, M. S. (2009). A synergistic model to enhance multicultural competence in supervision. *Counselor Education & Supervision*, 48, 204–221.

Schaefle, S., Smaby, M. H., Packman, J., & Maddux, C. D. (2007). Performance assessment of counseling skills based on specific theories: acquisition, retention and transfer to actual counseling sessions. *Education*, *128*(2), 262–273.

Steward, R. J., Neil, D. M., & Diemer, M. A. (2008). A concept of best practices in training school counselors. In H. L. K. Coleman & C. Yeh (Eds.), *Handbook of school counseling*. New York, NY: Taylor & Francis.

● APPENDIX A (PRACTICUM EVALUATION; CACREP 2016 STANDARDS)

Counseling Practicum Assessment of Counseling Skills

Professional School Counselor

School Counselor-in-Training Name ______________________________ Date: __________

Evaluator Name: ______________________________ Position: ________________

Directions:

For each of the performance areas, please use the following rating scale:

0 – *Unsatisfactory*	**1 – *Needs Improvement***	**2 – *Demonstrates Competency***	**3 – *Above Average***	***4 – *Not Demonstrated***	**5 – *Not Applicable***

*If the skill has not been demonstrated yet, please indicate approximately when you think the student will be able to demonstrate the skill.

Also, include any relevant comments addressing the intern's professional skill development.

Attendance: Adheres to agreed upon schedule and arrives on time.	0	1	2	3	4	5
Dress: Dresses appropriately for the work setting.	0	1	2	3	4	5
Organization: Organizes and completes work on time.	0	1	2	3	4	5
Rules: Understands and follows school rules and procedures.	0	1	2	3	4	5
Ethics: Follows ASCA ethical standards. (CACREP 2016 5.G.2.n; MPCAC 1.a)	0	1	2	3	4	5
Consultation: Works effectively with teachers. (CACREP 2016 5.G.2.b; MPCAC 1.e)	0	1	2	3	4	5
Consultation: Works effectively with parents. (CACREP 2016 5.G.2.b; MPCAC 1.e)	0	1	2	3	4	5
Consultation: Works effectively with administrators. (CACREP 2016 5.G.2.b; MPCAC 1.e)	0	1	2	3	4	5
Rapport: Establishes rapport with students. (CACREP 2016 5.G.3.f; MPCAC 1.e))	0	1	2	3	4	5
Basic Skills: Demonstrates basic skills in empathy, listening, and reflection. (CACREP 2016 5.G.2.3.f; MPCAC 1.e)	0	1	2	3	4	5
Effective Counseling: Designs and implements developmentally appropriate and effective strategies. (CACREP 2016 5.G.2.3.f; MPCAC 1.b)	0	1	2	3	4	5
Focus: Maintains appropriate focus and pacing.	0	1	2	3	4	5
Cultural Sensitivity: Understands students' worldview. (CACREP 2016 5.G.3.k; MPCAC 1.d)	0	1	2	3	4	5
Verbal Skills: Makes clear statements and questions that facilitate discussion.	0	1	2	3	4	5
Follow Through: Maintains an ongoing counseling relationship.	0	1	2	3	4	5
Progress: Effectively evaluates student progress.	0	1	2	3	4	5
Lesson Planning: Plans developmentally appropriate lessons. (CACREP 2016 5.G.3.c; MPCAC 1.c)	0	1	2	3	4	5
Management: Uses appropriate classroom management strategies.	0	1	2	3	4	5

What leadership characteristics or qualities has your practicum student exhibited in this half of the semester?

Please comment on the areas of strength for this student.

Please comment on the areas where development is needed.

Additional comments:

● APPENDIX B (INTERNSHIP EVALUATION; CACREP 2016 STANDARDS)

Evaluation #1 2016 CACREP STANDARDS

Counseling Internship Developmental Assessment of Counseling Skills

Professional School Counselor

School Counselor-in-Training Name ______________________ Date: __________

Evaluator Name: ______________________ Position: __________

Directions:

For each of the performance areas, please use the following rating scale:

0 – *Unsatisfactory*	1 – *Needs Improvement*	2 – *Demonstrates Competency*	3 – *Above Average*	*4 – *Not Demonstrated*	5 – *Not Applicable*

*If the skill has not been demonstrated yet, please indicate approximately when you think the student will be able to demonstrate the skill. Also, include any relevant comments addressing the intern's professional skill development.

Description						
Professional Behaviors						
Adheres to agreed upon schedule.	0	1	2	3	4	5
Arrives on time for internship.	0	1	2	3	4	5
Dresses appropriately for internship.	0	1	2	3	4	5
Demonstrates appropriate interpersonal relationships with colleagues and staff.	0	1	2	3	4	5
Meets and effectively communicates with primary site supervisor (and secondary supervisors, if applicable), demonstrating an openness and willingness to learn.	0	1	2	3	4	5
Demonstrates flexibility or adaptability.	0	1	2	3	4	5
Takes initiative in seeking out additional advice, resources, or supervision when needed.	0	1	2	3	4	5
Comments:						

Counseling Skill Development						
Effectively establishes rapport with students.	0	1	2	3	4	5
Communicates to student the nature and boundaries of the counseling relationship.	0	1	2	3	4	5
Demonstrates effective listening skills/techniques of personal/social counseling. (5.G.2.3.f)	0	1	2	3	4	5
Accurately reflects student's thoughts and feelings/techniques of personal/social counseling. (CACREP 2016 5.G.3.f; MPCAC 1.e)	0	1	2	3	4	5
Demonstrates an awareness and sensitivity to student's developmental stage and developmental context. (CACREP 2016 5.G.3.f; MPCAC 1.b & 1.d)	0	1	2	3	4	5
Demonstrates an awareness and sensitivity to student's cultural and contextual/systemic reality. (CACREP 2016 5.G.3.f; MPCAC 1.b & 1.d)	0	1	2	3	4	5
Identifies and assesses factors that are supporting or impeding student's academic, career, personal success. (CACREP 2016 5.G.3.d & h; MPCAC 1.d)	0	1	2	3	4	5
Identifies student's strengths and needs with contextual, cultural, and developmental awareness. (CACREP 2016 5.G.3.f; MPCAC 1.b & 1.d)	0	1	2	3	4	5
Comments:						

Management System/Accountability						
Demonstrates knowledge of school procedures and policies.	0	1	2	3	4	5
Demonstrates knowledge of community resources and referral sources. (CACREP 2016 5.G.2.k; MPCAC 1.e)	0	1	2	3	4	5
Comments:						

Evaluation #2

Counseling Internship Developmental Assessment of Counseling Skills

Professional School Counselor

School Counselor-in-Training Name ______________________________ Date: ______________

Evaluator Name: ____________________________________ Position: ____________________

Directions:

For each of the performance areas, please use the following rating scale:

0 – *Unsatisfactory*	1 – *Needs Improvement*	2 – *Demonstrates Competency*	3 – *Above Average*	4 – *Not Demonstrated*	5 – *Not Applicable*

Also, include any relevant comments addressing the intern's professional skill development

Description						
Professional Behaviors						
Able to make effective use of constructive feedback.	0	1	2	3	4	5
Accepts personal and professional responsibility and initiates action to resolve concerns.	0	1	2	3	4	5
Accurately self-appraises counseling skills and performance.	0	1	2	3	4	5
Works with his/her supervisor in monitoring student's progress.	0	1	2	3	4	5
Consistently adheres to the legal and ethical standards specific to school counseling (e.g., informed consent for counseling and groups). (CACREP 2015 5.G.2.n; MPCAC 1.a)	0	1	2	3	4	5
Demonstrates ability to maintain confidentiality with students, teachers, and colleagues.	0	1	2	3	4	5
Exercises patience with students while balancing and attending to the multiple tasks required of a school counselor.	0	1	2	3	4	5
Comments:						
Counseling Skill Development						
Counsels individual students and small groups of students with identified needs and concerns. (CACREP 2016 5.G.3.f; MPCAC 1.e & 1.f)	0	1	2	3	4	5
Demonstrates knowledge of strategies for implementing and coordinating peer intervention programs. (CACREP 2016 5.G.3.m; MPCAC 1.f)	0	1	2	3	4	5
Accurately reflects student's thoughts and feelings. (CACREP 2016 5.G.3.f; MPCAC 1.e & 1.f)	0	1	2	3	4	5
Consults effectively with parents or guardians, teachers, administrators, and other relevant individuals to improve student success. (CACREP 2016 2.b & 3.l; MPCAC 1.e & 1.g)	0	1	2	3	4	5
Implements strategies to promote equity in student achievement and college access (e.g., scheduling, small groups). (CACREP 2016 5.G.3.j; MPCAC 1.d & 1.g)	0	1	2	3	4	5

Actively participates in school meetings (e.g., IEP, SAP, parent)/ demonstrates understanding of school counselor's role in multidisciplinary meetings and in school leadership (e.g., writes 504 plans). (CACREP 2016 5.G.2.d; MPCAC 1.a, 1.d & 1.e)	0	1	2	3	4	5
Uses interventions to promote academic development (e.g., study skills). (CACREP 2016 5.G.3.d; MPCAC 1.g)	0	1	2	3	4	5
Teaches school/classroom units effectively and uses differentiated instruction strategies. (CACREP 2016 5.G.3.d; MPCAC 1.d)	0	1	2	3	4	5
Comments:						
Management System/Accountability						
Tracks time spent providing direct and indirect service to students. (CACREP 2016 5.G.3.0; MPCAC 1.j)	0	1	2	3	4	5
Uses accountability data to inform decision-making (e.g., needs assessment for small groups). (CACREP 2016 5.G.3.n & o; MPCAC 1.j)	0	1	2	3	4	5

Evaluation #3

Counseling Internship Developmental Assessment of Counseling Skills

Professional School Counselor

School Counselor-in-Training Name ______________________ Date: ____________

Evaluator Name: ______________________ Position: ____________

Directions:

For each of the performance areas, please use the following rating scale:

0 – *Unsatisfactory*	1 – *Needs Improvement*	2 – *Proficient*	3 – *Above Average*	4 – *Not Demonstrated*	5 – *Not Applicable*

Also, include any relevant comments addressing the intern's professional skill development.

Description						
Professional Behaviors						
Demonstrates developing self-confidence in the role of counselor.	0	1	2	3	4	5
Presents in a professional manner.	0	1	2	3	4	5

(Continued)

(Continued)

Consistently adheres to the ASCA ethics code. (CACREP 2015 5.G.2.n; MPCAC 1.a)	0	1	2	3	4	5
Comments:						
Counseling Skill Development						
Selects appropriate assessment strategies to evaluate student's academic, career, and personal/social development and interprets assessment information in a valid and relevant manner. (e.g., use of Naviance or Career Cruiser). (CACREP 5.G.1.e & 3.e; MPCAC 1.h, 1.i & 1.j)	0	1	2	3	4	5
Facilitates appropriate closure to counseling relationships. (CACREP 2016 5.G.3.f; MPCAC 1.e & 1.f)	0	1	2	3	4	5
Provides support for students who are transitioning to other sites, schools, etc. (CACREP 2016 3.k & g; MPCAC 1.d, e & g)	0	1	2	3	4	5
Demonstrates sensitivity when interacting with socioculturally diverse students and colleagues. (CACREP 2016 5.G.3.f; MPCAC 1.b & 1.d)	0	1	2	3	4	5
Demonstrates knowledge and skills to critically examine the connections between social, familial, emotional, and behavior problems and academic achievement. (CACREP 2016 5.G.3.h; MPCAC 1.b, d. h)	0	1	2	3	4	5
Implements student programs (e.g., peer helping, conflict resolution, time management, self-esteem). (CACREP 2016 5.G.3.b & m; MPCAC 1.e & f)	0	1	2	3	4	5
Comments:						
Management System/Accountability						
Advocates for learning and academic experiences and opportunities to promote student development. (CACREP 2016 5.G.2.a & f; MPCAC 1.a, e f, & g)	0	1	2	3	4	5
Demonstrates use of data to advocate for programs and students. (e.g., Intern assesses student achievement due to the lessons taught by intern and then advocates for program/curricula). (CACREP 2016 5.G.3.n & o; MPCAC 1.h, I & j))	0	1	2	3	4	5
Comments:						

LESSON 4

AMERICAN SCHOOL COUNSELOR ASSOCIATION NATIONAL MODEL

Stacey Havlik
Villanova University

School Counseling — How to Implement the ASCA National Model

"What is the role of the school counselor?"

Real Life

Student: "What do school counselors do?"

Counselor-in-Training: School counselors play important roles in helping students and supporting the mission of their schools. They focus on serving children and adolescents in three different areas of development: (1) personal/social, (2) academic, and (3) career (American School Counselor Association [ASCA], 2012b). Across these domains, they assist students facing emotional issues but also provide guidance to help them to be successful in school and prepare for careers. They work one on one with students, as well as provide group counseling and classroom lessons on various developmentally appropriate topics. School counselors work across different settings, including private and public schools and in elementary, middle, and high schools. According to Colette T. Dollarhide and Kelli A. Saginak (2012), "In general, school counselors must be able to provide counseling through prevention and intervention efforts, advocate for diversity and equity in education, and use diverse and multicultural perspectives to help students to develop academically, vocationally, and personally" (p. 3).

To help to ensure that school counselors are meeting the needs of all students, there is an organization called the American School Counselor Association (ASCA) that provides a clear description of what should be included in comprehensive school counseling programs. ASCA recommends that school counselors develop their programs around a national model of school counseling. This model includes a foundation, which contains the program's mission and related goals; a delivery system to provide direct and indirect services to students; a management system to organize programs through calendars and various assessments; and an accountability system to evaluate effectiveness of programs (ASCA, 2012b). Through these four areas, school counselors can develop evidence-based programs that successfully support students in their academic, personal/social, and career development.

Lesson Four

American School Counselor Association National Model

Stacey Havlik
Villanova University

Essential Question: What is the ASCA National Model and how do I use it in practice?

Objectives

Students will

- be able to identify the four quadrants of the ASCA National Model.
- demonstrate an understanding of each of the quadrants and how they apply to the role of the school counsellor.
- demonstrate an understanding of the reasons why the profession has a national model and standards.

CACREP Standards

- Knows roles, functions, settings, and professional identity of the school counselor in relation to the roles of other professional and support personnel in the school. (SC.A3)
- Understands current models of school counseling programs (e.g., American School Counselor Association [ASCA] National Model) and their integral relationship to the total educational program. (SC.A.5)
- Knows how to design, implement, manage, and evaluate a comprehensive school counseling program. (SC.O.3)

MPCAC Standards

- professional counselor identity, ethical behavior, and social justice practices
- human development and wellness across the life span

Materials

1. Provide students with a hard copy of the ASCA standards or the Web link to access them: http://static.pdesas.org/content/documents/ASCA_National_Standards_for_Students.pdf
2. Students should purchase, as a required text for the course (or at the onset of their program). the *ASCA National Model: A Framework for School Counseling Programs* (3rd ed.), Item Number: 289325, ISBN: 978-1-929289-32-5

Video Spark

https://www.youtube.com/watch?v=IxitBXjqjZM&feature=em-share_video_user

What do school counselors do?

Reflection Activity

Reflect on the question, "What do school counselors do?"

Bring this reflection to your field experience class for small-group discussion. One group member writes a few of his or her main discussion points on the board. Group members will then share their points with the class. After the activity, the instructor reviews all of the different responsibilities for school counselors based on what is written. This discussion leads into the purpose of the ASCA model.

● INTRODUCTION

The field of school counseling has changed and developed over the past few decades. School counseling started as a profession of vocational counselors, mostly teachers, who took on the role of counselor on top of their other responsibilities. It eventually evolved through the years toward a position where counseling became a sole task (Gysbers & Henderson, 2012; Schimmel, 2008). During the early years, when school counseling was in its infancy, there was a lack of definition and agreement on counselors' roles (Hatch, 2010). Because of the shifting roles of school counselors, over time, it became necessary to clearly define the roles and responsibilities of school counselors in order to move the profession forward. Therefore, in 2001, the governing board of ASCA agreed to develop a model of school counseling that would reflect national educational reform movements such as No Child Left Behind (Hatch, 2010). The first version of the model was published in 2003, providing a framework for comprehensive school counseling programs (ASCA, 2003). Presently, the model is in its third edition (ASCA, 2012b). In ensuring that school counselors are providing comprehensive services that meet the needs of all students, the question has moved from "What do counselors do?" to "How are students different as a result of what we do?" (ASCA, 2012b).

● THE ASCA NATIONAL MODEL

According to the American School Counselor Association (2012b), the purpose of the national model is to promote uniformity across school counseling programs; encourage programs to address the needs of *all* students; and highlight the field of school counseling as being integral to student success. In this sense, school counseling programs moved from being responsive in nature to comprehensive in meeting the needs of every student and positioning school counselors as a collaborative leaders in the school system. Accordingly,

> the ASCA National Model ensures equitable access to a rigorous education for all students; identifies the knowledge and skills all students will acquire as a result of the K–12 comprehensive school counseling program; is delivered to all students in a systemic fashion; is based on data-driven decision-making; and is provided by a state-credentialed school counselor. (ASCA, 2012b, p. xii)

The National Model essentially defines the profession of school counseling. It provides a standardized model for school counseling programs to follow that allows for flexibility so that school counselors can make the model fit their unique populations and programs. The model itself consists of four elements: the *Foundation*, *Management System*, *Delivery System*, and *Accountability System*. Through these areas, ASCA provides a framework for school counselors that establishes school counseling as an essential piece of the educational system (Dahir & Tyson, 2010).

Let's breakdown each of the four quadrants of the National Model.

Foundation. At the base of the model, the foundation lays the groundwork for school counseling programs. ASCA (2012b) states, "The school counseling program's foundation serves as a solid ground upon which the rest of the comprehensive school counseling program is built" (p. 21). The foundation defines what students (and the school) will get out of the school counseling program, as well as the professional expectations for school counselors. There are three components of the foundation system.

Program level. The first component is the program level, which focuses on developing beliefs, a vision, and mission statement, as well as program goals. On the program level, all school counseling programs should describe their beliefs about student achievement, school counselors' roles, and other relevant areas such as use of data and ethical practices. From these beliefs, school counseling programs should develop a vision statement, which focuses on the future direction of the program, as well as a mission statement that aligns with the program's vision and specifies the intent of the program. It is important that the school counseling mission and vision statements align with those of the school and demonstrate how the school counseling program fits into the broader educational mission. Lastly, the foundation of school counseling programs should include program goals that guide how the mission and vision will be met.

Student competencies. A second component of the foundation is student competencies, which include the ASCA Standards, as well as other student standards. These standards describe the knowledge, skills, and attitudes that students should have as a result of the school counseling program across three domains: Academic, Personal/Social, and Career (ASCA, 2004). The school district or state itself may also have standards in which the program should also align. We will discuss the ASCA standards in more detail a little later.

Professional competencies. The third component of the foundation is professional competencies, which includes school counselor professional competencies, as well as the ASCA Ethical Standards for school counselors. The ASCA School Counselor Competencies describe the knowledge, abilities, and skills that all school counselors should have in order to meet the needs of their school and students (ASCA, 2012a). These standards are aligned with the ASCA model and designed for self-assessment and professional development, as well as for school administrators and counselor educators to evaluate and determine benchmarks for counselors (ASCA, 2012a). Additionally, school counselors are obligated to follow the ethical standards for the profession (American Counseling Association [ACA], 2014). The purpose of the ethical standards is to guide the practices of professional counselors and those in training (ACA, 2014, p. 3).

Management system. The management system is essential to the delivery of the school counseling program. "The management component of the ASCA National Model provides organizational assessments and tools designed to manage a school counseling program" (ASCA, 2012, p. 41). This system describes how school counselors evaluate their time spent on various tasks, monitors achievement gaps, and uses data to inform the direction of the program. It highlights the importance of school counselors being intentional and organized with their time, as well as the development of plans of action to meet program goals. For example, the model provides a lesson plan template that recommends school counselors align lessons with the ASCA student standards, as well as learning objectives (ASCA, 2012, p. 55).

The management component highlights the need for school counselors to develop and publish calendars with information about the school counseling program for all stakeholders. They can use these calendars to promote their programs, to keep stakeholders abreast on what they are doing throughout the year, and to organize their week, month, and year. Essential to the management system is an advisory council. This council includes a group of key stakeholders who regularly gather to advise and review the school counseling program. By including stakeholders who are outside of the program, it provides an objective voice to make recommendations and promote accountability.

Delivery system. The delivery system includes the direct and indirect services provided to students. In this sense, "the delivery component focuses on the method of implementing the school counseling program to students" (ASCA, 2012, p. 83). Delivery of school counseling programming includes a curriculum, student planning, responsive services, as well as system support (ASCA, 2012). A school counseling core curriculum comprises of providing classroom and schoolwide activities, where counselors go into individual classrooms or gather large groups and teach units (Gysbers & Henderson, 2012, p. 73). When developing a curriculum, it is important that school counselors plan developmentally appropriate lessons (Vernon, 2010). Examples of possible topics include expressing feelings, managing anger, developing healthy relationships with peers and parents, promoting self-acceptance, identifying personal strengths, dealing with puberty, or working through peer pressure (Vernon, 2010). Lessons should be age appropriate and designed to align with the ASCA standards, as well as program goals.

Individual student planning is also a critical aspect of the delivery system for school counselors. In this role, school counselors support students in developing future plans and personal goals (Gysbers & Henderson, 2012, p. 78). School counselors work to "help all students plan, monitor and manage their own learning as well as to achieve academic, career and personal/social competencies aligned with school counseling core curriculum" (ASCA, 2012, p. 85). Through individual planning, counselors may discuss financial aid, college planning, course selection, requirements for graduation, academic advisement, and test scores related to interests and abilities (Dollarhide & Saginak, 2012, p. 81).

In addition to individual planning, an essential role in delivering the school counseling program is counseling and crisis response. Such response services require school counselors to work with students in individual or small-group settings to provide support for students on a range of academic, personal/social, or career development concerns. School counselors provide counseling to help students to overcome issues that are holding them back from success (ASCA, 2012b). Crisis response may be necessary when students have needs that must be immediately addressed. Often responding to crises involves a team of stakeholders as well. Within the delivery system, school counselors should also provide indirect student services, which may include providing referrals to community resources, consulting and collaborating with teachers, parents and other stakeholders.

Accountability system. Effective school counseling programs are "data-driven," meaning that data are collected across the program for purposes of evaluation, in order to assess student outcomes and determine whether the counseling program is meeting the stated goals (Hatch, 2013). According to the ASCA model (2012b, p. 99), "to achieve the best results for students, school counselors regularly evaluate their program to determine its effectiveness." There are three sections in the ASCA National Model in the accountability system: (1) data analysis, (2) program results, and (3) evaluation and improvement.

Data analysis. School counselors should collect data throughout the year on their programs. Gathering data can inform them how they are meeting the needs of students and where they can make changes moving forward. In the ASCA (2012b) model, it is recommended that counselors annually review both school profile data and use of time data. *School profile* data may include student achievement (i.e., test scores, grades), attendance (i.e., number of absences or tardiness), or behavior data (i.e., discipline records, counselor referrals, suspensions). *Use of time* data include an assessment of how the counselors are spending their time (e.g., the amount of time they are spending on indirect versus direct services for students). Both forms of data provide counselors with insight on areas they need to focus on, as well as where they can make adjustments and set goals moving forward.

Program results. Determining the effectiveness of school counseling programs requires that school counselors analyze results reports from data collected on interventions and programs run at the school. Counselors collect data on the interventions that they implement in the school. For example, they may conduct needs assessments, design pre- and posttests, and invite students to fill out program evaluations or feedback surveys on interventions such as small groups or classroom lessons. Through compiling the data collected, analyzing it, and creating reports that show trends in the data, counselors can assess the effectiveness of their programs, promote the impact of their programs, and plan ahead for the following school year. These data results should be publicized and shared so that all stakeholders can see the impact of the program (ASCA, 2012b, p. 51).

Evaluation and improvement. The last critical piece of the accountability system is evaluation and improvement. This includes a self-evaluation that school counselors complete, examining their programs' performance, as well as their own. It also includes an evaluation to be completed by an administrator, in order to offer an outside assessment of the counselor and program performance. Through these types of evaluations, school counselors can reflect on their programs, make appropriate adjustments, and receive feedback on how they can improve. The ASCA model provides school counselor competencies (ASCA, 2012a) that can also be used for evaluation and professional development purposes. These competencies describe the knowledge, abilities, skills, and attitudes that effective school counselors possess.

Themes. There are four important themes that run around the edges of the National Model. They are *leadership, advocacy, collaboration,* and *systemic change*. These four areas are critical to the everyday work of school counselors. First, school counselors are seen as leaders in the school, as they manage their programs and promote student achievement. They lead meetings, facilitate the development of programs, and provide consultation for staff. Second, they are considered advocates who fight to remove barriers for all students in their personal/social, academic, and career development. In doing so, they act with and on behalf of students. In some cases, they may have to be the voice for a student or parent to help meet their needs. Third, in order to ensure that programs are effectively meeting the needs of all students, collaboration is crucial. School counselors can work together with other key stakeholders inside and out of the school such as teachers, administrators, social workers, school psychologists, parents, coaches, or school nurses to ensure that there is a system of support available. Finally, school counselors work across school, family, and community systems to promote change and support student success. School counselors who identify barriers to success can advocate and lead toward systemic change. They can be a voice to change school policies or fight to transform state or district legislation that impedes student achievement. In order to be most effective, school counselors must embrace these four themes across all elements of their programs.

• CONCLUSION

In conclusion, since the field has gone through many changes, and only recently has adopted a national model, there are still schools who followed older models of school counseling, and school communities who are only familiar with the profession as they saw it many years ago (Dollarhide & Saginak, 2012, p. 75). Despite some resistance to using the ASCA model, research indicates that programs that align with the model, or related elements, have students with higher levels of achievement and higher graduation rates than programs that do not (Carey, Harrington, Martin, & Stevenson, 2012; Wilkerson, Perusse, & Hughes, 2013). When schools are not aware of comprehensive school counseling programs, counselors may get assigned more administrative duties (Gysbers & Henderson, 2012). Using this model, school counselors can audit and evaluate their programs and determine how to most effectively meet students' needs (Hatch, 2010). Therefore, the ASCA National Model is a valuable tool for standardizing the school counseling profession and providing a framework that schools can use to design comprehensive school counseling programs.

Activity: Reflect and answer this question: What factors do you think would hinder or help school counselors in implementing this model in their schools? Share this reflection with your field experience class.

____

____

____

____

____

The ASCA Standards

In order to determine what students should get out of a school counseling program, the ASCA standards were developed. They include the knowledge, attitudes, and skills that all students should have as a result of participation in a counseling program (ASCA, 2004). School counselors should align their programs and interventions with these standards. The standards are divided into three domains in which school counselors should focus: (1) academic, (2) personal/social, and (3) career. The academic standards focus on the knowledge, skills, and attitudes that students should acquire as a result of the school counseling program in their academic development. The academic standards are related to developing effective learning skills and mind-sets, enhancing learning and planning goals, and building connections between life and school. Examples of academic standards include the following: Standard A:A2.1—"Apply time-management and task-management skills" and Standard A:A3.3—"Develop a broad range of interests and abilities."

The career development standards emphasize the transition from school to career. The career standards focus on the how students are investigating the world of work, implementing strategies toward career goals, and acquiring knowledge and applying skills toward career goals. Examples of career standards include Standard C:B1.1—"Apply decision-making skills to career planning, course selection and career transition" and— C:C1.2 "Explain how work can help to achieve personal success and satisfaction."

The personal/social standards focus on the personal and social growth and development of students, as a result of the school counseling program. These standards include self-awareness and interpersonal skills, as well as being able to connect self-knowledge to developing goals and interacting with peers. These standards also address safety and survival skills. Examples of personal/social standards include Standard PS:B1.1—"Use a decision-making and problem-solving model" and PS:C1.8—"Learn about the emotional and physical dangers of substance use and abuse." The ASCA standards may not all be addressed in one year of schooling but may be met in different developmental ways across Grades K–12. The standards can be used as a way of assessing programs and determining and demonstrating how school counseling programs help students.

Activity: With a partner, discuss some specific topics that may arise at each level (high, middle, and elementary school) across each of the domains (academic, personal/social, and career).

____

____

____

____

Concluding Activity

Students will work in small groups (4–5 students in each group); have them decide which grade level they would like to address in this activity. Each group will select a topic that is relevant to their level (e.g., bullying in elementary or middle school, or SAT preparation in high school). Students will find three standards related to their topic and discuss how that may deliver the content to their population of students. They will then present this to the class.

• REFERENCES

American Counseling Association. (2014). *ACA code of ethics.* Retrieved from https://www.counseling.org/resources/aca-code-of-ethics.pdf

American School Counselor Association. (2003). *The ASCA National Model: A framework for school counseling programs* (1st ed.). Alexandria, VA: Author.

American School Counselor Association. (2004). *ASCA national standards for students.* Retrieved from http://static.pdesas.org/content/documents/ASCA_National_Standards_for_Students.pdf.

American School Counselor Association. (2010). *Ethical standards for school counselors.* Retrieved from https://www.schoolcounselor.org/asca/media/asca/Resource%20Center/Legal%20and%20Ethical%20Issues/Sample%20Documents/EthicalStandards2010.pdf

American School Counselor Association. (2012a). *ASCA school counselor competencies.* Retrieved from https://www.schoolcounselor.org/asca/media/asca/home/SCCompetencies.pdf

American School Counselor Association. (2012b). *The ASCA National Model: A framework for school counseling programs* (3rd ed.). Alexandria, VA: Author.

Carey, J., Harrington, K., Martin, I., & Stevenson, D. (2012). A statewide evaluation of the outcomes of the implementation of ASCA National Model: School counseling programs in Utah high schools. *Professional School Counseling, 16*(2), 89–99.

Dahir, C., & Tyson, L. (2010). The ASCA national standards: The foundation of the ASCA National Model. In E. Erford (Ed.), *Professional School Counseling* (2nd ed., pp. 166–176). Austin, TX: PRO-ED.

Dollarhide, C. T., & Saginak, K. A. (2012). *Comprehensive school counseling programs: K–12 delivery systems in action* (2nd ed.). Upper Saddle, NJ: Pearson.

Gysbers, N. C., & Henderson, P. (2012). *Developing and managing your school guidance & counseling program* (5th ed.). Alexandria, VA: American Counseling Association.

Hatch, T. (2010). The ASCA National Model: A framework for school counseling programs: One vision, one voice for the profession. In E. Erford (Ed.), *Professional School Counseling* (2nd ed., pp. 177–190). Austin, TX: PRO-ED.

Hatch, T. (2013). *The use of data in school counseling: Hatching results for students, programs, and the profession.* Thousand Oaks, CA: Corwin.

Schimmel, C. (2008). *School counseling: A brief historical overview.* Retrieved from http://wvde.state.wv.us/counselors/history.html

Vernon, A. (2010). Designing developmental guidance lessons. In E. Erford (Ed.), *Professional school counseling: A handbook of theories, programs & practices* (2nd ed., pp. 224–232). Austin, TX: PRO-ED.

Wilkerson, K., Perusse, R., & Hughes, A. (2013). Comprehensive school counseling programs and student achievement outcomes: A comparative analysis of RAMP versus non-RAMP schools. *Professional School Counseling, 16*(3), 172–184.

LESSON 5

DOCUMENTATION, CONFIDENTIALITY, AND INFORMED CONSENT

Susan Hansen
School-Counseling-Zone.com

Helen S. Hamlet

"My records have been subpoenaed . . ."

Real Life

A number of students in your school have taken part in demonstrations protesting violence between the youth of the city and law enforcement. Several students on your caseload have shared with you in a counseling session that they have attended these illegal protests. A representative from the local and state law enforcement visits you and has asked you to identify any students you may recognize from video of the demonstration and to share your case notes on any students involved in the protest.

Lesson Five

Documentation, Confidentiality, and Informed Consent

Susan Hansen
School-Counseling-Zone.com

Helen S. Hamlet
"My records have been subpoenaed . . ."

Essential Question: How do I document and keep records that are legal, ethical, and useful?

Objectives

Students will:

- demonstrate understanding of legal and ethical concerns regarding documenting their work as a school counsellor.
- demonstrate understanding of how to keep appropriate records and files.
- demonstrate understanding of ASCA ethical standards and state legal standards in regards to confidentiality and documentation.

CACREP 2016 Standards

- Demonstrate appropriate school counselor roles in consultation with families, P–12 and postsecondary school personnel, and community agencies (5.G.2.b)
- Demonstrate knowledge about legislation and government policy relevant to school counseling (5.G.2.m)
- Demonstrate knowledge of legal and ethical considerations specific to school counseling. (5.G.2.n)

MPCAC Standards

- Professional counselor identity, ethical behavior, and social justice practices

Video Spark

http://www.schoolcounselor.org/school-counselors-members/professional-development/annual-conference/2014-conference-webstream/first-lady-s-address

First Lady Michelle Obama addresses the ASCA Conference on July 1, 2014

• INTRODUCTION

While ASCA recommends a ratio of 250 students to one school counselor, the national average ratio of students to one counselor is approximately 500. The expectation that a school counselor can remember information on each student meeting is clearly unrealistic. Hence, documentation of our work activities is very important. It is important for multiple reasons: it enables counselors to keep current on students' personal, academic, and career development; to document how much time is spent providing services;

to document what services are provided; and to support accountability through data collection. ASCA's ethical standards clearly delineate the school counselor's role and responsibility. ASCA's standards regarding student records are as follows:

A.8. Student Records—Professional school counselors:

a. Maintain and secure records necessary for rendering professional services to the student as required by laws, regulations, institutional procedures, and confidentiality guidelines.

b. Keep sole-possession records or individual student case notes separate from students' educational records in keeping with state laws.

c. Recognize the limits of sole-possession records and understand these records are a memory aid for the creator and in absence of privileged communication may be subpoenaed and may become educational records when they are shared or are accessible to others in either verbal or written form or when they include information other than professional opinion or personal observations.

d. Establish a reasonable timeline for purging sole-possession records or case notes. Suggested guidelines include shredding sole possession records when the student transitions to the next level, transfers to another school, or graduates. Apply careful discretion and deliberation before destroying sole-possession records that may be needed by a court of law such as notes on child abuse, suicide, sexual harassment, or violence.

e. Understand and abide by the Family Education Rights and Privacy Act (Family Policy Compliance Office, 1974), which safeguards student's records and allows parents to have a voice in what and how information is shared with others regarding their child's educational records (ASCA, 2010).

● CONFIDENTIALITY

The trust developed in the counseling relationship is essential to the development of a working relationship between the student and the school counselor. To some degree, this trust rests on the counselor's ability to maintain confidentiality. The school counselor's ability to maintain confidentiality is informed by the ASCA ethical standards, school district policy, and federal and state law.

The American School Counseling Association (2014) clearly defines the parameters of confidentiality and the role of the school counselor. ASCA uses the term *confidentiality* as an ethical term. ASCA writes:

The role of the professional school counselor in regards to confidentiality is

- to support the students right to privacy and protect confidential information received from students, the family, guardians and staff members.
- to explain the meaning and limits of confidentiality to students in developmentally appropriate terms.
- to provide appropriate disclosure and informed consent regarding the counseling relationship and confidentiality.
- to inform students and the family of the limits to confidentiality when
    - student poses a danger to self or others.
    - court-ordered disclosure.
    - consultation with other professionals in support of the student, that is, colleagues, supervisors, treatment teams, and other support personnel.
    - privilege communication is not granted by state laws and local guidelines (e.g., school board policies).
- to keep personal notes separate from educational records and not disclose their contents except when privacy exceptions exist.

- to seek guidance from supervisors and appropriate legal advice when their records are subpoenaed.
- to assert their belief that information shared by students is "confidential" and should not be revealed without the student's consent.
- to adhere to all laws protecting student records, health information, and special services (i.e., HIPAA, FERPA, IDEA) (ASCA, 2014).

Confidentiality is a professional's promise or contract to respect students' privacy by not disclosing anything revealed during counseling except under agreed upon conditions. The moral principles of fidelity, nonmaleficence, and beneficence apply to students' rights to confidentiality. *Fidelity* is defined as allegiance or loyalty to which one is bound by pledge or duty. *Nonmaleficence* is defined as the ethical principle of doing no harm. *Beneficence* is defined as action that is done for the benefit of others. In applying the moral principle of fidelity, school counselors make explicit and implicit promises to students that they will actively work against disclosing students' secrets, except under agreed upon conditions. Without this assurance, most students would be hesitant to seek the help they need to improve their mental health. A student's trust in his or her counselors is violated when information is communicated without their knowledge and permission, or when information, including details beyond what is minimally required, is communicated to third parties.

School counselors are expected to adhere to the moral principle of nonmaleficence when trying to make decisions about communicating confidential information. In this process, counselors will clearly inform students regarding the conditions under which confidentiality may be breached. These conditions include, but are not exclusive to, if a student is in danger of harming self or others. However, confidentiality becomes more complicated in a school setting because state laws defining the limits of school counselor confidentiality differ.

In addition, at times, school counselors may need to share information with teachers or administrators in order to facilitate academic success. Since information in a school setting is shared on a "need to know" basis, the importance of clarity during the informed consent process cannot be stressed enough. If counselors break their promise of confidentiality or disclose information without students' consent, students may feel betrayed. As a result, they may lose trust in their counselors and hold back other personal information or they may prematurely terminate the counseling relationship. These actions could cause harm to students. The moral principle of beneficence raises interesting issues for school counselors. If students who would benefit from counseling learn that the school counselor shared information without student consent, they may not seek the very services they need. The maintenance of student confidentiality may be challenged by others who believe that they have a duty to assist the student and, thus, be fully informed. Community support for the school and school counseling may be diminished if parents believe school counselors withhold information vital to proper exercise of their parental duties.

School counselors do not give up their ethical obligation to apply the basic moral principles when counseling children and adolescents. However, they must apply these principles in developmentally appropriate ways and honor the rights of children and adolescents to make decisions while appropriately including their parents and school personnel.

FAMILY EDUCATIONAL RIGHTS AND PRIVACY ACT (FERPA)

The Family Educational Rights and Privacy Act (FERPA) is a federal law that addresses educational records not privileged communication. The following section will address privileged communication. FERPA provides parents with the right to access their child's educational records, seek to have the records amended, and have some control over disclosure of personally identifiable information from education records. When a student turns 18 years of age or enters a postsecondary institution at any age, these rights transfer to the student (Family Policy Compliance Office, 2015). School counselors' personal notes should be kept separate from FERPA regulated educational records.

Privileged Communication

Privileged communication is a legal term granted by federal or state statutes. Carolyn Stone (2014) of the ASCA Ethics Committee investigated the state statutes regarding confidentiality and privilege for school counselors. Stone indicated that "state statutes fall into one of four categories:

1. Unconditional privilege
2. Privilege with exceptions
3. Counselors are mentioned in statute with regard to confidentiality and privilege but the language does not specifically state school counselors
4. Mute on privilege for counselors" (p. 1).

Interestingly, the results of this research found important state-to-state specificity regarding privileged communication. For example, Texas specifically writes in its statute "Mental health counselors are the only counselors granted exceptions; school counselors do not qualifiy as mental health professionals under Rule 502." Conversely, North Dakota's Title 31: Judicial Proof; 31-01-06.1 states "For the purpose of counseling in a school system, any elementary or secondary school counselor possessing a valid North Dakota guidance credential . . . shall be legally immune from disclosing any privileged or confidential communication made to such counselor in a counseling interview. Such communication shall be disclosed when requested by the counselee." However, in the majority of states, school counselors are required to testify in court proceedings (Stone, 2012).

In summary, ASCA clearly supports the importance of confidentiality in the counseling relationship while stressing the importance of informed consent. This informed consent should include the potential breach of confidentiality in the following three situations: clear and imminent harm to self, clear and imminent harm to others, and if it is legally required. Additionally, it is critical that you know your state's statutes regarding privileged communication for school counselors.

Informed Consent

Informed consent is both a legal and ethical principle requiring school counselors to adequately disclose to students potential risks, benefits, and alternatives to proposed counseling. Minor students, however, cannot legally give informed consent, only their parents can. Although the majority of students served by school counselors cannot legally give informed consent, they can assent to counseling without parental consent. Some school districts or school principals have policies that require counselors to obtain parents' permission before beginning to counsel students, and others require counselors to seek permission if they see students for more than a specified number of counseling sessions (e.g., two or three). ASCA's ethical standards indicate that a person has a right to privacy; however, this must be accomplished within the laws and policies addressing confidentiality (Williams, 2007). Due to the ambiguity surrounding confidentiality, having a comprehensive knowledge of the school district's policies specific to informed consent and confidentiality are critical.

● DOCUMENTATION TIPS AND GUIDELINES

There is no way to give one absolute set of guidelines for documentation in a school counseling setting. Each district and each school may have its own policies, based on the needs of its students or community. Having said that, here are some things to consider.

Basic Considerations

First, check with your supervisor to find out if there is a specific procedure or set of guidelines already in place. If there is, please use it, but you may also want to consider the following items so you can be as efficient and effective as possible, and so you can be prepared in case legal or ethical dilemmas arise.

Unlike social workers and clinical counselors, whose documentation is considered "case notes" and may be read by various people, school counselors often keep "anecdotal notes," which are separate from the student's permanent record, and kept in folders in each counselor's private filing cabinet. I would encourage you to ask your supervisor ***in advance*** who has access to your files and who is allowed to see them upon request.

For instance, if a parent asks to see your notes, are you allowed (or required) to grant that request? Does your administration have the right to access your files? It's important to know this ahead of time.

Anecdotal Notes

If your records are considered anecdotal notes, then they are your personal property and are not to be shown to anyone, under any circumstances. When I worked in the public schools, I was taught that if I physically show my notes to one other person, the notes become public property and can no longer be considered confidential, so anyone can see them—they could even be printed in the newspaper. Even if I was subpoenaed, I was instructed to take my notes with me and read from them in court, but not to visually show them or turn them over to anyone.

If you are keeping anecdotal notes, you may want to consider including a simple, one-page summary of your time spent with a particular student, which you could refer to, or even make copies of, if a parent or your administrator requested the information. A sample of a summary like this is included later in this article.

When to Get More Detailed

If you are keeping anecdotal records, there are certain situations where you will want to take more detailed notes, usually on a separate page from your basic summary. These are typically the times when student safety is in question, or there may be legal involvement, and you are required to notify parents, administration, the school nurse, the police, or Child Protective Services (CPS) about something a student has told you. These situations will most often include the following:

- any question of a student's safety being at risk
- self-harm (such as cutting, eating disorders, etc.) or suicide attempt or plan
- threats of violence or harm to others, particularly at school
- drugs or weapons on campus; some off-campus drug use
- known or suspected abuse or neglect

- suspected or confirmed pregnancy
- sexual activity between minors and adults (even with consent)
- harassment, bullying, or discrimination
- cheating, stealing, particularly at school
- custody battles (because of potential legal involvement)
- angry or volatile parents in most any situation
- any other situation you feel uneasy about—better safe than sorry!

Which Details to Include

When you do need to get more detailed, here are some things to include in your documentation:

- the time and date that you spoke with the student
- exactly what the student said, in quotes, without paraphrasing or editorializing
- interventions that you used with the student at the time (processes you walked them through, worksheets you had them fill out, etc.)
- recommendations or suggestions that you made to the student
- follow-up calls or conversations you had with anyone else (parents, administrators, police, CPS, etc.) including time and date, who you spoke with, and the content of those conversations, also specifically quoting rather than paraphrasing what the other parties said when it seems significant
- any recommendations, referrals, or community resources you offered to the parents
- any other details you want to have in writing for future reference

Documenting on the Computer

If you are keeping your anecdotal records on a computer that is owned by the school, which is the case in some districts, please keep in mind that even if your records are considered confidential, they are still part of a bigger network and may be accessed by others. If you want more privacy than that, you may choose at certain times to hand write your notes and keep them in a locked filing cabinet.

Some districts are requiring counselors to do all of their documentation on the school's shared computer system, where it can be seen by other counselors, administration, and anyone with access to this system. While I believe this is ***a huge violation of ethics and confidentiality,*** it is the policy in some schools.

If your school requires this, I strongly encourage you to keep that documentation very general and minimal, and keep more detailed notes in student files, in a locked filing cabinet in your office. Ethically, informing students and parents about this computerized documentation system is important; they have a right to know in advance who will have access to their records.

Documentation at Different Grade Levels

If you are a high school counselor, you may not be required to keep track of every student you see, or those records may be kept on sign-up sheets in the reception area of the counseling department. If that is the case, the only time you will need to document specific information is when you have an exception to your regular confidentiality guidelines—in other words, if you need to notify parents, administration, or the school nurse about something, or make a CPS or police report.

If you are a school counselor anywhere in Grades K–8, you may be required to keep documentation of every student you see, as well as more specific and detailed notes in situations where safety or legality is a concern. Again, check with your supervisor in advance to see what is expected.

Documentation Options

If you are required to keep basic documentation of every student you see, whether for statistical purposes or accountability, one of the easiest ways to do this is to use a daily planner or calendar and just write in the names of the students you see each day, along with your other daily information. If you need to keep track of other basic information, such as how many students you see from each grade level, or on what subjects, you could make notations on your calendar such as

Sarah Jones, 6th gr., gossip Zach Garcia, 8th gr., scheduling Emily Miller, 4th gr., grief.

If you need a basic documentation list of all students you see, which you can then turn in to your supervisor or principal (and you don't want to make copies of your daily planner, which might contain other information you don't want made public), you can create a separate form that you can photocopy and turn in periodically.

This also means you can keep the vast majority of your documentation very brief and save the detailed note-taking for the times it's actually needed. Please see the sample **Record of All Students Seen** form below.

If you need to create separate folders for some or all of the students you see, I would recommend having one basic documentation sheet for each student that you could photocopy and turn in to a supervisor or administrator if needed, and that you keep additional anecdotal notes on separate pages, also stored in the student's folder. That way, the basic sheet is your "official documentation" and any additional notes are anecdotal records and are your private property, not to be shared. Please see the **Student Contact Sheet** form below.

You may need to document parent contacts as well, and I would certainly recommend it in any case where you are notifying parents about a safety issue or another touchy or controversial issue involving their child. In some schools, you will be asked to keep this as a separate record, and in others, it will be part of your regular daily documentation and can be listed along with student contacts or in your daily planner or calendar. I would suggest keeping track of parent contacts in the student's individual folder. If you need to make a separate log, please see the sample **Parent/Guardian Contact Log** form below.

If you are facilitating one or more support groups, you may also want to keep track of the students in your group, group attendance, and what topics or lessons you've covered in group. Please see the sample **Small-Group Log** form below.

Activity: Using your field experiences, complete each of the following forms. Discuss the completed forms in your field experience course.

- Student Contact Sheet (Appendix A)
- Individual Counseling Session Summary Form #1 (Appendix B)
- Individual Counseling Session Summary Form #2 (Appendix C)
- Parent/Guardian Contact Log (Appendix D)
- Parent/Guardian Consultation Form (Appendix E)
- Small-Group Log (Appendix F)

● REFERENCES

American School Counselor Association. (2010). *Ethical standards for school counselors*. Retrieved from https://www.schoolcounselor.org/asca/media/asca/Resource%20Center/Legal%20and%20Ethical%20Issues/Sample%20Documents/EthicalStandards2010.pdf

American School Counselor Association. (2014). *The school counselor and confidentiality*. Retrieved from https://www.schoolcounselor.org/asca/media/asca/PositionStatements/PS_Confidentiality.pdf

Council for Accreditation for Counseling and Related Program. (2014). *2016 standards*. Retrieved from http://www.cacrep.org

Family Policy Compliance Office. (2015). *FERPA for school officials*. Retrieved from http://familypolicy.ed.gov/ferpa-school-officials

Masters in Psychology and Counseling Accreditation Council. (2015). *Accreditation manual*. Retrieved from http://www.mpcacaccreditation.org/about/accreditation-manual

Stone, C. (2012). *Confidentiality, privileged communication and your legal muscle*. Retrieved from https://www.schoolcounselor.org/magazine/blogs/march-april-2012/confidentiality,-privileged-communication-and-your

Stone, C. (2014). *State statutes regarding confidentiality and privilege for the students of school counselors*. Retrieved from http://www.alaskaschoolcounselor.org/file_cabinet/download/0x00007a4dd

Williams, R. (2007). *To tell or not to tell: The question of informed consent*. Retrieved from https://www.schoolcounselor.org/magazine/blogs/september-october-2007/to-tell-or-not-to-tell-the-question-of-informed-c

APPENDIX A

Student Contact Sheet

Date: ____________________

Student Name	*Arrival Time*	*Time Left Office*	*No Show*

Student Name	*Arrival Time*	*Time Left Office*	*No Show*

● APPENDIX B

Individual Counseling Session Summary

NAME:____ **DATE:**__________________

SUBJECTIVE (Description of Presenting Concern): ______________________________________

____

OBJECTIVE (Topics discussed):

____ Academic Progress/Grades ____ Drugs/Alcohol

____ Friendships/Peers relationships ____ Home/Family

____ Postsecondary Transitioning ____ Discipline/Behavior

____ Other

Summary:

____

____

____

ASSESSMENT __ 1st Meeting __ No Change __ Improvement

Summary:

____

____

PLAN OF ACTION:

____ Academic intervention
____ Group counseling
____ Referral to outside resources
____ Individual counseling
____ Skill training
____ Actions to be taken by student

Summary:

____

____

Counselor's Plan of Action: ____ **None needed** ____ **Next Appointment**

____ Contact parents
____ SAP referral
____ Collaborate with school personnel
____ Contact outside resources
____ Referral for group (in school)
____ Other

Summary:

____

● APPENDIX C

Individual Counseling Session Summary

Date: ____________ Time (meeting starts): ____________ Time (meeting ends): ____________

Student's Name: ______________________________ Grade: ____________

Summary:

● APPENDIX D

Parent/Guardian Contact Sheet

Date: ____________________

Parent/Student Name	Phone	E-mail	Scheduled Meeting	Drop In	Topic

(Continued)

(Continued)

Parent/Student Name	*Phone*	*E-mail*	*Scheduled Meeting*	*Drop In*	*Topic*

● APPENDIX E

Parent/Guardian Consultation

Student Name: ______________________________ Date: ______________

Parent Name: ____

Contact requested by: ______________________ Date of request: ______________

E-mail: ______________ Phone call: __________ Note: ________ In person: ______

APPENDIX F

Small-Group Log

Date: ______________________ **Type of Group:** ______________________

Topic for This Group Session: ______________________

Student's Name	*Attended group*		*Notes*
	Yes	*No*	

(Continued)

(Continued)

Student's Name	*Attended group*		*Notes*
	Yes	*No*	

Lesson 6

ACCOUNTABILITY MATTERS: WHERE DOES ALL THE TIME GO?

Timothy A. Poynton
University of Massachusetts Boston

Real Life

Imagine yourself as a first-year school counselor, employed in your dream job in a school with colleagues you enjoy who value you. In the spring, you learn that the school board is considering eliminating one counselor position because there is a budget shortfall—and since you are the new counselor, that would be you. What could you do to advocate for your job? You could ask colleagues to speak about your value and contributions, but without "hard data" this is often not enough to sway a school board. Put yourself in the school board's shoes—they have a fixed amount of money to spend, and something needs to be cut.

Lesson Six

Accountability Matters: Where Does All the Time Go?

Timothy A. Poynton
University of Massachusetts Boston

Essential Question: Why would I want to document time spent providing interventions, and how do I do it?

Objectives

Students will

- demonstrate an understanding of why documenting interventions is important.
- demonstrate knowledge of different methods for documenting interventions.

CACREP 2016 STANDARDS

- Competencies to advocate for school counseling roles (5.G.2.f)
- Design and evaluation of school counseling programs (5.G.3.b)
- Use of data to advocate for programs and students (5.G.3.o)

MPCAC Standards

- Professional counselor identity, ethical behavior, and social-justice practices
- Counseling, consultation, and social justice advocacy theories and skills
- Ecological, contextual, multicultural, social justice foundation of human development

Video Spark:

https://www.youtube.com/watch?v=KspKFDD2Jl4

Accountability + Data = Achievement 2011

● INTRODUCTION

Documenting how school counselors spend their time is not a new phenomenon and is historically linked in the school counseling literature to accountability—often referred to as *time analysis*. Charles T. Dykstra (1973) described guidance reports he used to "give the faculty, administration, and board of education an awareness of the scope of guidance activities" (p. 151). M. M. Gubser (1974) also described time analysis data as one source of accountability data, in addition to behavioral and academic information from students. Similarly, Thomas Fairchild and Tracey Seeley (1994) described the use of time analysis procedures for accountability purposes. Janna Scarborough (2005) created the School Counselor Activity Rating Scale (SCARS), which is an instrument designed to highlight discrepancies between the amount of time a counselor actually spends in various activities in relation to the amount of time the counselor would prefer to spend in those same activities.

Documenting how a counselor spends his time throughout the day—"tracking" how time is spent—is drudgery perhaps, and does take time away from meeting directly with students. On the other hand, documenting the interventions a counselor provides throughout the day by keeping track of how her time is spent is also very useful as a proactive data collection strategy to arm counselors with useful information to engage in advocacy efforts for students and counselors and to assess alignment with modern models of school counseling practice.

Imagine yourself as a first-year school counselor, employed in your dream job in a school with colleagues you enjoy who value you. In the spring, you learn that the school board is considering eliminating one counselor position because there is a budget shortfall — and since you are the new counselor, that would be you. What could you do to advocate for your job? You could ask colleagues to speak about your value and contributions, but without "hard data" this is often not enough to sway a school board. Put yourself in the school board's shoes—they have a fixed amount of money to spend, and something needs to be cut. They need to know what is tangibly lost—how students, families, and the school community are affected—if you are not there next year. If you have been keeping track of how you spend your time providing programs, services, and counseling to students, you can concretely describe what the school community will lose if your position is cut. For example, you could provide a summary describing the amount of time you spend engaged in meeting students' needs that the school board values, something like "If we removed one counselor, there would be 142 fewer hours of college counseling, 38 fewer hours of anti-bullying education, 48 hours of consultation with parents . . . ." If you have been keeping track of how you spend your time, you will have the information you need to advocate for yourself. If you have not been proactively collecting this data, it will be much more difficult to advocate concretely—and will likely be too late to collect data that could help you.

Keeping track of how you spend your time can also help you see how well you are aligned to models of practice such as the American School Counselor Association (ASCA) National Model (2012), which asserts that at least 80% of a counselor's time is spent providing services directly or indirectly to students. Direct student services include implementing the school counseling core curriculum, responsive services, and individual student planning, and indirect services include things such as consultation, collaboration, and referral. No more than 20% of a counselor's time should be spent on things such as meetings and "other duties as assigned," such as lunch or hall duty, or anything counselors may be asked to do that does not require a master's degree in counseling.

When you think about all the reasons that may exist to spend a little of your time keeping track of how you spend it, they all lead to benefits in helping you advocate. Tracking your time can help you advocate for counselors to spend more time in appropriate activities and less time in inappropriate activities. It can help you advocate for not only keeping the same number of counselors, but justify increasing the number of counselors. Documenting the interventions school counselors provide is also one way to understand student needs and provides for developing an understanding of how to better meet them. For example, if all of the school counselors in the school are spending 25% of their time meeting with students reactively in mediating peer conflicts, this may indicate a more proactive, whole-school approach to improving interpersonal relations is needed. Also, if counselors are spending too much time in noncounseling responsibilities, documenting it alongside interventions can highlight the discrepancy in concrete ways.

● HOW TO TRACK HOW YOUR TIME IS SPENT

There are many ways you can document how your days are spent, and what is most important is finding a system that works for you, in the context you work within, that gives you the information you need to effectively advocate. Whichever system best meets these criteria will be the right system for you. One feature of school counseling that presents unique challenges in terms of documenting how our time is spent is that our days often evolve in ways we never planned. This means that whatever system we might choose needs to be able to somehow account for this. Elaborated below are some ways people have tracked their time along with the possible benefits and challenges each has in terms of implementation in school counseling practice.

Handwritten Calendar

Before the proliferation of computers and related technology tools, records were kept in some form of handwritten form. For keeping track of time, a calendar was often used as it provided for a logical way of both planning for how time would be spent in the future, and documenting how it actually was spent. In my own school counseling practice, I had one of those desk blotter calendars where I recorded appointments. At the end of the school year, at my principal's request, I would go through the calendar to summarize the number of student contacts I had. I have to admit I loathed doing this, as it was mind-numbingly dull work to do. In retrospect, I could have done things more proactively to get more out of my effort—for example, I could have coded each appointment with a reason (e.g., crisis intervention, academic, personal/social), and used those to get a sense of how many student contacts I had across the year in each code. If I would have taken just a little bit of time each month to summarize the contacts, it would have made the task of the end-of-year summary less arduous—and I could have also seen how student needs changed or remained the same each month.

The handwritten calendar was easy to use, and it was not too intrusive on my day-to-day work with students—in fact, my schedule of future meetings was also the same place I recorded unplanned meetings with students made it relatively pain free to use, most of the time. Since I did not always meet with students in my office, I did have to remember to then write down those student contacts—something I have to admit I did not always remember to do. To summarize, the benefits of using a paper-pencil type of calendaring system are intuitive and relatively easy to incorporate into school counseling practice, while the challenges are summarizing the resulting information easily in meaningful ways.

Since we now live with technology embedded in most facets of our lives, the remaining examples of ways to track time will leverage those technologies—and will be focused on those I have explicitly seen school counselors using in practice. There are time-tracking apps that exist online and for smartphones that may hold promise for school counselors that are not reviewed here—I would encourage you to explore and see how these might be adapted to school counseling practice!

Electronic Calendars

A natural extension of the paper-pencil calendars are online calendars (e.g., Google Calendar) and other computer-based calendars (e.g., Microsoft Outlook). You are likely using a calendar like one of these already! Since the Microsoft Outlook calendar and Google Calendar are among the most popular, these will be reviewed in more detail—other calendaring apps are likely very similar in terms of functionality, making the concepts described below applicable beyond these two. Google Calendars, which are currently free to use, are relatively ubiquitous—if you have a Gmail account already, you have a Google Calendar. In the Google Calendar, you can relatively easily create events using a menu-driven approach, or can "quick add" events using shorthand, such as "Collaboration Teacher SP 11:33a–12:14p." In the Outlook Calendar (which is not free, but comes alongside the Outlook Email client when purchased), creating events is similar to that of a Google Calendar, but there is slightly less flexibility when creating calendar entries. For example, Outlook presents time in 15- or 30-minute intervals; if you want to quick add an event in Outlook with time intervals that are different from the 15- or 30-minute intervals, you have to manually edit the calendar entry to put in more precise times—which makes the quick add not so quick.

One way to summarize the information you have input in Google and Outlook calendars is to simply search your calendar for keywords—but that does require that you have defined those keywords ahead of time. Doing so will help you more easily summarize the information in your calendar. Think of the keywords as codes or tags; these will provide a way of categorizing your calendar entries that makes them more meaningful when you search for them later. For example, you can create a code called *SCCC* that represents time you spend in the school counseling core curriculum, which you then use each time you make a calendar entry when you plan on implementing curriculum. Later, when you search your calendar for SCCC, the search results will show you all entries containing that code, which you can then add up to calculate how much time was spent implementing curriculum. With all of that explained, you probably see some challenges with this system. As of this writing, there is no easy way to summarize all time spent, or all time spent in specific coded activities—you have to manually add up all the time spent. It may be worth noting that Outlook Calendars can be exported to an Excel file, where you could then have Excel calculate the amount of time spent across all entries or within categories of entries, but that is beyond the scope of what can be elaborated in this lesson. There is an add-in called the Time Elapsed Analysis & Reporting System (T.E.A.R.S) for Excel that you could purchase (currently $3.99) that automates the process of exporting and analyzing Outlook Calendar data. Developed by school counselor educator Russ Sabella, you can find information about this add-in at schoolcounselor.com/tears/.

To summarize, the benefits of using calendars such as those provided by Google or Microsoft Outlook are that they are somewhat easily incorporated into school counseling practice and can be used for both planning and time tracking. The challenges of these calendars are that analyzing the resulting information can still be cumbersome, and you may be limited in your calendaring software options by the technology environment provided by your school.

Activity: Use an electronic calendar to document your activity for at least one day at your internship.

Online Forms

Online forms (AKA online surveys), such as those provided by Google and SurveyMonkey (among many others), can provide a useful platform for documenting how a counselor's time is spent. Using online forms like these can be used to do more than just document how your time was spent; they can also be used to serve as a notekeeping system as well, where the resulting data are housed in an easily searchable spreadsheet or database. In addition, some of these online form providers also provide some basic analyses with the click of a button—both Google and SurveyMonkey do, for example.

Once you have chosen an online form service provider, an online form can be constructed to collect information for each "event" you would like to document. I would recommend collecting the following information, at a minimum: student name or initials, date, amount of time spent on the activity, the reason (or "code") for the activity/meeting/counseling session, and a place for notes or summary of the activity. There may be other information you would like to collect, such as a referral source or the number of students in group activities, but remember that the longer the form is, the longer it will take for you to complete it.

With the form complete, you can then start recording information on how your time is spent using the form, with the added benefit of having a searchable electronic file cabinet of sorts for notes and meetings with students. Having the information recorded like this in a spreadsheet or database format makes it very easy to retrieve and analyze information. For example, imagine you have a meeting with the parents of a student you have met with six times over the past 3 months. To prepare for the meeting, you could sort your spreadsheet by student name, locate the student, and print out that section of the spreadsheet for your meeting (you could also accomplish this by applying a filter to your spreadsheet). Analyzing how your time is spent may be a little more involved. As I mentioned earlier, Google and SurveyMonkey do provide basic analyses of data collected using their systems. For example, a Google form could be summarized in one click of the mouse button, but it would only be able to provide limited information, such as how many student contacts you had for each student reason. The built-in analysis functions are typically not useful for summarizing how time is spent in various activities because they cannot (currently) disaggregate data. However, if the resulting spreadsheet data can be opened in Microsoft Excel, there is an Excel add-in designed for school counselors, EZAnalyze, that can quickly display disaggregated data (Poynton, 2007).

Online forms have some advantages over calendars in terms of tracking time—information is more easily retrievable and summarized if the form is constructed correctly. Furthermore, if all of the counselors in a school or district use the same form, the resulting information is also easier to summarize at the school or district level as well. One disadvantage to using online forms is that you will probably need to use the forms in addition to a calendar because the forms cannot be used for planning. If you use the forms for notekeeping, you also need to understand the ethical, legal, and practical considerations when doing so, which vary not only across states, but across districts within the same state.

Activity 1: Discuss the ethical and legal considerations in keeping notes on your counseling work with students. Read Lynn Merlone (2005) before responding.

Activity 2: With your internship group members, create an online form for documenting how your time is spent at internship and use it for at least one day.

EZAnalyze TimeTracker

The EZAnalyze TimeTracker (Poynton, 2012) was developed explicitly as a tool to be used by school counselors for tracking time and keeping notes. A specialized Microsoft Excel spreadsheet, the TimeTracker was designed to be a free tool to help school counselors track their time in detail to measure the "dose" of interventions that students received while also allowing counselors to see how well their practice aligns with the ASCA National Model. The TimeTracker also does a little more than just track time—it also allows for notes to be kept within the system and provides a variety of reports.

The first step in using the TimeTracker is to add student names and student ID numbers. Instead of entering all of this information by hand, it is recommended that the information be retrieved from the school's student information system and then copied and pasted into the TimeTracker. The use of ID numbers as they are represented in the student information system is crucial, because using the same number in both systems allows for the merging of their data. For example, imagine you have implemented a new set of classroom-based lessons on prosocial behavior and want to assess the impact on discipline referrals. You could export the data on discipline referrals from the student information system, export the TimeTracker data, and merge the datasets together with a tool such as SPSS (IBM, 2014) or EZAnalyze (Poynton, 2007). With the merged data, you could calculate a variety of statistics to assess the impact, such as a correlation between the time students spent in the prosocial behavior lessons and discipline referrals. The second step in setting up the TimeTracker involves editing the "reasons" lists—the codes that define the specific categories of time you will track in terms of time spent with students and time spent in other activities not in direct contact with students. The TimeTracker comes prepopulated with codes derived from the ASCA National Model (2005) but is completely customizable. Most counselors find that they need to add to the list or modify existing codes to capture elements of their work that are unique to their school.

The final step in setting up the TimeTracker is to create groups of students for any planned curriculum or counseling group activities. While this can be done using a point-and-click interface within the TimeTracker, it is cumbersome and time consuming if you are creating groups for every student in the school. There is a tool within the TimeTracker to create groups en masse, and is designed to work with information retrieved from a student information system that can be copied and pasted into the TimeTracker (just like student names and IDs). For example, if you implement a school counseling curriculum on a schoolwide basis and provide the curriculum to students in homerooms, you could export the student names, IDs, and homeroom location from the student information system, and copy and paste that information into the TimeTracker to create groups en masse—each homeroom location would be the group's name.

With the TimeTracker set up, you can track how your time is spent in one of two ways: with a timer where you click a start and stop button, or you can input time in a manner similar to how you would in an online form. The TimeTracker also distinguishes between tracking time spent with students directly and what is dubbed *counselor time*, or time not spent directly with students. An interesting dilemma of sorts was brought to my attention by TimeTracker users—How do you "count" parent phone calls? In early versions of the TimeTracker, this time had to be categorized as time not spent with students (counselor time) because it was not appropriate to count the time as time with a student. This was a dilemma because I truly believe that helping students very often means involving parents in the process to effect lasting change. I solved this dilemma by adding an "indirect time" function to the TimeTracker, where you could associate time not spent directly with students with a student name. Many counselors have found this addition to be helpful because it allowed them to stop using their handwritten phone logs to document parent contact and instead use this function in the TimeTracker to serve that purpose.

The TimeTracker also generates a variety reports: a summary report that provides a detailed overview of how time has been spent; an individual student report that can be printed and brought to meetings to help organize your own thoughts or share with parents; a daily activity report that shows all recorded activity for a single day; a group counseling report that can help you track attendance in group sessions; an indirect time report that summarizes all time spent on behalf of students but not in direct contact with them; a report that provides a list of all the students you have seen, or have yet to see; and a reason report that lists all the students you have seen for a specific, selected reason. All of these reports can be generated for a selected time frame, or for all recorded data. If you would like to learn more about the TimeTracker, there are video tutorials, a user manual, and online documentation available at www.ezanalyze.com/tutorials.htm.

While I would be the first to admit I am biased toward school counselors using the TimeTracker, that does not mean it is the perfect tool for everyone. The benefits of using the TimeTracker are that it is explicitly designed for school counselors, provides both notekeeping and time-tracking functions, and allows for data to be exported for use in traditional data analysis programs. The drawbacks to using the TimeTracker are that it requires a version of Microsoft Excel that supports the Visual Basic for Applications programming language (VBA), sometimes referred to as *macros*, and summarizing data across counselors is not as easy to accomplish as it is with online forms.

Activity: View the video tutorials at http://www.ezanalyze.com/tutorials.htm regarding EZAnalyze TimeTracker initial setup, basic use, and reports. Compare and contrast what you imagine using the TimeTracker would be like against your experience using a calendar and an online form.

Other Ways to Track Time

The methods for documenting how time is spent elaborated above are not an exhaustive list, but are the most common in my opinion. Other tools I have heard counselors use for their time-tracking purposes are various student information systems, including Hallways ($150, http://www.ihatepaperwork.com/hallways) and noteCounselor ($49/year, http://www.notecounselor.com/).

● REFERENCES

American School Counselor Association. (2005). *American School Counselor Association National Model: A framework for school counseling programs* (2nd ed.). Alexandria, VA: Author.

Dykstra, C. T. (1973, November). Accountability: The Monthly and Yearly Guidance Report. *The School Counselor, 21*(2), 151–153.

Fairchild, T. N., & Seeley, T. J. (1994). Time analysis: Still an important accountability tool. *School Counselor, 41*(4), 273–280.

Gubser, M. M. (1974, March). Performance-based counseling: Accountability or liability? *School Counselor, 21*(4), 296–302.

IBM Corp. (2014). *IBM SPSS Statistics, Version 23.0.* Armonk, NY: Author.

Merlone, L. (2005). Record keeping and the school counselor. *Professional School Counseling, 8*(4), 372–376.

Poynton, T. A. (2007). *EZAnalyze Version 3.0* [Computer software and manual]. Retrieved from http://www.ezanalyze.com

Poynton, T. A. (2012). *EZAnalyze TimeTracker* [Computer software and manual]. Retrieved from http://www.ezanalyze.com

Scarborough, J. L. (2005). The School Counselor Activity Rating Scale: An instrument for gathering process data. *Professional School Counseling, 8*(3), 274–283.

PART II

DIVERSITY AND ADVOCACY

Lesson 7: Social Justice

Lesson 8: English Language Learners

Lesson 9: Working With Lesbian, Gay, Bisexual, and Queer Students

Lesson 10: Working With Transgender and Gender Nonconforming Students

LESSON 7

SOCIAL JUSTICE

Krista Malott
Villanova University

"Striving for social justice is the most valuable thing to do in life."

—Einstein

Real Life

In examining school data, you note several academic struggles for the English Language Learner (ELL) youth at your high school. There is a disproportionate rate of special education placement of ELL youth; a high rate of dropout of certain ELL students (when you disaggregate the data, you see it's mainly Mexican American boys, at the 9th-grade level); and high rates of expulsion for ELL boys (when you look up specifics for the last few years of expulsions, you realize that the majority of those boys were Black). In addition, you see a low rate of college attendance for ELLs who are excelling at school, and when you do a bit more research, you realize those youth without citizenship are the ones who do not go on to attend college (likely due to the inability to obtain government loans to fund their education).

Lesson Seven

Social Justice

Krista Malott
Villanova University

Essential Questions: What is the role of the school counselor in facilitating social justice for students? What groups might experience social injustices in our school systems? How do dominant norms relate to social injustices? How do we act (what do we do) to increase justice in our settings? What barriers might be holding us back from social-justice action?

Objectives

Students will

- increase knowledge of social-justice competencies and skills.
- increase knowledge of the school counselor role in addressing injustices.
- increase knowledge and awareness of the various social identities possessed by oneself and youth in the school.
- increase understanding of the ways certain social groups may experience oppression in the school.
- increase student knowledge and awareness of dominant norms.
- increase understanding of the link between dominant norms and social injustices.
- demonstrate competence in identifying and applying skills for use in unjust scenarios.
- identify barriers that impede effective social-justice action.
- identify solutions to overcoming barriers to social-justice action.

CACREP Standards

- Demonstrate an understanding of the multicultural and pluralistic characteristics within and among diverse groups nationally and internationally. (2.2.a)
- Demonstrate multicultural counseling competencies. (2.2.c)
- Demonstrate an understanding of the impact of heritage, attitudes, beliefs, understandings, and acculturative experiences on an individual's view of others. (2.2.d)
- Demonstrate an understanding of the effects of power and privilege for counselors and clients. (2.2.e)
- Demonstrate an understanding of the help-seeking behaviors of diverse clients. (2.2.f)
- Demonstrate an understanding of the impact of spiritual beliefs on clients' and counselors' worldviews. (2.2.g).
- Demonstrate knowledge of strategies for identifying and eliminating barriers, prejudices, and processes of intentional and unintentional oppression and discrimination.

MPCAC Standards

- human development and wellness across the life span
- counseling, consultation, and social-justice advocacy theories and skills
- ecological, contextual, multicultural, social-justice foundation of human development

Video Spark

https://www.ted.com/talks/bryan_stevenson_we_need_to_talk_about_an_injustice?language=en

Bryan Stevenson: We need to talk about an injustice

● INTRODUCTION

Social-justice counseling has been defined as promoting the dignity and human development of clients who are experiencing marginalization through helping them gain equal access to benefits, opportunities, and resources (Chung & Bemak, 2012; Counselors for Social Justice, 2011; Goodman et al., 2004). Scholars have noted social-justice advocacy as the most essential task for the modern school counselor, with social justice-advocate as a necessary role in supporting students in achieving educational, social, and academic success (Bailey, Getch, & Chen-Hayes, 2007; House & Martin, 1999). The call for social-justice work is echoed by national organizations such as the American School Counselor Association (American School Counselor Association [ASCA], 2004, 2005) and the Education Trust (2009).

Social-justice action by school counselors can take many forms. School counselors can lead school reform efforts to challenge educational inequities such as achievement gaps stemming from the less than ideal learning environment that is prevalent in many schools (Marbley, Malott, Flaherty, & Frederick, 2010). They may aid youth in accessing quality educational health, and mental health services when necessary, or bring in experts to provide anti-oppression trainings or interventions (Bemak & Chung, 2005; Cox & Lee, 2007). In addition, they can advocate with, or for, a student who is experiencing discrimination that impedes his or her opportunities, such as ethnic or racial discrimination by a teacher, or speak out against policies or practices that are biased toward a certain population within the school (Dixon, Tucker, & Clark, 2010).

Hence, social-justice action requires various counselor skills and knowledge, with examples including collaboration, consultation, self-and-other critical awareness (regarding one's own and others' social identities, world views, and related experiences of privileges, power, and oppression), dialogic abilities (to inquire about, and dialogue regarding, social injustices), social action, and advocacy (Brady-Amoon, Makhija, Dixit, & Dator, 2012; Ratts, Singh, Nassar-McMillan, Butler, & McCullough, 2015). To this end, professional school counselors can serve as agents for social change by using the American Counseling Association's (ACA) advocacy competencies (see Appendix A) as a framework for executing social-justice advocacy strategies (Ratts et al., 2015). The proposal that school counselors incorporate the advocacy competencies into their practice seems timely given their endorsement in 2003 by the ACA Governing Council (2003, p. 90). Incorporating advocacy competencies into practice requires acquisition of knowledge, skills, and increased self-awareness on social-justice constructs.

This set of five activities in this section draws from evidenced-based practices in higher education (Malott, Hall, Sheelymoore, Krell, & Cardaciotto, 2014) to apply social-justice constructs to school counselor training. In specific, active learning strategies (Sutherland & Bonwell, 1996; Prince, 2004) are applied to increase knowledge and skills in social-justice action in the school setting. *Collaborative* and *problem-based learning* (Allen, Donham, & Bernhardt, 2011; Groccia & Buskist, 2011) will be used across the following sessions, whereby you will be asked to initially reflect on the materials and then work in small groups during your internship class to more deeply explore and apply social-justice constructs and to address complex, real-world problems.

● ACTIVITY I: EXPLORING THE SCHOOL COUNSELOR ROLE

Step I. Introducing Essential Social-Justice Concepts

Read the social-justice resources in Appendix A and identify additional policies or mission statements available in your professional world that relate to social justice and advocacy. Using this information as a resource, develop a set of social-justice constructs that is important to you. Type up, print out, and bring your social-justice constructs list to your field experience class. Tape and hang this set of important social-justice constructs on the classroom walls, making the print large enough for students to wander and read each construct from a distance (note, you may want to make a separate set of these as a handout for students who may have physical limitations to walking).

Here are some suggested concepts for wall hangings (see Appendix A for specified examples and copies of some of these resources):

- all or essential parts of "The ACA Advocacy Competencies: A Social Justice Advocacy Framework for Professional School Counselors" (Ratts, DeKruyf, & Chen-Hayes, 2007)
- essential parts of the "Multicultural and Social Justice Counseling Competencies" (MSJCC) (Ratts et al., 2015)
- social-justice and advocacy-related tenets of the ASCA National Model (2012)
- any essential university, department, program-specific, and state and regional policies or mission statements related to social justice and advocacy
- social-justice or advocacy-related standards in the Council for Accreditation of Counseling and Related Educational Programs (CACREP)
- essential social-justice terms with definitions of social-justice concepts (e.g., *social injustice, advocacy, collaboration, consultation, equity versus equality*, etc.)
- one or two inspirational quotes that embody and illustrate the school counselor role as a social-justice change agent
- levels or continuum of possible social-justice action (see Appendix A)
- levels for possible school counselor social-justice advocacy, with examples (see Appendix A)

Step II. Activity Reflection to the Wander-and-Read Activity

After you have read the wall hangings, reflect on the social-justice concepts and answer the reflection questions. Then briefly (e.g., 15 minutes) discuss the listed concepts to verify understanding of the concepts and to deepen learning. Here are some reflection questions:

- Taken as a whole, what are your thoughts or reactions to these wall hangings and statements?
- Which one most stood out to you?
- Which one do you have a question about?
- How might you summarize your role as a social-justice advocate?
- Who are we advocating for?
- What feelings come up for you regarding stepping into a social-justice advocacy role?
- What do you feel you still need to learn, before effectively stepping into this role?

Step III. Applying Social-Justice Concepts: The Social-Justice Quiz

The Social-Justice Quiz (below) asks you to apply the social-justice concepts more deeply. You may do the quiz independently and then share it when you are in your field experience course, or the quiz may be done in small groups during class. Students are encouraged to use the list of social-justice concepts they (and their group) previously developed to help them answer the questions. The professor may act as a consult, to clarify questions and misunderstandings.

Group Quiz: Making Meaning of Social-Justice Concepts (see also Appendix B)

1. Imagine you are a school counselor who is delivering a 1-minute presentation to your colleagues defining your role as social-justice change agent. What do you say in that 1 minute to clearly explain that role (and make sure to back it up with one or more standards to support any claim).

   ____

   ____

   ____

   ____

2. One of your roles entails system's advocacy. Give an example of two (2) social injustices you have learned about in certain schools or districts that stem from *systems'* issues. Note several ways you might address such issues to enact systemic changes.

   ____

   ____

   ____

   ____

3. What is the difference between advocating *for,* advocating *with*, and empowering a student to *advocate for self?*

   ____

   ____

   ____

   ____

   a. What is the benefit and disadvantage of each, and how will you know which is best to use?

      ____

      ____

      ____

4. Discuss and write down the difference between equity and equality (referring back to those definitions). Explain and write how this relates to social justice.

   ____

   ____

   ____

   ____

5. Consider the following case: Your student Jose, 13, is a predominantly Spanish-speaking student who was placed into special education courses due to the teacher's perspective that Jose is "low-functioning." Special education referral is often determined, in this school district, through teacher opinion, and when testing is done, it is done in English (with assessments created by U.S. citizens, premised on U.S. dominant cultural norms, to determine students' abilities). You have noticed a pattern of similar referrals from this and several other teachers. However, you know that in Jose's home, as the oldest household member with some English skills, he assumes all responsibilities for managing details related to his parents' business, advocating for his parents' rights, and managing bills—hence, you suspect Jose is experiencing teacher misunderstanding or bias and has been incorrectly placed.

   a. First, name four advocacy skills you can use to aid Jose.

      ____

      ____

      ____

   b. Write one way you could advocate for change at each of the following levels: (1) micro-level: student level, (2) micro-level: systems, and (3) macro-level: public information level.

      1) ____

      ____

2) ____

____

3) ____

____

6. Write a sentence you would actually use to directly address the teacher who referred this student.

____

____

____

____

7. Imagine the teacher was resistant (very closed) to your above intervention, blaming the student for the issue. Explain how you can overcome such resistance from your colleague.

____

____

____

____

8. Identify the kinds of evidence, including school data, you can use to determine which student groups may be experiencing social injustices in your setting (refer again to the definition of *social injustice*, if necessary).

____

____

____

____

9. Discuss and summarize in writing what is most important about today's activity, and what questions or concerns remain.

____

____

____

____

Step IV. Review and Discuss Answers

● ACTIVITY II. EXPLORING SOCIAL GROUPS AND THEIR LINK TO SOCIAL JUSTICE

Introduction

Brainstorm responses to the question, "What groups might experience social injustices in our school systems?" Describe certain injustices you have seen or experienced in real contexts and consider various causes of those injustices (e.g., the use of biased testing, whereby academic and aptitude tests privilege youth from wealthier families, due to having greater access to resources such as travel, museums, concerts, tutors, well-funded and high-quality early childhood education).

Step I. Fill Out a Social Identities' Reflection Chart (see example in Appendix C)

Afterward, discuss at length in your field experience course. Examples of questions are

- What most stood out to you?
- What surprised you?
- Which identities were unknown to you? New for you?
- Which did you add? Tell us about those.
- What does it mean to know there are some identities you never think about?
- What thoughts or feelings came up for you around privileges experienced based on a social group identity?
- What thoughts or feelings came up for you around oppression experienced based on a social group identity?
- How do issues of oppression and privileges become parts of systems in a school?
- How do you apply this discussion to your future role as a social-justice advocate in the schools?

● ACTIVITY III: IDENTIFYING DOMINANT CULTURAL NORMS

Introduction

Organizations are premised on a certain set of norms, often those that are dominant norms inherent across society—as reflected in social media, our laws, and our educational systems. These norms stem from persons who create organizations, and such norms are used to shape the policies, practices, and unspoken assumptions and expectations leaders in that setting have of others. Often, we are completely unaware of these norms, and especially unaware that others' have differing, and at times conflicting, norms. This can result in criticizing, or even pathologizing and punishing, those whose norms do not fit the dominant norms of the system itself.

Step I. Brainstorming Norms

Brainstorm and write, in groups, a list of dominant cultural norms (see examples of prompts in Appendix D). Share lists, discussing overlap and disagreement, to create a final, agreed upon list. Then compare it to an official list of dominant cultural norms (an example is in Appendix E).

Step II. Exploring the Nature and Effect of Dominant Cultural Norms

Examples of prompts to verbally reflect upon, or write about

- Where do these norms come from?
- How did you learn these?

- How have they embedded themselves in systems (e.g., educational, political, community, health-care, counseling) or systemic practices (e.g., laws and policies)?
- How might they lead to social injustices?
- Do we all fit into these norms?
- What happens when someone does not fit into certain norms (how you felt, when you haven't fit into a certain norm, for instance)? How are they treated? Can you give concrete examples?
- How do dominant cultural norms affect expectations about how our youth in schools should behave?
- How do these norms affect who we hire? Who gets to become a counselor, a teacher?
- How do dominant cultural norms influence school norms and policies (think about: curriculum selection, school culture/atmosphere, creation of standardized testing, discipline policies, college admission policies, etc.)?

Step III. Case Examples of Social Injustices Related to Dominant Cultural Norms

Identify the dominant norms and assumptions and how they are impacting the youth and effecting a social injustice. Identify the dominant norm or assumption of the adult, and state how you would intervene and advocate in each case (see case examples in Appendix F).

● ACTIVITY IV: PRACTICE IN SOCIAL-JUSTICE ACTION

Introduction

Recall prior readings and handouts created and viewed for social-justice counseling, and consider how they can be applied to specific real-world cases.

Step I. Exploring Cases and Solutions

Review various social-justice cases (see Appendix G for case examples), and in groups of three, read and discuss the cases. Using directives for social-justice counseling, come up with and write down on one of the blank pieces of paper school counselor solutions to each dilemma. Create solutions using certain skills or levels of intervention. Examples of skills might include consultation and collaboration in client advocacy. Indicate which level you intervened in, providing a summary of those levels for reference (e.g., see Appendix A, Examples of Social-Justice Related Wall Hangings).

Step II. Identifying Best Solutions

Exchange and review "solutions" proposed for a case. Order solutions from the most to least effective and come up with an explanation as to what about the "most" effective solution made it so. Repeat this process with each case.

ACTIVITY V. IDENTIFYING BARRIERS TO SOCIAL-JUSTICE ACTION

Introduction

There are many barriers, some real, some self-imposed, to effecting real change through the school counselor advocacy role. Sometimes, people are simply frightened to speak up against the norm, for instance, and often due to the fear of backlash—such as critique or dislike from others, to the more serious fear of losing one's job. Other times, there are actual systemic issues—such as certain policies and procedures put in place, that seem to act as barriers that prevent us from effectively making social-justice change happen.

Step I. The Card Activity

Take an index card and consider all prior readings or discussions related to the school counselor's role as a social-justice advocate. Then, write what you see as two major barriers to social-justice action in your future roles as a school counselors—one should be a personal barrier (self-imposed) and one an external barrier.

Step II. Exploring Ideas

Exchange cards with a person who is not standing next to you. Repeat this process five more times. Form groups of three and review the possible barriers written on the cards. Select two to focus on—one that is self-imposed and one that is externally imposed. Have them identify and write down solutions to each.

Step III. Discussing Barriers and Solutions

Read and present the barrier and solution. Consider the following questions afterward:

- What were the barriers and solutions you have read?
- How did you relate to these?
- What if we allow barriers to get in the way and we do not act—what are the consequences?
- What solutions are missing?
- What "issues" or barriers are not named?

REFERENCES

Allen, D. E., Donham, R. S., & Bernhardt, S. A. (2011, Winter). Problem-based learning. *New Directions for Teaching and Learning, 2011*(128), 21–29.

American School Counselor Association. (2012). *American School Counselor Association National Model: A framework for school counseling programs* (3rd ed.). Alexandria, VA: Author.

Bailey, D. F., Getch, Y. Q., & Chen-Hayes, S. (2003). Professional school counselors as social and academic advocates. In B. T. Erford (Ed.), *Transforming the school counseling profession* (pp. 411–434). Upper Saddle River, NJ: Merrill Prentice Hall.

Bemak, F., & Chung, R. C-Y. (2005). Advocacy as a critical role for urban school counselors: Working toward equity and social justice. *Professional School Counseling, 8,* 196–202.

Brady-Amoon, P., Makhija, N., Dixit, V., & Dator, J. (2012). Social justice: Pushing past boundaries in graduate training. *Journal for Social Action in Counseling and Psychology, 4*(2), 85–98.

Chung, R. C.-Y., & Bemak, F. (2012). *Social justice in counseling: The next step beyond multiculturalism.* Thousand Oaks, CA: Sage.

Counselors for Social Justice. (2011). The Counselors for Social Justice (CSJ) code of ethics. *Journal for Social Action in Counseling and Psychology, 3,* 1–21.

Cox, A. A., & Lee, C. C. (2007). Challenging educational inequities: School counselors as agents of social justice. In C. C. Lee (Ed.), *Counseling for social justice* (2nd ed., pp. 3–14). Alexandria, VA: American Counseling Association.

Dixon, A. L., Tucker, C., & Clark, M. A. (2010). Integrating social justice advocacy with national standards of practice: Implications for school counselor education. *Counselor Education and Supervision, 50*(2), 103–115.

Duan, C., & Brown, C. (2016). *Becoming a multiculturally competent counselor.* Thousand Oaks, CA: Sage.

Education Trust. (2009). *The new vision for school counselors: Scope of the work.* Retrieved from https://edtrust.org/resource/the-new-vision-for-school-counselors-scope-of-the-work/

Goodman, L. A., Liang, B., Helms, J. E., Latta, R. E., Sparks, E., & Weintraub, S. R. (2004). Training counseling psychologists as social justice agents: Feminist and multicultural principles in action. *The Counseling Psychologist, 32,* 793–837. doi:10.1177/0011000004268802

Groccia, J. E., & Buskist, W. (2011, Winter). Need for evidence-based teaching. *New Directions for Teaching and Learning, 2011*(128), 5–11.

House, R., & Martin, P. J. (1999). Advocating for better futures for all students: A new vision for school counselors. *Education, 119,* 284–291.

Malott, K. M., Hall, K. H., Sheelymoore, A., Krell, M. M., & Cardaciotto, L. (2014). Evidence-based teaching in higher education: Application to counselor education. *Counselor Education & Supervision, 53,* 294–305.

Marbley, A. F., Malott, K. M., Flaherty, A., & Frederick, H. (2010). Three issues, three approaches, three calls to action: Multicultural social justice in the schools. *Journal for Social Action in Counseling and Psychology, 3,* 59–73.

McClintock, M. (2000). How to interrupt oppressive behavior. In M. Adams, W. J. Blumenfeld, R. Castaneda, H. W. Hackman, M. L. Peters, & X. Zuniga (Eds.), *Readings for diversity and social justice* (pp. 483–485). New York, NY: Routledge.

Prince, M. (2004). Does active learning work? A review of the research. *Journal of Engineering Education, 93*(3), 223–231.

Ratts, M. J., DeKruyf, L., & Chen-Hayes, S. F. (2007). The ACA advocacy competencies: A social justice advocacy framework for professional school counselors. *Professional School Counseling, 11*(2), 90–97.

Ratts, M. J., Singh, A. A., Nassar-McMillan, S., Butler, S. K., & McCullough, J. R. (2015). *Multicultural and Social Justice Counseling Competencies.* Retrieved from http://www.multiculturalcounseling.org/index.php?option=com_content&view=article&id=205:amcd-endorses-multicultural-and-social-justice-counseling-competencies&catid=1:latest&Itemid=123

Stone, D. (2002). *Policy paradox.* New York, NY: W. W. Norton.

Sutherland, T. E., & Bonwell, C. C. (1996). *Using active learning in college classes: A range of options for faculty.* San Francisco, CA: Jossey-Bass.

● APPENDIX A

Examples for Social-Justice Related Wall Hangings

- Suggested definitions of *social-justice concepts*
  - Social Injustice: "the unequal access (inequality) to resources, rights, and opportunities" (Duan & Brown, 2016, p. 332)
  - Equity vs. Equality: Equity implies fairness, and equality implies the same treatment or equal distribution of resources. Hence, equality is giving all people the exact same things or treating all people the same. Judging or treating all children the same (treating them "equally") is only fair if every child has had equal access to all resources and opportunities and treatment

in society across their life spans. As an example, using the same standardized assessment tool across all districts in the nation may seem logically to be fair (e.g., "equal" treatment), but this does not take into account the fact that many youth, such as those living in poverty, have been systematically denied equal access to many community and educational resources that wealthier communities have. They have experienced *inequity* in their lives. Hence, those students who performed poorly on their exams should be provided *greater* resources and supports than those who performed well, to establish equity. Equity must first be established before equality can be achieved (Stone, 2002).

- Tools/skills related to advocacy, as taken from various advocacy models and standards. Some examples might include collaboration; consultation; referral; communication skills, such as those to broach and discuss social-justice issues such as privilege and oppression; communication skills to advocate against social injustice; ability to critically analyze data and evidence showing achievement gaps; ability to communicate and disseminate essential resources or information; ability to recognize and address resistance to social-justice change.

- Inspirational and instructional quotes—one example is "School counselors working as social-justice advocates are educational leaders who challenge the status quo, use data to increase access and address equity for all students, and provide services in classrooms and communities" (Ratts et al., 2007, p. 91).
- Social-justice or advocacy-related standards in the Council for Accreditation of Counseling and Related Educational Programs (CACREP). Two examples are
  - CACREP School Counseling Diversity and Advocacy standards F.2 and F.3
    - F.2. [a school counselor] Advocates for the learning and academic experiences necessary to promote the academic, career, and personal/social development of students.
    - F.3. [a school counselor] Advocates for school policies, programs, and services that enhance a positive school climate and are equitable and responsive to multicultural student populations.
- Levels of social-justice action: On a continuum, from actively working against social-justice solutions (such as remaining silent, or joining others in thwarting efforts at social justice), to working for social justice by educating self, supporting others who are actively fighting, or becoming active (such as speaking up, interrupting injustice), to being proactive (developing groups and policies and norms and practices that increase justice (Harro, 1986; McClintock, 2000).
- Levels for possible school counselor social-justice advocacy, with examples: See more examples in the book, *ASCA National Model: A Framework for School Counseling Programs* (ASCA, 2012).
  - Micro-level
    - Student-level advocacy: Advocate with or for a student, to help him or her remove barriers or to access resources and opportunities; or use consultation, collaboration, or referrals to help students overcome barriers or access resources and opportunities.
    - School or community level: Collaborate with a local group or organization to create an advocacy plan.
    - Systems-level advocacy: Identify a problem within a system, including the values, norms, policies,and laws of a workplace, and work with others through collaboration and consultation to affect change in a specific system.
  - Macro-level
    - Public information: Collaborate with community to inform the public of issues related to human dignity. Ways to communicate are through school reports, vision or mission statement, results reports, school committees, and collaboration with advisory councils or community groups.
    - Social or political advocacy: Advocate for change at a level that addresses policy, laws, and legislation. Present at boards, in front of state or national legislation, or state and national involvement in professional association.

● APPENDIX B

Group Quiz: Making Meaning of Social-Justice Concepts

Continue using the wall hangings as a reference; work in a group to answer these questions to the best of your ability. You will hand responses in as a group, but each student must share in writing at least one response to the below answers.

1. Imagine you are a school counselor who is delivering a 1-minute presentation to your colleagues defining your role as social-justice change agent. What do you say in that 1 minute to clearly explain that role (and make sure to back it up with one or more standards to support any claim). Discuss and write a summary here.
2. One of your roles entails system's advocacy. Give an example of two (2) social injustices you have learned about in certain schools or districts that stem from *systems'* issues. Note several ways you might address such issues to enact systemic changes.
3. What is the difference between advocating *for*, advocating *with*, and empowering a student to *advocate for self?*
   a. What is the benefit and disadvantage of each, and how will you know which is best to use?
4. Discuss and write down the difference between *equity* and *equality* (referring back to those definitions). Explain and write how this relates to social justice.
5. Consider the following case: Your student Jose, 13, is a predominantly Spanish-speaking student who was placed into special education courses due to the teacher's perspective that Jose is "low-functioning." Special education referral is often determined, in this school district, through teacher opinion, and when testing is done, it is done in English (with assessments created by U.S. citizens, premised on U.S. dominant cultural norms, to determine students' abilities). You have noticed a pattern of similar referrals from this and several other teachers. However, you know that in Jose's home, as the oldest household member with some English skills, he assumes all responsibilities for managing details related to his parents' business, advocating for his parents' rights, and managing bills—hence, you suspect Jose is experiencing teacher misunderstanding or bias and has been incorrectly placed.
   a. First, name four advocacy skills you can use to aid Jose.
   b. Write one way you could advocate for change at each of the following levels: (1) micro-level: student level, (2) micro-level: systems, and (3) macro-level: public information level.
   c. Write a sentence you would actually use, to directly address the teacher who referred this student.
6. Identify the kinds of evidence, including school data, you can use to determine which student groups may be experiencing social injustices in your setting (refer again to the definition of *social injustice*, if necessary).
7. Discuss and summarize in writing what is most important about today's activity, and what questions or concerns remain.

● APPENDIX C

Social Identities' Reflection Chart*

Social Identity Category	*My identity label*	*Salient (important to me: I think about this often)*	*Never thought about this identity*	*I experience discrimination or barriers to opportunities due to this identity*	*I experience privileges and power due to this identity*
Social class					
Race (skin tone)					
Ethnicity (cultural traditions, origins, language use, etc.)					
Sex					
Sexual orientation					
Gender identity (internal identity)					
Religion					
Age					
Ability/ disability					
Age					
Language					
Other:					

*Adapted from R. Hardiman and B. Jackson (2007), Conceptual foundations for social justice education. In M. Adams, L. A. Bell, & P. Griffin (Eds.), *Readings for diversity and social justice* (pp. 35–66). New York, NY: Routledge.

● APPENDIX D

Prompts for Eliciting Dominant Cultural Norms

Identify norms that are implied in the following ways:

- Consider major media outlets that highlight "The most beautiful people in the world." What is the appearance/aesthetic for the majority of persons considered "most beautiful"? Also to consider: body type, gender norms, skin color, and hair texture.
- Media images of persons who are considered to be the most powerful and successful in society—What do the majority of those persons tend to look like? Their gender? "Normative" behaviors? How is *powerful* defined in society? Success?
- Famous figures who represent the most "normal" or "all-American" person—Consider traits of those persons (e.g., usually the majority are White, Christian, heterosexual, middle class, cisgendered [their gendered behaviors and appearances align with their sex]).
- Statements that imply what or who is "normal." Here are some examples:
    - "She's as American as apple pie."
    - "She's the girl next door."
    - "He's an all-American guy."
    - "They're a traditional family."
    - "This is great/classical music (who created that music?)."
    - "These works of art/literature are by the 'greats' (who is largely considered a 'great' in literature?)."
    - "I wish she had a 'normal' name; hers is so hard to pronounce!"

● APPENDIX E

Norms, Worldviews, or Assumptions of Dominant U.S. Culture

Norm/Worldview	*Traits*
Rugged individualism	Independence/self-reliance and autonomy most valued and rewarded; consider oneself and personal gains/losses when making decisions (rather than "sacrifice personal needs to maintain relationships")
Helping value	Seek help (rather than hiding problems to avoid shame/save face)
Competition	Being first most important; accomplishments before relationships; winner-loser dichotomy; assertiveness or, even, aggressiveness
Action orientation, locus of control	Belief that we control our destiny; efforts to control nature and others; must take control of/act and "do something" in all situations
Communication	"King's English" grammatical rules; tradition as written (rather than oral/storytelling); direct communication (say what you want, think; look someone in the eyes); emotional restraint, never raise one's voice
Holidays/traditions	Christian-based, with European and masculine origins

Norm/Worldview	*Traits*
History	Based on male, European immigrant histories; Emphasis on British empire; history of White males as leaders; premised on Western (Roman/Greek, Judeo-Christian) traditions
Protestant work ethic	Doing more important than "being." Work before play; those who are poor are only poor because they are lazy—hence, *meritocracy*, or the belief that hard workers all have equal access to resources/opportunities
Emphasis on scientific mind	Objective, linear, rational thinking; emphasis on the truth of quantitative (belief in truth of numbers over other forms of evidence)
Status, power, and authority	Worth = wealth; value placed on the ownership of spaces, properties, goods (rather than relationships/community or shared ownership); work is our identities; those with status/power seen as White; those who are non-White are considered minorities even if in the majority
Time	Adherence to strict time schedules; time as linear and a commodity (spent/used/saved)
Future orientation	Plan for future/future focus; delay gratification—sacrifice today for tomorrow; progress as always best; "tomorrow will be better"
Family structure	Nuclear (father, mother, two children) as ideal; heteronormative; paternalistic—husband breadwinner, head of household; wife as subordinate to husband; children should have own rooms
Aesthetics	Based on European culture/art/literature (Mozart, Shakespeare as superior); woman's beauty as white skin, blond, tall, thin—"Barbie"; others considered exotic or unattractive; attractiveness of men based on intellect, power, economic status
Religion	Christianity the norm; anything beyond Judeo-Christian traditions seen as foreign; intolerance for beliefs beyond a single god concept

Adapted from Brown & Landrum-Brown, 1995; Ponterotto, Casas, Suzuki, & Alexander, 2010.

● APPENDIX F

Case Examples of Dominant Cultural Norms

Case #1: Mrs. Myers, 10th-grade math teacher, casually notes to the counselor one day during lunch that she "has issues" with the group of African American students who have recently enrolled at the school (their own school had been closed, and they were being bused to this school). She described them as "Rude—refusing to look me in the eye when I talk to them, and disrespectful, they are so loud, they talk over their peers as well as me. I sent one out of the room yesterday, for the second time, and the principal expelled him."

(Note to instructor: Mrs. Myers is expressing dominant-culture communication norms that define politeness as low-volume of voice, turn taking when speaking, looking someone in the eye when speaking to them as a sign of respect.)

Case #2: Mr. Lyons, new 6th-grade teacher, noted that he finds his Asian and Latino students (who are all recent immigrants) in his class to be "apathetic," explaining that when he asks a question, they refuse to speak up or offer an answer, and even when he calls on them, they often refuse to answer. He notes their grades, based on class participation, are being affected, and he asks you to call his parents to let them know of this problem. (Note to instructor: Mr. Lyons is expressing culturally informed values that prioritize the expression of one's knowledge over the unified/collectivistic needs of the class as a whole. The students may come from cultures that consider sharing one's knowledge to be "boasting" and shaming to peers who may not know the answers.)

Case #3: Mrs. Smith, 10th-grade teacher, asked students to create family genograms. She noted that she is getting student "attitude" and refusals to complete genograms. When you look at the assignment, you see that she has given them a genogram chart that asks them to specifically identify a nuclear family—for example, a mom, a dad, and siblings only. You are aware of the fact that several kids in the class do not know who their father is, one is from an adoptive family, one has had limited contact with family throughout his life (he lives in a foster home), while others have several parents and extended family members they would want to name as family. (Note to instructor: Mrs. Smith has premised her assignment on the dominant normative assumption of family as biological, heterosexual, and nuclear in nature, without recognizing the potential trauma issues that may emerge for some students related to family histories and events.)

Case #4: Mr. Lumbardo, the principal, creates a policy that all teachers, staff, and students are to wear "standard" hairstyles. This prohibits braids, afros, and other (what he calls) "non-standard" hairstyles. (Note to instructor: Mr. Lumbardo has created a policy that punishes, pathologizes, or targets students with curly hair, who are mainly Black students. The type and nature of hairstyles targeted are particularly specific to African American styles. The decision pathologizes members' natural hair, with an expectation or assumption that curly hair can or should be styled according to dominant White norms.)

• APPENDIX G

Examples of Social-Justice Cases

Case I. A parent comes to you one day to complain that his son, who is African American, was passed over for advanced placement/college prep courses. She notes that many other parents of color were saying the same about their children. When you investigate, you find that all AP courses are predominantly filled with White students. When you inquire about this, the teachers assert that the students of color come from "bad feeder schools" and "aren't properly prepared" to take AP courses. However, you know this to be factually untrue, that students of color came from all feeder schools.

Case II. You notice a distinct gap in the college-going rate for first generation college goers, as compared to youth whose parents attended college. When those first-gen kids do attend college, they seem to drop out at higher rates, particularly for students of color.

Case III. You notice a distinct lack of parent participation in various school activities, including college-going night, from parents who live in poverty. You are also aware that those families live across town (and there is a poor public transportation system), and that many parents work multiple jobs that do not allow them to take time off from work to attend school events. One day you suggest to a teacher that the school should take offer a parent-event in those families' neighborhood, and the teacher replies, "Are you crazy? There's no way I'd go to that place!"

Case IV. In examining school data, you note several academic struggles for the English Language Learner (ELL) youth at your high school. There is a disproportionate rate of special education placement of ELL youth, a high rate of dropout of certain ELL students (when you disaggregate the data, you see it's mainly Mexican American boys, at the ninth-grade level), and high rates of expulsion for ELL boys (when you look up specifics for the last few years of expulsions, you realize that the majority of those boys were Black). In addition, you see a low rate of college attendance for ELLs who are excelling at school, and when you do a bit more research, you realize those youth without citizenship are the ones who do not go on to attend college (likely due to the inability to obtain government loans to fund their education).

LESSON 8

ENGLISH LANGUAGE LEARNERS

Malti Tuttle
Auburn University

Leonissa Johnson
Clark Atlanta University

Real Life

"I've never prepared a lesson for students whose first language is not English. I feel nervous about what to do."

"The student (English Language Learner) had trouble with his classwork. I don't know if he was getting all the support he needed."

"The student kept getting in trouble for leaving his seat and not raising his hand. I am not sure if he understood the directions. I want to think through the best way to help."

These are the voices of counselors-in-training (CITs) who questioned their skills and ability to effectively advocate for English Language Learners (ELLs). CITs often lack formal training or awareness of the academic, social/emotional, or career needs of ELLs. Without knowledge and experiences with this population, CITs may lack self-efficacy and confidence as practitioners and advocates. Current barriers cited by CITs include anxiety when preparing and delivering lessons for new arrival ELLs, ambiguity when evaluating culturally appropriate supports for ELLs, and uncertainty about "best practices" to support this student population. This chapter was designed to reduce CIT anxiety in working with ELLs. We hope that by increasing CIT knowledge about the needs, policies, and processes that impact English Language Learner schooling experiences, they will grow in confidence as school counselor advocates.

Lesson Eight

English Language Learners

Malti Tuttle
Auburn University

Leonissa Johnson
Clark Atlanta University

Essential Question: What do school counselors need to know about working with English Language Learners?

Objectives

Students will

- demonstrate an understanding of the definition of English Language Learners.
- explore the identification and assessment processes for English Language Learners.
- recognize the factors that influence English Language Learner experiences in school.
- implement advocacy interventions to support English Language Learners.

CACREP Standards

- School counselor roles as leaders, advocates, and systems change agents in P–12 schools (5.G.2.1)
- School counselors' roles in consultation with families, P–12, postsecondary school personnel, and community agencies (5.G.2.b)
- School counselors' roles in school leadership and multidisciplinary teams (5.G.2.d)
- Interventions to promote academic development (5.G.3.d)
- Skills to critically examine the connections between social, familial, emotional, and behavioral problems and academic achievement (5.G.3.h)
- Strategies to promote equity in student achievement and college access (5.G.3.k)

MPCAC Standards

- human development and wellness across the life span
- ecological, contextual, multicultural, social-justice foundation of human development
- assessment of human behavior and organizational/community/institutional systems

Video Spark

https://www.youtube.com/watch?v=5HU80AxmP-U

English language learners: Culture, equity, and language (NEA Priority Schools Campaign)

● INTRODUCTION

According to the National Center for Education Statistics (NCES) approximately 4.4 million students in U.S. public schools (9.2%) were identified as English Language Learners during the 2012–2013 school year (National Center for Education Statistics [NCES], 2015). This represented a steady increase since 2002. English Language Learners have unique needs. School counselors are called to implement programming that provides access and equity for all students (American School Counselor Association [ASCA], 2012b). This chapter explores the needs, experiences, and potential supports you can provide these pupils through your work as a school counselor.

Activity: What I Think and What I Think Now

Reflection is a significant and strategic form of the learning process. During class, write down ideas and questions you may have on your own thoughts, experiences, and beliefs about linguistically diverse learners. It is important to recognize our own biases as school counselors in order to grow as practitioners. Before moving forward with the class, spend 5 minutes writing your thoughts in the "What I Think" section. Throughout the class session, come back to reflect on your thoughts. At the end of the class session, write your thoughts in the "What I Think Now" section about what you have learned about English Language Learners and how are you different from the knowledge you acquired.

What I Think	*What I Think Now*

● LINGUISTICALLY DIVERSE LEARNERS

Who Are English Language Learners?

During the 2012–2013 school year, approximately 4.4 million students were identified as English Language Learners (NCES, 2015). English Language Learners are students whose first language is not English and live in a country in which the predominate language is English. English Learners are in the process of learning English and that process can be supported with specific teaching and learning experiences (U.S. Department of Education [DOE], 2015).

English Language Learners represent a heterogeneous and complex group of students. The majority of these pupils were born in the United States to at least one parent born in another country (Migration Policy Institute, 2011). The cultural and linguistic backgrounds of these pupils vary. Approximately 70% of ELLs speak Spanish as a first language; however, the other 30% of students converse in over 150 different languages including Chinese, Vietnamese, and Haitian/Creole.

English Language Learners attend school in most U.S. states. In 2008, half of the English Learner population enrolled in elementary schools. In 2012–2013, California reported the largest English Language Learner enrollment, with approximately 1,500,000. Other states documented sizeable English Learner populations. Ariel Ruiz Soto, Sarah Hooker, and Jeanne Batalova (2015) reported that states with historically large immigrant populations such as Texas, Florida, New York, and Illinois each had English Language Learner enrollments of over 100,000. "New Destination" states like North Carolina, Georgia, Arkansas, and Tennessee saw 200% increases in English Language Learner student populations since 1990. English Language Learners have diverse needs. Factors such as socioeconomic status, immigration status, family changes, and acculturative stressors can greatly influence their school experiences.

BICS Versus CALP

Sonia Nieto (2002) argued that students enter U.S. schools with two goals: learn English and learn English subject matter. These processes require English language acquisition. Jim Cummins (1984) developed a framework of the English language acquisition process. First, individuals acquire basic interpersonal communication skills (BICS). After one or two years of exposure, individuals acquire social language. This language encompasses basic interpersonal language, such as greetings, slang, cultural references, and discussion. At this level, the speaker relies heavily on contextual clues, pictures, and gestures to support understanding (Cook, Boals, & Lundberg, 2011). While social language is an important part of an English Learner's experience, language used in the process of learning requires a different type of linguistic skill. Cummins (1984) defined this language as cognitive academic language proficiency (CALP). Speakers at this level understand more complex grammar and technical vocabulary and can use decontextualized reading and language. As pupils progress in school, they rely more heavily on CALP for academic achievement (Cook et al., 2011). Acquisition of CALP takes 5 to 7 years for English Language Learners. This timetable can provide a challenge for ELLs who need time to acquire these skills for academic success. The acquisition of BICS and CALP can be supported by implementation of English Learner education service programs.

Activity: Learning in a New Language

Instructions: English Language Learners often learn in a language other than their primary tongue. We will watch or listen to a recording of someone speaking in a language other than English. Take notes about the information the speaker is discussing.

Processing questions: Are there any questions about what you heard? What was it like listening to or watching the recording? How would you feel if you were responsible for learning the information? What would have helped you understand the information while watching or listening?

Factors That Influence English Language Learners School Experiences

English Language Learners are a heterogeneous group of students. A number of contextual factors impact their ability to adjust to school settings in the United States. Contextual dynamics such as socioeconomic status, family changes, acculturation, and previous learning experiences each impact ELL school proficiencies.

Socioeconomic Status. The American Psychological Association Presidential Task Force on Immigration (2012) explained that many immigrant youth live in two parent households, in which both are employed. Socioeconomic status was also influenced by the countries of origin in which English Language Learners originated. Mark Mather reported that individuals from countries such as India, Philippines, China, Korea, Canada, and Europe were the least likely to live at risk of poverty. Latino youth and refugee children from Iraq, Somalia, Sudan, and Yemen were at greatest risk for poverty (Mather, 2009). Children from families at most risk of poverty were less likely to take part in preschool or have access to health care (American Psychological Association [APA], 2012).

Immigration Status. Immigration status within linguistically diverse families is complex. Individuals immigrate to other countries in order to reunite with family, find work, or seek refuge (APA, 2012). In 2008, the Migration Policy Institute reported that 78% of English Language Learners in kindergarten through fifth grade were born in the United States. Sixty percent of middle and high school English

Language Learners were also born in the United States. These students were second generation immigrants and in many cases U.S. citizens. The majority of these pupils were born in the United States to at least one parent born in another country (Migration Policy Institute, 2011). Other English Language Learners may be immigrants or refugees. These students may suffer trauma from the harsh conditions of the journey to the United States, or loss of home or relatives. If families enter the United States without documentation, they may face the threat of deportation. While each individual's status is unique, the stressors of a particular status or immigration experience can impact on all members of a family (Suárez-Orozco, Suárez-Orozco & Todorova, 2008).

Family Changes. English Language Learners are parts of family systems (Suárez-Orozco et al., 2008). These systems may expand across many cities, states, and countries for linguistically diverse students. One or no parents may travel with some English Language Learners to the Unites States due to circumstances or limited resources, forcing students to move in with unfamiliar relatives or friends. These changes yield new family arrangements (Suárez-Orozco et al. 2008). If parents later follow, strains in parent–child relationships can develop due to changes in the family structure and the child's evolved individual identity. English Learner student's identity may be influenced by new U.S. gender, race, authority, and material expectations. As students mature into adolescents, they may think and behave in more individualistic and less familial patterns, which can lead to intergenerational conflict (James, 1997; Suárez-Orozco, Onaga, & de Lardemelle, 2010).

Acculturative Stressors. Acculturation is a process that involves interaction between two cultural groups, which results in changes in both parties (Berry, 2001). English Language Learners may have to adapt to cultural changes and differences in U.S. schools and communities. These distinctions in culture can impact student learning experiences. "Communication, cognition, language, behavior, affinity toward the individual or the group, and relationships with authority figures are several important domains where culture can influence teacher-student and teacher-parent interactions" (Chamberlain, 2005, p. 200). These tensions can be a source of stress for linguistically diverse students.

Formal Schooling Experiences. Exposure to language can influence academic achievement. Donna Ford (2012) explained that English Learners have diverse academic backgrounds. The Migration Policy Institute reported that 40% of middle and high school English Learners were born outside of the United States; these students include immigrants and refugees (Migration Policy Institute, 2011). Some English Learners experience interrupted schooling before starting school in the United States. Other ELLs received regular, formal language training in their home countries. Varied schooling experiences mean that ELLs may grasp academic content at different rates (Ford, 2012). Formal schooling experiences may inform the progress that English Learners make in U.S. classrooms. Education services that support English Learners are imperative to their overall academic success.

What Is ESOL?

In 1965, the U.S. Supreme Court ruled that public schools must provide students affected by Limited English Proficiency (LEP) with the supports needed to meaningfully participate in educational programs and services. Congress also enacted the Equal Educational Opportunities Act (EEOA) requiring public schools and state educational agencies to "overcome language barriers that impede equal participation by students in their educational programs" (U.S. Department of Justice [DOJ] & U.S. Department of Education [DOE], 2015, p. 5). The DOE administers the English Language Acquisition, Language Enhancement and Academic Achievement Act, also known as Title III, Part A of the Elementary and Secondary Education Act of 1965. Federal funds are awarded to school districts to improve the education of English Learners. As a result, school districts are legally obligated to provide specific information, processes, and procedures to English Learners.

How are students identified? Students in need of language services must be identified within the first 30 days of the school year. Public schools are required to have an identification process in place (DOJ & DOE, 2015). School districts often begin this process by utilizing a Home Language Survey (HLS).

This instrument helps school personnel collect data about the language background of enrolling students. Data from the HLS highlight pupils who should be referred for an English Language Proficiency (ELP) assessment (DOJ & DOE, 2015). The assessment measures student proficiency in listening, speaking, reading, and writing in English. ELP scores help school officials determine which students should receive English Language services. Parents or guardians must be notified within the first 30 days of the school year of the identification, testing, and placement decisions. Notification must occur in writing and in a language parents or guardians can understand. If written translation is not possible, school districts must provide free, oral interpretation of the written information (DOJ & DOE, 2015).

Language Assistance Programs. English Language Learners are served via diverse programs. School districts receiving Title III funds can choose the English Language programs that best meet their needs, however these programs must be supported by educational theory and research and demonstrate student language acquisition within a reasonable period of time (DOJ & DOE, 2015). Individual student factors such as age, grade level, academic background, language, and English proficiency level must also be considered when making placement decisions. The amount of support students receive varies based on proficiency level. The most common theoretically supported programs include English as a Second Language (ESL), Structured English Immersion (SEI), Transitional Bilingual Education (TBE), and Dual Language programs.

English as a Second Language (ESL) programs are designed to teach English skills. Students are explicitly taught the techniques and methods utilized in the English language. Pupils are also exposed to the academic vocabulary needed to comprehend instruction in various disciplines within U.S. schools (DOE, 2015). Instruction typically occurs in English.

Structured English Immersion (SEI) programs immerse students into a classroom where all instruction occurs in English. Students are taught by trained educators with ESL or SEI credentials. The goal is for students to acquire English so that they will be proficient in a mainstream, English-only classroom (DOE, 2015).

Transitional Bilingual Education (TBE) programs begin instruction in a student's primary language. English skills are introduced, developed, and maintained. As students proceed through the program, the amount of English instruction increases and the primary language instruction decreases until students can transition into an all-English instructional program (DOE, 2015; Ochoa & Rhodes, 2005; Thomas & Collier, 2002).

Dual Language or two-way language programs are designed in order for students to gain proficiency in two languages. Students are instructed in their primary language and in English. Typically dual language classes are composed of both primary English speakers and speakers with other primary languages (DOE, 2015; Ochoa & Rhodes, 2005; Thomas & Collier, 2002).

Activity: English Language Learner SOL Scavenger Hunt

Explore the website of a local school system. Try to find answers to the following questions:

- Which languages are served in the school district?
- How are students in the setting identified for English Language Learner placement?
- What assessments are utilized in the placement process?
- What language standards are used in the setting?
- Describe the type of English Language Learner programming utilized in the school system.

● SCHOOL COUNSELOR ADVOCACY

It is imperative for school counselors to gain understanding of English Language Learners, the challenges they face, and how to become allies and advocates, especially since language poses a barrier to building relationships between schools and linguistically diverse students and families (Aydın, Bryan, & Duys, 2012). Therefore the first step prior to counseling English Language Learners would be to consult research such as journal articles, websites, media, and individuals to acquire knowledge regarding their local and global communities. This allows the school counselor to gain insight into the community's worldview such as privilege, assumptions, and biases (Ratts, Singh, Nassar-McMillan, Butler, & McCullough, 2015). The purpose of consulting research is to provide a deeper lens to examine which diverse populations are in the United States and local regions, the rationale for moving to the area, challenges faced by each group, and recognizing how the role of the school counselor can support their needs.

Additionally, school counselors who proactively consult research for knowledge are on the forefront of understanding who their students are, gaining leverage to build relationships, and advocating for students' needs. The benefit of this step is that when the school counselor makes contact with the student or parents, it is evident the school counselor has a sincere and genuine interest in supporting and advocating for the student. This will also allow the school counselor to show his or her investment in the student's success since it will be apparent the school counselor is aware of the possible needs and challenges the student may be facing.

Knowledge acquired from research on English Language Learners provides the school counselor with information to help advocate for students in their communities (Trusty & Brown, 2005). Once research has been conducted and school counselors are aware of the needs of English Learners, they are able to move forward, knowing what types of advocacy are needed for their particular students. The American School Counselor Association (ASCA) specifically has two position statements, "The School Counselor and Cultural Diversity" and "The School Counselor and Equity for All Students," which speak to advocating for diverse and multicultural student needs and provide direction for school counselor advocacy (www.schoolcounselor.org/school-counselors-members/about-asca-%281%29/position-statements). All school counselors are strongly encouraged to be familiar with the ASCA position statements for the purpose of recognizing how to provide support and advocacy.

Advocacy is a critical component in supporting English Language Learners since these students often do not seek help on their own (Aydın, Bryan, & Duys, 2012; Montgomery, Roberts, & Growe, 2003). Additionally, English Learners may not know what services and supports are available or needed, so school counselors should advocate on their behalf (ASCA, 2012). Therefore, school counselors should provide services specifically to support English Learners and collaborate with stakeholders within the community. Below are examples of how school counselors can advocate for these students.

Academic Advocacy. English Language Learners may have a difficult time understanding the academic culture and demands. School counselors are in the position to identify difficulties and challenges by advocating for appropriate class placement and educational services. For example, high school counselors should assist students with appropriate class placements and postsecondary planning since the students may not have a full grasp of appropriate requirements and classes to take (Montgomery et al., 2003). Also, school counselors can proactively meet with students to discuss what differences and challenges they might be experiencing in the academic setting since their previous schooling may not have been set up as the current school or perhaps they did not receive educational services prior to arriving in the United States.

School counselors should ensure English Language Learners have access to school services and programs that allow them to participate with their English-speaking peers such as inclusionary services, gifted services, and extracurricular opportunities. The U.S. Department of Education created the English Learner Tool Kit for State and Local Education Agencies (SEAs and LEAs), which provide checklists and resources detailing appropriate programs and services needed for English Learners. Additionally, school counselors can advocate for programs, services, and inclusionary systems if they are not be provided in their school setting. Data collection of student needs may be utilized and results provided to stakeholders for specific programs and services to be implemented.

Career Readiness Advocacy. Linguistically diverse learners may not have the knowledge of careers or the skills needed for career planning. Therefore, school counselors should speak to English Language Learners about the importance of careers, career opportunities, and skills needed for these vocations. School counselors can advocate for students to take particular high school courses that provide training for future careers. Career planning would be important to discuss with students since undocumented students may not be able to receive scholarships, college acceptance, or join the armed forces. Therefore, students will need to acquire skills to assist them for lives after high school. School counselors could advocate for students to participate in apprenticeship programs where they learn work skills. Also it would be important for school counselors to partner with parents to discuss career planning for their students and express respect for their cultural expectations of their children. School counselors should recognize many cultures have expectations for their children based on several factors, such as gender, and therefore school counselors should be mindful of the family's cultural beliefs.

Social-Emotional Advocacy. English Language Learners may encounter social-emotional stressors needing school counselor support and advocacy. The backgrounds and reasons English Learners immigrate to the United States are significantly different. Various examples include some students may be refugees and facing trauma, have difficulty making friendships due to language, socioeconomic issues, or may possibly transition without any concerns (Goh, Wahl, McDonald, Brissett, & Yoon, 2007). Often students may be the only English speakers in their families therefore may be called upon to provide translation services for their parents and families causing the students to take on additional roles (Seddon, 2015). As advocates, school counselors should speak with the students to address these concerns as well as seek support from community resources while consulting with stakeholders such as teachers and parents.

Additionally, school counselors could collect data about English Language Learners' needs such as family changes, trauma histories, attendance, or sense of belonging. The data collected would inform the school counselors, teachers, parents, and stakeholders about types of interventions and programs needed. Further support would then be provided through school counseling interventions such as small-group counseling, individual meetings, and services from outside agencies. School counselors can also support English Language Learners by connecting them with extracurricular activities which would give them an opportunity to meet other students and utilize their English language skills. This would also provide opportunities to interact with others, feel connected to a group, and build a sense of belonging.

Activity: Who Is Present?

Consult journal articles, websites, and individuals in the community from different countries who speak another language prior to the next class. Find out which cultural groups are identified in the United States, in the state, and in the local community. Students may utilize the Census Bureau website (www.census.gov/prod/2013pubs/acs-22.pdf) and Migration Policy Institute (www.migrationpolicy.org/programs/data-hub/state-immigration-data-profiles). Look for languages spoken, historical background of the countries, and reasons to immigrate to the United States. Students will present their findings to the class to discuss possible challenges students may encounter, counseling interventions to assist students, and advocacy interventions.

____

____

____

____

____

____

Debriefing/Group Processing

Student advocacy is powerful and meaningful for students, parents, school counselors, and all stakeholders. Throughout this lesson, there have been significant amounts of reflection, research, and advocacy activities. If in a class setting, share your reflections from the class session. If reading on your own, reflect on your experiences from this chapter's activities. Together, the class will answer and discuss the following questions. If you are reading this alone, reflect on your own responses.

The following questions guide the debriefing process:

What did you know and what do you now know?

How are you different after learning and researching English Language Learners?

How will the knowledge you acquired show up in your counseling skills?

What strategic practices as a social-justice advocate can you implement in support of English Language Learners?

• REFERENCES

American Psychological Association Presidential Task Force on Immigration. (2012). *Crossroads: The psychology of immigration in the new century*. Retrieved from http://www.apa.org/topics/immigration/report.aspx

American School Counselor Association. (2012a). *The ASCA National Model: A Framework for School Counseling Programs* (3rd ed.). Alexandria, VA: Author.

American School Counselor Association (2012b). *The school counselor and equity for all students*. Retrieved from https://www.schoolcounselor.org/asca/media/asca/PositionStatements/PS_Equity.pdf

Aydın, N. G., Bryan, J. A., & Duys, D. K. (2012). School counselors' partnerships with linguistically diverse families: An exploratory study. *School Community Journal, 22*(1), 145–166.

Berry, J. J. (2001). A psychology of immigration. *Journal of Social Issues, 57*(3), 615–631.

Brown, M. T., & Landrum-Brown, J. (1995). Counselor supervision: Cross-cultural perspectives. In J. G. Ponterotto, J. M. Casas, L. A. Suzuki, & C. M. Alexander (Eds.), *Handbook of multicultural counseling* (3rd ed.; pp. 263–286). Thousand Oaks, CA: Sage.

Chamberlain, S. P. (2005). Recognizing and responding to cultural differences in the education of culturally and linguistically diverse learners. *Intervention in School and Clinic, 40*(4), 195–211. Retrieved from http://search.ebscohost.com/login.aspx?direct=true&db=a9h&AN=16266007&site=ehost-live

Cook, H. G., Boals, T., & Lundberg, T. (2011). Academic achievement for English learners: What can we reasonably expect? *Kappan, 93*(3), 66–69. Retrieved from https://www.wida.us/get.aspx?id=485

Cummins, J. (1984). Language proficiency, bilingualism and academic achievement. In P. Richard-Amato & M. Snow (Eds.), *Academic success for English Language Learners: Strategies for K-12 mainstream teachers* (pp. 76–86). New York, NY: Longman.

Ford, D. Y. (2012). Culturally different students in special education: Looking backward to move forward. *Exceptional Children, 78*(4), 391–405.

Goh, M., Wahl, K., McDonald, J., Brissett, A., & Yoon, E. (2007). Working with immigrant students in schools: The role of school counselors in building cross-cultural bridges. *Journal of Multicultural Counseling and Development, 35*, 66–79.

Hays, D. G. & Singh, A. A. (2012). *Qualitative inquiry in clinical and educational settings*. New York, NY: Guilford Press.

James, D. C. S. (1997). Coping with a new society: The psychosocial problems of immigrant youth. *Journal of School Health, 67*(3), 98–101.

Mather, M. (2009). *Children in immigrant families chart new path*. Washington, DC: Population Reference Bureau. Retrieved from http://www.prb.org/pdf09/immigrantchildren.pdf

Migration Policy Institute. (2011). *English language learners and their performance in U.S. schools* [Video File]. Retrieved from http://www.migrationpolicy.org/multimedia/english-language-learners-and-their-performance-us-public-schools

Migration Policy Institute. (2015). *State immigration data profiles*. Retrieved from http://www.migrationpolicy.org/programs/data-hub/state-immigration-data-profiles

Montgomery, P. S., Roberts, M., & Growe, R. (2003). *English Language Learners: An issue of educational equity*. Lafayette, LA: University of Louisiana Press.

National Center for Education Statistics. (2015). *English Language Learners*. Retrieved from http://nces.ed.gov/programs/coe/indicator_cgf.asp

NEA Priority Schools Campaign. (2012, January 20). *English Language Learners: Culture, equity and language* [Video File]. Retrieved from https://www.youtube.com/watch?v=5HU80AxmP-U

Nieto, S. (2002). We speak many tongues: Language diversity and multicultural education. In P. Richard-Amato & M. Snow (Eds.), *Academic success for English Language Learners: Strategies for K–12 mainstream teachers* (pp. 133–149). New York, NY: Longman.

Ochoa, S. H., & Rhodes, R. L. (2005). Assisting parents of bilingual students to achieve equity in public schools. *Journal of Educational and Psychological Consultation, 16* (1/2), 75–94. doi: 10.1207/s1532768xjepc161&2_5

Ponterotto, J. G., Casas, J. M., Suzuki, L. & Alexander, C. M. (Eds.). (2010). *Handbook of multicultural counseling* (3rd ed.). Thousand Oaks, CA: Sage.

Ratts, M. J., Singh, A. A., Nassar-McMillan, S., Butler, S. K., & McCullough, J. R. (2015). *Multicultural and social justice counseling competencies*. Retrieved from http://www.multiculturalcounseling.org/index.php?option=com_content&view=article&id=205:amcd-endorses-multicultural-and-social-justice-counseling-competencies&catid=1:latest&Itemid=123

Seddon, J. (2015). School counselor support for the academic, career, personal, and social needs of ELL students. *Culminating Projects in Community Psychology, Counseling and Family Therapy* (Paper 8). Retrieved from http://repository.stcloudstate.edu/cpcf_etds/8

Ruiz Soto, A. G., Hooker, S. & Batalova, J. (2015). *Top languages spoken by English language learners nationally and by state* (Report No. 4). Washington, DC: Migration Policy Institute.

Suárez-Orozco, C., Onaga, M., & de Lardemelle, C. (2010). Promoting academic engagement among immigrant adolescents through school-family-community collaboration. *Professional School Counseling 14*(1), 15–26.

Suárez-Orozco, C., Suárez-Orozco, M. M., & Todorova, I. (2008). *Learning a new land: Immigrant students in American society*. Cambridge, MA: Belknap Press.

Thomas, W. P., & Collier, V. P. (2002). *A national study of school effectiveness for language minority students' long-term academic achievement*. Retrieved from http://www.eric.ed.gov/ERICDocs/data/ericdocs2sql/content_storage_01/0000019b/80/29/d4/52.pdf

Trusty, J., & Brown, D. (2005). Advocacy competencies for school counselors. *Professional School Counseling, 8*(3), 259–265.

U.S. Department of Education. (2015). *Developing programs for English Language Learners: Glossary*. Retrieved from http://www2.ed.gov/about/offices/list/ocr/ell/glossary.html

U.S. Department of Justice, & U.S. Department of Education. (2015). *Dear colleague letter: English Learner students and Limited English proficient parents*. Retrieved from http://www2.ed.gov/about/offices/list/ocr/letters/colleague-el-201501.pdf

Lesson 9

WORKING WITH LESBIAN, GAY, BISEXUAL, AND QUEER STUDENTS

Critical Lessons for School Counselors

Theodore R. Burnes
Antioch University, Los Angeles

Real Life

Maxwell is a 2nd year, Native American, heterosexual male school counseling student in his master's program and on his school counseling internship in a high school. One of the students on his caseload, Liam, has recently come out to him as questioning his sexual orientation. Liam has had some sexual feelings toward other men in his homeroom class, and has begun to explore his feelings by entering chatrooms online to meet other gay, bisexual, and questioning men. Maxwell is providing Liam individual counseling services and quickly realizes that Liam's educational experiences may be compromised by experiences of bullying that are happening inside and outside of the school. In some instances, Liam noted that school personnel who have witnessed bullying events haven't done anything. Liam also notes that his sex education class has been difficult for him, in part because the teacher has told all the male students in the class (the sex education classes at the school are separated by gender) that they have to be respectful and careful when having sex with women for the first time, assuming that all students in the class were sexually attracted to women.

Lesson Nine

Working With Lesbian, Gay, Bisexual, and Queer Students

Critical Lessons for School Counselors

Theodore R. Burnes
Antioch University, Los Angeles

Essential Question: How can I best meet the needs of lesbian, gay, bisexual, and queer (LGBQ) students?

Objectives

Students will

- demonstrate techniques that are culturally appropriate when working with LGBQ students.
- demonstrate a sensitivity to and awareness of LGBQ student's worldview.

CACREP 2016 STANDARDS

- Techniques of personal/social counseling in school settings (5.G.3.f)

MPCAC Standards

- Human development and wellness across the life span
- Counseling, consultation, and social-justice advocacy theories and skills
- Ecological, contextual, multicultural, social-justice foundation of human development

Video Spark

https://www.google.com/webhp?sourceid=chrome-instant&ion=1&espv=2&ie=UTF-8#q=Ted+talk+tania+israel

Bisexuality and Beyond (Tania Israel)

Helen Hamlet and Theodore Burnes (2013) have identified ways for school counseling interns to learn the numerous ways that sociocultural diversity is a part of professional school counseling and the school counseling internship experience. Like Maxwell in the case above, interns will aid in the development of a school counseling program that celebrates various social and cultural aspects of diversity. Although various cultures have traditionally been defined through identities centered on race, ethnicity, or gender, expanded definitions include a variety of different aspects including socioeconomic status and sexual orientation (Sue & Sue, 2015). Through these school counseling training experiences, interns will begin to facilitate and engage with resilience, privilege, and oppression that these students experience. One specific group of students with whom these school counselors will engage with are lesbian, gay, bisexual, and queer (LGBQ) students. *Sexual orientation* refers to an individual's social, emotional, and/or physical attraction to someone of the same sex, another sex, or multiple sexes (Diamond & Butterworth, 2008; Fassinger & Arsenau, 2007). This attraction has multiple components that overlap, but should be understood as distinct facets, including sexual identity, which is a part of sexual orientation. *Sexual identity* is the label that individuals use to describe their identity, often (but not always) influenced by culture, environment, and community. Although there has been consistent documentation that these identities and attractions are often fixed within individuals, there is a growing documentation that highlights a series of identities that are relatively stable, may be fluid, and can change over time (Manley, Diamond, & van Anders, 2015). Specifically, these identities demonstrate a stability in terms of labeling and attraction; however, there may some fluidity in terms of who one is attracted to and how those attractions manifest over time (e.g., physical attraction, emotional attraction, behavioral engagement). Subsequently, the term *queer* has some origins in academic settings and is a label often used by individuals with a fluid identity (Stombler, Baunach, Simonds, Windsor, & Burgess, 2013). The queer identity has often been used both to politicize one's identity and also as an assault on the hurtful use of the term by non-LGBT individuals in historical contexts. Individuals also often use this label to be inclusive of their attractions to transgender individuals and represent a nonbinary understanding of their attractions.

It is important to note that chapters in this text have differentiated chapters for working with LGBQ students from working with transgender and gender nonconforming (LGBQ) students. Although many group the five letters in the *LGBTQ* acronym together due to their transcending of gender norms and experiences of physical, verbal, societal, and vocational harassment, scholars have noted the importance in differentiating sexual orientation and gender identity (Diamond & Butterworth, 2008). Those individuals who identify as transgender may not have any similarities, community, or identity politics related to those individuals who identify as lesbian, gay, bisexual, or queer (DePaul, Walsh, & Dam, 2009).

The school counseling model made by the American School Counselor Association (ASCA) helps school counselors and school counseling interns to develop a program in their school that is comprehensive, has a strong foundation, and is data driven (2012). School counseling interns can work collaboratively with their supervisors using the ASCA model when working with LGBQ students to ensure that various ecological levels of the school counseling program meet the needs of LGBQ students. Further, school counseling interns' social-justice advocacy can ensure systemic change of various levels of the educational system to ensure that issues of sexual orientation are ingrained in multiple ecological levels. This chapter provides school counseling interns with suggestions and strategies for utilizing cultural competence with LGBQ students into the ASCA model.

• THEORETICAL UNDERSTANDINGS OF LGBQ STUDENTS IN SCHOOL SYSTEMS

Contemporary understandings of sexual orientation have produced a critique of educational and counseling discourses for using outdated and conflated definitions of sex, sexual orientation, and gender identity (Burnes & Stanley, in press). When examining the intersections between sexual orientation school counseling, it is important for school counselors working with LGBQ students to understand common language related to the identity and psychological well-being of these students. As language in LGBQ communities consistently changes and evolves, to define all necessary language for competent school counseling practices with LGBQ communities would be outside the scope of this chapter; I suggest the comprehensive glossary in the *Competencies for Counseling with Lesbian, Gay, Bisexual, Queer, Questioning, Intersex, and Ally Individuals* put forth by the American Counseling Association (ACA, 2013). These various terms related to sexual identity and expression can help school counselors to understand that sexual orientation can impact the school counseling process in numerous and complex ways.

As competent school counselors, using developmental theory and practice in working with LGBQ students is reflective of school counselors' ethical standards (American School Counselor Association [ASCA], 2010). Many students will begin to understand notions of sexual attraction as early as late childhood (Broderick & Blewitt, 2010); however, such developmental processes may be severely impacted by environmental factors. For example, the detrimental impact of bullying and incident-based hate crimes has been documented by scholars to negatively impact LGBQ adolescents' well-being (Hillard, Love, Franks, Laris, & Coyle, 2014). Further, recent research has suggested that lack of social support from families and peers may negatively impact LGBQ students' social (Bowen & Bourgeois, 2001), emotional (Almeida, Johnson, Corliss, Molnar, & Azrael, 2009), and academic (DePaul et al., 2009) self-esteem and self-efficacy. Joseph P. Robinson, Dorothy L. Espelage, and Ian Rivers (2013) note that, in comparison to a sample of heterosexual youth, there are stronger relationships between emotional distress (and subsequent emotional development), sexual identity, and peer victimization for LGBQ youth, and these relationships are influenced by an LGBQ youth's gender.

Although LGBQ students may utilize school counseling services for many different reasons, there is continual documentation (e.g., Israel, Gorcheva, Burnes, & Walther, 2008) that counselors may tend to incorrectly interpret LGBQ individuals' reasons for counseling based on their identities (e.g., a school counselor does not ask about sexual orientation or sexual identity when it is an issue; a school counselor may assume heterosexuality unless a student corrects the counselor or students reveal their own LGBQ identity). Scholars (e.g., Cole, 2009) have noted the complexity of how identities for individuals with differing degrees of marginalization and privilege. Some LGBQ students may find themselves having to "prioritize" one identity over the other (e.g., identifying as a Black male, rather than as a Black gay male) when these students possess intersecting marginalized identities. Further, schools that have a Gay-Straight Alliance (GSA) may be welcoming for White students, but LGBQ may experience racism in these environments and thus feel marginalized from a space that could be a source of support for them. Thus, the numerous complexities of working with LGBQ students' identities necessitate that school counselors assess how a client's unique combinations of marginalized and privileged identities impact his or her respective worldviews, environments, and relationships. Further, LGBQ students have unique stressors based on their sexual identities that are often uniquely impacted by other marginalized identities such as class, gender, ethnicity, and race. These intersecting identities, then, impact their mental health and wellness inside and outside of the school setting. Scholars (e.g., Hillard et al., 2014) have documented some of these stressors, including heterosexism by teachers or school administrators, physical violence, fear of violence and discrimination in the forms of physical harassment, or verbal harassment.

• USING THE ASCA MODEL TO CELEBRATE LGBQ STUDENTS

School counselors can consider the context of their clients' unique social and cultural frameworks in the building and maintenance of culturally informed school counseling. Specifically, school counselors and school counseling interns like Maxwell can utilize the ASCA model as a framework to consider how their school counseling program may need to be adapted, changed, or updated so as to celebrate a diverse continuum of sexual expression and to serve LGBQ students effectively. The following section identifies strategies for school counselors to adapt their programs accordingly.

Foundation. When developing school counseling programs, school counselors should develop a mission statement that explicitly states that their school is a welcoming place for individuals with diverse gender identities. ASCA's (2014) position statement on working with LGBTQ youth in schools can be a framework for developing a school counseling program that combines LGBTQ affirmative practice with the understanding of the effects of discrimination, privilege, and marginalization of all a student's unique combination of identities. School counselors can also help to make LGBQ students feel supported by infusing issues of sexual orientation into the school community. Celebrating the history and culture of LGBQ communities is one way to help students learn about resources available to LGBQ people in the students' geographic area (e.g., LGBT community centers, coffee shops, bars) and, as well, websites and Internet-based sources that may provide assistance in students learning about LGBQ identities in a context that is more anonymous. It is imperative that school counselors and school counseling interns make sure to thoroughly review websites that are listed as resources for any member of the school's community so as not to provide inaccurate information.

As school counselors assess their own competencies in working with LGBQ students, the need for appropriate continuing education and training becomes paramount (Goodrich, Harper, Luke, & Singh, 2014). In the absence of supervisors with competency in working with LGBQ students, school counseling interns should identify opportunities to seek additional training and experiences to work in the P–12 educational setting (e.g., additional coursework, professional conference presentations, workshops and training given at local, state, national, or international levels).

Service Delivery. As bullying attitudes and behaviors are disproportionately reflected toward LGBQ students in comparison with their non-LGBQ peers, the need for school counseling interns to deliver comprehensive services that affirm LGBQ individuals and communities in their school becomes paramount so as to provide concrete actions that an attitude of celebration of LGBQ identities in school is the norm and not the exception. Making sure that counseling services use affirmative language and counseling processes is necessary in order to achieve this goal, including questions related to (a) how the multiple facets of students' sexual identities (e.g., behaviors, emotions, attractions, fantasies, physical experiences, and sexual expressions) come together and intersect, (b) how the student came to connect with a LGBQ identity in their developmental experiences (if applicable), (c) the process (if applicable) of the student's sharing of an LGBQ identity with other people (the school counselor can ask about sharing this identity in multiple ecological domains, including family, extracurricular sports teams, school personnel, home life, etc.), (d) how the process of coming out has impacted the student's mental health and well-being. School counselors should also inquire as to how a student's cultural, familial, and societal identities may cause stress as they interact with a student's LGBQ identity. For example, a Mexican American male student may have disclosed his bisexual identity to his family and thus may lack a vital support system to buffer against ethnic discrimination.

For school counselors conducting individual and group counseling sessions working with LGBQ clients, it is important that they routinely self-assess their competence level. Many school counseling trainees may lack specific training in working with LGBQ students; such lack of training is not specific to the discipline of school counseling and is true of many different mental health disciplines (Luke, Goodrich, & Scarborough, 2011). Thus, school counselors' learning about LGBQ individuals and communities to increase their knowledge, attitudes, and skills will be able to positively impact their skills with respect to the counseling process. Recent guidelines for psychological practice with LGBQ clients note that psychologists should recognize that the families of LGBQ people might include people who are not legally or biologically related (American Psychological Association [APA], 2012, p. 18). Utilizing these guidelines, school counselors should apply theories of ecology (e.g., "family of choice," understanding self-acceptance; Fassinger & Arsenau, 2007) and the use of ecological frameworks to aid in the conceptualization of LGBQ students.

For example, Liam may exhibit anxiety-related symptoms, such as "my stomach feels numb like parts of my body are disconnected from other parts" and poor concentration as he decides to come out as bisexual to his family. Thus, Maxwell can ask Liam questions related to who is in Liam's community (*Who do you consider family? Can you tell me why this person is family to you?*), questions related to how and to what extent family have helped Liam (*Can you tell me about a specific instance when a family member has helped you through a difficult time?*), and questions related to clients' relationship to their unique relationship to culture (*I know that we all have different ways that we engage with culture and the world around us. What are ways that you engage with your culture?*). Further, Maxwell can ask Liam questions in a counseling interview from a strength-based approach. Specifically, Maxwell can assess what Liam's strengths are as he develops his bisexual identity, what Liam values in himself, and what are strengths and social support that Liam would like to cultivate as he deepens his resilience and his connection to his bisexual identity.

School counseling interns may want to implement the school counseling core curriculum lessons as part of their training and as part of their school counseling program's service delivery model. Such experiential activities can be helpful in working with students who may not have the cognitive capacity or emotional maturity to engage in conversation about abstract topics such as sexual orientation (Broderick & Blewitt, 2010). In one such activity, students sit by themselves with a piece of paper and a writing instrument. School counseling interns ask students to write the names of four people in their life—any four people—on the piece of paper. Next, students are instructed to pick two of the names and circle them. They can pick any two of the four names that they want to circle. Once everyone has circled, the school counseling interns announces that the student has come out as lesbian, gay, bisexual, or queer, to the four people on their respective list. Further, on the list, the students are told that the two people whose names that they circled have had a positive reaction, and the two names that were not circled have had a negative reaction. Students then cluster into small groups of two to four students; they are asked to process what it would be like if these were the reactions that these people had in real life. In a subsequent large-group process, it is helpful for the school counseling intern to discuss how it is often difficult to predict the ways that people might react to such identity disclosure.

As part of the service delivery domain of a school counselor's program, Kristopher Goodrich, Amney Harper, Melissa Luke, and Anneliese Singh (2013) urged professional school counselors and school counseling interns to work within multiple levels of the school system to facilitate in-service trainings and workshops on working with LGBQ students, staff, and administration. They suggested including domains on language and on policies for including diversity about sexual practices and identities in gendered spaces (e.g., school dances, sex education classes). Further, making sure that LGBQ students have specific resources available for their career development and college readiness is also important.

Management. Hamlet and Burnes (2013) note that the school counseling internship is a developmental process in which interns should be able to incorporate their own increasing bodies of knowledge and feel supported by their supervisor as they develop skills of managing programs that serve the needs of a diverse student body. When school counselors engage in the management of their school counseling programs, they should consider the needs of LGBQ students in a variety of ways. First, it is helpful to initially examine the nondiscrimination policies within the school to ensure that sexual orientation is included in the policy (Almeida et al., 2009). Further, school counselors can also work with administrators to establish an advisory council of counselors, faculty, staff, and administration that can be responsive to issues of sexual identity diversity and issues of intentional inclusion of sexual orientation issues into schools. Additionally, school counselors can begin collecting data related to incidence of anti-LGBQ attitudes, behaviors, or practices. Further, making sure that various members of a school's health care team—intervention advisors, school counselors, psychologists, nutritionists, and social workers—can create collaborations that will translate into long-term partnerships to develop a LGBQ-affirmative environment for the school.

In managing their school counseling program, school counseling interns can design, implement, and evaluate in projects that highlight understanding, celebration, and sensitivity of LGBQ students. In conjunction with their supervisors, such projects could include designing and implementing an assembly presentation or a school counseling core curriculum lesson in sexual fluidity or how to be an ally to lesbian, gay, bisexual, or queer students. Further, school counseling interns can also create advocacy groups or task forces within the school focused on drafting and editing discrimination policies that could be added to the school's philosophy and mission statement.

Accountability. ASCA (2012) documented the importance of school counselors not only designing innovative strategies to collect data within their school counseling programs, but also using data to show how school counseling programs have impacted student well-being and facilitated student success. When analyzing and interpreting data about their programs, school counselors' interpretation should be carefully checked and audited for homophobic, biphobic, or anti-queer biases and assumptions, including those that are heterosexist (e.g., assuming pronoun usage when speaking about someone's attractions or partners), and may include biases about sexual roles, norms, and behaviors. The ways that some LGBQ students' transcending of certain gender norms should also be explored and taken into careful consideration when interpreting peers, as many LGBQ students transcend societal gender roles and norms similar to their transgender, genderqueer, and gender nonconforming peers.

Finally, school counselors and school counseling interns must recognize that interpreting results and providing feedback to school and district administrators about the mental health and well-being of LGBQ students must be accompanied by feedback about the harsh realities of LGBQ students' experiences in school environments. Specifically, noting how data can be used to identify strategies for systemic change at the school or district levels can be helpful in school counseling interns' education about how to create affirmative environments for LGBQ students at multiple levels.

● CONCLUSION

This article has identified the ways that school counselors can utilize the ASCA model to serve LGBQ students. Further, the article identified the multiple ways that school counseling interns are able to implement specific interventions at individual, group, classroom, school, and district levels that utilize frameworks of social justice and cultural competence. As issues of sexual orientation and sexual expression continue to be a topic of continued importance worldwide given the expansion of LGBQ issues in the media, it is important for school counselors and school counseling interns to bring issues of sexual diversity to the forefront of their school community's minds so as to increase understanding.

● REFERENCES

Almeida, J., Johnson, R. M., Corliss, H. L., Molnar, B. E., & Azrael, D. (2009). Emotional distress among LGBT youth: The influence of perceived discrimination based on sexual orientation. *Journal of Youth and Adolescence, 38*(7), 1001–1014.

American Counseling Association. (2013). Association for Lesbian, Gay, Bisexual, and Transgender Issues in Counseling Competencies for Counseling with Lesbian, Gay, Bisexual, Queer, Questioning, Intersex, and Ally Individuals. *Journal of LGBT Issues in Counseling, 4*(3), 135–159. doi:10.1080/15538605.2010.524839

American Psychological Association. (2012). Guidelines for psychological practice with lesbian, gay, and bisexual clients. *American Psychologist,67*(1), 10–42.

American School Counselor Association. (2014). *Position statement on working with LGBTQ Youth: The Counselor's Role.* Retrieved from https://www.schoolcounselor.org/asca/media/asca/PositionStatements/PS_LGBTQ.pdf

American School Counselor Association. (2012). *The ASCA National Model: A framework for school counseling programs* (3rd ed.). Alexandria, VA: Author.

American School Counselor Association. (2011). *The professional school counselor and the promotion of safe schools through conflict resolution and bullying/harassment prevention.* Retrieved from http://www.schoolcounselor.org/files/PS_Bullying.pdf

American School Counselor Association. (2010). *Ethical standards for school counselors.* Retrieved from http://www.schoolcounselor.org/asca/media/asca/Resource%20 Center/Legal%20and%20Ethical%20Issues/Sample%20 Documents/EthicalStandards2010.pdf

Bowen, A. M., & Bourgeois, M. J. (2001). Attitudes toward lesbian, gay, and bisexual college students: The contribution of pluralistic ignorance, dynamic social impact, and contact theories. *Journal of American College Health, 50*(2), 91–96.

Broderick, P. C., & Blewitt, P. (2010). *The life span: Human development for helping professionals* (3rd ed.). New York, NY: Pearson/Prentice Hall.

Burnes, T. R., & Smith, S.R. (in press). Queering personality assessment: Intersections between personality assessment, sexual orientations, and gender identity. In S.R. Smith & R. Krishnamurthy (Eds.), *Diversity-sensitive personality assessment.* New York, NY: Routledge.

Burnes, T. R., & Stanley, J. S. (in press). *Teaching LGBT psychology: Queering innovative pedagogy and practice.* Washington, DC: American Psychological Association.

Cole, E. R. (2009). Intersectionality and research in psychology. *The American Psychologist, 64,* 170–180.

Collins, P. H. (2009). Forward: Emerging intersections—Building knowledge and transforming institutions. In B. T. Dill & R. E. Zambrana (Eds.), *Emerging intersections: Race, class and gender in theory, policy and practice.* New Brunswick, NJ: Rutgers University Press.

Crenshaw, K. (1991). Mapping the margins: Intersectionality, identity politics, and violence against women of color. *Stanford Law Review, 43*(6), 1241–1299.

DePaul, J., Walsh, M., & Dam, U. (2009). The role of school counselors in addressing sexual orientation in schools. *Professional School Counseling, 12*(4), 300–308. doi:http://dx.doi.org/10.5330/PSC.n.2010-12.300

Diamond, L. M., & Butterworth, M. (2008). Questioning gender and sexual identity: Dynamic links over time. *Sex Roles, 59,* 365–376.

Fassinger, R. E., & Arsenau, J. R. (2007). "I'd rather get wet than be under that umbrella": Differentiating the experiences and identities of lesbian, gay, bisexual, and transgender people. In K. J. Bieschke, R. M. Perez, &

K. A. Debord (Eds.), *Handbook of counseling and psychotherapy with lesbian, gay, bisexual and transgender clients* (2nd ed; pp. 19–50). Washington, DC: American Psychological Association.

Goodrich, K. M., Harper, A. J., Luke, M., & Singh, A. A. (2013). Best practices for professional school counselors working with LGBTQ youth. *Journal of LGBT Issues in Counseling*, *7*(4), 307–322.

Hamlet, H. S., & Burnes, T. R. (2013). Development of the Counseling Intern Developmental Assessment-School Counseling Form (CIDASC). *Counseling Outcomes Research and Evaluation, 4*(1), 55–71.

Hillard, P., Love, L., Franks, H. M., Laris, B. A., & Coyle, K. K. (2014). "They were only joking": Efforts to decrease LGBTQ bullying and harassment in Seattle public schools. *Journal of School Health*, *84*(1), 1–9.

Israel, T., Gorcheva, R., Burnes, T. R., & Walther, W. A. (2008). Helpful and unhelpful therapy experiences of LGBT clients. *Psychotherapy Research, 18*(3), 294–305.

Kosciw, J. G., Palmer, N. A., & Kull, R. M. (2015). Reflecting resiliency: Openness about sexual orientation and/or gender identity and its relationship to well-being and educational outcomes for LGBT students. *American Journal of Community Psychology, 55*, 167–178. doi:10.1007/s10464-014-9642-6

Luke, M., Goodrich, K. M., & Scarborough, J. L. (2011). Integration of the K–12 LGBTQI student population in school counselor education curricula: The current state of affairs. *Journal of LGBT Issues in Counseling*, *5*(2), 80–101.

Manley, M. H., Diamond, L. M., & van Anders, S. M. (2015). Polyamory, monoamory, and sexual fluidity: A longitudinal study of identity and sexual trajectories. *Psychology of Sexual Orientation and Gender Diversity, 2*(2), 168–180. doi:http://dx.doi.org/10.1037/sgd0000098

Meyer, I. H. (2003). Prejudice, social stress, and mental health in lesbian, gay, and bisexual populations: Conceptual issues and research evidence. *Psychological Bulletin, 129,* 674–697.

Robinson, J. P., Espelage, D. L., & Rivers, I. (2013). Developmental trends in peer victimization and emotional distress in LGB and heterosexual youth. *Pediatrics, 131*(3), 423–430.

Stombler, M., Baunach, D. M., Simonds, D., Windsor, E., & Burgess, E. O. (Eds.). (2013). *Sex matters: The sexuality and society reader* (4th ed.). New York, NY: W.W. Norton.

Sue, D. W., & Sue, D. (2015). *Counseling the culturally diverse: Theory and practice* (7th ed.). New York, NY: Wiley.

Toomey, R. B., Ryan, C., Diaz, R. M., Card, N. A., & Russell, S. T. (2010). Gender-nonconforming lesbian, gay, bisexual, and transgender youth: School victimization and young adult psychosocial adjustment. *Developmental Psychology, 46*(6), 1580–1589. doi:10.1037/a0020705

LESSON 10

WORKING WITH TRANSGENDER AND GENDER NONCONFORMING STUDENTS

Critical Lessons for School Counselors

Theodore R. Burnes
Antioch University, Los Angeles

Real Life

> *Rayann is a 2nd year, African American, cisgender female school counseling student in her master's program and on her school counseling internship in a middle school. One of the students on her caseload, Parker, has recently come out to her as questioning her gender identity. Assigned male at birth, Parker has "known I was a girl since I was five or six." Rayann is providing Parker individual counseling services, but quickly realizes that other aspects of Parker's educational experiences may be increasingly difficult for Parker. The middle school does not have gender neutral restrooms, and there is no mention of gender diversity in the school's various policies. Rayann remembers learning a bit about specific cultural norms and values for transgender individuals in some of her school counseling classes; however, she is not sure how to apply some of this knowledge so that she can advocate for students like Parker while she is on her internship.*

Lesson Ten

Working With Transgender and Gender Nonconforming Students

Critical Lessons for School Counselors

Theodore R. Burnes
Antioch University, Los Angeles

Essential Question: How can I best meet the needs of transgender and gender nonconforming students?

Objectives

Students will

- demonstrate techniques that are culturally appropriate when working with transgender and gender nonconforming students.
- demonstrate a sensitivity to and awareness of transgender and nonconforming student's worldview.

CACREP 2016 STANDARDS

- Techniques of personal/social counseling in school settings (5.G.3.f)

MPCAC Standards

- Human development and wellness across the life span
- Counseling, consultation, and social-justice advocacy theories and skills
- Ecological, contextual, multicultural, social-justice foundation of human development

Video Spark

http://tedxtalks.ted.com/video/Trans-Liberation-is-for-Everybo

Trans Liberation is for Everybody (Anneliese Singh)

• INTRODUCTION

There is increased documentation to support the need for school counseling interns to learn the numerous ways that diversity and multiculturalism are a part of school counseling programs and, thus, the school counseling internship experience (Hamlet & Burnes, 2013). Like Rayann in the case above, interns will engage with and serve students of a variety of different cultural expressions and identities; through these engagements, interns will understand the wide experiences of resilience, privilege, and oppression that these students experience. One specific group of students with whom these school counselors will engage with is transgender and gender nonconforming (TGNC) students. The American Counseling Association (2010) has defined *gender* as "set of social, psychological, and emotional traits, often influenced by societal expectations, that classify an individual as feminine, masculine, androgynous, or other" (p. 158). Terms such as *transgender* and *gender nonconforming* (TGNC) refer to students whose physical body may not match the gender identity and/or gender expression that students know themselves to be. Thus, the impact of gender socialization may have implications for TGNC students that can result in experiences of marginalization and oppression.

The school counseling model made by the American School Counselor Association (ASCA) helps school counselors develop a comprehensive, data-driven program (American School Counselor Association [ASCA], 2012). When working with TGNC students, school counseling inters can work collaboratively with their supervisors using the ASCA model to ensure that the needs of TGNC students are met at various ecological levels of the school counseling program. The following chapter provides school counseling interns with strategies and suggestions for infusing cultural competence with TGNC students into this model.

● THEORETICAL UNDERSTANDINGS OF TGNC STUDENTS IN SCHOOL SYSTEMS

When conceptualizing the intersections between school counseling and gender identity, it is important for school counselors working with TGNC students in schools to understand common language related to the identity and psychological well-being of LGBT people. Further, scholars (Kosciw, Palmer, & Kull, 2015) have noted the importance of differentiating TGNC students' identities from the identities of their LGB peers. Although the four letters in the *LGBT* acronym are often grouped together due to their collective transcending of gender norms and experiences of verbal, physical, vocational, and societal harassment, those individuals who identify as TGNC may not have any similarities, community, or identity politics related to those individuals who identify as lesbian, gay, or bisexual.

As language in TGNC communities consistently changes and evolves, to define all necessary language for competent psychological assessment practices with LGBT communities would be outside the scope of this chapter; however, we suggest the comprehensive glossary put forth by the *Competencies for Counseling with Transgender Clients* put forth by the American Counseling Association in 2010. Although there has been consistent documentation that gender identities are often fixed within individuals, there is a growing documentation that highlights a series of identities that are relatively stable, may be fluid, and can change over time. These various understandings of gender identity help school counselors to understand the numerous and complex ways that gender and sexual orientation can impact the school counseling process. Further, more contemporary understandings of gender identity have produced a critique of educational and counseling discourses for using outdated and conflated definitions of sex, gender, and gender identity.

As competent school counselors, taking a developmental approach in working with TGNC students is also important as is reflective of school counselors' ethical standards (ASCA, 2010). Many students will begin to understand notions of gender as early as 5 years of age (Broderick & Blewitt, 2010); however, such developmental processes may be severely impacted by environmental factors. Scholars have consistently documented the detrimental impact of incident-based hate crimes and bullying on TGNC children's well-being (Brill & Pepper, 2008). Further, recent research has suggested that families may be the instigators of some insidious trauma for children (Burnes, Dexter, Richmond, Singh, & Cherrington, 2016). As children mature into adolescence, scholars have suggested that TGNC young adults are questioning, forming, and experimenting with their various, intersecting identities as a major developmental task in order to achieve a cohesive sense of self. For TGNC adolescents who are in supportive school environments, maladaptive coping may emerge through behaviors such as self-injury, accelerated sexual behavior, or avoiding professionals (e.g., doctors, school administrators) who may further cause them suffering through aggressive acts. Kate Richmond, Theodore Burnes, Anneliese Singh and M. Ferrera (2016) note that as their peers begin to engage in the developmental task of peer relationships and the development of social competencies, it may be difficult for the TGNC adolescent to form such relationships, and they may isolate themselves for fear of further ridicule, bullying, or traumatic incidence.

Singh, Sarah Meng, and Anthony Hansen (2014) have articulated the resilience of TGNC youth in finding social support networks through online communities, communities that support them in identifying their own gender, and reframing mental health challenges as they navigate relationships with family and friends.

Although TGNC students may utilize school counseling services for many different reasons, there is continual documentation that counselors may tend to incorrectly interpret LGBT individuals' reasons for counseling based on their identities (e.g., a school counselor does not ask about transgender, gender queer, or gender nonconforming identity when it is an issue; a school counselor tends to overly focus on TGNC identity with a TGNC student when it is not the focus of counseling; Singh & Burnes, 2009). Compounded with issues related to being TGNC, scholars (e.g., Cole, 2009; Burnes & Chen, 2012) have noted the complexity of intersecting identities for individuals with differing degrees of marginalization and privilege. For TGNC students who possess intersecting marginalized identities, they may often find themselves having to draw alliances with one identity over the other (e.g., identifying as a Black male, rather than as a Black *trans* male), which fall short in understanding the complexity of such issues, especially when working in applied settings with diverse populations (Collins, 2009; Crenshaw, 1991). Thus, the numerous complexities of working with TGNC students' identities necessitate that school counselors to assess how a client's unique combinations of marginalized and privileged identities impact their respective worldviews, environments, and relationships.

In addition, TGNC students have a unique set of stressors based on their marginalized statuses that are often compounded by other marginalized identities such as race, class, and gender that impact their mental health and wellness inside and outside of the school setting. Scholars (e.g., de Jong, 2015) have highlighted some of these unique stressors, including fear of violence and discrimination in the forms of physical harassment, verbal harassment, or actual physical violence. Richmond, Burnes, and Kate Carroll (2012) note that transgender individuals are almost four times as likely to experience physical harassment as the general population. Further, Russell Toomey, Caitlin Ryan, Rafael Diaz, Noel Card, and Stephen Russell (2013) note that there are specific issues that impact the coming out process for youth who are LGBT, including homelessness, family rejection, and increased incidence of major depression disorder and suicidal ideation.

• USING THE ASCA MODEL TO CELEBRATE TGNC STUDENTS

The building and maintenance of culturally informed school counseling can aid school counselors in considering the context of their clients' unique social and cultural frameworks. Specifically, school counselors and school counseling trainees like Rayann can utilize the ASCA model as a framework to consider how their school counseling program may need to be adapted, changed, or updated so that they can serve TGNC students effectively. The following section identifies strategies for school counselors to adapt their programs accordingly:

Foundation. When developing school counseling programs, school counselors should develop a mission statement that explicitly states that their school is a welcoming place for individuals with diverse gender identities. Singh and Burnes (2009) urge school counselors to use the ASCA model (ASCA, 2005) to create systems that foster community pride and support for TGNC students. School counselors can also help to make TGNC students feel supported by infusing gender diversity issues into the school community. Celebrating the history and culture of TGNC communities is one way to help students learn about transgender historical figures and the past and present struggles that transgender individuals have met when undergoing their fight for civil rights. Further, as school counselors assess their own competencies in working with transgender students, the need for appropriate continuing education and training becomes paramount. School counselors should identify experts in their area who have the relevant scope of practice to be gender specialists and consult with them about opportunities in their area to gain additional knowledge, training, and experience.

Service Delivery. A comprehensive initial counseling assessment (Morrison, 2014) is vital to this approach, including questions related to (a) how the student came to connect with a TGNC identity in his or her developmental experiences, (b) the process (if applicable) of the student's sharing a TGNC identity with others (the school counselor should ask about this sharing of identity in multiple arenas, including school, home life, family, and extracurricular sports teams), and (c) how the process of coming out has impacted the student's mental health and well-being. School counselors should also inquire as to how a TGNC client's identity may cause stress as it interacts with other cultural, familial, and societal identities. For example, how has an African American client who has come out to her ethnic community as a genderqueer person lost her community due to transphobia and thus lacks a vital support system to buffer against racism?

For school counselors conducting individual and group counseling sessions working with TGNC clients, such a process would involve knowledge of how issues of gender has been found to impact the client's development, ability to utilize the school's resources (e.g., gendered bathrooms, gendered extracurricular activities), and overall expression (e.g., assertiveness, ability to form relationships, self-esteem, avoidance). Also, school counselors should assess how clients' TGNC identities may cause stress that interacts with other cultural, familial, and societal identities. The need to understand both a client's lived and perceived experiences of gender and gender discrimination should also be carefully considered.

Many school counseling trainees may lack specific training in working with TGNC students; such lack of training is not specific to the discipline of school counseling and is true of many different mental health disciplines (Burnes, Rowan, & Paul, 2016). Thus, asking clients questions related to who is in their community ("Who do you consider family? Can you tell me why this person/these people are family to you?"), related to how and to what extent family have helped the client ("Can you tell me about a specific instance when a family member has helped you through a difficult time?"), and related to clients' relationship to their unique relationship to culture ("I know that we all have different ways that we engage with culture and the world around us. What are ways that you engage with your environment? How about your culture?"). Further, asking clients questions in a clinical interview from a strength-based approach is equally important. Specifically, what is going well, strengths, and what they value in themselves helps people to comprehensively understand how their culture, environment, and context impact their personality and overall functioning. Finally, knowing how to use affirmative language when speaking of sexual orientation and gender identity has been documented as a critical process (Morrison, 2014).

Counselors should apply theories of ecology (e.g., "family of choice," LGBT culture and community; Fassinger & Arsenau, 2007) and the use of ecological frameworks to aid in the conceptualization of LGBT clients. Recent guidelines for psychological practice with LGB clients note that psychologists should recognize that the families of LGBT people might include people who are not legally or biologically related (APA, 2012, p. 18). In a case example, an 18-year-old African American female presents inability to sleep and poor concentration as she decides to come out as lesbian to her family. As part of her clinical interview, the assessor notes that she exhibits nervousness as she explains her situation. However, as the assessor asks the client about her cultural support networks, the client is able to identify (and subsequently remember) the various sources of social support and close friends that she has upon whom she calls often.

School counselors who are conducting individual counseling sessions, group counseling sessions, or facilitating lessons may choose to engage in more experiential activities as part of their service delivery model. Such activities can prove helpful in working with younger students who may not have the cognitive capacity to engage in strict conversation about abstract topics such as gender identity (Broderick & Blewitt, 2010). Burnes and Hovanesian (2016) note a variety of activities for use with groups learning about gender diversity.

Activity

One such activity, the *Gender vs. Sexual Orientation Worksheet* (see Appendix A), can be helpful in facilitating conversation in a classroom lesson. Each student engaging in the activity needs a printed worksheet and a writing instrument. Attendees are instructed to look at each of the five continua and to "place" themselves on the continua where they believe they are by marking themselves with an *X*. Attendees can then break into small groups and be given structured prompts to discuss what they feel comfortable sharing.

As part of the service delivery domain of a school counselor's program, Singh and Burnes (2009) urged school counselors to work within multiple levels of the school system to facilitate consciousness-raising trainings on issues faced by transgender students for teachers, staff, and administration. They suggested including domains on language and working through school-specific issues affecting transgender students (e.g., bathroom issues, bullying). Such training often creates space for dialogue about LGBTQ youth in the schools and sends messages to other school and district personnel that the school counseling office is a supportive space for these students.

Management. When school counselors consider the needs of TGNC students in the management of their school counseling programs, it is helpful to initially examine the nondiscrimination policies within the school to ensure that gender identity is included in the policy (Singh & Burnes, 2009). Often, school counselors will find that the policies in their school include the federally protected category of "gender," but that they must advocate to add "gender identity" in order to provide specific accountability on transgender issues. Using the ASCA model as a guide, school counselors can also work with administrators to establish an advisory council of counselors, faculty, staff, and administration that can be responsive to transgender issues. This task force should first take on the necessary job of ensuring gender-neutral bathrooms or single-stall bathrooms that TGNC students may access safely, as scholars have noted how public bathrooms can be a source of trauma and violence for TGNC students (Burnes, Rowan, & Paul, 2016).

Additionally, school counselors can begin collecting data related to incidence of transphobic attitudes, behaviors, and practices. In delivering these educational meetings, school counselors can use these data to promote systemic change within their schools, other schools, and community-based organizations that work with the school's students on mental health issues. These types of collaborations can translate into long-term partnerships that can be called upon to develop a TGNC-affirmative environment for the school.

School counseling interns can engage in projects in their school that highlight sensitivity, understanding, and celebration of TGNC students in conjunction with their supervisors. Such projects could include developing and implementing a lesson or assembly presentation in transgender issues or drafting and editing discrimination policies that could be added to the school's philosophy and mission statement. Hamlet and Burnes (2013) note that the school counseling internship is a developmental process in which trainees should be able to incorporate their own increasing bodies of knowledge and feel supported by their supervisor as they develop an awareness of diverse student bodies.

Accountability. ASCA has documented the importance of school counselors not only collecting data about their school counseling programs, but also to use the data to show how programs have impacted student achievement. In addition to culturally competent data collections and the selection (or modification) of assessment instruments, school counselors should also be careful in their interpretation and writing of reports when conducting assessment that includes the experience of TGNC students. The interpretation of test data for any student must be done from a framework of ethical decision-making that includes cultural knowledge, attitudes, and skills (Burnes & Smith, 2016). School counselors' interpretation should be carefully checked and audited for gender biases and assumptions, including those that are transphobic, cissexist (e.g., assuming pronoun usage for all students, assuming individuals who play on a particular sports team were all assigned female at birth), and may include biases about gender roles, norms and behaviors. Such auditing should particularly occur with computer-aided analysis of traditional school-based assessments, given the basis for interpretive statements may not be clear (Lichtenberger, 2006, pp. 19–32). Finally, school counselors must recognize that interpreting results and providing feedback to school and district administrators about the mental health and well-being of TGNC students must be accompanied by feedback about the harsh realities of TGNC students in many schools throughout the globe.

CONCLUSION

This lesson has identified the ways that school counselors can utilize the ASCA model to serve TGNC students. Further, it is important for school counselors to provide specific interventions that utilize frameworks of social justice and cultural competence. As literature on transgender youth and school counseling continues to slowly increase but is still nascent, Singh and Burnes (2009) urge school counselors and school counseling trainees to contribute to the practice and research literature with TGNC students in order to understand how to best meet their needs. These needed theoretical and empirical additions to the counseling literature will help to build application-focused resources of school counseling practice with TGNC youth.

REFERENCES

American Counseling Association. (2010). Counseling competencies with transgender clients. *Journal of LGBT Issues in Counseling, 4*(3), 135–159. doi:10.1080/15538605.2010.524839

American School Counselors Association. (2012). *The ASCA National Model: A framework for school counseling programs* (3rd ed.). Alexandria, VA: Author.

American School Counselors Association. (2010). *Ethical standards for school counselors.* Retrieved from http://www.schoolcounselor.org/asca/media/asca/Resource%20 Center/Legal%20and%20Ethical%20Issues/Sample%20 Documents/EthicalStandards2010.pdf

Brill, S. A., & Pepper, R. (2008). *The transgender child: A handbook for families and professionals.* San Francisco, CA: Cleis Press.

Broderick, P. C., & Blewitt, P. (2010). *The Life Span: Human development for helping professionals* (3rd ed.). New York, NY: Pearson/Prentice Hall.

Burnes, T. R., & Chen, M. (2012). Multiple identities of transgender individuals: Incorporating a framework of intersectionality to gender crossing. In R. Josselson & M. Harway (Eds.), *Navigating multiple identities: Race, gender, culture, nationality and roles* (pp. 113–127). New York, NY: Oxford University Press.

Burnes, T. R., Dexter, M. D., Richmond, K., Singh, A. A., & Cherrington, A. (2016). The experiences of transgender survivors of trauma who undergo social and medical transition. *Traumatology, 99,* 1–10.

Burnes, T. R., & Hovanesian, P. N. T. (2016). Teaching as psychoeducation: Psychoeducational group design and implementation in LGBTQ psychology. In T. R. Burnes & J. L. Stanley (Eds.), *Teaching LGBTQ Psychology: Queering innovative pedagogy and practice.* Washington, DC: American Psychological Association.

Burnes, T. R., Rowan, S., & Paul, P. (2016). Clinical supervision with TGNC clients in health service psychology. In A. A. Singh & l. m. dickey (Eds.), *Psychological practice with transgender and gender nonconforming clients.* Washington, DC: American Psychological Association.

Burnes, T. R., & Smith, S.R. (in press). Queering personality assessment: Intersections between personality assessment, sexual orientation, and gender identity. In S.R. Smith and R. Krishnamurthy (Eds.), *Diversity-sensitive personality assessment.* New York, NY: Routledge.

Cole, E. R. (2009). Intersectionality and research in psychology. *The American Psychologist, 64,* 170–180.

Collins, P. H. (2009). Forward: Emerging intersections—Building knowledge and transforming institutions. In B. T. Dill & R. E. Zambrana (Eds.), *Emerging intersections: Race, class and gender in theory, policy and practice.* New Brunswick, NJ: Rutgers University Press.

Crenshaw, K. (1991). Mapping the margins: Intersectionality, identity politics, and violence against women of color. *Stanford Law Review, 43*(6), 1241–1299.

de Jong, D. (2015). "He wears pink leggings almost every day, and a pink sweatshirt . . .": How school social workers understand and respond to gender violence. *Child & Adolescent Social Work Journal, 32*(3), 247–255.

Eubanks-Carter, C., & Goldfried, M. R. (2006). The impact of client sexual orientation and gender on clinical judgments and diagnosis of borderline personality disorder. *Journal of Clinical Psychology, 62*(6), 751–770. doi: 10.1002/jclp.20264

Fassinger, R. E., & Arsenau, J. R. (2007). "I'd rather get wet than be under that umbrella": Differentiating the experiences and identities of lesbian, gay, bisexual, and transgender people. In K. J. Bieschke, R. M. Perez, & K. A. Debord

(Eds.), *Handbook of counseling and psychotherapy with lesbian, gay, bisexual and transgender clients* (2nd ed; pp. 19–50). Washington, DC: American Psychological Association.

GLAAD-Movement Advancement Project. (2012). *An ally's guide to terminology: Talking about LGBT people and equality.* Retrieved from http://www.glaad.org/publications/talkingabout/terminology

Hamlet, H. S., & Burnes, T. R. (2013). Development of the Counseling Intern Developmental Assessment-School Counseling Form (CIDASC). *Counseling Outcomes Research and Evaluation, 4*(1), 55–71.

Lichtenberger, E. O. (2006). Computer utilization and clinical judgment in psychological assessment reports. *Journal of Clinical Psychology, 62*(1), 19–32.

Maddux, J. E. (2002). Stopping the "madness": Positive psychology and the deconstruction of the illness ideology and the DSM. In C. R. Snyder & S. J. Lopez (Eds.), *Handbook of positive psychology* (pp. 13–25). London, England: Oxford University Press.

Meyer, I. H. (2003). Prejudice, social stress, and mental health in lesbian, gay, and bisexual populations: Conceptual issues and research evidence. *Psychological Bulletin, 129,* 674–697.

Morrison, J. (2014). *The first interview* (4th ed.). New York, NY: Guilford Press.

Richmond, K., Burnes, T. R., & Carroll, K. (2012). Lost in trans-lation: Interpreting systems of trauma for transgender clients. *Journal of Traumatology, 18*(1), 45–57.

Richmond, K., Burnes, T. R., Singh, A. A., & Ferrera, M. (2016). Assessment and treatment of trauma with transgender and gender nonconforming clients: A feminist, strength-based, social justice approach. In A. A. Singh & l. m. dickey (Eds.), *Psychological practice with transgender and gender non-conforming clients.* Washington, DC: American Psychological Association.

Riggle, E. D. B., Whitman, J. S., Olson, A., Rostosky, S. S., & Strong, S. (2008). The positive aspects of being a lesbian or a gay man. *Professional Psychology: Research and Practice, 39*(2), 210–217.

Singh, A. A., & Burnes, T. R. (2009). Creating developmentally appropriate, safe counseling environments for transgender youth: The critical role of school counselors. *Journal of LGBT Issues in Counseling, 3*(3), 315–334.

Singh, A. A., Meng, S., & Hansen, A. (2014). "I am my own gender:" Resilience strategies of trans youth. *Journal of Counseling & Development, 92*(2), 208–218.

Toomey, R. B., Ryan, C., Diaz, R. M., Card, N. A., & Russell, S. T. (2010). Gender-nonconforming lesbian, gay, bisexual, and transgender youth: School victimization and young adult psychosocial adjustment. *Developmental Psychology, 46*(6), 1580–1589. doi:10.1037/a0020

● APPENDIX A

Directions

As you can see from this diagram, which represents only a few of the aspects of sex and gender, identity is composed of multiple, independent factors and each factor has multiple places that individuals can inhabit.

Print a copy of this worksheet, which contains five different spectra. Mark where you see yourself on each spectra by marking your place with an *X* on each line.

Biologic Sex (anatomy, chromosomes, hormones)

Male **Intersex** **Female**

Gender Identity (psychological sense of self)

Man **Third Sex, Trans, Bigender, Gender Queer, Other** **Woman**

Gender Expression (communication of gender)

Masculine **Androgynous** **Feminine**

Sexual Orientation (identity of erotic response)

Attracted to Women **Attracted to Both, Neither, Trans, Gender Queer, Other** **Attracted to Men**

Sexual Behavior (sexual behavior)

Sex with Women **Sex with Both, Trans, Gender Queer, Other,** **Sex with Men**

PART III

CRISIS PREVENTION AND INTERVENTION

Lesson 11

IDENTIFYING AND REPORTING CHILD ABUSE AND NEGLECT

"Consult, consult, consult."

Counselor-in-Training:

Amelia, a fifth-grade student, met with me today. Her teacher referred her because Amelia seems to be discouraged. The teacher indicated that Amelia might need some support and wasn't quite sure what was going on with her.

Amelia reported having an argument with her father this morning. She indicated that he grabbed her and shook her really hard. Amelia cried and said that her dad has a short fuse. Amelia showed me marks on her arms where her dad grabbed her. I told Amelia that I would have to reach out for assistance for her and that you and I would work on this with her.*

Supervisor:

"Hi Amelia—thank you for meeting with Ms. Field Experience student and me. I understand you are having a really tough morning. Let's talk about it."

*Ms. Field Experience and her supervisor called ChildLine to report this incident.

Lesson Eleven

Identifying and Reporting Child Abuse and Neglect

"Consult, consult, consult."

Essential Question: How do I report suspected child abuse and/or child neglect?

Objectives

Students will

- know the prevalence of child abuse and neglect.
- demonstrate knowledge of how to report and also how to access relevant resources in the reporting process.

CACREP Standards

Student will

- demonstrate knowledge about the school counselor's roles and responsibilities in relation to the school emergency management plans and crises, disasters, and trauma. (G.5.2.e)
- demonstrate an understanding of the legal and ethical considerations specific to school counseling. (G.5.2.n)
- demonstrate an understanding of legislation and government policy relevant to school counseling. (G.5.2.m)
- demonstrate use of techniques of social/personal counseling in school settings. (G.5.3.f)
- demonstrate use of skills to critically examine the connection between social, familial, emotional, and behavior problems and academic achievement. (G.5.3.h)

MPCAC Standards

- professional counselor identity, ethical behavior, and social justice practices
- human development and wellness across the life span
- ecological, contextual, and social-justice foundations of human development
- counseling, consultation, and social-justice advocacy theories and skills

Video Spark

http://tedxtalks.ted.com/video/What-does-being-nice-have-to-do

What does being nice have to do with child abuse prevention? (Lesley Taylor)

● INTRODUCTION

The prevalence of child abuse and neglect in the United States is increasing (American School Counselor Association [ASCA], 2015). The numbers of children being abused or neglected is staggering. In 2013, there were approximately 3.5 million referrals of children being abused or neglected as compared to 3.4 million referrals in 2012 (Child Welfare Information Gateway, 2015; Centers for Disease Control and Prevention, 2014). Of the 3.4 million referrals, the Child Welfare Information Gateway estimated that 679,000 children were victims of maltreatment. For these victims, the Child Welfare Information Gateway (2015) identified the following prevalence rates: neglect (79.5%), physical abuse (18%), sexual abuse (9%), psychological maltreatment (8.7%), medical neglect (2.3%), and other type of maltreatment (10%).

Who is reporting this child abuse and neglect? The U. S. Department of Health and Human Services (HHS), Administration of Children and Families (2014) reported that professionals made 61.6% of alleged abuse and/or neglect reports. In 2013, the largest percentage of child abuse and/or neglect reports were made by legal and law enforcement personnel reported (17.5%), education personnel (17.5%), and social services personnel (11%). Although laws may vary from state to state on the specifics of reporting child abuse, ***school counselors are identified as mandated reporters by Federal legislature—the Child Abuse Prevention and Treatment Act of 1974.***

• THE LAW AND CHILD ABUSE AND NEGLECT REPORTING

The Child Abuse Prevention and Treatment Act (CAPTA) of 1974, as amended by the CAPTA Reauthorization Act of 2010, is Federal legislation that provides guidance to states by defining the minimum standard (acts or behaviors) (U.S. Department of Health and Human Services [HHS], 2014). The following are relevant terms and definitions provided by the U.S. Department of Health and Human Services, Administration for Children and Families (HHS, 2014).

Child: A person who has not attained the lesser of (a) the age of 19 or (b) except in the case of sexual abuse, the age specified by the child protection law of the state in which the child resides.

Child Maltreatment: The CAPTA definition of child abuse and neglect is, "at a minimum: Any recent act or failure to act on the part of a parent or caretaker which results in death, serious physical or emotional harm, sexual abuse or exploitation; or an act or failure to act, which presents an imminent risk of serious harm."

Child Protective Services Agency (CPS): An official agency of a state having the responsibility to receive and respond to allegations of suspected child abuse and neglect, determine the validity of the allegations, and provide services to protect and serve children and their families.

Child Protective Services Agency (CPS) Response: CPS agencies conduct a response for all reports of child maltreatment. The response may be an investigation, which determines whether a child was maltreated or is at risk of maltreatment and establishes if an intervention is needed. The majority of reports received investigations. A small, but growing number of reports receive an alternative response, which focuses primarily upon the needs of the family and usually does not include a determination regarding the alleged maltreatment(s).

Investigation: A ***type of CPS response*** that involves gathering of objective information to determine whether a child was maltreated or is at risk of maltreatment and establishes if an intervention is needed. Generally includes face-to-face contact with the alleged victim and results in a disposition as to whether or not the alleged maltreatment occurred.

Maltreatment Type: A particular form of child maltreatment that received a CPS response. Types include medical neglect, neglect or deprivation of necessities, physical abuse, psychological or emotional maltreatment, sexual abuse, and other forms included in state law.

Medical neglect: A type of maltreatment caused by failure of the caregivers to provide appropriate health care of the child although financially able to do so, or offered financial or other resources to do so.

Neglect or deprivation of necessities: A type of maltreatment that refers to the failure by the caregiver to provide needed, age-appropriate care although financially able to do so or offered financial or other means to do so.

Physical abuse: Type of maltreatment that refers to physical acts that caused or could have caused physical injury to a child.

Psychological or emotional maltreatment: Acts or omissions—other than physical abuse or sexual abuse—that caused or could have caused—conduct, cognitive, affective, or other behavioral or mental disorders. Frequently occurs as verbal abuse or excessive demands on a child's performance.

Sexual abuse: A type of maltreatment that refers to the involvement of the child in sexual activity to provide sexual gratification or financial benefit to the perpetrator, including contacts for sexual purposes, molestation, statutory rape, prostitution, pornography, exposure, incest, or other sexually exploitative activities.

Keep current! The definitions above are generated by federal mandate. Other regulations, procedures, definitions, and mandated reports vary from state to state. In addition, the states are continually updating and revising legislature. For example, during the 2014 legislative session, the National Conference of State Legislatures reported that at least 294 child-welfare bills were proposed. Of these 294 bills, approximately 100 bills were enacted in 34 states. The 100 legislative bills addressed child abuse investigations, child sexual abuse, confidentiality and information sharing, definitions and health care (National Conference of State Legislatures, 2014).

● IDENTIFYING CHILD ABUSE AND NEGLECT

Warning Signs of Abuse

School counselors are mandated reporters of child abuse and neglect or suspected child abuse and neglect. Hence, regardless of whether a counselor has concrete information about abuse and neglect or not, they are mandated to report the ***suspicion*** of child abuse and neglect. For example, a student may come into the office and share information that leads the counselor to suspect that abuse has occurred. It is important to be cognizant of the role of the counselor at this point in the identification process. School counselors do not investigate whether child abuse or and neglect has taken place. However, it is important for school counselors to be aware of the warning signs of child abuse and neglect. Warning signs of abuse and neglect will vary greatly from one child to another. The following from the Mayo Clinic (2015) are example of behaviors that may be warning signs of abuse:

Physical abuse signs and symptoms:

Unexplained injuries, such as bruises, fractures, or burns

Injuries that don't match the given explanation

Untreated medical or dental problems

Sexual abuse signs and symptoms:

Sexual behavior or knowledge that's inappropriate for the child's age

Pregnancy or a sexually transmitted infection

Statements that he or she was sexually abused

Emotional abuse signs and symptoms:

Delayed or inappropriate emotional development

Loss of self-confidence or self-esteem

Social withdrawal or a loss of interest or enthusiasm

Neglect signs and symptoms:

Poor growth or weight gain

Poor hygiene

Lack of clothing or supplies to meet physical needs

Eating a lot in one sitting or hiding food for later

When neglect is a concern, school counselors or the school counselor in collaboration with the school social worker should provide the family with information about available resources to help in case the neglect is due to financial constraints. If the neglect continues, then a report should be made.

● RECOGNIZING DISCLOSURES: (PREVENT CHILD ABUSE NEW YORK, 2009)

Very seldom will a child disclose abuse immediately after the first incident has occurred. Victimized children often experience a great sense of helplessness and hopelessness and think that nobody can do anything to help them. Also, victimized children may try to make every attempt to protect an abusive parent. Or, they may be extremely reluctant to report any abuse for fear of what the abuser may do to them. Typically, a child may not report abuse for months and even years, particularly if the abuser is someone close to the child.

Sometimes an outcry may not be verbal but portrayed in a drawing left behind inadvertently for the teacher, the counselor, or a trusted relative to see. Another form of outcry may be seen in a child who will frequently go to the school nurse complaining of vague, somatic symptoms, often without organic basis, hoping that the nurse will guess what has happened. This way, in their minds, they have not betrayed nor will they be punished, since they did not directly report the abuse. Some children, while totally reluctant to report or discuss the abuse, may be more willing to express their apprehensions and anxieties about the perpetrator or the home situation. In some cases, abused children will make an outcry that may take the extreme form of a suicide gesture or attempt.

Children may disclose abuse in a variety of ways. They may blurt it out to you, especially after you have created a warm nurturing environment. They may come privately to talk directly and specifically about what is going on. But often they may be more obtuse by employing one or more of the following:

Indirect Hints: "My brother wouldn't let me sleep last night." "My babysitter keeps bothering me." A child may talk in these terms because he/she hasn't learned more specific vocabulary, feels too ashamed or embarrassed to talk more directly, has promised not to tell, or for a combination of these reasons. Appropriate responses would be invitations to tell you more, such as "Is it something you are happy about?" and open-ended questions such as "Can you tell me more?" or "What do you mean?" Gently encourage the child to be more specific. It is important that the child use his/her own language, and that no additional words are given to the child.

Disguised Disclosure: "What would happen if a girl told someone her mother beat her?" "I know someone who is being touched in a bad way." Here the child might be talking about a friend or sibling, but is just as likely to be talking about her/himself.

Encourage the child to tell you what he/she knows about the "other child." It is probably that the child will eventually tell you about whom he/she is talking.

Disclosure with Strings Attached: "I have a problem, but if I tell you about it, you have to promise not to tell anyone else." Most children are all too aware that some negative consequences will result if they break the secret of abuse. Often the offender uses the threat of these consequences to keep the child silent. Let the child know you want to help him or her. Tell the child, from the beginning, that there are times when you too may need to get help with the problem. In order to help him or her, it may be necessary to get some special people involved. The fact that the child has chosen this particular moment to disclose is important. Usually, they will agree to seek help if you talk about it ahead of time. Assure the child that you will respect his or her need for confidentiality by not discussing the abuse with anyone other than those directly involved in getting help. And, if you can explain the process to them, it may help with their initial fear.

● RESPONDING TO DISCLOSURES: (PREVENT CHILD ABUSE NEW YORK, 2009)

In school, if a child discloses during a lesson, acknowledge the child's disclosure and continue the lesson. Afterward, find a place where you can talk with the child alone. It is best to present child abuse curricula before a playtime or recess so that you have a natural opportunity to talk with children privately if they come forward.

Before notifying anyone outside of your school or agency, you or another designated person should sit down in a quiet room without interruptions and speak with the child. If a child has chosen you as the person in whom to confide, you should take the time to speak with the child about the problem. If that is not possible, ask the child if she/he would feel comfortable discussing it with someone else. If the child indicates that he/she wants to tell you, you must make every effort to listen and support the child. She/he may not trust another enough to tell them.

Multiple interviews should be avoided. The child will have to share the story with many others. When you speak with the child, sit down together, assure him/her that you are concerned and want to know more and that it's alright to tell you. Go slowly, allowing the child to explain as much as he/she can. Do not suggest in any way that any particular person may have done something to him/her or that the child was touched in any particular way. Let the child talk as much as possible.

Explain, in age-appropriate language, that the law requires you to make a report if any child discloses abuse and that the law is there to protect them. Describe for them who will be involved, for example, the social worker, principal, and the CPS caseworker.

When Talking to the Child, DO

- Find a private place to talk with the child.
- Sit next to the child, not across a table or desk.
- Use language the child understands; ask the child to clarify words you don't understand.
- Express your belief that the child is telling you the truth.
- Reassure the child that it is not his/her fault, and that he/she is not bad and did nothing to deserve this.

- Determine the child's immediate need for safety.
- Let the child know you will do your best to protect and support him/her.
- Tell the child what you will do, and who will be involved in the process.

When Talking to the Child, DON'T

- Disparage or criticize the child's choice of words or language.
- Suggest answers to the child.
- Probe or press for answers the child is unwilling to give.
- Display shock or disapproval of parent(s), child, or situation.
- Talk to the child with a group of interviewers.
- Make promises to the child, about "not telling" or about how the situation will work out.

To Report or Not to Report?

If you have a reasonable suspicion that abuse has occurred, you should report. When in doubt, report.

What Is the Reporting Process?

The American School Counselor Association (ASCA, 2015; Appendix A) identifies reporting abuse and neglect as the legal, ethical, and moral responsibility of the counselor. In addition, all 50 states require teachers and school personnel to report suspected child abuse. With this clear legal, ethical, and moral responsibility in mind, gaining clarity of the laws, requirements, and procedures for mandated reports is essential. Importantly, the regulations and agencies for identifying and reporting child abuse and neglect vary from state to state. Thus, each state will have its own child welfare system designed to investigate child abuse and neglect reports. The name of child welfare systems varies from state to state. Be knowledgeable about the procedures and systems in your state. Below is an example of the process:

The Reporting Process

- Consult with your supervisor (if available).
- Consult a colleague to discuss the situation.
- Provide oral report to intake worker at the state's Department of Social Services (DSS) or use the state's online system (if available).
- If an oral report was made, complete written report. (Forms are state specific.)
- Mail written report within 48 hours to DSS.
- Information to have available when reporting
  - identifying information and current location of the child (name, sex, birth date, address, school, school grade)
  - parent/guardian identifying information
  - nature and extent of the abuse and/or alleged neglect
  - information regarding past abuse/neglect to the child or other children in the family

● NATIONAL CHILD ABUSE REPORTING RESOURCE

Childhelp

Childhelp is a national organization that provides crisis assistance and other counseling and referral services. The Childhelp National Child Abuse Hotline is staffed 24 hours a day, 7 days a week, with professional crisis counselors who have access to a database of 55,000 emergency, social service, and support resources. All calls are anonymous. Contact them at 1.800.4.A.CHILD (1.800.422.4453) (Childhelp, 2015).

The National Children's Advocacy Center (NCAC)

"**The NCAC** models, promotes, and delivers excellence in child abuse response and prevention through service, education, and leadership." NCAC uses a multidisciplinary team approach in response to child abuse. This model "recognized that in order for the United States to effectively respond to this issue that a unique public-private partnership was essential, and that the various agencies and departments responsible for the protection of children must be united in a collaborative effort to respond with the recognition that no one agency by itself could assure the protection of children. Only by working as a multidisciplinary team could we effectively respond to child abuse. . . . Currently, this approach has been widely adopted as a best practice in responding to child sexual abuse in the United States. Throughout the United States, there are now more than 950 Children's Advocacy Centers, which served more than 270,000 children during 2009, and this model has now been implemented in more than 25 countries throughout the world" (NCAC, 2015).

● REFERENCES

American School Counselor Association. (2015). *The school counselor and child abuse and neglect prevention* (ASCA Position Statement). Retrieved from https://www.schoolcounselor.org/asca/media/asca/PositionStatements/PS_ChildAbuse.pdf

Centers for Disease Control and Prevention. (2014). *Child maltreatment*. Retrieved from http://www.cdc.gov/violenceprevention/pdf/childmaltreatment-facts-at-a-glance.pdf

Child Abuse Prevention and Treatment Act (CAPTA) of 1974, Pub. L. 93-247.

Childhelp. (2015). *Childhelp National Child Abuse Hotline*. Retrieved from https://www.childhelp.org/hotline/

Child Welfare Information Gateway. (2015). *Child abuse and neglect statistics*. Retrieved from https://www.childwelfare.gov/topics/systemwide/statistics/can/

Council for Accreditation for Counseling and Related Program. (2014). *2016 standards*. Retrieved from www.cacrep.org

Masters in Psychology and Counseling Accreditation Council. (2015). *Accreditation manual*. Retrieved from http://www.mpcacaccreditation.org/about/accreditation-manual

Mayo Clinic. (2015). *Child abuse symptoms*. Retrieved from http://www.mayoclinic.org/diseases-conditions/child-abuse/basics/symptoms/con-20033789

National Children's Advocacy Center. (2015). *Multidisciplinary team*. Retrieved from http://www.nationalcac.org/about/multi-team.html

National Conference of State Legislatures. (2014). *2014 child welfare legislative enactments*. Retrieved from http://www.ncsl.org/research/human-services/2014-child-welfare-legislative-enactments.aspx

Prevent Child Abuse New York. (2009). *Identifying and reporting child abuse and neglect: A mandated reporter handbook*. Retrieved from http://www.preventchildabuseny.org/files/3413/2580/4980/Mand%20Rep%20handbook%20PCANY.pdf

U.S. Department of Health and Human Services. (2014). *Definitions of child abuse and neglect*. Retrieved from https://www.childwelfare.gov/topics/systemwide/laws-policies/statutes/define/

● APPENDIX A

American School Counselor Association (ASCA) Position Statement

The School Counselor and Child Abuse and Neglect Prevention

(Adopted 1981; revised 1985, 1993, 1999, 2003, 2015)

It is the school counselor's legal, ethical, and moral responsibility to report suspected cases of child abuse and neglect to the proper authorities. School counselors work to identify the behavioral, academic, and social/emotional impact of abuse and neglect on students and ensure the necessary supports for students are in place.

The Rationale

The National Child Abuse and Neglect Data System (NCANDS; 2014) indicated a significant rise in reported child abuse and neglect incidents in recent years. This increase presents a public issue that must be addressed through advocacy for child protection. A child who is a victim of abuse and neglect may experience consequences including, but not limited to, immediate physical and/or emotional harm, the inability to build healthy relationships, increased likelihood of being abused by another perpetrator, or becoming an abuser and lowered self-worth.

The U.S. Department of Health and Human Services, Administration for Children and Families (2014) has defined maltreatment as "A particular form of child maltreatment determined by investigation to be substantiated or indicated under state law." Types include

- physical abuse
- neglect or deprivation of necessities
- medical neglect
- sexual abuse
- psychological or emotional maltreatment
- and other forms included in state law

The School Counselor's Role

School counselors are among those mandated by the Child Abuse Prevention and Treatment Act (CAPTA) of 1974 (Public Law 93-247) to report suspected abuse and neglect to proper authorities and are critical in early detection and recognition of abuse. It is imperative that school counselors gain essential knowledge of policies and referral procedures by staying current on reporting requirements and state laws. Laws and definitions pertaining to child abuse and neglect vary among states; therefore, school counselors should commit themselves to become familiar with and abide by Child Protective Services (CPS) laws in their respective state (see a summary of state laws pertaining to child abuse and neglect at www.schoolcounselor.org/school-counselors-members/legal-ethical).

In addition to mandated reporting, school counselors

- understand child abuse and neglect and its impact on children's social/emotional, physical and mental well-being;
- provide interventions that promote resiliency, healthy interpersonal and communication skills, and self-worth;

- make referrals to outside agencies for child or family support when appropriate;
- engage families in the school community;
- identify barriers and limitations that affect healthy family functioning and may lead to child abuse or neglect; and
- identify instances of child abuse and neglect and respond on both individual and systemic levels.

ASCA recognizes it is the absolute responsibility of school counselors to serve as child advocates. Responsible action by the school counselor can be achieved through the recognition and understanding of the problem, knowing the reporting procedures, and participating in available child abuse information programs. School counselors play an integral role in helping to promote child welfare by providing direct and indirect student services. Those services include advocating for students' needs by addressing issues that could affect their academic, personal, and social/emotional well-being.

● SUMMARY

School counselors are a key link in the child abuse prevention network. It is their responsibility to report suspected cases of child abuse or neglect to the proper authorities. School counselors must be able to guide and assist abused and neglected students by providing appropriate services. School counselors are committed to providing high-quality services to children who are victims of abuse and neglect with research-based intervention techniques.

Lesson 12

SUICIDE ASSESSMENT, PREVENTION, AND POSTVENTION

Diane Shea
Holy Family University

"Yesterday . . . History: Tomorrow . . . Mystery: Today is Gift"

One of the most difficult incidents that I experienced in teaching prospective school counselors took place when an intern came to class and shared that a student in her school had committed suicide during the previous week. This is a topic we often might discuss academically but when the reality hits, no textbook can alleviate the pain that touches families, friends, students, teachers, and other school personnel.

The numbers can become overwhelming. According to the most recent statistics from the Centers for Disease Control and Prevention as reported by the American Association of Suicidology (AAS; 2013), in 2011, suicide was the second leading cause of death for adolescents between the ages of 10 and 24. This is up from the previous data, which listed suicide as the third leading cause of death in that age group. In the 2011 data, 4,822 youth died by suicide. Based on the results of the Youth Risk and Behavior Survey, the AAS summarized that in the previous year, 15.8% of high school students seriously considered suicide and 12.8% had a plan for completion. Translating these numbers to a high school with 1,000 students, approximately 158 students might have contemplated suicide and 128 might actually have a plan. How can you as a school counselor make a difference in preventing a suicide? How might you assess for a potential suicide? What will you do in the event that such a tragedy does occur?

The Council for Accreditation of Counseling and Related Educational Programs (CACREP) has updated its 2016 standards to require that assessment courses prepare counselors to understand how to assess the risk of suicide. One classroom lesson will not make you an expert. But we must begin somewhere.

Lesson Twelve

Suicide Assessment, Prevention, and Postvention

Diane Shea
Holy Family University

"Yesterday . . . History: Tomorrow . . . Mystery: Today is Gift"

Essential Questions: What can I do to assess the risk for suicide in order to prevent it, and what should I do in its aftermath?

Objectives

Students will

- demonstrate an understanding that school counselors are mandated reporters.
- be able to distinguish between facts and myths associated with suicide.
- recognize the warning signs that might be indicative of suicide.
- demonstrate the ability to intervene with a potentially suicidal student.
- become familiar with reliable assessment instruments that are used to screen for suicidal ideation.
- have a postintervention plan in the event of a suicide in schools.

CACREP (2015) Standards

- procedures for assessing risk of aggression or danger to others, self-inflicted harm, or suicide (7.c)

MPCAC Standards

- assessment of human behavior and organizational/community/institutional systems
- human development and wellness across the life span
- ecological, contextual, multicultural, social-justice foundation of human development

Video Spark

https://www.youtube.com/watch?v=dTeytkxlDt8

Kevin Hines, Jumped off Golden Gate Bridge and Survived INT

As Kevin attested, the moment he leapt from the Golden Gate Bridge he realized he did not want to die. Had he been a student in your school, would you have recognized him to be a student at risk? What do you know about suicide? Would you have a tool to assess the danger? What would you do in the event that a student in your school does complete a suicide?

● PRETEST

To begin, let's see if you can sort out facts from myths. Take a minute and see how many of these questions you can answer. These questions and answers were adapted from various sources (American Association of

Suicidology, 2013; Australian Government Department of Veterans' Affairs Crisis Services, Inc., n.d.; Doan, Roggenbaum, & Lazear, 2003; Opalewski, 2008; Achilles, Gray, & Moskos, 2004; Poland, 1989). (These could be presented as a PowerPoint or given as a handout.)

● MYTH OR FACT?

M/F

1. Teens who talk about suicide rarely actually follow through with completing a suicide.
2. Confronting teenagers about suicide will increase the risk of them committing suicide.
3. Most teenagers who talk about suicide really do want to die.
4. Talking to a troubled person about suicide will put ideas into that person's head.
5. People who attempt suicide and survive are just seeking attention; they seldom ever try it again.
6. Troubled teenagers who drink or use drugs as an escape are less likely to complete suicide to escape from their problems.
7. Talking about suicide in the classroom and educating students about suicide gives them ideas of how to kill themselves and will promote suicidal ideas and suicidal behavior.
8. Parents are often unaware of their child's suicidal behavior.
9. Once a person decides to die by suicide, there's nothing anyone can do to stop them.
10. People who think about completing suicide usually give one or more warnings of their intention.
11. The tendency toward suicidal behavior is inherited.
12. Among teenagers, more girls than boys try to kill themselves.
13. A teenager who talks about suicide is unlikely to go through with it.
14. If a person has a religious belief that suicide is wrong that belief will prevent the person from committing suicide.
15. Death by firearms is a leading cause of suicide.

● ANSWERS

1. Myth: The possibility of discussion lowers the risk of completion: Eighty percent of teenagers who kill themselves have gave definite warnings of their suicidal intention.
2. Myth: Asking a person directly about suicide will lower his or her anxiety, opens the possibility of communication, and lowers the risk of that person acting impulsively.
3. Myth: Testimony from survivors of suicide attempts indicates that they usually don't want to die. They see no other option to make things better, but the decision is made with a great deal of ambiguity.
4. Myth: It is highly unlikely that by bringing up the topic of suicide you will be planting the idea in a person's head. More likely, if the person has had suicidal thoughts, you are opening the door for that person to talk about his or her feelings.

5. Myth: For each suicidal attempt a person makes, the likelihood of a suicidal completion increases.
6. Myth: The use of drugs and alcohol may decrease a person's inhibitions, and a suicide completion may become more likely if that person already has suicidal thoughts.
7. Myth: Talking about suicide in the classroom gives students an opportunity to explore their feelings and talk about them with a trusted adult. Research supports that students are more likely to talk to their school counselors about a friend who might have expressed suicidal thoughts and refer that friend to the counselor.
8. Fact: Most teenagers are more willing to talk with their peer group than their parents. Research suggests that as many as 86% of parents were not aware that their son or daughter thought about suicide.
9. Myth: Persons who are suicidal often have mixed feelings and often send out verbal and/or behavioral clues. Many suicides are preventable.
10. Fact: As many as 80% of persons who committed suicide told at least one other person about their thoughts.
11. Myth: Although there may be a predisposition to depression, there is no genetic evidence to support that suicide is inherited. However, if a family person commits suicide, this may model a destructive way to deal with stress and depression.
12. Fact: Suicide is more common in men but women make more attempts. This is also true for teenagers. It is likely because females tend to use less lethal means such as overdosing on drugs while males are more likely to use a handgun on themselves.
13. Myth: The majority of teenagers who attempted or completed suicide have given verbal clues.
14. Myth: While a person's religion may teach that suicide is wrong, and the person may even believe that it is wrong, she or he may not see any other way to relieve her or his pain.
15. Fact: Death by a gun accounts for approximately 60% of all suicides.

● REFLECTION/DISCUSSION

How well did you do? What questions do you have?

____

____

____

____

____

● RISK FACTORS AND WARNING SIGNS

There are warning signs and psychiatric factors that may put a person at risk for suicide. These may include depression, substance abuse, persons with eating disorders, and persons with borderline personality disorders. However, these risk factors are suggestive of possible underlying factors (Gangwisch, 2010; Rudd et al., 2006).

The Suicide Prevention Resource Center (n.d.) also suggests other possible **biopsychosocial risk factors**:

- a person with a previous history of trauma or abuse
- a person with a family history of suicide
- a person who has made a previous suicide attempt

There are also **environmental risk factors** to consider:

- job or financial loss
- relational or social loss
- easy access to lethal means
- a local cluster of suicide that may have a contagious influence

Likewise there may be **sociocultural risk factors** to consider:

- a stigma that might be associated with seeking mental health professionals
- a religious belief that suicide is a noble resolution
- barriers to accessing mental health and substance abuse treatment

The more immediate warning signs are even brighter red flags that must not be ignored. James Gangwisch (2010) suggested that such **warning signs** are more observable and immediate indications and/or symptoms of possible suicidal behavior. Paul G. Quinnett (2009) advises that the more signs that are observed, the greater the risk. These signs can be direct such as a person saying that "I really don't want to live any longer," "I think I am going to kill myself." They can also be behavioral including giving away one's prized possessions, acquiring a gun, stockpiling pills, or even a sudden interest or even disinterest in religion. Situational clues such as a death of a loved one or financial insecurity may also be a clue.

The American Association of Suicidology identified specific behaviors that warrant immediate attention:

- A person is threatening to hurt or kill himself or herself.
- A person is looking for the means to commit suicide such as seeking pills or guns.
- A person is talking about or writing about death, dying, or suicide.
- A person expresses a feeling of hopelessness.
- A person is acting recklessly or is engaging in reckless activity, seemingly without thought.
- A person says she or he feels trapped like there is no way out.
- A person is withdrawing from family, friends, or society.
- A person displays anxiety or agitation and either is unable to sleep or sleeps most of the time.
- A person displays extreme mood changes.
- A person expresses that he or she has no reason to live and has no purpose in life.

● PROTECTIVE FACTORS

While risk factors may increase the likelihood of a person committing suicide, there are other protective factors that may actually decrease the likelihood even if she or he is at an elevated risk (Nock et al., 2013; Walsh & Eggert, 2007).

The Suicide Prevention Resource Center (n.d.) lists the following as important protective factors:

- effective clinical care for mental, physical, and substance use disorders
- easy access to a variety of clinical interventions and support for help seeking
- restricted access to highly lethal means of suicide
- strong connections to family and community support

- support through ongoing medical and mental health care relationships
- skills in problem-solving, conflict resolution, and nonviolent handling of disputes
- cultural and religious beliefs that discourage suicide and support self-preservation

(The above points could be presented as a PowerPoint or given as a handout.)

REFLECTION/DISCUSSION

Have you ever experienced a friend who exhibited any of these signs? How did you feel? What was your response? If not, how do you think you would feel and why?

____

____

____

____

____

WHAT SHOULD YOU DO?

To begin, you, as a perspective school counselor, have a unique role in the efforts to prevent suicide. Recall the *Eisel vs. Montgomery County Board of Education* case (1991). Nicole Eisel told some of her friends that she was going to kill herself. The friends reported this to the two school counselors, but when the counselors questioned Nicole, she denied the allegation. The counselors did nothing further. Shortly after that, Nicole and one of her friends did commit suicide. Nicole's parents took the case to court. In the end, the court ruled that although the school counselors did not have a legal duty to ***prevent*** suicide, they did have the duty to do use ***reasonable means to try to prevent it***. In this case, school counselors had the duty to inform the parents.

In the Eisel case, the decision was made on the basis of the in loco parentis doctrine (Stone, 2003). This means that educators, including school counselors, are legally standing in for the parents and must use reasonable care to protect students. Educators are gatekeepers. A gatekeeper is anyone who may be in the position of recognizing the warning signs that someone may be contemplating suicide. In a school situation, gatekeeper programs are offered to all school personnel. This may include teachers, cafeteria aides, and even janitors. I suggest that you are a leading "gatekeeper above other gatekeepers."

There is a renewed emphasis on schools planning and implementing suicide awareness and prevention programs (Ward & Odegard, 2011). For example, on June 26, 2014, the governor of Pennsylvania signed into law Act 71 making it mandatory that, beginning with the 2015–2016 school year, every school in the state is required to adopt age-appropriate youth suicide awareness and prevention policies. The Pennsylvania Department of Education was required to develop a model suicide awareness and prevention curriculum and make materials available to the public. That model curriculum is now available online (www.education.pa.gov/Documents/K-12/Safe%20Schools/Act%2071/Youth%20Suicide%20Education%20Awareness%20and%20Prevention%20Curriculum.pdf).

However, according to the American Foundation for Suicide Prevention (AFSP), there are only four other states that mandate such suicide prevention policies (American Foundation for Suicide Prevention [AFSP], 2015). Nonetheless, even if your state is not one of the five that requires such ongoing education, I strongly suggest that you look into receiving more formal training in a recognized and research-based suicide prevention program. As a trainer in one specific program, Question, Persuade, Refer (QPR; Quinnett, 2009), I make suggestions from that framework. Please view these brief clips—a brief introduction to QPR:

https://www.youtube.com/watch?v=MIIu0Zm_NvM

https://www.youtube.com/watch?v=CB0kV_XMeWA

Ask THE Question

Even if a school counselor recognizes some of the warning signs, she or he may often feel insecure in addressing a student. How do you ask a person if she or he is possibly suicidal? Quinnett (2009) suggested, just ask! It is probably easier to ask less directly with something like, "Have you ever wished that once you go to sleep that you would never wake up?" However, Quinnett (2009) would have you be more direct. Consider these questions:

- "You look pretty upset. Are you having any thoughts of death or suicide?"
- "Have you been thinking about ending your life?"
- "Have you ever wanted to stop living?"
- "You know, when people are as upset as you seem to be they often wish they were dead. I'm wondering if this is how you are feeling now."
- "Are you thinking about killing yourself?"
- "You look pretty miserable, I wonder if you ae thinking about suicide?"

Practice Asking

Turn to a student near you. Look him or her in the eye and ask each of the above questions. Do it slowly. Then switch partners.

● REFLECTION/DISCUSSION

What were you feeling when you asked the questions? Was it easy or hard? What questions do you have?

____

____

____

____

____

It is important that when you ask the question, you do so respectfully and sympathetically. Remember that by asking the question, you are opening the door for that person to express her or his feelings. However, as Quinnett (2009) pointed out, there is a way NOT to ask the question. How do you think a person might react if you said something like this?

"You're not going to do something crazy like committing suicide are you?"

____

____

____

Formalized assessment. Short of the direct verbal question, a counselor may want to screen for the possibility of suicidal ideation either individually or in a group setting. In this case, the school counselor should have access to standardized questionnaires that can be used to assess for suicidal ideation. I will only mention two.

- Suicidal Ideation Questionnaire (SIQ), William M. Reynolds, PhD: The SIQ is useful for screening adolescents for suicidal ideation—one aspect of suicidal behavior that may point to suicidal intentions. The SIQ can be administered either individually or in a group setting. It can be used in both clinical and school settings. It can be administered individually or in a group setting. There are two versions of the SIQ. One is a 30-item format for students in Grades 10 to 12. The second version is 15-item SIQ-JR, for students in Grades 7 to 9. Both forms use a 7-point scale to assess the frequency of suicidal thoughts and ideas. The SIQ can be obtained from Psychological Assessment Resources Inc. (http://www3.parinc.com/).
- The Reynolds Adolescent Depression Scale, 2nd ed. (RADS-2 [two versions]) and Reynolds Adolescent Depression Scale, 2nd ed. Short Form (RADS-2:SF): This instrument is useful for screening depressive symptoms and severity of depression. The long form is a 30-item format and the short form is a 10-item format. Both forms contain critical items which are suggestive of clinical severity that warrant immediate attention. The RADS-2 instruments can be obtained from PAR Inc. (http://www4.parinc.com/Products/Product.aspx?ProductID=RADS-2)

Although not a formal assessment, David A. Opalewski (2008) offers the following acronym **SLAP** as a short guide for counselors. However, know this does NOT take the place of a formal clinical assessment.

- **S Specificity**: Ask, "Is there a plan? The more specific the plan, the more serious the student may be about following through with the specific plan.
- **L Lethality**: Ask yourself about how lethal the plan may be.
- **A Availability**: Ask if the person has acquired the means and/or how available the means may be.
- **P Proximity**: Consider the proximity of helping resources near where the plan might take place. Where is a hospital, police station, EMS office? The more remote to places such as these, there is less likelihood that the person will be discovered and the more serious she or he may be.

● YOU BE THE JUDGE

Laura Madison and Corey Vas (2003) presented different scenarios for students to evaluate possible risk factors for suicide. I adapted the following scenarios from their research. Read each situation below. Consider the risk factors, warning signs, and possible protective factors. Then rank each one from highest (1) to lowest (4) in terms of the likelihood of suicide.

1. Peter is a 38-year-old man. He has a wife, Betty and a 6 year-old daughter, Alina. They have been happily married for 8 years. However, he was working as district manager for a chain restaurant and just found out today that he was being laid off after working at the same company for 9 years. He does not know how he is going to tell Betty and Alina that daddy just lost his job. There are already financial concerns and worse. Peter finds himself thinking that perhaps Betty and Alina might be better off if he were dead so they could collect on the insurance money.

2. Jessie is a 22-year-old student in her junior year at college. She has been dating her boyfriend, Dave, for the last 3 years. Last night, he told her he was seeing someone else and didn't really love Jessie. Jessie's self-concept was based on her idea that she and Dave would get married and they would spend their life together. Her own parents had divorced when she was 12, and she had a very difficult time with the divorce. Both parents have since remarried. Right after the divorce,

Jessie found some of her mother's pain meds and took "a few pills" but nothing serious happened to her and she never told anyone about it.

3. Maria Carmen is a 19-year-old female who comes from a very religious family. She is a sophomore in college. Recently she "came out" to them and told them she is a lesbian. Her father said he would disown her and would no longer pay her tuition. She felt ostracized by the rest of the family. Maria Carmen wonders how she will be able to continue in and pay for school. Her friends noted disturbing changes in her behavior. She could hardly sleep and wasn't eating. She can't concentrate on schoolwork, and she has stopped doing things with her friends. Her friends encouraged her to see the counselor. She did go and reluctantly followed her counselor's advice and saw a doctor about beginning medication.
4. Kevin is a 59-year-old man who works as a real estate agent. His salary is based on commission. He has been divorced three times. As a result of his last divorce, he lost his house and status in the community. Because of the recession and poor economy, house sales have fallen off and he is in financial difficulty. He has missed his child-care support payment for the last three months. One of the things that he enjoys is to take his favorite gun to the shooting club after work and shoot a few rounds as a way to blow off steam. On the way home, he stops at the local bar stop and has a few beers "to help him relax." Yesterday, after this routine he called his friend and asked him to come over. When the friend came, Kevin gave him his favorite gun.

• REFLECTION/DISCUSSION

How did you rank the scenarios? Why? What did you consider?

____

____

____

____

____

(Suggested rankings: Ranking of 1 (highest likelihood of suicide): Scenario #4—due to substance abuse problem, ready access to firearms, giving away prized possession; ranking of 2 (high likelihood of suicide): Scenario #2—strong predictors being previous attempt with pills and break up of a long-term relationship; ranking of 3 (moderate likelihood of suicide): Scenario #3—does have protective factors being in treatment and friends who care; ranking of 4 (least likely of the four scenarios): Scenario #1—(does have protective factors of having a family for support.)

These rankings are somewhat arbitrary since there are so many other factors that might come into play. Hopefully this exercise will generate a good discussion.

Remember, as a professional school counselor, if a student is formally assessed and the suicidal score is highly elevated, or responds to your questioning with a "yes" to your direct questioning, you have an obligation to do something. You will need to be prepared to share in that person's pain. What will you do?

Persuading a Person to Stay Alive

Although this is not a formal QPR training, there is much that can be learned from that framework. You will need to listen to the person without judgement. Sometimes a person may even pose the question,

"Don't I have a right to die?" Your role as a school counselor is not to answer that question. You want to persuade the student that you care and want to help. It is important to remember that suicide is a permanent solution to a temporary problem. Remember, take all threats of suicide seriously!

It goes without question that you have informed the student about the **limits of confidentiality**. This should happen at the **beginning** of a session. You must inform the student that everything that will be discussed is confidential with three exceptions. If she or he reports that someone is (or has been) seriously hurting or abusing, someone will be notified. If she or he reports that she or he plans on hurting herself or himself, someone will be notified. If she or he reports that she or he intends to harm another person, someone will be notified. Make sure you ask something such as "Do you understand that it's OK to talk about most things here but that these are three things we must talk about with other people?" This is part of informed consent.

Here are a few points to consider. Once a student has expressed suicidal thoughts, NEVER leave that student alone. Don't tell her or him to walk to the principal's office. Go with her or him. Depending upon school protocol, you should contact the student's parent(s). You may even consider using some form of a no-suicide contract.

No-Suicide Contracts. A no-suicide contact is a written agreement that a person consents to that she or he will seek help in the event of suicidal impulses (Weiss, 2001). Scott Poland (1989) offered an example for a school situation:

> I ___________, a student at ___________________ school, take the responsibility for my welfare, and I agree not to harm myself in any way. I understand that if I am having suicidal thoughts, I agree to call my counselor __________________ (name) at _____________ (phone number). If I cannot reach my counselor, I will call the crisis hotline at _______________ (phone number), or I will tell the nearest adult and get help for myself. (p. 83)

There is a great deal of controversy regarding the use of such no-suicide contracts (Edwards & Harries, 2007). Lack of research regarding their efficacy is often mentioned as an argument against their use (Lewis, 2007; Weiss, 2001).

However, Lisa Lewis (2007) suggested that such an intervention does have the possibility of helping to build a therapeutic alliance. While there are many debates regarding for the use of such "contracts," I have seen a third grader put in his own printing a brief "promise" that he wouldn't hurt himself. I suggest that such contracts should be tailored to the individual. For sure, these contracts are not legally binding. In a school setting, both pros and cons to should be considered as a possible way to relieve the student.

Quinnett (2009) emphasized the importance of building rapport. If a student in your office is having suicidal thoughts, that student needs to be listened to—REALLY listened to. Try to remain calm and try to normalize feelings. Say something like "I'm here with you. I care. I'll help you get through this. Don't use platitudes like "I understand what it is that you're going through," or "It will be better tomorrow." Try to instill the notion that the situation may be very serious and even desperate but not hopeless.

Refer to an Appropriate Outside Person or Agency

In many school situations, teachers will refer students directly to you, the professional school counselor. But it is not your role to provide the treatment that is necessary. You have either assessed formally or informally the lethality risk and need to inform the parent(s) or guardian(s). Most parents will be grateful and willing to get the help that their daughter or son may need. Some schools have a policy to refer the student directly to a crisis center. You will need to know your school policy. You will need to have a list of emergency numbers.

There have been a few occasions when parents wanted to minimize the emergency. I have suggested that something should be documented. Poland (1989) provided a sample verification of an emergency conference. You school may want to use this sample and modify it to the uniqueness of your school:

I, or we, _____________, parents of _______________, were involved in a conference with school personnel on _______________. We have been notified that our child is suicidal. We have been further advised that we should seek some psychological/psychiatric consultation immediately from the community. We have been provided with a list of community services. The school district has clarified its role and will provide follow-up assistance to our child to support the treatment services form the community. (p. 198)

● PRACTICE

Put the following role-plays on separate pieces of paper. Pair students up. Give one role play to one student and the other is a friend. *Read only what is in italics to the friend.* The student with the role-play reads the rest to herself or himself. After giving the student enough time, instruct the friend to come and say hello. Afterward, have students switch roles using a different role-play.

Role-Play 1

You are a 16-year-old girl who lived in New York City. Last year your parents divorced and your dad remarried. You had to move with your dad to a small town in New Jersey. You are now enrolled in a small high school with only 200 students. You are talking to one of the few friends that you have made.

Your friend doesn't know this yet but your grades are falling and you are crying every day. You tried to tell your dad and new stepmom that you were feeling terrible, but they said that things would get better if you would just give it some time.

You don't like this small-town atmosphere and your best friend is your sister Tiffany but she is going away to college in the fall, which made her feel even worse

Toward the end of your conversation with your friend, tell her or him that **"last night, I gave my sister my birthstone ring, since I wouldn't need it anymore."**

Role-Play 2

You are an 18-year-old and a senior in high school. You will be graduating in May. You had planned a career in medicine and have applied to a number of colleges but so far you have not been accepted into any of them.

Your friend does not know that you feel like your world is falling apart. You have also been arguing with your mother and father because they want you to go into the family car-dealership business. You are talking with one of your friends but the friend does not know that you recently quit the swim team, which you really used to enjoy. You have felt increasingly tired, irritable, and lost 10 pounds. You prefer to be alone and rarely call any of your friends. Your GPA has dropped from 4.0 to 2.5 this last semester. You are having thoughts about killing yourself and you have access to your father's gun.

Toward the end of your conversation with your friend tell her or him that **"I want to leave my guitar with you because I won't need it anymore. I know you will take care of it."**

Role-Play 3

You are a 14-year-old student living with your father. Six months ago, your mother died of cancer and your life hasn't been the same since her death. However, you have been doing OK on school. You are good at putting up a good front and your grades are As and Bs. You are on the track team and have lots of friends. Your friend just called you.

Your friend does not know that while you are skilled at putting up a good front on the outside, you are feeling completely miserable on the inside. You had a girlfriend (boyfriend) last year but that person broke up last night because she (he) thought the relationship was getting too serious. You feel devastated so you found a bottle of your dad's scotch and drank a glassful. The more you drank, the more hopeless you felt. You are now considering taking a bottle of Tylenol.

Toward the end of your conversation with your friend tell her or him that **"I just can't take it anymore."**

Role-Play 4

You are a 25-year-old college graduate and have been married for two years. Your husband's job required that you relocate from Boston to a small town in Iowa. You have been living there for 6 months. This move has been very hard for you. Your family and extended family live over 1,200 miles away and you miss them very much and you're not happy with your husband's new job.

One of your best friends from college is visiting you for the weekend and the two of you are driving to the store.

Your friend does not know that you and your husband have been arguing more. You have recently been diagnosed with multiple sclerosis and you have not been sleeping through the night. You have begun to drink more as a means of coping. You had these kinds of feelings during your senior year in college, considered committing suicide by taking an overdose of pain pills. You have begun to stockpile your pain medication and have plenty of alcohol at home. To you, suicide seems like a viable option.

During your conversation you say to your friend, **"It's not worth it anymore."**

● REFLECTION/DISCUSSION

Were you able to ask the *Q*uestion, try to *P*ersuade your student or friend to stay alive and agree with your making some *R*eferral to a professional? How did you feel doing these role plays?

____

____

____

____

____

● POSTVENTION

As R. D. Parsons (1996) noted nearly 20 years ago, a student suicide is tragic. However, he went on, "What may not be so clear is that suicide not only kills victims, but victimizes and 'kills' many of those who were touched by their lives and, consequently, by their deaths" (p. 77). When such a heart-breaking event occurs, too often schools have not developed procedures to minimize confusion and emotional distress on the part of other students, teachers, and other school personnel. Kerrie Fineran (2012) advised that, if this is the case, school counselors should become actively involved in putting procedures in place. In addition to reducing the emotional distress, these postvention activities should be geared at reducing the likelihood of a contagion effect as well as trying to help the school return to a normal routine

(Aguirre & Slater, 2010). Beverly Celotta (1995) urges that the procedures be put in writing. They should identify the leader and members of a crisis team. Only an identified school person should communicate with the media. A number of districts have published postvention plans that are available online. In particular, I recommend looking at the Yavapai County Educational Services Agency (2013) detailed handbook (available at ycesa.com/files/Postvention.pdf).

At a Safe Schools conference, Stephen E. Brock (2003) briefly outlined a postvention protocol. He suggested the following activities:

- Verify death has occurred and that it is a suicide death. This could be done through the coroner's office.
- Contact the crisis response team. The members should include crisis intervention specialists such as school counselors, psychologists, a media liaison, and security personnel.
- Determine how the death will impact students in the school and whether they might already have information about the death. Assess the impact of the suicide on the school; determine if students are likely to learn about the death and how they may cope.
- Be in touch with the family of the student suicide victim to express sympathy, offer support, verify facts, and identify those students who are most likely to be affected by the suicide death.
- Ask the family members what information about the death can or should be shared. Verify facts, address possible rumors and excessive detail about the mode of suicide.
- Decide how to communicate information. Make sure not to sensationalize the suicide and do not glorify or vilify the victim.
- Identify which students are most likely to be affected by the suicide. Typically, this includes those who were physically proximal to the death or who were emotionally close to the suicide victim.
- Begin crisis intervention services. These services may include walking through the victim's class schedule, meeting separately with the victim's close friends, establishing drop-in counseling centers, and facilitating disidentification with the suicide victim in order to avoid a contagion affect.
- Determine the appropriateness of any memorial activities. If there are any, they should not romanticize or sensationalize the death. Students should not view suicide as a way to obtain incredible amounts of attention.

Suicide is a terrible tragedy. Unfortunately, there are no easy answers. The best made plans will never be able to erase the pain. As future school counselors, I can only suggest that you keep in touch with your own emotions and develop your own wellness plan.

● REFERENCES

Achilles, J., Gray, D., & Moskos. (2004). Adolescent suicide myths in the United States. *The Journal of Crisis Intervention and Suicide Prevention, 25*(4), 1–3.

Aguirre, R. T. P., & Slater, H. (2010). Suicide postvention as suicide prevention: Improvement and expansion in the United States. *Death Studies, 34,* 529–540. doi:10.1080/07481181003761336

American Association of Suicidology. (2013). *Youth suicide fact sheet.* Retrieved from http://www.suicidology.org

American Foundation for Suicide Prevention. (2015). *Policy news.* Retrieved from http://www.afsp.org/advocacy-public-policy/policy-news-updates/pennsylvania-adopts-bill-requiring-comprehensive-suicide-prevention-policies-in-schools

American Foundation for Suicide Prevention, & Suicide Prevention Resource Center. (2011). *After a suicide: A toolkit for schools* (Suicide prevention). Newton, MA: Education Development Center. Retrieved from http://crisisservices.org/suicide-prevention/myths-facts/

Australian Government, Department of Veterans' Affairs. (n.d.). *Suicide awareness quiz.* Retrieved from http://at-ease.dva.gov.au/suicideprevention/learn-more-about-suicide/test-what-you-have-learnt/

Brock, S. E. (2003, May). *Suicide postvention.* Paper presented at the DODEA Safe Schools Seminar. Retrieved from http://www.dodea.edu/dodsafeschools/members/seminar/SuicidePrevention/generalreading.html#2

Celotta, B. (1995). The aftermath of a suicide: Postvention in a school setting. *Journal of Mental Health Counseling, 17*, 397–412.

Council for Accreditation of Counseling and Related Educational Programs. (2015). *2016 CACREP standards*. Retrieved from http://www.cacrep.org/wp-content/uploads/2012/10/2016-CACREP-Standards.pdf

Crisis Services. (n.d.). *Myths & Facts*. Retrieved from http://crisisservices.org/suicide-prevention/myths-facts/

Doan, J., Roggenbaum, S., & Lazear, K. (2003). *Youth suicide prevention school-based guide (c/p/r/s)—True/False 1: Information dissemination in schools—The facts about adolescent suicide* (FMHI Series Publication #219-1t). Tampa, FL: Department of Child and Family Studies, Division of State and Local Support, Louis de la Parte Florida Mental Health Institute, University of South Florida.

Edwards, S., & Harries, M. (2007). No-suicide contracts and no-suicide agreements: A controversial life. *Australian Psychiatry, 15*, 484–489. doi:10.1080/10398560701435846

Eisel vs. Board of Education of Montgomery County, 324 Md. 376, 597 A. 2d 447 (Md. Ct. App. 1991). Retrieved from http://www.leagle.com/decision/1991700324Md376_1672.xml/EISEL%20v.%20BOARD%20OF%20EDUCATION

Fineran, K. (2012). Suicide postvention in schools: The role of the school counselor. *Journal of Professional Counseling: Practice, Theory and Research 39*, 14–28.

Gangwisch, J. E. (2010). Suicide risk assessment. *Psychiatry, 21*, 113–119.

Lewis, L. M. (2007). No-harm contracts: A review of what we know. *Suicide and Life-Threatening Behavior, 37*, 50–57.

Maples, M. F., Packman, J., Abney, P., Daugherty, R. F., Casey, J. A., & Pirtle, L. (2005). Suicide by teenagers in middle school: A postvention team approach. *Journal of Counseling & Development, 83*, 397–405.

Nock, M. K., Deming, C. A., Fullerton, C. S., Gilman, S. E., Goldenberg, M., Kessler, R. C., . . . & Ursano, R. J. (2013). Suicide among soldiers: A review of psychosocial risk and protective factors. *Psychiatry, 72*, 97–125.

Opalewski, D. A. (2008). *Answering the cry: A suicide prevention manual for schools and communities*. Chattanooga, TN: National Center for Youth Issues.

Parsons, R. D. (1996). Student suicide: The counselor's postvention role. *Elementary School Guidance & Counseling, 31*, 77–80.

Poland, S. (1989). *Suicide intervention in the schools*. New York, NY: Guilford Press.

Quinnett, P. G. (2009). *Suicide: The forever decision*. New York, NY: Crossroad.

Rudd, M. D., Berman, A. L., Joiner, T. E., Nock, M. K., Silverman, M. M., Mandrusiak, M., . . . & Witte, T. (2006). Warning signs for suicide: Theory, research, and clinical applications. *Suicide and Life-Threatening Behavior, 36*, 255–262.

Stone, C. (2003). Suicide: A duty owed. *ASCA School Counselor*. Retrieved from http://www.schoolcounselor.org/magazine/blogs/march-april-2003/suicide-a-duty-owed

Suicide Prevention Resource Center. (n.d.). *Risk and protective factors for suicide*. Retrieved from https://www.ok.gov/odmhsas/documents/Suicide%20Risk%20and%20Protective%20Factors.pdf

Walsh, E., & Eggert, L. L. (2007). Suicide risk and protective factors among youth experiencing school difficulties. *International Journal of Mental Health Nursing, 16*, 349–359. doi: 10.1111/j.1447-0349.2007.00483.x

Ward, J. E., & Odegard, M. A. (2011). A proposal for increasing student safety through suicide prevention in schools. *The Clearing House, 84*, 144–149. doi:10.1080/00098655.2011.564981

Weiss, A. (2001). The no-suicide contract: Possibilities and pitfalls. *American Journal of Psychotherapy, 55*, 414–419.

Yavapai Educational Services Agency. (2013). *Postvention: A practical guide for responding to death, serious injury and other unexpected events affecting a school*. Retrieved from http://ycesa.com/files/Postvention.pdf

Lesson 13

CRISIS MANAGEMENT

Cheri Lovre
Crisis Management Institute

> *"Having experienced the unthinkable, the one thing I would urge all school leaders to do is get prepared. The key is awareness and readiness."*
>
> —Randy Wright, Chairman of the Board of Education, McCracken County Public Schools, Paducah, Kentucky

Real Life

It is a quiet Monday at your high school. A call comes in from the local police station that there has been a bank robbery at the bank two blocks from your school. The person who held up the bank had a gun. He is a male, average height and weight, wearing a navy blue hoodie. The robbery suspect has not been apprehended. The school's emergency plan must go into effect.

At this time of the day, students are all over campus. The marching band is on the field practicing. Students who are at gym are currently on the lower field playing soccer. Some students are in the cafeteria at lunch while others are in the library.

Knowing the crisis management plan prior to a crisis is essential. Field experience students will have reviewed the plan and will work with their supervisor in this situation.

Lesson Thirteen

Crisis Management

Cheri Lovre
Crisis Management Institute

"Having experienced the unthinkable, the one thing I would urge all school leaders to do is get prepared. The key is awareness and readiness."

—Randy Wright, Chairman of the Board of Education,
McCracken County Public Schools, Paducah, Kentucky

Essential Question: How are crises handled in schools?

Objectives

Student will demonstrate an understanding of crisis management and crisis management strategies used in schools.

Students will

- demonstrate an understanding of the school counselor's roles and responsibilities in relation to the school emergency management plans and crises, disasters, and trauma. (2.e)
- demonstrate an understanding of the legal and ethical considerations specific to school counseling. (2.n)

MPCAC Standards

- professional counselor identity, ethical behavior, and social-justice practices
- human development and wellness across the life span
- ecological, contextual, multicultural, social-justice foundation of human development

Video Spark

http://www.cmionline.com/supporting-youth-after-suicide/

Supporting Youth After Suicide

● INTRODUCTION

When counselors consider what might constitute a school crisis, a range of circumstances might come to mind. While many would be consistent throughout all schools, there are also possible variations based on the culture of the community. For purposes of this chapter, we'll consider school crises to be events that destabilize the school environment or disrupt trust or sense of safety and security of either parents or students. One helpful way of approaching this is to separate school crises into three categories: (1) catastrophic events, (2) tragedies or crises, and (3) destabilizing events.

Catastrophic events are those that occur on school grounds and pose a threat to life or that involve a loss of life during the school day. These events involve mobilizing an immediate response by school staff while waiting for first responders to arrive. Natural disasters requiring shelter-in-place or evacuation fall into this category as well.

School crises or tragedies are those events that occur outside of the school environment, such as a student or staff death over the weekend. No life was at threat of loss during school hours, so the response is focused on meeting the needs of grieving youth and students who will be returning to school the following day or Monday.

Destabilizing events are those situations that disrupt the trust or sense of safety and security for parents and students, such as a sexual abuse case involving a staff member and a student or the collateral damage caused by teacher strikes. Although schools often don't think to mobilize a crisis response team for such events, team members are often very well suited to help craft communications and devise action plans that can help limit some of the damage and perhaps use the opportunity this event provides to foster good relations and closer communication with families.

Before You Put the Plan in Place, Have the People in Place.

A plan is just a collection of ideas on paper. Crisis response capacity is entirely dependent on the people who will put that plan into action. While this chapter deals with the planning component, it is critical to acknowledge the process that has to be in place in order for the plan to work. Although everyone in the building needs to take ownership in their part of crisis response, it is particularly important that there is substantive training for the team of people who will respond to support that building, as well as training for administrators and counselors.

The Bigger Picture—Teams to Have in Place

Every building needs a **rapid response team**, which is that group of people in each building who have specific assignments about what they'll do if there is threat to life or limb within a building. That is not the focus here, but needs to be mentioned as all of these teams need to operate seamlessly in those events that call for their mobilization. The rapid response team within a building includes administrators, those with medical expertise, and those who can help manage security and stem the spread of the emergency zone.

Flight team (school-based crisis response team) refers to those who will "fly at a moment's notice" to meet the needs of a building that is recovering from a tragedy, crisis, or overwhelming event. Many districts call these the *Crisis Response Team*. Flight team members are those who have had special training in how to help a building recover in the aftermath of critical events. These may be school counselors, school psychologists, school social workers, nurses or med techs, and others who would have a heart for the emotional recovery for students and staff. The flight team may be called into events that involve the rapid response team. For instance, if a building has an event and has to evacuate, the flight team could be called to staff the student-family reunification center. More often, this team comes into a school to provide grief support in the aftermath of the loss. Tasks include setting up safe rooms, supporting teachers in the rooms with the "empty desk," reading announcements to students in those classrooms where teachers are reluctant to do so.

The **safe room** is more of a concept than a place. Safe rooms refers to a safe place set aside for students who either wish to gather with one another in their grieving or who wish to have time with an adult who will listen. It is not a place specifically for counseling, and best practice is for the safe room to be run by incoming school counselors, psychologists, nurses, and/or social workers from other districts or at least from other buildings so the home building can have people in their usual roles. This allows the building counselor to be in his or her private room, available to those youth who self-disclose child abuse, sexual abuse, or suicidal ideation in the safe room. Our goal is to provide additional support leaving the home school counselor available to students who present with unique needs.

Safe rooms are usually in the library of the school, but other spaces can also work. Auditoriums and cafeterias and gymnasiums definitely do not work! The safe room is staffed by the flight team with the hope that the building counselor can be in his or her room for the students who need 1:1 counseling. It has a range of activities to facilitate both the grieving process as well as the sharing of memories. The safe room should never be referred to as a place for "those who are having trouble with this event." Grief comes with a natural need for people to gather together, and the safe room provides that opportunity. Too, by getting students who are more profoundly grieving out of the classrooms and into their own space, those students who are less affected and are ready to get back into academics can do so without their teachers being divided in trying to support students who are grieving while teaching.

Having flight team members who can readily respond and have the skill and capacity to set up safe rooms is really the heart of most crisis response. Having a plan is just another three-ring binder on the shelf. Having people who have the capacity to carry that plan out is essential for effective crisis response!

● COMPONENTS OF A CRISIS DAY ACTION PLAN

Cheri Lovre, director of Crisis Management Institute (CMI), says crisis plans need to be clear enough to give direction in the midst of the event, but flexible enough to meet a range of types of circumstances that can't be predicted. Because we've segregated the general topic of crisis into three categories, that means that you'll need three different plans to address each type (Crisis Management Institute [CMI], 2016).

The primary starting place is that communications need to happen immediately, and the very first needs include three tracks: engagement between the impacted school and the central office administration, communications to staff, and communications between the impacted school and responders coming in from other schools or districts. That needs to roll as soon as you know there is a likelihood that the flight team will be activated. The next step in communications is considering what and when to notify parents of what happened and what you're doing and will do in response. Finally, depending on the event, there may also be a need for broader communications with the community and, particularly, media. At least the district, staff, and flight team communications would start immediately upon hearing of the event, and then the other two would vary more, depending on the nature of the circumstance.

If the timing is such that you can call together a few key people in the evening, by all means do so. If the event unfolds as buses are rolling in the morning, the plan has to be modified. Begin writing the probable student announcement right away—- don't wait till morning. There will be new details and challenges. Do all you can the night before if possible.

Next is outlining steps for getting through the day. Start with a small meeting with administration and mental health folks (counselors, school psychologists, school social workers, etc.) and go from that into an all-staff meeting before school. At that meeting, don't just share facts and your expectations about how the day will go—give staff time to talk in small groups to identify their concerns so you know what they most want to feel supported. Give them the student announcement so they can begin to imagine reading it to their students. That is one possible time for giving them a little small-group conversation time, because the announcement is what many dread the most. Ask what any have heard from social media or other sources that might be surprise statements by students. Give teachers language for answering difficult expected questions.

When school starts, teachers read the announcements to their students and may take time for an activity like letting students create cards for the family, and then when most are ready to head into academics, the few that aren't ready in any classroom can go to the safe room, which remains open all day.

One great way of providing support to staff is to stagger safe room staff lunch breaks to coincide with staff lunch times and go talk informally with staff. It is also helpful to have flight team members go down the halls a couple of times to offer each teacher a short break. Few will take advantage of it, but teachers often say that, once they really knew they could have a break if they needed it, they felt more anchored for the rest of the day.

Also on crisis day, call together any teams or clubs or activities in which the deceased student participated rather than having those students be uncomfortable for weeks or months until their sport starts to have the chance to talk about what it means to them to lose this person.

After school, hold an all-staff meeting again, keeping it fairly brief, but doing a check in with all of them. What went well? What didn't? What would they like for tomorrow? What surprised them? Lessons learned?

Often staff say they're too tired to meet, but it makes a huge difference in giving you the understanding of what they need for the next day, so if for no other reason, it is helpful to have that. Truth be told, though, it is psychologically very helpful for them as well. Often those who need it most are apt to say they just want to go home, so the best practice is that administration make it essentially mandatory with exceptions for extenuating circumstances, such as one individual who has an important medical appointment.

Notification and Announcements

Probably the greatest challenges or the causes for difficulties during the response are related to communication and information. It is helpful for people to know as soon as possible that a crisis has occurred so they can begin to psychologically prepare first for their own needs and then for those of their students. It is extremely rare that anyone complains of getting too much information. On the other hand, it is extremely common that people are stressed or frustrated because they've received too little.

Here are some general guidelines about giving information to anyone at times of crisis:

- When telling someone over the phone of a loss that is very close for that individual (loss of a family member, classroom student, or someone with whom they work closely), it is helpful to ask whether the person is alone and suggest that they sit down. This is the beginning of helping someone with psychological preparedness for receiving terrible news. Even if they're alone and you need to tell them, that kind of question immediately communicates the gravity of your coming message.
- Begin with a sentence of warning. "I have tragic news," or, "I'm sorry I have bad news," or, "It is really difficult to have to tell you this," or in a group, "Please may I have everyone's attention. . . . we have tragic news to share that impacts all of us at ______ High School."
- Give the facts in a kind, but clear way. *"Last night around 7:30, So-and-So died in a car wreck."* Begin with who died, when, and how. Then pause briefly to let that sink in. The next part of sharing information depends on the receiver of the information and the situation—is this is a classroom or staff meeting? On the phone? Will this person have to support others or is this just information for this person to begin to process? (CMI, 2016)

If on the phone with an individual

- As soon as you convey the information, let the person know that you have time to remain on the phone with her or him for a while as she or he begins to make decisions about what needs to happen next. *"I know that it will take a few minutes for you to know what you need most right now, so let me stay with you for a few minutes on the phone while we try to figure out what will help most right now."*
- Next steps might be helping the person identify who might be able to come be with him or her, who needs to know, and whether you could make some calls that would be helpful.

- Before you hang up, let him or her know that you'd like to check back with them before long, and consider doing a call-back in a couple of hours to make sure the person has been able to begin to make some calls or whatever would be appropriate given the situation.

If addressing a classroom

- After giving the facts, acknowledge that there is a range of feelings and reactions that people have at times like these, and that there isn't a "right" way to feel. We all just need to respect one another and accept that different people will have different reactions. Also point out that feelings are transitory. What any of them feel tomorrow may be quite different than how they feel today, and that as we work our way through this, what helps most is for us to just support one another unless someone is thinking about doing something dangerous to self or others. When that becomes an issue, peers need to find adult help quickly to be sure that everyone stays safe.
- Mention that you'll take some time for class discussion in a moment, but first you want to let them know more about what the school is putting in place.
- Next, talk about the kinds of support that will be available for students over the next few days. The heart of these responses is the safe room, which is a place for students to gather together. In many cultures, gathering together to share memories is an important aspect of grieving. There is a strong social need to gather in the groups in which one knew the deceased. That means that those who were all on a sports team together with him or her will need to gather as a group, and those who were in an after-school club together will need to gather in that configuration. The safe room is a place for students to collect to share that process, no matter how they knew the person who died. They'll usually find their own natural groupings once they get to the safe room. So in the announcement, describe the safe room only as a gathering place for students who want to share memories or just be together. Take the focus off the counseling aspect of this, and for sure, don't speak of it as a place for students who are "having trouble with this." Making that kind of statement discourages much of the healthiest use of the room—providing for one of the important aspects of grief.
- Let them know how they'll be receiving further information. Will you have a website page for students, staff, and parents? (Recognize that anything you have on the Web can be found by media and "outsiders," so you'll have to be judicious about what is said, but this is one great way to keep information flowing.)
- Then, to start class discussion, you might try any of these:
  - *So let's begin talking about this. Maybe a few of you would share how you first heard about his or her death?*
  - *What kinds of things did any of your parents or loved ones do that was helpful?*
  - *How was it coming into school? Were you looking forward to being able to be with one another?*
  - *What troubles you most?*
  - *Can you think of things that the school could do that would help?*
  - *Are there things I could do that would help?*
  - *What do you wish adults understood about how this is for you?*
- After the announcement and discussion, teachers might want to allow students to make cards or write letters to the family. There are other activities teachers can lead as well. When most students are ready to return to academics, those few who are not can then walk down to the safe room. (CMI, 2016)

How do we tell staff?

For those of us old enough to remember, there was once a time when we could wait until teachers came into school in the morning to tell them of a student death, or perhaps wait until we had all pertinent information and the beginnings of a response plan before we called staff to let them know of a death. But with the dawning of e-mail, texting, and Facebook, we lost that luxury.

Perhaps one of the most disconcerting ways for a teacher to hear that a student in her classroom has died is by having her son or daughter show it to her on Facebook. Dealing with a loss of this sort is often new for the teacher, and a major immediate concern is, "How will I manage my classroom? How will I help all of my students?"

Important things we can encourage administrators to do in this regard include these:

- Let all school staff know as soon as possible that the following day will likely be a crisis response day so they have the time to do their own psychological preparation.
  - Even if you can't confirm the death or share the name, at least they heard it first from you, not from Facebook.
  - Let them know how they'll receive further information.
  - Have these calls be in person, not voice recordings. If no one answers the phone, don't leave the death announcement in voice mail; let them know it is very urgent and have the person return the call.
- When confirmed, let them know the facts (who died, how, and when) and pause to let them digest that much; then let them know there will be a before-school meeting when they'll learn more information.
  - You can let them know supports you expect to be in place for them:
    - additional information at the morning meeting
    - flight team (crisis response team) support for a safe room
    - flight team support for reading the announcements to students for those teachers who would like it
    - a flight team person to be in the classroom that will have an empty desk (all of them, if the incident caused more than one death and/or injury, and/or in the case of middle and high school, following the student schedule/s to all classes on the first day back).
    - If there is other support that you're expecting, mention it.
  - You might also let him or her know that you will send e-mail updates if you have any between now and that meeting.
  - You might ask whether there is anyone on staff for whom the listener is concerned—anyone they would think might need extra support.
  - Let them know who to call if something comes up that they think is important to convey.

How and what to tell parents?

It is very customary for students to bring home a letter to parents, including basics about what happened, perhaps a copy of the announcement read to students, and a thumbnail of how the school responded. Give them information on who to call if they have questions and include tips for parents on the back. Our website (www.cmionline.org) has guidelines for talking with children about a range of kinds of events, and as long as copyright information is left intact, and nothing is changed, those can be included in what is sent home to parents (CMI, 2016).

Two critical caveats

Always be sure the administrator in your building has approved any written communications you're sending out, and depending on the district, she or he may be expected to run it past either the superintendent or, in larger districts, the public information officer. The other caveat is that anything you send out is apt to end up in the hands of media, so write it with that in mind and remind all who are editing or approving it of the same.

When the event unfolds during the day

Sometimes the timing of the event makes it very difficult to give staff advance information in order to give them time to collect themselves before facing their class. If at all possible, send runners to each room and ask the teacher to step out into the hallway to talk and give them the information in the same kind of format as listed above. If possible, give each a moment to adjust and have something written that has bullet points of facts or an announcement to read to their classrooms. If at all possible, do not e-mail these messages, come over the PA, and have the teachers hear the information at the same moment they need to be able to support their students.

Here is an example of a very insightful response. On 9/11, a principal in New Jersey realized that some of his teachers and students were apt to have the head of household working in the towers. He went on the PA and said to all that, although it was earlier in the year than when they have their first fire drill, he wanted teachers to have their students line up and walk out to where they will need to go when they practiced the drill later in the month. Although teachers were very surprised, all did so, and when students were all lined up in the football field, he brought all of the teachers into the center of the field to talk with them. Of course, teachers whose spouses were working in the towers self-identified, and many could also in the moment identify students with a parent who worked in the towers. They then decided how teachers would talk about this with their students and what support the school could arrange for those students who self-identified as having a parent working in the towers.

Also on 9/11, another school filtered their database for all parent and emergency contact phone numbers that included New York City area codes. Because cell phones were not yet so ubiquitous, student records included landline numbers for parent work numbers. In that same school, the local police took all license plate numbers at parking lots for the commuter trains and busses into the city and ran lists of names. Police stopped by with additions to the list several times during the day so the principal could look through those names to determine whether any of them might be parents of students in the school. That gave him the opportunity to choose a staff person who could be in the office when he called each student down to let them know that he wanted them to know that there was an emergency in New York City, that we didn't have confirmed information about much of it, but that he wanted them to hear that much privately and let them call the other parent or decide about going back to class.

Community

Any time a school has a loss that activates the flight team (crisis response team), it is worth considering whether to also make a public statement about the circumstance. This is a case-by-case call. If it is decided that a public statement will be made, be sure the family knows and receives a copy before it goes public.

Consider including the following, depending on the event:

- Open with a statement of condolence to the family.
- Mention the shock it was to those at school, if so.
- List the heroic efforts and the kindnesses that have been extended to the school with appreciation.
- Share any special efforts that were made by police or first responders or others who are outside of the school setting but were helpful.
- Give appreciation for ways students have been helpful to one another or displayed exemplary behavior, and to staff who have provided support to students.
- Talk about the supports that have been made available to staff, students, and parents and what additional supports are expected.
- Mention how updates will be released.
- Mention where people can find a list of resources or how they might refer anyone about whom they're worried.
- Let them know how to give information to the school if they are concerned about a student.

There are other important dimensions about community communications. If media are involved, it is critical to get all of the major points you want parents to know and believe reflected in media coverage as much as possible. For example, following a bus accident, you can do a terrific job of helping students get past their fears about riding on the bus, and they may be all ready to ride. But if the media are posing questions that raise parent concerns, just a couple of onerous questions to their children can rekindle the fear you've managed. Kids are very loyal to their parents' feelings and opinions, particularly when it involves negative emotion.

Because of that, consider that any effort that goes into helping parents and community support your plan is time well spent. And recognize that community perception is driven much more by media than by the district's good efforts.

If media are stirring the pot negatively, there are two things that can help. One is to give them the article you'd like them to print. They'll wordsmith it if they use it, or perhaps will only use parts, but they're busy people and will often use what they're given. You might also include bullet point content that gives them a starting place on several key factors. Journalistic writing is different from all other writing, though, and it is critical that you put the most important factors first, down to the least important. The other is to call them on the negative outcomes for students of media sensationalism. In one town where four students died by suicide in a very short period of time, media were interviewing parents who were angry and placing blame. The district asked for a meeting with all media organizations in their area and pointed out that, to stem this tragic cascade of events, students needed hope and support, and parents needed helpful information and resources. A very clear statement that the school viewed the negative media coverage as such a major factor that they felt that further losses could result directly because of that coverage, and that if another student died, we'd be asking for another meeting, that entirely turned the tide on coverage. Nobody wants to be blamed for a student suicide and implicating them made that clear.

Basics of Grief

Most of the time, students and staff will be grieving a loss, so an understanding of grief is critical. Too, often when the incident is something that involves a destabilizing circumstance, elements of grief may be present, but the loss is, for instance, a loss of faith in the goodness of people or a loss of trust in staff, or a loss of respect for a group.

Dr. Alan Wolfelt has written several books about grief, all of which are clear, concise, and helpful. He uses the concept of "tasks of grief" as opposed to stages, which is a helpful concept, because we don't just have grief happen to us in stages. We have to do our part of the work in order to process grief. The following is an adaptation of his approach, making it more school specific.

The first need we all have in order to process loss is to **know the truth of what happened.** That means that all students need to hear an announcement that is primarily the same information. In elementary schools, it may be appropriate to have two different announcements simply to take in developmental levels of students in different grades, but we have to remember that all students will be riding the bus together or playing at recess with students from other classes, so that makes it important to read the announcements to all classes, not just those who have students who personally know the child. Another reason for reading the announcements to all students is that there is no way for schools to know which students in other classes know the deceased through church or other associations.

Once students have heard what has happened, there is often a need for them to **put their own words to their perceptions and reactions.** That means the teachers need to make room for discussion before heading into academics, and the length of that discussion time needs to be determined by the needs of the students.

There is a social component to grief, so we need to **gather together with others in the context of how we knew that person and share memories.** That is the main function of the safe room, and that's why we call teams on which the student played together the first day back to school rather than waiting for that sport to begin.

Although we often fail to recognize it, the **meaning** that one gives a death determines many things of great importance. Even children as young as three or four years old give death meaning. One child whose parent was a loving and kind parent might give that parent's death the meaning that God wanted to take him because he was a good person to help out in heaven. Another child from a more dysfunctional home might see his parent's death as God's punishment for bad behavior.

This makes it really important to use different questions when we're working with youth. Instead of so often asking "How do you feel?" try, "What does it mean to you that your (whomever) has died?" When we ask how a child feels, we get an answer that is temporary—how she or he is feeling in the moment, and we can almost predict what the feelings are likely to be. When we ask what it means, however, we are gaining insight into how the child will relate to future deaths, whether the child feels she or he is somehow to blame (particularly with younger children who are in the developmental stage of magical thinking, this is critical), whether they now feel there is no God when previously they did. The possibilities of meanings are endless, and some meanings young ones give a death can mar their positive self-image or leave them in ongoing anxiety about losing the remaining parent and so on.

All cultures have some kind of **tribute** or activity to mark the loss of life, and it is universal because it has such critical function in the wellness of its people. It provides a time to gather together, to take note of who that person was in the community, why they'll be missed, and so on. Life tributes are wonderful for students of all ages, tailored to meet their developmental needs. The life tribute also marks the time when the school begins moving forward from the formal time of shared grief, noting that individual grief will continue for some time.

Finally, because grief *does* go on for some time, it is important to plan for **long-term follow-up** that is appropriate to the impact for those closest to the child or staff person who died. Put a tickler in your calendar for around 48 weeks from the event—about a month before the first anniversary. That will be a time to check in, at least informally, with those for whom the anniversary may bring up unfinished grief. Other dates to consider will be the deceased's birthday and any other important dates.

When your school responds to a student or staff death, if you're finding ways to give students and staff the opportunity to do each of these "tasks" as outlined above, you're covering the basics of grief really well.

One caveat here: If there were students who witnessed the death or saw things that could give one bad dreams or flashbacks, their needs will be very different from those who are grieving; in fact, they'll probably struggle and perhaps misbehave in the safe room because being around others who are grieving often throws them into reexperiencing the trauma until they've had professional help to "move" the memory into a part of the brain that allows greater control over thoughts. If you know students witnessed an event, give them their own space to talk; ask them not to share graphic details with others (because then those who hear about it may also begin to struggle with trauma). It will likely be more helpful for them to talk about what happened in the event than to explore emotions, which are likely entirely overwhelming. To ask traumatized youth to go back through the event and label their emotions is often retraumatizing. Stay with more cognitive and left-brain questions than right-brain or emotionally laden conversation and be sure to make appropriate referrals for youth who need help with traumatic memories.

Self-Care/Counselor Wellness

This is one area where we almost always cut corners is with self-care. The positive aspect of this is that, as school counselors, we figure it is more important to meet the needs of children and that we'll take care of ourselves later. The same is true for teachers. Administrators are often the least likely to pay attention to self-care because their responsibilities are great and varied, and they attained the positions they have by being so willing to work so very hard. Usually what happens is all the adults make it through the event, and the trips to the emergency rooms begin about six weeks after the event. That's about how long we can run on adrenaline before something gives. Either our psyche or our body wants to begin to cave unless the situation has greatly improved. Here are some ways you can protect yourself from that kind of reaction.

1. Before something happens, put in place all of the resources and support you can.

The most effective organization for flight teams is to have countrywide or regional teams. No city is big enough to be able to just depend on their own response capacity (think 9/11 when every single school in New York was in crisis or the recovery from Hurricane Katrina). Bring in all of the support you can for the first few days and try to save your energies for the longer-term recovery. Although major parts of the recovery efforts (safe rooms, announcements, activities related to the event) are over within a week or so, there will usually be long-term issues and struggles that surface, and by then, help is long gone and it's all on your shoulders. Mobilize all the help you can early on and save your energies for later.

2. Before you have a crisis, create two little self-care boxes for yourself. One is what you need when you hear there is a crisis—that might be a few of your favorite tea bags and your favorite kind of chocolate to put in your pocket as you head into the day. The second one is what is waiting for you when you get home from the first day. That might have bath salts, your favorite relaxing CD, whatever it is that you could do that would help you relax when you finally get home after what will seem like—and may literally be—a very long day.

3. Talk now with your partner/spouse/family members/friends about what you think you might want from them when you've had to manage crisis at school. Of course you can't know for sure, but let them know whether you'd like phone calls or not, whether you think you'll want company, or the relief of a totally quiet evening. Giving them ideas also gives them permission, and that's a win for everybody.

4. Take some time to list off all your favorite things to do and then reflect on each one. How often do you do the things that you enjoy? The things that sustain you? Has work gobbled you up or do you still exercise and do yoga or ride bikes or whatever you've ever done that helps you feel healthy? The stronger you are going into a crisis, the better you'll weather it when it happens.

5. Have that same conversation with some of those at work with whom you feel closest, and all of you can share how you want to support one another. As the building counselor, it would also be terrific if your principal would give you some time to do some anticipatory work with your staff so you could do the same thing. Introducing the concept ("Let's think ahead of time what we might want . . .") and then giving staff time to talk in small groups would be really effective; then ask each small group to tell the whole group ideas they had. This is the kind of thing that doesn't have to become policy or written down, the power of it is recording their statements on flip charts in the room so people can look at common ideas and threads. It would be a great topic several times a year, even if just for a few minutes each time.

● CRISIS DAY GUIDELINES FOR COUNSELORS

Crisis Management Institute

Students know where to find you in your office and that there may be more benefit to your being there than helping to staff the safe room. Any students who have check-in programs with you still need their chance to check in. If you are in your office, those students who are most in need of having some one-to-one time with you have a chance to do so. If you are in the safe room or moving about the school, sometimes those students are a bit at loose ends. Keeping the chaos level down is best facilitated by having as little disruption as possible and providing a stable environment. That includes knowing that you're still there for them in the same way.

The purpose of the safe room is to allow students to talk among themselves while they try to give meaning to the loss. If there are students who are particularly disturbed or in need of counseling support from you, the flight team will send them to you if they come into the safe room. It is not the flight team's goal to take over your role; it is their goal to facilitate a space where students who are not ready to return to academics can congregate and begin healthy grieving. It will be very helpful for them to be able to send you those students who are most devastated.

Try not to overextend yourself too much today. The flight team is probably only here for one or a few days. You will be picking up the pieces for a long time to come. Staff and students will be turning to you for some time. Consider turning anything over to the flight team you can for today—ask whether your needs are within their scope.

Invite those students about whom you are concerned to stop by your office during the day. Have notes inviting students to your office delivered to students' rooms during the day or hand them out to the teachers at the before school staff meeting.

The flight team usually sets up meetings for specific groups with whom the deceased was closely involved. This often includes sports teams, debate, drama, or other special activities in which the deceased person participated. The team members have ideas as to what makes those meetings work well and what some of the pitfalls tend to be. It is very helpful if you can participate in those group meetings, because long after the flight team is gone, those groups will still be grieving. If you are there at the initial meeting, they identify with you as already knowing what they're going through (CMI, 2016).

Encourage teachers to keep lists of those students whose behavior, academic performance, or attendance changes in the near future, or any students of concern. You may want to organize some informal "lunch bunches" or some more formal grief groups as a follow-up to this event.

The two staff people most apt to be overworked and given least space for their own needs around these kinds of events are the counselor and the administrator in charge. People have come to depend on the counselors in many ways, and this is apt to be a very demanding time. Go on record with your staff as being a "regular" person with real needs, and ask for support or breaks when you need them.

There is information further back in the manual suggesting guidelines for planning memorial activities. It would be helpful for you to read that, especially if you will end up being the person who oversees the planning of that activity with students. Feel free to call on flight team members for suggestions or as sounding boards. There are some wonderful outcomes of having a memory activity—we suggest it almost ALWAYS. There are some pitfalls to be avoided, too.

Be kind to yourself and ask the flight team to help in any way you wish! Your school is fortunate to have you, especially now.

● TO SPEAK OR NOT TO SPEAK? THAT IS THE QUESTION!

Crisis Management Institute

Often when a death occurs, administrators are uncertain of what to have teachers say to students. When the cause of death is other than an accident or terminal illness, it often seems even more difficult to know whether to talk about it at all, or perhaps not bring it up to the students.

Often there are aspects of a death about which we are not free to comment because of an investigation or perhaps issues that complicate whether we feel free to discuss the death with students. There are some compelling reasons not to buy into the knee-jerk reaction of "Don't say anything." Often what we really mean is "Don't say anything specific about the cause of death because that is a sticky issue." Here are several considerations as you work toward a decision about what to have teachers say and not say or whether to say anything at all.

For starters, the more difficult the circumstances of the death, the more likely it is to spawn anxiety, curiosity, anger, gossip, and rumors. We often think that if we don't bring it up, and if the kids don't bring it up, maybe it isn't an issue for them. Nothing is more likely to be further from the truth. In actuality, students read our nonverbal language just as well as our verbal messages and are often respectful of the boundaries we set for ourselves. But that doesn't in any way mean that they aren't worried, that they aren't anxious, that they aren't spreading rumors, or that they aren't talking about it among themselves.

What we do when we refuse to discuss difficult issues with students is drive the conversation underground. Without our joining in the discussion, students only have one another for support, and their youth equates to very little wisdom. So what we do is leave them more vulnerable in so many ways because we don't influence their conversation or contemplation with any wisdom or adult guidance or influence.

Another consideration is the opportunity we have at these difficult times in students' lives to do a range of very positive things:

- By being a part of the discussion, we can encourage students to be their most mature, "very best selves," in this time and help them see the deleterious effects of rumors.
    - "When things like this happen, we really may not have the facts right at first, even though information is flying around on texts and social media. So, while we're waiting for the official statement on this, we can really be contributing to some of the problems we see by guessing what happened and stating it as truth. Making up what we think might be true." (CMI, 2016)
    - Reinforce that part of the reason for this is that, if we can KNOW what happened, we could try to stay safe from it, we can put it to rest in some way. Not knowing is the most difficult of all!
    - In the interim, while we wait for more official word, what we CAN talk about is what kind of impact this has on our school, on the community. Students can talk about what they wish adults understood about what is difficult about being a kid these days.
    - We can acknowledge that, in order to grieve or make sense of frightening events, it is helpful to talk, and while there may be aspects of this event that we cannot talk about, we certainly can look at what troubles the students and help them brainstorm ways of coping.
- If the death was unintentional, but caused by another student, we have the opportunity to help students have empathy for how difficult this must be for, for instance, the driver of the car who survived his friend's death. This doesn't mean we promote acceptance of drunk driving, but rather that we make room for both the anger at a student having made a dangerous decision while also acknowledging that revenge toward that student continues the cycle of negativity.
    - State the obvious. This is about the facts: who died, who is reported to have been driving according to news sources, what is being investigated.
    - If that information hasn't been reported by media, you can talk about the fact that it takes a while for investigations sometimes. But acknowledge that via social media, students may have much more information than we have.
    - Acknowledge that it is easy at times like this to think that you are hearing "the truth" when, in fact, details are often erroneous in early stages.
- If the death was gang related, we have a terrific opportunity to influence those students who might be on the verge of joining a gang to make a much more life-affirming decision. Often, we're afraid to address the issue at all because we don't want to either support gang activity or even perhaps make a statement about gangs.
    - State the obvious. You can certainly announce the death; you can also confirm that news sources are saying it was a gunshot wound. At this point, unless media have released names of those accused, it is fine to just acknowledge that they may have lots more information through social media than the school has from officials at this point, and that it would be most helpful for them not to spread that information around until you have official word.
    - The next part is critical. "When things like this happen, we have a range of reactions, which can include sadness, fear, anger, and a desire for revenge. All of these are common reactions, and

the anger is acceptable, but you are still responsible for your reactions, and using violence or hurtful behaviors is not!"

  - The difficult questions students might ask ("Was it a gang thing?") can be answered by noting that parts of this—including cause of death, guilt or innocence of a suspect, for example—will be answered by others. That is the job of law enforcement and the courts.
  - The focus of the discussion then moves away from cause of death (which we may not know for sure initially) to examining how we cope and survive difficult times. This is the time to "bridge" the conversation to, "What is it like for us that these things happen?" and let students talk about their fears.

Something for us to remember is that the very first step in the tasks of grieving, according to Dr. Alan Wolfelt, is to "hear the truth." The reason that matters so much is that the circumstances of the death determine the quality of our grief. Grief feels different if the death was an act of nature or a terminal illness than if it was of human intent. Remembering this allows us to have more patience with students who are really blaming and perhaps creating rumors. Often this is what they do to try to gain a sense of control and begin to be able to grieve.

In nearly any death, the sketchier the details, the more students need a safe place to talk—one that allows adults to temper their thoughts with wisdom. Here are a few statements and questions that are fairly universal and work in a range of circumstances:

- "It is easy to want to blame someone else, but let's look at what happens if we're blaming the wrong person. Someone who didn't do this. What have we done to that person? Let's take a moment to listen to several of you talk about a time that others were saying something that wasn't true about you and what that was like."
- "What do you wish adults understood about the ways in which this is difficult for you all right now?"
- "Sometimes it helps if we can do something rather than just talk about it. If we were going to do one thing right now, what might that be?" (Students often collect money or do fundraisers for the family, or they might form a chapter of Students Against Drunk Driving or that sort of thing.) (CMI, 2016)

The critical thing to remember is that, just because we don't talk about it doesn't mean the kids won't. And we need to remember—we teach them just as much by what we **don't** say as by what we **do**. In these times of increasing complexities in our lives, students benefit from knowing that school staff wants to create a safe place. If we don't talk with students at times such as when they've lost a friend, how can we expect they'll come to tell us that they've heard someone is planning to shoot up the school? This is our opportunity to create an open and trusting climate.

● REFERENCES

Center for Loss & Life Transition, Dr. Alan Wolfelt: http://www.centerforloss.com/

Crisis Management Institute (CMI), Cheri Lovre (2016): www.cmionline.org; info@cmionline.org

CRISIS MANAGEMENT INSTITUTE PO Box 331 * Salem, OR 97308 * (503) 585-3484

Lesson 14

SUBSTANCE ABUSE

"Prevention is key. Intervention is required. Treatment can work."

Denise Horton
Alcohol and Drug Control Officer and EAP for Fort Dix Army Support Activity

Real Life

Amber is a 12-year-old eighth-grade student. Her friends have come to you to tell you that they are worried about Amber. They think she is meeting an older boy in the park after school and getting high. Amber's friends report that she doesn't want to hang out with them very much anymore. Amber is an excellent student, and there has been no change in her grades. She presents as mature for her age, and adults tend to treat her as if she were older. Amber is an only child and has close relationships with both of her parents. Her parents are divorced, and she "floats" between the two houses.

Lesson Fourteen

Substance Abuse

"Prevention is key. Intervention is required. Treatment can work."

Denise Horton

Alcohol and Drug Control Officer and EAP for Fort Dix Army Support Activity

Essential Question: What are signs and symptoms of substance abuse in children?

Objectives

Students will

- recognize signs/symptoms to intervene as early as possible.
- recognize fetal alcohol signs.
- provide awareness on levels of prevention.

CACREP Standards:

- Recognize signs and symptoms of substance abuse in children and adolescents as well as the signs and symptoms of living in a home where substance use occurs. (G.5.s.2.i)

MPCAC Standards

- assessment of human behavior and organizational/community/institutional systems
- human development and wellness across the life span
- ecological, contextual, multicultural, social-justice foundation of human development

Video Spark

http://www.tedmed.com/talks/show?id=309096

Why do our brains get addicted? (Nora Volkow)

● INTRODUCTION

Addressing the complexities of substance abuse in students and their families is challenging and requires significant thought and consultation. Each state has laws regulating confidentiality, informed consent, and other aspects of working with individuals whose lives are impacted by substance abuse. In addition, each school district will have specific policies and procedures concerning substance abuse. And last, but far from least, are the ethical standards and responsibilities of the professional school counselor. Hence, it is essential to know the state laws and the school district's policies and procedures and remain grounded in the ASCA ethics.

This note of caution is very important in light of the prevalence of underage drinking and substance abuse in adolescents. In 2013, the National Survey on Drug Use and Health reported that 23% of youth ages 12 to 20 years drink alcohol and 14% reported binge drinking in the past 30 days (Substance Abuse and Mental Health Services Administration [SAMHSA], 2014). SAMHSA (2015) reported "An estimated 1.3 million U.S. adolescents ages 12 to 17 had a substance use disorder in 2014 (5% of all adolescents). The 2014 rate of past-month illicit drug use was 3.4% among those ages 12 to 13, 7.9% among youth ages 14 to 15, and 16.5% among youth ages 16 to 17" (p. 1). Importantly, these statistics are numbers representing individual students. Some are as young as 12. The role of the professional school counselor is to best meet the needs of these students. In addition, meeting the needs of all students through prevention programs and education is fundamental to the role of the school counselor.

• PREVENTION

Prevention is often an aspiration rather than a goal. As the saying goes—goals are dreams without deadlines. With high-stakes testing and other demands on student time, the school counseling core curriculum is not necessarily a consistently scheduled part of a student's educational experience. Without the scheduled time or deadline, prevention is overlooked until a crisis or tragedy occurs. When in reactive mode, systems tend to put into place a "one-and-done" program or a brief program implemented post event. As school counselors, it is at this point that leadership comes into play. Advocate for the integration of the school counseling core curriculum and the necessity to have it in the school's required curriculum and schedule.

The Institute of Medicine reports that there are universal, selective, and indicated strategies. Universal prevention refers to applying a broad brush intervention or activity to all. The school counseling core curriculum addresses universal prevention. Selective prevention is targeted prevention that narrows the intervention to higher at-risk groups and people. Small groups in schools may address selective prevention. Indicated prevention refers to applying strategies to those who already have experienced some level of problem secondary to use or abuse of a substance. Professional school counselors working with individual students and student assistance programs address students who have experienced some difficulty with substance use/abuse. Each school will approach prevention based on the needs and characteristics of their stakeholders.

Evidenced-based interventions are best practice. SAMHSA (2016) provides a list of evidence based programs and their accompanying website information. Some of the evidenced-based programs are California Healthy Kids Resource Center, the Campbell Collaboration, and ChildTrends. SAMHSA's website is www.samhsa.gov/ebp-web-guide/substance-abuse-prevention.

• INTERVENTION

School counselors provide intervention through a comprehensive counseling program that addresses the needs of all students. When working with students whose lives are impacted by substance abuse, a holistic approach is considered best practice. Hence, physical, spiritual, socioemotional, and cultural issues are to be assessed and the role of each given consideration. Once the counseling relationship is established, trust is built and all aspects of the student's life are considered, the school counselor can then expand their use of strategies. Cognitive, behavioral strategies and motivational interviewing techniques are recommended for at-risk students. Also, in accordance with the school district's policy and procedure, refer the student to the student assistance program.

• CHILDREN OF ALCOHOLICS, FAMILY RULES, AND ROLES

According to the National Association of Children of Alcoholics (NACA), there are approximately 17 million children under the age of 18 with a parent who has alcoholism. Chances are strong that you will come in contact with a number of children in families who live with this secret at home. NCAC has provided a resource that gives us a glimpse into the everyday world of these children. This resource is letters from children talking about their experiences as children in families with alcoholism. The letters are well worth reading. Once you go to the NCAC website (www.nacoa.org/), on the left hand side (currently at the bottom of the list) is a section called "Just for Kids."

Many writers like Claudia Black and Robert Ackerman note the family system carries high levels of shame and denial. Rules that allow the substance using or abusing person to continue to use or abuse a substance include what goes on in the house stays among family only, what's happening isn't really real so do not trust what you see, and no one has the right to express what is really felt. There is a quiet unspoken acceptance of unacceptable behavior (Ackerman, 2002; Black, 2002).

In addition to this closed family system, each family member plays a role. Think of the HERO as proof that the family is OK. This is the captain of the team, the head cheerleader, the perfect child. The CLOWN tells jokes, creates comic relief, and distracts the family. The SCAPEGOAT is the child who gets blamed for everything that is wrong. The LOST CHILD is what it sounds like. No one knows this child is a part of the family. Being aware of the roles of the family is important for school counselors because these children can be very skillful at hiding the issue and protecting the family.

● CASE STUDIES

- Tommy is a 10-year-old boy who was missing several days of school. His dad is a businessman who travels a lot away from home. Mom is a stay-at-home mom. After a child neglect investigation by the state family services, it was learned that Tommy was caring for his two siblings and not attending school because mom was drinking daily.

Critical checkpoint—In the school setting, who needs to know about Tommy's family situation? How would you help?

- Courtney could not retain her math facts in first grade. The child study team could not determine what was creating her memory problems. An in-depth assessment from a neuro-developmental specialist revealed that Courtney had signs and symptoms of fetal alcohol syndrome.

Critical checkpoint—As the school counselor, how could you provide support for Courtney?

These two scenarios identify two important facts. Addiction is a family disease, and children are impacted through environmental causes as well as direct physical transmission.

● ACTIVITY

At times, it may be necessary to make a report of child abuse or neglect due to substance abuse in the family. Be familiar with the number and agency in your state to report child abuse. Do a mock report with another person so you know all the information details required to make a report.

● ADOLESCENT SUBSTANCE ABUSE

Adolescence is probably the most difficult age group in which to recognize abuse. What adolescent is NOT going through changes? Peer groups become more relevant and "understanding" than parents ever were. Developmentally, the need to explore and take risks is a part of learning. I am not going to list the drugs adolescents are currently using because they are constantly changing and shifting. However, I will provide you with an excellent resource that stays as current as possible (e.g., today is March 7, 2016, and the website was last updated on March 7, 2016.) The website is the National Institute on Drug Abuse for Teens and is sponsored by the National Institute of Health (teens.drugabuse.gov/interactives-and-videos).

● CASE STUDIES

Marijuana or Marijuana—No Problem

Roger was a 16-year-old student referred to counseling by his single-parent father. He had "caught" him using marijuana. Roger's parents divorced when Roger was 10 years old because of mom's drinking. Roger's relationship with his father was aloof and distant. Roger was an only child. Roger was depressed, isolating himself, and stopped participating in activities.

Critical checkpoint—Marijuana users are supposed to be "mellow" right? Substance abuse changes the brain in ways we are just beginning to understand. Roger's case pointed to many risk factors. Roger may be at risk for hurting himself, suicide, or suicide ideation. Make it a point to ask adolescents about their intentions and history of any type of suicidal behavior frequently.

Alcohol and an Adolescent's Social Life

Colin was an 18-year-old high school senior. He already has an academic scholarship for college and plans to "relax and enjoy the rest of senior year." Colin's approach to enjoying senior year is to do quite a bit of partying. He was at a party with some people he didn't know really well and did not pay attention to how many drinks he had that night. Not remembering how he got home, he woke to his mom knocking on the door with the police. He was being escorted to a local police department. At 180 pounds at 9 a.m., his blood alcohol was twice the legal limit. He was being questioned about an assault.

Critical checkpoint—Could this incident be prevented? School policies against alcohol on school property, early and frequent interventions with students and faculty encouraging health and wellness, and education about the effects of alcohol could be implemented. Identifying at-risk students (such as Roger and Colin) is important although not always possible.

Prescription Abuse

The National Institute for Drug Abuse (NIDA) reports that "Prescription drugs and over-the-counter drugs are among the most commonly abused drugs by 12th graders, after alcohol, marijuana, and tobacco. While past-year nonmedical use of sedatives and tranquilizers decreased among 12th graders over the last 5 years, this is not the case for the nonmedical use of amphetamines or opioid pain relievers." More than half of the 12th-grade students surveyed reported getting the drugs from friends or buying them from a friend or relative. NIDA (2015) reported that the prevalence of using the Internet to get drugs was negligible. Prescription and over-the-counter drugs are easily accessible to students.

Ever hear of pharm parties? Teens know. Robo hits? Both legal and over-the-counter medications are collected by young people to have at parties. Adolescents are using pharmaceuticals (pharm) and items like Robitussin (Robo) in conjunction with alcohol to get high. The problem comes from teens believing if given by a doctor or you can buy it over the counter, it cannot be harmful. Visit NIDA for Teens (teens.drugabuse.gov/peerx) to learn all you need to learn about abuse of drugs used for hyperactivity, pain relief, or cough and cold remedies.

The Adolescent Language of Drugs

Adolescents speak their own language. Drug-related language is varied so as to keep it out of view of adults. Labels for street drugs vary by region, neighborhood, or cultural group. The activity below provides extensive information on current drug terms and street names.

● ACTIVITY

Learn the common street names for most commonly abused drugs. NIDA's information on commonly abused drugs was updated in Oct 2015 (www.drugabuse.gov/sites/default/files/commonly_abused_drugs_august_2015.pdf).

● ACTIVITY

Talk to local law enforcement to discover what drugs are most found in your area.

● ACTIVITY

Go to the Drug Enforcement Agency website (www.dea.gov/index.shtml) to learn about an annual prevention campaign called Red Ribbon. Plan a Red Ribbon event.

● CONCLUSION

Working with families is extremely gratifying. This chapter was written to be a practical guide to help you help families. Issues of shame, denial, and silence can be dealt with through acceptance, honesty, and calling it what it is—a disease that can get better. With trained, caring listeners and helpers, families can thrive. Prevention is key. Intervention is required. Treatment can work.

With love and thanks to my family—

● TERMS

Addiction: obsessive/compulsive use of a substance despite continuing adverse consequences

Tolerance: ingesting more and more of a substance to reach desired effect

Withdrawal: changes in the body after cessation of a substance

Abuse pattern of behavior over a period of time that creates disruption in any area of living

Dependence: continued abusive use of a substance despite significant problems; can be physical and/or psychological

Cross-tolerance: resistance to drugs that comes from similar pharmacological classification

Route of transmission: method of ingestion a drug

Drug classifications: pharmacological effects of drugs in similar categories

Acute and chronic effects: short- and long-term ways substance impact health and well-being

● REFERENCES

Ackerman, R. (2002). *Perfect daughters: Adult daughters of alcoholics.* Deerfield Beach, FL: Health Communications.

Black, C. (2002). *It will never happen to me: Growing up with addiction as youngsters, adolescents, adults* (2nd ed.). Center City, MN: Hazelden.

Center for Application of Prevention Technology. (2015, September 30). Retrieved from http://www.samhsa.gov/capt/

Center for Substance Abuse Treatment. (2014). *Improving cultural competence* (Treatment Improvement Protocol [TIP] Series, No. 59). Rockville, MD: Substance Abuse and Mental Health Services Administration. Retrieved from http://www.ncbi.nlm.nih.gov/books/NBK248428/

Centers for Disease Control and Prevention. (2015, July). *Competency-based curriculum guide.* Retrieved from http://www.frfasd.org/Comp Guide.html

National Institute for Drug Abuse, NIDA for Teens. (2015, October 23). *The science behind drug abuse.* Retrieved from http://teens.drugabuse.gov/

Volkow, N. (2014). *Why do our brains get addicted?* [Video file]. Retrieved from http://tedmed.com/talks/show?id=309096

LESSON 15

THE SCHOOL COUNSELOR AND BULLYING PREVENTION

"What Is YOUR Role?"

Christy W. Land
University of West Georgia

Lauren Moss
Kutztown University of Pennsylvania

Real Life

Things seem to be unfolding well as you acclimate to your new role of "professional school counselor" until several days in a row students start coming into your office reporting a number of students "picking" on them on the bus and at the bus stop. You report their claims to administration, but your principal and assistant principal indicate that the bus driver should handle the reports. The reports continue over several days, and as you try to decide what to do next, the student reports start to include incidence of teasing and unkindness in the lunchroom, locker room, and hallways. Finally a parent contacts you and angrily indicates that the "bullying" her child is experiencing at school "needs to stop, NOW"!

Lesson Fifteen

The School Counselor and Bullying Prevention

"What Is YOUR Role?"

Christy W. Land
University of West Georgia

Lauren Moss
Kutztown University of Pennsylvania

Essential Question: What is the school counselor's role in the implementation of schoolwide bullying prevention initiatives?

Objectives

Students will

- demonstrate an understanding of bullying behaviors and associated physical, social, and emotional impact of involvement in bullying.
- understand the school counselor's role in bullying prevention.
- apply components of effective bullying prevention programs and interventions.
- develop knowledge of assessing schoolwide bullying prevention needs and interventions.

CACREP Standards

- School counselor roles as leaders, advocates, and systems change agents in P–12 schools (5.G.2.a)
- Qualities and styles of effective leadership in schools (5.G.2.j)
- Legal and ethical considerations specific to school counseling (5.G.2.n)
- Core curriculum design, lesson plan development, classroom management strategies, and differentiated instructional strategies (5.G.3.c)
- Techniques to foster collaboration and teamwork within schools (5.G.3.l)
- Use of data to advocate for programs and students (5.G.3.o)

Video Spark

http://www.cbsnews.com/video/watch/?id=7381364n

Bullying: Words Can Kill

• INTRODUCTION

Bullying among young people is a common and complex problem which may be most effectively addressed through the implementation of schoolwide bullying prevention initiatives that work to effectively change the overall school climate to one in which bullying is not tolerated (Davis & Nixon, 2011; Farrington & Ttofi, 2010; Goodwin, 2011; Pergolizzi et al., 2009; Serwacki & Nickerson, 2012; Young et al., 2009). *Bullying* is typically defined by researchers as aggressive behavior characterized by repetition of actions and an imbalance of power (Crothers & Kolbert, 2004; Espelage & Swearer, 2003;

Farrington & Ttofi, 2010; Olweus, 2007). Previously, scholars in the field described bullying behaviors as teasing and dismissed such behaviors as a part of normal childhood development (Stockdale, Hangaduambo, Duys, Larson, & Sarvela, 2002). However, characteristics of bullying distinguish such behavior from typical childhood nuances (Whitted & Duper, 2005). According to Dan Olweus, a leading scholar around research on the topic of bullying, a person is bullied or harassed when he or she is exposed, repeatedly and over time, to negative actions on the part of one or more other persons, and is unable to defend him or herself. Specifically, Olweus defined a negative act as one that intentionally attempts to inflict, or inflicts, injury or harm to another person. Unique to the school setting, the definition of bullying includes the presence of an imbalance of power where a more powerful young person oppresses a less powerful young person repeatedly over a prolonged period of time (Farrington & Ttofi, 2010; Olweus, 2007). Accordingly, the two characteristics that distinguish bullying behavior from other forms of aggressive behavior are an imbalance of power and repetition of actions over time (Crothers & Kolbert, 2004; Olweus, 2007; Pergolizzi et al., 2009).

The effects of bullying may range from loss of opportunity to loss of life. Depression, suicidal ideation, isolation, low self-esteem, and lack of hope are just a few of the characteristics evident in young people victimized as a result of bullying (Klomek et al., 2008; Lieberman & Cowan, 2011; Pranjic & Bajraktarevic, 2010). Anat Brunstein Klomek and colleagues (2008) and Sabaha Dracic (2009) found that frequent exposure to bullying was directly related to high risk of depression, suicidal ideation, and suicide attempts compared to students not victimized. These scholars note anxiety, feelings of being unsafe, loss of concentration, migraine headaches, inability to start or finish a task, and fear of going to school as consequential of repeated bullying.

• BULLYING PREVENTION

School officials may believe that bullying is not a problem in *their* school as teachers and administrators typically only witness about 4% of bullying incidents (Goodwin, 2011; Green, 2007). Moreover, many schools have multiple pressing problems to address, such as academic performance and standardized testing and, therefore, may unintentionally overlook obvious signs and acts associated with bullying (Green, 2007). Therefore, a critical first step to bullying prevention in schools is to eliminate the culture of denial, which should be followed by establishing an effective schoolwide bullying prevention initiative acceptable to all stakeholders (Austin, Reynolds, & Barnes, 2012; Goodwin, 2011; Serwacki & Nickerson, 2012; Whitted & Dupper, 2005).

What Is Bullying Prevention?

Many bullying prevention programs are based on the false assumption that the best way for victims to handle bullying is to utilize better coping mechanisms (Austin et al., 2012; Farrington & Ttofi, 2010; Whitted & Dupper, 2005). Effective anti-bullying programs are comprehensive and enlist the help and support of multiple stakeholders, including school staff, community members, parents, and students (Farrington & Ttofi, 2010; Serwacki & Nickerson, 2012; Whitted & Dupper, 2005). Furthermore, effective schoolwide bullying prevention programs work to change the school climate so that bullying behavior is viewed as socially unacceptable (Goodwin, 2011; Lieberman & Cowan, 2011; Serwacki & Nickerson, 2012; Whitted & Dupper, 2005).

Scholars have identified program components that are effective in reducing bullying and victimization and components that prove ineffective. David P. Farrington and Maria M. Ttofi (2010) conducted a meta-analysis of 44 anti-bullying program evaluations, all including data that permitted calculation for the effect size for bullying or victimization, and found that overall, schoolwide bullying prevention programs are effective in reducing bullying and victimization. The results of the meta-analysis, which systematically reviewed 26 years of bullying intervention research, indicated that on average bullying decreased by approximately 22% and victimization by approximately 19% when a schoolwide bullying prevention program was in place (Farrington & Ttofi). The researchers determined specific interventions and components of anti-bullying programs to decrease both bullying and victimization while other components negatively affect bullying reduction as evidenced by an increase in reported victimization. The researchers found the following program elements to be associated with a decrease in both bullying and victimization: (a) parent trainings and meetings; (b) disciplinary methods; (c) increased playground supervision, classroom management; (d) classroom rules; and (e) the duration and intensity of the program for the young people and the school staff (Farrington & Ttofi, 2010; Serwacki & Nickerson, 2012; Whitted & Dupper, 2005). Specifically, parent trainings, disciplinary methods, and duration and intensity of the program were shown to be most effective in decreasing victimization (Farrington & Ttofi, 2010; Serwacki & Nickerson, 2012; Whitted & Dupper, 2005). The results of Farrington and Ttofi's meta-analysis revealed that anti-bullying programs which utilized "work with peers" to be directly correlated to an increase of victimization for the young people that were bullied and in turn should not be used as an intervention (Crothers & Kolbert, 2004). To take case in point, bringing the bully and victim together for a peer mediation intervention only heightened the imbalance of power leading to future victimizations by the bully (Whitted & Dupper, 2009).

Disciplinary methods were an intervention component that was significantly associated with a decrease in both bullying and victimization (Farrington & Ttofi, 2010; Serwacki & Nickerson, 2012). Stan Davis and Charisse Nixon (2011) maintain that how schools plan and implement disciplinary actions make a difference. Disciplinary methods may include a range of firm sanctions such as having serious talks with the bullies, sending them to the principal, and depriving them of privileges. Davis and Nixon (2011) and Anita Young and colleagues (2009) found that when schools implement the following steps bullying behavior is most likely to decrease:

- Involve students and staff in the development of rules, expectations, and consequences for bullying related behaviors.
- Develop a schoolwide climate that is positive, warm, and nurturing that imposes fair consequences in a positive context.
- Develop a schoolwide rubric for addressing specific bullying behavior.
- Use smaller, consistent consequences and develop a progressive discipline process for addressing more serious actions.
- Have a schoolwide reporting system in place that addresses retaliation or threat of retaliation for reporting.

Based on Farrington and Ttofi's (2010) findings, anti-bullying programs need to be intensive and long lasting to have the greatest impact on this troubling issue (Goodwin, 2011). The most effective schoolwide anti-bullying programs and initiatives will be a collaborative and comprehensive effort between the school, families, and the community (Davis & Nixon, 2011; Serwacki & Nickerson, 2012; Young et al., 2009). David R. Whitted and Kathryn S. Dupper (2009) argue that one of the most common mistakes that schools make is implementing partial programs due to time constraints resulting in inadequate and sporadic ineffective interventions. Newer bullying prevention programs should be inspired by existing programs and should include the specific components that were found to be effective in decreasing both bullying and victimization (Farrington & Ttofi, 2010).

• TECHNOLOGY AND BULLYING

Although the standard definition of *bullying* with regard to relational terms remains the same regardless of context, the platform upon which bullying behavior takes place for students in the present may look vastly different from what bullying behavior looked like to current teachers, staff, parents, and administrators when they were school age. Elementary, middle, and high youth of today face relational challenges that extend beyond the classroom, playground, and neighborhood into the ever-evolving landscape of the Internet. The emergence of the Internet as a space occupied largely by youth has shifted movement of traditional types of bullying, such as teasing and name-calling, to bullying behaviors supported by a virtually endless buffet of websites and applications. This reality is intensified by students' ability to access and modify digital media and the dangerous capacity to spread damaging information at lightning speed in a form of abuse commonly known as cyberbullying.

The American School Counselor Association (ASCA) supports the Olweus Bullying Prevention Program's cyberbullying prevention curricula for Grades 3 to 12 (Limber, Kowalski, & Agatston, 2008, 2009). In this curriculum, Limber and associates indicate that *cyberbullying* occurs when children and youth use technology such as text messaging, Internet sites, and cell phones to bully others. Although technology is constantly evolving, with youth remaining on the cutting edge of how to apply current technology for both positive and devastating social interaction, ASCA (2012a) recommends several general strategies for school counselors and others to help keep cyberbullying in check.

Technology Awareness

ASCA (2012a) and Stopbullying.gov, a federal government website managed by the U.S. Department of Health & Human Services, offer suggestions regarding how adults can decrease the likelihood of cyberbullying. For example, remaining aware of technology and the way in which students are using technology is important (ASCA, 2012a, U.S. Department of Health & Human Services, n.d.). Specifically, keeping computers in open access areas and remaining aware that students can access the Internet from a variety of sources such as mobile phones, iPod touch devices, and handheld gaming devices will help adults remain in touch with students' technology. Seeing this type of awareness from adults keeps youth mindful that adults may review their online communications if there is reason for concern, perhaps mitigating poor technology use decision-making.

Communication Is Critical

By engaging students in regular conversation about their online presence and reinforcing the importance of responsible technology use, school counselors can begin to normalize dialogue about students' technology-supported activity. Furthermore, best practice for school counselors involves encouraging students to report any instances of online bullying they witness and to tell a trusted adult if they, or someone they know, become the victim of cyberbullying, cyberstalking, or other illegal or upsetting online behaviors (ASCA, 2012a). Overall, talking with children about the seriousness of online activity and cyberbullying, including the possibly devastating consequences for anyone involved, is critical for developing students' awareness of the issue of cyberbullying.

When Cyberbullying Occurs

Overall, it is important for school counselors to be sure students feel empowered to report instances of cyberbullying rather than feeling compelled to respond to instances of cyberbullying. Also, it is wise for parents and students to save (print or screen capture) any posts messages that may otherwise be deleted. When parents contact the school regarding instances of cyberbullying, school counselors rely heavily on local school policy administration to determine the most appropriate course of action. Instances of cyberbullying often occur outside of the school context, but the effects of actions that occurred online are brought into the school setting due to the emotional turmoil suffered consequentially. In such cases, the school counselor should work with students and families to report instances of bullying to the appropriate authorities. For example, sending vulgar language violates the terms and conditions of many e-mail services, Internet providers, websites, and applications. Students or parents can contact these websites or companies directly to get help blocking the perpetrator or removing offensive content (ASCA, 2012a).

However, if the school district's Internet network was used for reprehensible purposes, the school is likely obligated to respond consequentially, and typically works closely with administration to be sure victims and their families feel supported in disclosing such instances and also that appropriate intervention is provided for students demonstrating bullying behaviors. In the most severe situations, the U.S. Department of Health & Human Services (n.d.) indicates that cyberbullying can be considered a criminal offense, particularly if it includes

- threats of violence,
- child pornography or sending sexually explicit messages or photos,
- taking a photo or video of someone in a place where he or she would expect privacy, or
- stalking and hate crimes.

If any of the aforementioned behaviors are reported, the school counselor should work with local school administration to contact police regarding appropriate reporting procedures.

THE SCHOOL COUNSELOR'S ROLE IN BULLYING PREVENTION

The American School Counselor Association (ASCA) National Model for school counseling provides a framework for school counseling programs to reflect a comprehensive approach to program implementation (ASCA, 2012b). The ASCA National Model not only answers the questions "What do school counselors do?" but requires school counselors to respond to the question, "How are students different as a result of what we do?" (ASCA, 2012b). The American School Counselor Association position statement on bullying indicates that professional school counselors recognize the need for all students to attend school in a safe, orderly, and caring environment that promotes a positive school climate and fosters growth (ASCA, 2012b). Furthermore, the American School Counselor Association National Model emphasizes that professional school counselors are leaders in the school and community who serve as advocates for students and work in collaboration with other stakeholders to remove barriers to student success (ASCA, 2012b).

The American School Counselor Association (2012b) states that "school counselors should possess the knowledge, abilities, skills and attitudes necessary to plan, organize, implement and evaluate a comprehensive, developmental, results-based school counseling program that aligns with the ASCA National Model (p. 148). Professional school counselors practicing as social-justice change agents advocating for the implementation of schoolwide bullying prevention efforts align with many of the ASCA school counselor competencies.

COLLABORATION WITH ADMINISTRATORS AND STAFF FOR THE IMPLEMENTATION OF SCHOOLWIDE BULLYING PREVENTION INITIATIVES

School counselors as "change agents" must work closely with administrators to implement schoolwide bullying prevention policies and initiatives (ASCA, 2012b; Austin et al., 2012; Young et al., 2009). ASCA believes that "although the school principal serves as the head of the school and is ultimately responsible for student success, the school counselor plays a critical role in making student success a reality" (2012b, p. 17). Therefore, in this role of change agent, professional school counselors must work with administrators as a team to help teachers and other support staff to understand personal characteristics of their students and the role they may play in bullying and the overall school climate (Austin et al. 2012). Administrators need school counselors' perspectives on the overall school climate, and school counselors require administrative support. Whitted and Dupper (2009) argue that for bullying prevention initiatives to be successful administrators must openly demonstrate support of the initiatives which should be integrated into the overall school curriculum in order to obtain buy-in from school personnel.

Further, teachers will benefit from the school counselor's skills and knowledge related to bullying (ASCA, 2012b). Young et al. and Richard Lieberman and Katherine Cowan (2011) noted that bullying is a schoolwide issue; therefore, a comprehensive systemic approach requires the support and collaboration from all school personnel to effectively address the issue. Moreover, school counselors must work in collaboration with administrators to train staff members to understand bullying behavior and know the steps necessary to effectively deal with bullying (Green, 2007). Additionally, school personnel must be educated on the theoretical rationale on which schoolwide bullying prevention initiatives are based (Crothers & Kolbert, 2004).

Laura M. Crothers and Jered B. Kolbert (2004) suggested that school personnel overlook incidents of bullying due to the common misconception that bullying is a harmless rite of passage among young people (Robinson, 2010). Young et al. (2009) recommend that specific bullying prevention and intervention goals be created and added to the school's overall improvement plan. Administrators and staff can then identify specific work plans to address the issue of bullying and collect data to measure the effectiveness of interventions implemented schoolwide. Further, researchers found that students do not believe that the intervention strategies utilized by teachers will help the situation; therefore, often students fail to report bullying behavior (Crothers & Kolbert; Robinson, 2010; Young et al., 2009). Young and colleagues suggested establishing an anti-bullying website, monitored by the administrators and school counselors, which allows students to report bullying incidents anonymously.

School counselors must work with other stakeholders to challenge injustices when administrators work to maintain the status quo (Griffin & Steen, 2013). Therefore, school counselors must be able to effectively challenge injustices and question authority who is refusing to address barriers to success (Bemak & Chung, 2008). School counselors can use data as a transformative tool and share with administrators and staff to understand educational issues that prevent students from being successful and to evaluate and improve school counseling programs and initiatives such as bullying prevention (ASCA, 2012b; Young et al., 2009). Young et al. found that collecting, analyzing, and sharing data led to increased support from administrators and teachers for schoolwide bullying prevention initiatives and other school counseling services (ASCA, 2012b).

● COLLABORATION WITH PARENTS AND COMMUNITY MEMBERS FOR THE IMPLEMENTATION OF SCHOOLWIDE BULLYING PREVENTION INITIATIVES

School–family–community collaboration is defined as "collaborative relationships in which school counselors, school personnel, students, families, community members and other stakeholders work jointly to implement school and community based programs and activities that improve student academic achievement directly within schools, and indirectly by attending to the needs that may be hindering students and families from these accomplishments" (Griffin & Steen, 2010, p. 77). Furthermore, the focus on serving students and families must move beyond individual challenges to external factors that are barriers to success (ASCA, 2012b; Griffin & Steen, 2010; Lieberman & Cowan, 2011; Young et al., 2009).

Sheila Austin and colleagues (2012) recommend that agencies that have an identified role in crime prevention and intervention be a part of a local school's bullying prevention efforts. Specifically, it is recommended that secondary school resources, such as coaches and other enrichment teachers, be an integral component of schoolwide bullying prevention efforts (Austin et al., 2012; Lieberman & Cowan, 2011). Such components promote school and community involvement and encourage students to develop a sense of community and connectedness. Furthermore, when young people have strong connections with adults, they tend to be more resilient and are less likely to be emotional wounded if bullied (Davis & Nixon, 2011).

Farrington and Ttofi (2010) findings suggest that efforts should be made to educate parents about the harmful effects associated with bullying behavior through parent educational workshops and meetings, as this intervention was shown to significantly decrease rates of both bullying and victimization (Lieberman & Cowan, 2011). The more immersed parents become with regard to bullying the more likely they will be to inquire about their children's experiences fostering an opportunity for open and effective communication if victimization occurs.

Activity: What Does Bullying Look Like? (Case Study)

Participants will demonstrate an understanding of bullying behaviors and associated physical, social, and emotional impact of involvement in bullying through the examination of a relevant case study. The participants will identify and discuss the potential impact of bullying behavior on the student's academic, personal/social, and career-oriented development. The participants will discuss the school counselor's role and potential course of action for the case study.

Materials

- "I Am Not Going to School" Case Study
- "If This Were My Student" Worksheet

● "I AM NOT GOING TO SCHOOL": A CASE STUDY

You are a professional school counselor at a middle school. You are contacted via phone by a parent of a sixth grader, Claire Smith. "Mrs. Smith" shares she is concerned her daughter "Claire" is avoiding coming to school and she is at her "wits end." Mrs. Smith states for the last month, several times a week, Claire wakes up saying that she does not feel well and is unable to go to school. Claire complains of headaches, stomachaches, and dizziness. Mrs. Smith explained she finally took Claire to her pediatrician earlier in the week and the doctor found no underlying physical ailments to explain Claire's physical symptoms. However, during the visit, the doctor suggested Mrs. Smith talk to Claire about how she is feeling emotionally and inquire if there are any concerns with her friends, peers at school, or teachers.

Much to Mrs. Smith's surprise on the car ride home from the doctor, Claire opened up to her mother that someone she considered a close friend posted a horrible comment about Claire on social media that many of her friends and classmates saw and commented on the post, and now all of the sixth grade "hates her." Claire told her mother that many of students have been saying hurtful things to her, excluding her from the lunch table for the last month, and even aggressively pushing past her in the hallway. Mrs. Smith tells you that she feels awful for not realizing this was going on. She is asking for your help with the situation. In your role as a professional school counselor, how do you proceed?

● "IF THIS WERE MY STUDENT" WORKSHEET

Based on your school's definition of *bullying*, do you believe that Claire is being bullied? Why or why not?

____

____

Is Claire exhibiting symptoms associated with involvement in bullying? If so, what?

____

____

First, I would: ____

____

Then, I would: ____

____

Next, I would: ____

____

I would consult and collaborate with the following stakeholders; ______________________

____

Questions I have are: ____

____

Overall thoughts about Claire's case: ______________________________________

____

____

Procedures

1. The instructor will review the following definition of *bullying*: A person is bullied or harassed when he or she is exposed, repeatedly and over time, to negative actions on the part of one or more other persons and is unable to defend him or herself (Olweus, 2007).
2. The instructor will facilitate a discussion of bullying behaviors, asking the following questions: What are some of incidents of bullying you have observed or encountered? What are some examples of physical, verbally, and relational bullying?
3. The instructor will review the harmful effects associated with involvement in bullying behavior to include the impact on academic performance, social/emotional functioning, and overall mental health.

4. Participants will review and briefly discuss the accompanying case study. The instructor may facilitate a large-group discussion or divide the class into small breakout groups for discussion based on the number of participants.
5. Individuals will complete the "If This Were My Student" worksheet.

Processing

- In your setting, how will you establish a schoolwide definition of *bullying*?
- How will you educate and raise awareness with stakeholders on the importance of prioritizing bullying prevention?
- As a school counselor how will you educate various stakeholders on the harmful effects associated with involvement in bullying?

Activity: How to Determine Bullying Prevention Needs

Participants will consider the state of bullying at a given setting by analyzing available data and discussing applicable data with professionals and preprofessionals in order to draft a student survey for a specific school setting that could be used by a school counselor to gain further insight into appropriate bullying prevention needs and interventions.

Materials

- School data (attendance data, bullying report data, etc.)
- Paper/pencil or computer

Procedures

1. Consider your current field experience placement. Discuss presenting bullying needs or issues with classmates, on-site supervisor, and/or university supervisor.
2. Think about your observations in the school and existing school data in a way that begins to offer you a "whole picture" about how bullying manifests at the school in question (i.e., What form of bullying most often takes place? Where are most incidences of bullying occurring? To whom do students most often report incidence of bullying?).
3. As you analyze the data (i.e., school attendance data, bullying reports, discipline reports, etc.), consider your impressions, discuss your thoughts with others, and record any themes or questions you have about the nature and reporting of bullying at the given setting.
4. Determine questions you still have about bullying in the given setting (i.e., Why aren't students reporting incidence of bullying to teachers? Why are most reported cases of bullying occurring in the locker room? What indicators prompt a student to report a bullying incident rather than ignore it?).
5. Based on the exploratory steps above, draft a brief survey that could be given to students in your setting to help the school counselor more specifically determine appropriate bullying prevention needs and interventions.

Processing

- What themes stuck out to you when reviewing the data?
- What were you able to infer from the data?
- What questions lingered even after discussing the data and your anecdotal impressions with professionals and/or preprofessionals in the school counseling field?
- Based on "gaps" in the data, what survey questions did you draft that would help a school counselor more specifically determine the school's bullying prevention needs and appropriate interventions?

Activity: Bullying Prevention Toolbox

Participants will identify interventions to support effective schoolwide bullying prevention programs. Participants will also pinpoint strategies to work with individuals and in small-group settings to prevent bullying in their setting. The interventions and lessons will be based on the ASCA National Model.

Materials

- Sticky notes (several for each participant)
- Whiteboard and marker
- ASCA standards, mindsets and behaviors

Procedures

1. The facilitator will discuss components of effective bullying prevention program and ASCA's position at bullying prevention. The following article, "Schoolwide Bullying Prevention," may serve as a resource for discussion: https://www.schoolcounselor.org/magazine/blogs/july-august-2011/schoolwide-bully-prevention (Burnham, 2011).
2. The facilitator will share two or three examples of bullying prevention interventions. (e.g., a schoolwide bullying prevention kick-off week, a classroom guidance lesson on conflict resolution).
3. The facilitator will write the following on a whiteboard or poster board: "What is in your bullying prevention toolbox?"
4. The facilitator will distribute several sticky notes to each participant and instruct they will have 3 minutes to brainstorm an effective bullying prevention intervention or lesson. At the end of the 3 minutes, the participants will place their sticky notes on the whiteboard under the question "What is in your bullying prevention toolbox?"
5. As a large group, the participants will discuss the interventions on the sticky notes and place them in the following categories: schoolwide interventions, classroom lessons, and individual or small-group interventions.
6. Next, the facilitator will divide the large group into small working groups based on the aforementioned categories. The working groups will use the ideas from the "sticky note storm" to construct two lessons plans for their given categories.
7. Each work group will share with the large group the lesson or activity their group designed.

Processing

- What is an effective schoolwide bullying prevention intervention at the elementary-school level?
- What type of small group could you implement at the middle or high school level to address bullying prevention?
- What teaching trainings or professional development workshops would you offer at your school to address bullying prevention?
- What types of parent workshops would you implement in your school to support the school's bullying prevention initiatives?

Activity: Collaboration Is Key

Participants will consider stakeholders who could serve as bullying prevention partners at a targeted site (i.e., field experience placement site).

Materials

- Poster board or butcher paper
- Markers

Procedures

1. Consider your current field experience placement or another school setting with which you are familiar.
2. On your poster board or butcher paper, create a visual map of all the stakeholders you can think of for the setting in question. This should involve school-based stake holders (e.g., teachers, administrators, support staff, students, parent–teacher association members) in addition to community stake holders (e.g., parents, community leaders, local organizations, local businesses, local political leaders, religious organization leaders).
3. Use the following symbols on your visual stakeholder map to denote various stakeholder characteristics: a star (*) by stakeholders who have *critical involvement* in bullying prevention initiatives (i.e., administrators); a dollar sign ($) by stakeholders who control potentially available *financial resources* to fund bullying prevention efforts; a plus sign (+) by stakeholders who may possibly be able to offer time in support of bullying prevention efforts; an arrow (>) by stakeholders who possess a particular skill, talent, or expertise that could be utilized in support of bullying prevention initiatives; and a question mark (?) for stakeholders who you would consider involving in bullying prevention initiatives but you are not sure what they can contribute.
4. Think about the bullying problems at this school and the school's bullying prevention needs. This could be preventative in nature (i.e., increasing kindness and facilitating continued appropriate bullying incident reporting) or responsive to a current urgency related to bullying (i.e., a sudden increase in severity or number of bullying incident reports). Record these needs and problems.
5. Considering the needs and problems you recorded, take an inventory of the stakeholder poster you created.

6. Blend the drafted needs and stakeholder poster to draft a *Collaborative Bullying Prevention/ Intervention Plan* for the school in focus. Take into account how you can best leverage all stakeholders in a way which capitalizes on available resources and involves those with a vested interest in improving the state of the school's bullying circumstances.

7. Share your Collaborative Bullying Prevention/Intervention Plan with a school counselor, school counselor educator, or counselor-in-training. Elicit feedback around how you might improve your plan.

Processing

- When taking an inventory of stakeholders for your given community, what surprised you? For example, were there any stakeholders you originally overlooked or stakeholders that you feel should be involved in bullying prevention initiatives, yet you felt unsure how to integrate them?
- How did you experience the process of writing your Collaborative Bullying Prevention/ Intervention Plan? What did you find challenging? What did you find exciting?
- Which parts or steps of your Collaborative Bullying Prevention/Intervention Plan do you think would be easiest and most difficulty to implement? Why?

Activity: What Is Your Digital Footprint?

Participants will identify a social media awareness project to implement at their field experience site to demonstrate the power of posting to various social media platforms.

Materials

- Whiteboard
- Markers
- Computer/Internet Access

Procedures

1. The facilitator will spark a discussion about the professional school counselor's role in the prevention of cyberbullying and the importance of leaving a positive digital footprint. Special attention should be placed on using social media outlets as a form of positive communication and interaction. The facilitator may want to use resources from stopbullying.gov to further introduce this topic.

2. The facilitator will write the words *Social Media Awareness Project* in a large white circle on the whiteboard. The participants will brainstorm various ways that they can bring awareness to positive social media interaction at the field experience sites.

3. Participants should write their brainstorming ideas around the circle on the board.

4. The instructor should facilitate a discussion of the brainstorming ideas to help participants narrow down a social media awareness project that they can implement at their own field experience site.

5. If time allows, participants should start to work on their social media awareness projects.

6. Some examples of projects may include a "Post Something Positive Challenge" or "A Picture Is Worth a Thousand Words"—How many likes can my picture get?

Processing

- What follow-up activity or lesson can you implement in your setting after you have put into action your social media awareness project?
- What are some additional strategies and interventions that professional school counselors can implement in their settings to promote positive interactions online?
- How can professional school counselors educate various stakeholders on cyber safety?

REFERENCES

American School Counselor Association. (2012a). *Prevent and address cyberbullying behaviors*. Retrieved from https://www.schoolcounselor.org/magazine/blogs/may-june-2012/prevent-and-address-cyberbullying-behaviors

American School Counselor Association. (2012b). *The ASCA National Model: A framework for school counseling programs*. Alexandria, VA: Author.

Austin, S. M., Reynolds, G. P., & Barnes, S. L. (2012). School leadership and counselors working together to address bullying. *Education School Leadership, 133*(2), 283–291.

Bemak, F., & Chung, R. C. (2008). New professional roles and advocacy strategies for school counselors: A multicultural/social justice perspective to move beyond the nice counselor syndrome. *Journal of Counseling and Development, 86,* 219–227.

Burnham, B. (2011). *Schoolwide bullying prevention*. Retrieved from https://www.schoolcounselor.org/magazine/blogs/july-august-2011/schoolwide-bully-prevention

Crothers, L. M., & Kolbert, J. M. (2004). Comparing middle school teachers' and students' views on bullying and antibullying interventions. *Journal of School Violence, 3*(1), 17–34.

Davis, S., & Nixon, C. (2011). What students say about bullying. *Education Leadership, 9,* 18–23.

Dracic, S. (2009). Bullying and peer victimization. *Materia Socio Medica, 21*(4), 216–221.

Espelage, D. L., & Swearer, S. M. (2003). Research on school bullying and victimization: What have we learned and where do we go from here? *School Psychology Review, 32*(3), 365–383.

Farrington, D. P., & Ttofi, M. M. (2010). School-based program to reduce bullying and victimization. *Campbell Systematic Reviews, 6,* 1–149.

Goodwin, B. (2011). Bullying is common and subtle. *Educational Leadership, 69*(1), 82–84.

Green, G. (2007). Bullying: A concern for survival. *Education, 128*(2), 333–338.

Griffin, D., & Steen, S. (2010). A social justice approach to school counseling. *Journal for Social Action in Counseling and Psychology, 3*(1), 74–87.

Klomek, A. B., Sourander, A., Niemela, S., Kumpulainen, K., Piha, J. Tamminen, T., . . . & Gould, M. S. (2008). Childhood bullying behaviors as a risk for suicide attempts and completed suicides: A population-based birth cohort study. *Journal of the American Academy of Child Adolescent Psychiatry, 48*, 254–261.

Lieberman, R., & Cowan, K. (2011). *Bullying and youth suicide: Breaking the connection*. Retrieved from http://www.readbag.com/nasponline-resources-principals-bullying-suicide-oct2011

Limber, S., Kowalski, R. M., & Agatston, P. W. (2008). *Cyber bullying: A prevention curriculum for grades 6–12*. Center City, MN: Hazelden.

Limber, S., Kowalski, R. M., & Agatston, P. W. (2009). *Cyber bullying: A prevention curriculum for grades 3–5*. Center City, MN: Hazelden.

Olweus, D. (2007). *Bullying prevention program teacher guide*. Center City, MN: Hazelden.

Pergolizzi, F., Richmond, D., Macario, S., Gan, Z., Richmond, C., & Macario, E. (2009). Bullying in middle schools: Results from a four-school survey. *Journal of School Violence, 8,* 264–279.

Pranjic, N., & Bajraktarevic, A. (2010). Depression and suicide ideation among secondary school adolescents involved in school bullying. *Primary Health Care Research & Development, 11*, 349–362.

Robinson, K. (2010). Bullies and victims: A primer for parents. *Helping Children at Home and School, 3,* 1–3.

Serwacki, M., & Nickerson, N. B. (2012). *Guide to school-wide bullying prevention programs.* Retrieved from http://gse.buffalo.edu/gsefiles/documents/alberti/Bullying%20Prevention%20Program%20Guide%20-%20FINAL%203.16.12.pdf

Stockdale, M. S., Hangaduambo, S., Duys, D., Larson, K., & Sarvela, P. D. (2002). Rural elementary students', parents', and teachers' perception of bullying. *American Journal of Health Behavior, 26,* 226–227.

U.S. Department of Health & Human Services. (n.d.). *Cyber bullying.* Retrieved from http://www.stopbullying.gov/

Whitted, K. S., & Dupper, D. R. (2005). Best practices for bullying preventing or reducing bullying in schools. *Children and Schools, 27*(3), 167–177.

Young, A., Hardy, V., Hamilton, C., Biernesser, K., Sun, L.-L., & Niebergall, S. (2009). Empowering students: Using data to transform a bullying prevention and intervention program. *Professional School Counseling, 12*(6), 413–420.

PART IV

SKILLS/INTERVENTIONS

Lesson 16

CLASSROOM BEHAVIORAL OBSERVATIONS

". . . becoming part of the furniture"

Real Life

A counselor-in-training is asked to observe a second-grade student in a self-contained regular education classroom. The teacher requested the observation. The referral sheet indicated that "Christopher seemed fine at the beginning of the year, but now seems to have attentional issues. He is off-task quite a bit and cannot sit still."

The observations took place over 2 days. Day 1: Christopher was off-task approximately 78% of the time. During a 30-minute observation, he went to the coat area four times and touched his coat and backpack. The teacher called him back to his table, and he returned immediately. He was off-task, demonstrating behaviors such as chatting with classmates, looking out the window, for example. Day 2: Christopher was off-task approximately 92% of the time. During circle time, Christopher returned to his desk six times, put his hands inside of the desk, was redirected by the teacher and returned to circle time.

The counselor-in-training then met one-on-one with Christopher. The counselor gathered information about Christopher's current grade, the return from summer, and so on. Christopher shared that his parents were not living together anymore and his older two brothers (who attended the same school) now lived with his dad, while he and his younger sister (preschool) moved to a new apartment and live with mom. Christopher reported that he was not allowed to take many things with him because the apartment was small. He also reported that this is the first time he is taking the bus and coming to school without his brothers. Christopher then explained that one of his brothers "sneaks" little toys from home to him; he keeps them in his desk and feels better if he can touch them.

The report of this observation and the follow-up interview with the student indicated that Christopher was experiencing anxiety due to a familial situation and that his behavior may be a manifestation of a current stressor. This observation demonstrates the importance of behavioral observation and a holistic approach to working with students.

Lesson Sixteen

Classroom Behavioral Observations

". . . becoming part of the furniture"

Essential Question: How do I competently observe behavior and generate information that facilitates student success?

Objectives

Students will

- demonstrate use of information from behavioral observations while they critically examine the connections between social, familial, emotional, and behavior problems and academic achievement.
- demonstrate use of information from behavioral observations in developing strategies that promote equity in student achievement.
- demonstrate techniques for collaboration and teamwork through their participation in the comprehensive evaluation process.

CACREP Standards

- Demonstrate skills to critically examine the connections between social, familial, emotional, and behavior problems and academic achievement. (5.G.3.h)
- Demonstrate strategies to promote equity in student achievement. (5.G.3.k)
- Demonstrate techniques to foster collaboration and teamwork within schools. (5.G.3.l)

MPCAC Standards

- human development and wellness across the life span

Video Spark

https://www.teachingchannel.org/blog/2014/08/14/observation-challenge-what-do-you-see/

An Observation Challenge: What Do You See?

• CLASSROOM OBSERVATIONS: A 3-PHASE LEARNING EXPERIENCE

Phase 1: Knowledge—Read the material provided in this chapter and use the IRIS website for additional information and examples.

Phase 2: Skill—Do two classroom observations at your site. Coordinate with your site supervisor the scheduling of those observations. Post the two observations on the online learning management system.

Phase 3: Reflection—Read your colleagues observations. Blog constructive feedback to your colleagues on the strength of their observations and also on how to improve their observations.

• INTRODUCTION

Behavioral observations are a source of invaluable information and an opportunity for collaboration. Teachers, school psychologists, administrators, special education specialists, and other professionals in the school setting often rely on the school counselor to do behavioral observations. The purpose for an observation varies widely. Observations may stem from academic performance, behavioral concerns or a teacher's request for feedback. Observations are often part of a student's comprehensive evaluation that ultimately determines if a student is eligible for services or accommodations. Hence, this is a very important skill and the information generated from observations is significant. However, the difficulty and level of specificity required in observing student behavior is often underestimated. To produce reliable data, the counselor-in-training should receive training and do classroom observations as part of their field experience. Performing accurate observations require a specific set of skills. This lesson will teach how to do behavioral observations, the various methods of observations with specific guidelines, and includes a field experience requirement implementing what has been learned.

What is a behavioral observation? In order to make sound decisions regarding students, decisions must be based on reliable information. Behavioral observation is a widely used method of behavioral assessment. Behavioral observations systematically measure the frequency, duration, and context of behavior through observing and recording the behavior. Behavioral observations focus on collecting data and information on objective behaviors. Perceptions, motivations, and possible hypotheses are not included in a behavioral observation.

Creating a naturalistic context for observations. School counseling departments have a culture of their own. Some tend to be out and about—in the hallways, in the cafeteria, in classrooms. Some tend to do most of their work in their office. (Discussion: What is the culture of your site?) Creating the natural context of school counselors in the classroom can be the first step in being able to do accurate behavioral observations. The goal of a behavioral observation is to have students behave as they would if the school counselor was not in the room. One way to accomplish this is for the students to be comfortable and familiar with the school counselor in the classroom. The counselor is just part of the normal classroom environment and is less likely to change behavior patterns.

The Referral: Having a referral form for behavioral observations will provide the counselor with the information needed to focus on behaviors of concern. Counselors are often approached in the hallway, in meetings, on the way to the restroom—and asked to attend to a student situation. I often refer to these interactions as "drive-bys." Having teachers complete a form prompts them to focus, provide the reason for the referral, and to be specific. If the teacher's concerns about the student are amorphous, going into the observation with that knowledge also guides the format the observation will take.

Place and Time: Best practice recommends that observations take place in a variety of settings. These settings include the classroom, the cafeteria, the playground, physical education class, sports practices, and the library. In addition, the time of observations should also vary. Students' behavior can vary greatly first thing in the morning, before lunch, after lunch, and the last period of the day.

Observational Methods: There are multiple approaches to recording behavior. These methods are narrative, event recording, interval sampling, and rating scales. The behavior of other students or the norm for the classroom should be noted. Examples of each method are included in this chapter. In addition, sample forms are included for your use.

Narrative recording is a written descriptive account of a student's behavior. In essence, it is a running record of everything the child does. Narrative recordings are open ended and provide a comprehensive picture of the student's behaviors, responses, context, and interactions. There are multiple approaches to narrative observations. This chapter provides forms for each of the observation methods.

Event/Frequency recording observes when a specific behavior takes place and records the frequency of the behavior. Event recording is very useful when observing behavior that has a discrete beginning and ending. John Hintze, Robert Volpe, and Edward Shapiro (2002) write that event recording works well for behaviors such as throwing paper airplanes or raising of a hand during class.

Duration recording observes behaviors that do not have a discrete beginning and ending. For example, duration recording would be appropriate for behaviors such as being off-task or having a tantrum. Hence, the occurrence of the behavior and the duration of the behavior are recorded.

Interval recording examines whether or not a specific behavior is occurring at predetermined intervals (for example, every 2 minutes). It is considered a shortcut procedure and used most often when time and resources are not available. Interval recording can be used to observe behaviors such as reading during a reading assignment. There are multiple approaches to interval recording. Two approaches are whole-interval recording and partial-interval recording. Whole-interval recording requires the target behavior to be present throughout the entire interval. Partial-interval recording records if the behavior occurred anytime during the interval.

Rating scales provide a more structured technique for observing and recording behavior.

Factors to Consider and Document During Observations

1. Purpose of the observation—student behavior, teacher management and teaching style, class content, class format. The purpose of the observation will drive which observational method will be used.
2. Context—Physical set-up of the classroom, number of students, time of day, classroom atmosphere, academic content, type of instructional activity, student grouping. Context greatly impacts human behavior thus information on the environment is essential.
3. Behaviors observed—In addition to the targeted behavior to be observed (as identified in the purpose of the observation), interactions between the student and teacher and interaction with peers may be included in an observation.

Writing Up the Observation

Behavioral. Behavioral. Behavioral. The importance of a behavioral observation without extraneous impressions or perceptions cannot be stressed enough. Information from observations of students must be accurate, behavioral, and professionally written.

● ONLINE OBSERVATION LESSON RESOURCE

This resource is one of the best educational sites I have found. It is also free and available to all students and educators. The lesson on observations cannot be beat!

Resource: http://iris.peabody.vanderbilt.edu/iris-resource-locator/?term=behavior-classroom-management

Classroom Observation Lesson: Using the Web resource above, complete the IRIS Resource Center "Behavior and Classroom Management," Section: Case Studies—Measure Behavior. Read the Case Study Unit and answer the questions after each case study.

Materials: Sample forms are provided in Appendix A, B, and C. Also, the IRIS Center provides multiple forms to be used for classroom observations.

● REFERENCES

Council for Accreditation for Counseling and Related Program. (2014). *2016 standards*. Retrieved from www.cacrep.org

Hintze, J. M., Volpe, R. J., & Shapiro, E. S. (2002). Best practices in the systematic direct observation of student behavior. *Best Practices in School Psychology, 4,* 993–1006.

IRIS Center, Peabody College Vanderbilt University. (2015). *Behavior and classroom management*. Retrieved from http://iris.peabody.vanderbilt.edu

Masters in Psychology and Counseling Accreditation Council. (2015). *Accreditation manual*. Retrieved from http://www.mpcacaccreditation.org/about/accreditation-manual

● APPENDIX A

Narrative Observation Sample Form

Student Name: ______________________________ **Grade:** ______________

Class Observed: ____________________ **Teacher:** ______________________

Referral reason for observation:

____

____

____

____

Behavioral Observation	*Notes*

● APPENDIX B

A-B-C Observation Sample Form

Student Name: ______________________________ **Grade:** ______________

Class Observed: ____________________________ **Teacher:** ______________

Referral reason for observation:

____

____

____

____

Antecedent	**Behavioral**	**Consequence**
Teacher asks students to line up to go to the library.	Joe (student being observed) stays at his desk and looks through his books.	Teacher redirects Joe and tells him to join the other students.

● APPENDIX C

Frequency Observation Sample Form

Student Name: ______________________________ **Grade:** ______________

Class Observed: ______________________ **Teacher:** ______________________

Referral reason for observation:

____

____

____

____

X = Behavior occurrence; O = Non-occurrence

Identified Behavior (examples)	*(e.g., 30-Minute Class) 9:05—9:35*	*(e.g., 30-Minute Class) 11—11:30*	*(e.g., 30-Minute Class) 1:15—1:45*	*(e.g., 30-Minute Class) 2:30—3:15*
Twirling and flipping hair	XXXX	XX	XX	XXXXX
Distracting neighbors (e.g., talking to them)	XXX	XXXX	XXXXX	XXXXXX
Banging pencil/pen	X	O	O	O
Walking around the classroom	O	O	O	O

● APPENDIX D

Duration Observation Sample Form

***A stopwatch is helpful with this type of observation.**

Student Name: ______________________________ **Grade:** ______________

Class Observed: ______________________ **Teacher:** ______________________

Referral reason for observation:

____

____

____

____

Identified Behavior: Off-task	*(e.g. 30-minute class) 9:05—9:35*	*(e.g. 30-minute class) 11—11:30*	*(e.g. 30-minute class) 1:15—1:45*	*(e.g. 30-minute class) 2:30—3:15*
e.g., Looking out window				
e.g., Putting color pencils in the order of the rainbow				
e.g., Pencil sharpening				

● APPENDIX E

Interval Observation Sample Form

Student Name: ______________________ **Grade:** ______________

Class Observed: ____________________ **Teacher:** ______________

Referral reason for observation:

____

____

____

____

(e.g., 1-minute intervals over a 15-minute observation)

Minute #	*Interval #*										*Observations*
	1	**2**	**3**	**4**	**5**	**6**	**7**	**8**	**9**	**10**	
1											
2											
3											
4											
5											
6											
7											
8											
9											
10											
11											
12											
13											
14											
15											

LESSON 17

SCHOOL COUNSELING CORE CURRICULUM AND HOW TO WRITE A LESSON PLAN

"If Plan 'A' didn't work, the alphabet has 25 more letters! Stay cool."

—hatchbuck.com

Real Life

Intern: "When I was doing the Orientation Checklist, one item I was having difficulty gathering information about is the school counseling core curriculum. My site supervisor said that there is one, but she cannot tell me exactly where it is. Some counselors in the office say it is in the district office. While other counselors say, 'There really isn't one. And besides, the schedule doesn't allow time for us to go into the classroom very often.' I know some of the other interns have located the K–12 school counseling core curriculum."

Faculty Supervisor: "Districts vary on whether they have an identified school counseling core curriculum, whether time is set in the schedule for that curriculum, and the level of administrative support for its implementation."

Lesson Seventeen

School Counseling Core Curriculum and How to Write a Lesson Plan

"If Plan 'A' didn't work, the alphabet has 25 more letters! Stay cool."

—hatchbuck.com

Essential Question: What is the school counselor's role in curriculum development and how do I write a lesson plan?

Objectives

Students will

- demonstrate an awareness of the importance of curriculum design, lesson plan development, and differentiated instructional strategies.
- demonstrate ability to collaborate with teachers in order to develop interdisciplinary curricula and lesson plans.
- demonstrate ability to implement the school counseling core curriculum.
- demonstrate the ability to write standards-based lesson plans.

CACREP 2016 Standards

- Demonstrate understanding of curriculum design, lesson plan development, classroom management, and differentiated instructional strategies (5.G.3.c)
- Demonstrate ability to implement techniques of academic, career, and person/social counseling in a school setting (5.G.3.f)
- Demonstrate techniques to foster collaboration and teamwork within schools (5.G.3.l)
- Demonstrate the skills to critically examine the connections between social, familial, emotional, and behavior problems and academic achievement (5.G.3.h)

MPCAC Standards

- Assessment of human behavior and organizational/community/institutional systems

Video Spark

https://www.youtube.com/watch?v=fUXdrl9ch_Q

good teamwork and bad teamwork (ants, crabs, and penguins)

http://tedxteen.com/talks/tedxteen-2014-london/259-josh-valman-challenge-convention

Challenge Convention (Josh Valman)

INTRODUCTION

Developing and implementing a school counseling core curriculum takes (a) collaboration and teamwork, (b) the ability to challenge the norm through leadership, (c) courage, and (d) knowing how to write a lesson plan. This lesson is going to provide you with information about developing a school counseling core curriculum and will teach you how to write a lesson plan.

SCHOOL COUNSELING CORE CURRICULUM

The American School Counselor Association (ASCA) National Model (2012) provides standards for the school counseling core curriculum. These are national standards that provide the foundation for your school counseling core curriculum. The ASCA standards address curriculum meeting the needs of students in their academic development, career development, and their personal/social development. In addition, many (but not all) states have standards for social and emotional curricula. Check your state Department of Education's website for information regarding these standards.

As the chapter title indicates, school districts may not have a comprehensive PreK–12 school counseling core curriculum. Some districts may have the curriculum but are not implementing them due to time constraints, budget constraints, or a host of other reasons. Unfortunately, when a comprehensive school counseling core curriculum is not being implemented, what often happens are what is known as the "one-and-done" events. These educational programs (albeit implemented with good intents) tend to be reactive (once an event or tragedy has occurred) or if preventatives are adrift without mooring. The effectiveness of these programs is variable at best.

Development of a PreK–12 developmental, comprehensive school counseling core curriculum is the key to presenting a cohesive educational program. Best practice in education is to prepare the student for the content to be taught, teach the content, follow up on the presented content, assess student knowledge and effectiveness of the lesson, revise the lesson, and teach again as needed.

Collaboration and teamwork: Collaboration with administrators and faculty is essential to the implementation of a comprehensive school counseling core curriculum. There are two reasons collaboration and teamwork are essential: (1) scheduling and (2) interdisciplinary curricular development. Scheduling is challenging and can be problematic. Many schools do not schedule time to implement a school counseling core curriculum. Hence, it requires collaboration with administrators to schedule time into the already overscheduled time in the students' day. Advocacy and education regarding the importance of the school counseling core curriculum to academic, career, and personal success are an important part of this discussion.

Interdisciplinary curricular development and implementation is an underutilized strategy to achieve the goal of meeting the academic, career, and personal/social standards. One lesson I learned about school counseling core curriculum implementation was that I did not have to do it all by myself. And, in fact, couldn't do it by myself due to lack of time and resources. Working with the teachers, your colleagues, not only facilitates curriculum coverage, but it also provides an opportunity for teamwork. The more school counselors become part of the team and are perceived as team players, the more likely it is that teachers will understand the role of the school counselor and the importance of the school counseling core curriculum and gain clarity on the goals and rationale for making time in their busy schedule to collaborate. Interdisciplinary lesson plans are provided at the end of this chapter to illustrate this collaborative approach.

Challenge the norm through leadership: Although leadership has always been part of the role of the school counselor, an increased awareness of the importance of leadership is seen throughout current literature. At times, school counselors work within a system that does not have or may not utilize an existing comprehensive, developmental school counseling core curriculum. As with most norms, they evolve over time and become an accepted standard. So—let's challenge this norm.

Using the ASCA National Model and state standards as a guiding educational practice, presenting the importance and need for the school counseling core curriculum is essential. Many school counselors are hesitant to take a leadership role—but times have changed. The role of the school counselor requires leadership skills. These skills include advocating for the students' needs to be met. Students now more than ever need and deserve to have a developmentally appropriate school counseling core curriculum addressing their academic needs, their careers need in today's global economy, and their ability to be socially and personally successful.

How do school counselors accomplish this? Collect data, get out of the office, and be a positive presence in the school day. Be seen, collaborate with administrators and faculty, and stand tall—be a leader. If you aren't as strong a leader as you would like to be right now, use the "fake it until you make it" strategy. Hold your head high, do your homework, be prepared, and be an excellent listener. As you gain experience, your leadership skills will evolve. Leadership will be discussed fully in a later chapter in this book.

Courage: I added courage because many school counseling interns face writing their first lesson plan and teaching for the first time in a classroom when they are required to implement a classroom school counseling core lesson. At one time, you had to be a teacher before you could be a school counselor. That is no longer a requirement in most states. Hence, this is an opportunity to implement a strategy we often teach our students—"let's reframe!" Teaching classroom school counseling core lessons provides school counselors with an opportunity to develop new skills—both people skills (e.g., classroom management) and academic skills (developing curriculum and writing lesson plans). Classroom management is covered later in this book.

● HOW TO WRITE A LESSON PLAN

A lesson plan is a guide, a manual, and a road map. It is the documentation of what content is to be taught and how it will be taught. Lesson plans are your friends. As you write your lesson plan, you "own" the information, the process, and the activities that you will be implementing in the classroom. Making the information your own increases your confidence in the classroom and, ultimately, may increase the success of the lesson. If it doesn't increase the success of the lesson, it will provide you with information on what did not work, what did work, and what needs to be changed. Writing lesson plans are worth the time and effort invested in the process. Once you have taught a lesson or two, you will truly understand the importance of preparation. Students know when you are prepared and when you aren't. Providing a model for competent, confident behavior is a lesson in itself. Preparedness also reduces stress.

Step One: Pre-Planning for Writing a Lesson Plan

- Identify standards: Prior to writing a lesson plan, you will identify the standards to be addressed in the school counseling core curriculum. These standards will include the ASCA National Standards and, if available in your school district or state, local or state standards. With these standards and the developmental grade level of your students, you will begin to write your lesson plan.
- Interdisciplinary or not? Many schools do not have time set aside for a school counseling core curriculum. Hence, school counselors often seek opportunities to collaborate and partner with subject area teachers in order to develop educational experiences that will cover the subject area content and the school counseling core curriculum content.
- If the school district has a lesson plan format, follow the school district's practice. If not, the following lesson plans include all of the major components required and serve as a model for you to follow. The three samples of lesson plans below address each of the grade-level bands (K–5, 6–8, 9–12).

Activity:

What standards are used for the school counseling core curriculum in your school district?

____

____

____

Is time scheduled in student schedules for implementation of the school counseling core curriculum? If not, what interdisciplinary opportunities are available for collaboration between content areas and the school counseling core curriculum?

____

____

____

Does the school district have a preferred or required lesson plan format? If so, what is the required content of the lesson plan?

____

____

Step Two: Lesson Plan Title

Lesson Plan Title: Inclusion/Exclusion—A Science Experiment

> Use a name that will be meaningful to you and provides enough keywords for other educators who may look at it. This lesson is an interdisciplinary level. It covers content in both the science and the school counseling core curriculums.

Step Three: Grade Level: 3rd and/or 4th Grades

> List the developmentally appropriate grade level(s) for the lesson content and activities.

Step Four: Learning Objectives

> Learning objectives are the specific measurable and objectives goals set of the lesson.

- Students will learn to empathize with and relate to one another through the common experiences of being included in and excluded from different social settings. Students recognize when others are being excluded and think of ways to include everyone.
- Students will be able to see, through a science experiment, what being excluded looks like and what being included looks like and how we can apply that to their daily lives and relationships.

Step Five: Standards (ASCA and/or State Standards)

Curriculum standards identified by the American School Counseling Association and/or your local, state, or school district.

16.1.5.A: Examine the impact of emotions and responses on view of self and interactions with others.

16.1.5.C: Identity adverse situations which all people encounter and healthy ways to address.

Step Six: Duration of Lesson: 45 Minutes

Identify how much time will be needed to complete the lesson.

Step Seven: Required Materials

List all materials required. Prior to lesson, confirm that you have all the materials needed. Having all of your supplies at hand will increase your confidence in implementing the lesson and will also free up your attention to student learning and classroom management.

- Large, clear, shallow container
- Water
- Pepper
- Bar of soap or liquid detergent
- Sugar
- Copy of exclusion/inclusion page
- Pencil

Step Eight: Anticipatory Set (Lead-In)

Preparing students for a lesson is best practice. This provides you with the opportunity to get the student's attention, encourage interest in the topic, and set the foundation for what will take place.

In this lesson, we will be talking about *inclusion* and *exclusion*. Does anyone know what those words mean? (Wait and listen.) Inclusion is when you feel included in a group of people. When you are included, you feel like you are welcomed and you belong. Exclusion is the opposite of inclusion. When you are excluded, you feel like the group is avoiding you or leaving you out.

Step Nine: Step-By-Step Procedure

Provide specific step-by-step directions for the lesson. Practicing the lesson is a good idea and reduces missteps when working with students.

Directions: Fill a large, clear, shallow container with water. Sprinkle pepper in the middle of the water. Squirt some liquid soap into the water. The pepper will separate and move to the edges of the container when you add the soap. Add a tablespoon of sugar into the middle of the water. It will take about five minutes for the sugar to attract the pepper.

- Ask the following questions:
  - Have you ever tasted soap? What does it taste like?
  - What is happening to the pepper?
  - Do you think this demonstrates exclusion or inclusion?
  - Why do you think the soap has this effect on the pepper? (The soap forms a film on the water surface. The soap film repels the pepper).
  - Was this reaction instant or delayed?
  - When you have been bitter toward someone or someone has been bitter toward you, what has your reaction been?
  - Now I am going to put a tablespoon of sugar in the middle of the water.
  - What do you think will happen to the pepper?
  - Does this demonstrate inclusion or exclusion?
  - Has anyone ever been mean to you, like the soap, and then turned nice, like the sugar?
  - Is the reaction time the same as the soap reaction time? Why? (The sugar reaction is slower. It takes time for the sugar to dissolve in the water. Once it does dissolve, the chemistry of the water changes. The sugar draws the pepper away from the edges. It attracts the pepper rather than repelling it.)
  - How can you relate to the experience?

Wrap-Up: We have seen that the soap and sugar had opposite effects on the pepper. Soap has a bitter or sour taste. When we are bitter or sour toward others, they avoid us. Just like the pepper was repelled by soap, negative words or behavior will repel people. Sugar has the opposite effect. Sugar taste sweet and pleasant. When we are kind and positive, we attract others to us.

Step Ten: Assessment

Assessment will measure student learning and inform the effectiveness of the lesson.

- informal observation of students during presentation
- informal asking of questions during the experiment
- formal assessment of the worksheet given to the students about inclusion/exclusion

Step Eleven: Accommodations

Accommodations will be provided in accordance with the students' IEPs.
Lesson used with permission from: © Chandra Verbic, Nashville, TN.

Activity: The counseling department has been asked to implement a school counseling core curriculum unit on conflict resolution. Using the SAMPLE Lesson Plan Format (Appendix A), develop two class lessons addressing conflict resolution. Share with your small group or post on the courseware platform.

Three additional sample lesson plans are available in the Appendix B, C, and D.

This sample lesson plans were developed by Anthony Musumeci, an educator extraordinaire.

REFERENCES

American School Counselor Association. (2012). *The ASCA National Model: A framework for school counseling programs* (3rd ed.). Alexandria, VA: Author.

Council for Accreditation for Counseling and Related Program. (2014). *2016 standards.* Retrieved from www.cacrep.org

Masters in Psychology and Counseling Accreditation Council. (2015). *Accreditation manual.* Retrieved from http://www.mpcacaccreditation.org/about/accreditation-manual

Verbic, C. (2014). *Inclusion Exclusion: A science experiment.* Retrieved from http://cjayneteach.com/blog/2013/11/18/preventing-invisibility-guest-post/

APPENDIX A

Sample Lesson Plan Format

Lesson Plan Title:
Grade Level:
Learning Objectives:
Standards:
Duration of Lesson:
Required Materials:
Introduction to Lesson:

(Continued)

(Continued)

Step-by-Step Procedure:
Assessment:
Accommodations:
Follow-up:
Counselor Notes to Self re: Future Changes in Lesson Plan:

● APPENDIX B

Sample Lesson Plan: Post-Secondary Planning

by Anthony Musumeci

Sample Lesson Plan: Post-Secondary Transition—Goal Setting

Title—Finding the Right Fit for You After High School

Subject/Course—School Counseling Core Curriculum

Grade level—9th

Standards—16.1.12.D (Incorporate goal setting into college, career, and other life decisions.)

Objective—Students will be able to identify what type of high school classes or electives will help guide them toward their future—whether it is college, a career, or life decisions after high school.

Essential question—What does your future entail after high school? Do you know how to obtain your ideal future while in high school? Do you know how to set goals for yourself to obtain these goals?

Duration—One or two 50-minute class periods

Materials—Website, "careertest.net," high school course selection book

Instructional Strategies

Do now: When you think of your future after high school, what feelings come to mind? Are you worried or excited? If worried, move to one side of the room and excited move to the other. If unsure, stand in the middle.

Next, use student movement to generate a discussion about student feelings regarding their future after high school and ask them, "Regardless of how you feel, do you know how to set goals to get what you want after high school?"

Next, students will use the careertest.net website and answer 68 multiple choice test questions (will take 10 minutes) that stem from the Carl Jung personality test. The test will help students identify who they are and will help guide them into professions that best suit their personality.

Students will then group themselves with other students who had similar test scores.

After students take the test, they will be given a handout that lists professions that best fit their personality. Students will discuss in their groups the professions and identify certain professions that interest them the most.

Wrap-Up

Students will discuss the following: "Why is it important to set goals for yourself?"

To wrap up, students will fill out a graphic organizer helping them with creating goals using the high school course selection guide. Students will use the rest of the period and next day to complete graphic organizer and then present to the class what career they chose, college or post-high school education they will use to get their goal, and what classes they will take (electives included) to help them achieve their future goal.

Assessment

- observation of students during the class activities
- participation in the class discussion
- a graphic organizer helping students create goals
- class presentation about their goals and future steps toward those goals

Accommodations

Accommodations will be provided in accordance with the students' IEPs.

● APPENDIX C

Sample Lesson Plan: Interdisciplinary History and School Counseling Core Curriculum

by Anthony Musumeci

Title—How Communication Impacted the Outcome of the Civil War

Subject—Eighth-grade U.S. History and School Counseling Core Curriculum

Standards—16.2.8.c (Analyze factors that impact communication.)

Objective—Students will be able to identify the impact Morse code had on getting information to and from Lincoln and his generals during the Civil War.

Essential Question—On a scale of 1 to 10, rank the impact Morse code had on the North's victory over the South in the Civil War.

Duration—One 50-minute class period

Materials—Video titled, *America: The Story of Us* (http://www.history.com/shows/america-the-story-of-us)

Instruction of the Lesson

Do now—With a partner, provide two or three reasons why people use Twitter today? Next, guide student answers to the quickness with which information is gained these days and ask the following—What is the benefit of to gain information quickly? Predict why gaining information in wartime would be so valuable to winning a war.

Next, students will view a 10- to 12-minute clip from the, *America: Story of Us* that shows how the North used technology—specifically Morse code—to win the war against the South.

Students will record two or three reasons that Morse code was valuable to the North in winning the war.

Next, students will use the interactive whiteboard to identify specific impacts Morse code and students must identify what does and does not belong.

Next, students will record notes from the interactive whiteboard about the impact Morse code had on winning the Civil War.

Wrap-Up—In your wrap-up section in your notes, answer the following questions for an end of class discussion:

- On a scale of 1 to 10 (1 = no impact; 10 = great impact) rank the impact Morse code had on North winning Civil War.
- Choose one word to describe North's use of Morse code and provide one or two sentences explaining your word choice.

Assessment

- Observation of students during the class activities
- On a scale of 1 to 10 (1 = no impact; 10 = great impact) rank the impact Morse code had on North winning Civil War.
- Choose one word to describe North's use of Morse code and provide one or two sentences explaining your word choice.

Accommodations

Accommodations will be provided in accordance with the students' IEPs.

• APPENDIX D

Sample Lesson Plan: Post-Secondary Transition

by Anthony Musumeci

Title—Hard and Soft Communication Skills

Subject—School Counseling Core Curriculum

Grade level—8th

Standards—13.2.8.A: Identify effective speaking and listening skills used in a job interview.

Objective—Students will be able to compare and contrast "hard" and "soft" skills when preparing for job interviews.

Essential Questions

- What are soft skills and hard skills?
- Identify hard skills you think you could be good at for a prospective employer.
- How would you describe the importance of soft skills?

Duration—One 50-minute class period

Materials—Interactive whiteboard

Instructional Strategies

Do Now: In order to keep a job, you will need to have "hard" and "soft" skills. (Surgeon needs to know how to operate on your body; math teacher needs to know how to solve equations). Discuss the following question with a neighbor sitting next to you:

- Which contractor do you want working on your home to build a new bedroom for you? Why?
- One that is pleasant, comes on time to meet you and go over the job, and can answer all your questions and does not seem to be in a hurry to go to the next job?

  OR

- One that shows up late, looks over the job quickly, and leaves you with an estimate on how much job will cost by barely answering any of your questions.

After neighbor and class discussion on the question above, explain to students that, despite having the knowledge to do a job, it isn't always going to get you the job.

Next, show a 15-minute interactive whiteboard lesson/lecture where students will record notes on the definitions of *hard* and *soft skills*.

Wrap-Up

Students will interact with the whiteboard by examining multiple examples of hard and soft skills. There will be a T-chart labeled ***hard*** and *soft,* and they must accurately slide over the skills that belong in the hard and soft categories.

Once students have shown an understanding of the difference between the two skills sets, students will answer a *3–2–1 activity* that answers the following questions into their notes for an end of class discussion:

- List *3* types of soft skills that employers are looking for in a new employee.
- Identify within yourself *2* hard skills you could be good at for a prospective employer.
- Provide *1* word that best describes soft skills and two- or three-sentence explanation of your word choice.

Assessment

- Observation of students during the class activities
- List 3 types of soft skills that employers are looking for in a new employee.
- Identify within yourself 2 hard skills you could be good at for a prospective employer.
- Provide 1 word that best describes soft skills and a two- or three-sentence explanation of your word choice

Accommodations

Accommodations will be provided in accordance with the students' IEPs.

Lesson 18

CLASSROOM MANAGEMENT

"Why won't they behave?"

Tricia Walsh Coates
Kutztown University of Pennsylvania

Real Life

Melissa, a counselor-in-training, has worked endlessly on preparing her school counseling core curriculum lesson on stress management for the seventh-grade students. The lesson plan looks great—comprehensive, grade-level appropriate, and interesting. As Melissa enters the classroom, she greets the students. She is well received, and the beginning of the lesson goes well. She is teaching the students a relaxation technique for breathing through a stressful situation. Three of the girls begin to laugh, roll their eyes, and look around the classroom. They then start to mock other students. The other students become uncomfortable and begin to disengage from the lesson. Melissa cannot get the students back to the lesson. The rest of the class period the students have chats with each other and act out while Melissa tries to regain control and continue on with her lesson. She is very upset and isn't sure where she went wrong.

Lesson Eighteen

Classroom Management

"Why won't they behave?"

Tricia Walsh Coates
Kutztown University of Pennsylvania

Essential Question: How can I facilitate a community of learners in a potentially disruptive classroom environment?

Objectives

Students will

- demonstrate an understanding of classroom management models to better facilitate student learning.
- demonstrate a working knowledge of restorative practice circles as a tool for student engagement.

CACREP Standards

- Understand core curriculum design, lesson plan development, classroom management strategies, and differentiated instructional strategies.
- Understand interventions to promote academic success.
- Identify techniques of personal/social counseling in school settings.

MPCAC Standards

- assessment of human behavior and organizational/community/institutional systems
- human development and wellness across the life span
- ecological, contextual, multicultural, social-justice foundation of human development

Video Spark

http://www.pbs.org/newshour/bb/new-approach-discipline-school/

To curb conflict, a Colorado high school replaces punishment with conversation.

● INTRODUCTION

In a show of commitment to First Lady Michelle Obama's Reach Higher Campaign, a local school district has asked their K–12 school counselors to speak to classes about postsecondary education opportunities. The Reach Higher Initiative focuses on the effort to inspire all students in the United States to "take charge of their future" by creating a long-term plan for attending postsecondary schooling after graduation (www.whitehouse.gov/reach-higher). Counselors in the district respond to the challenge by planning and developing activities for the Reach Higher Initiative. Middle-level counselors in the district decide to engage students in a classroom discussion centering on career goals and gender segregation. One goal is to have middle-level students identify careers that are nontraditional for their gender. Counselors are tasked with holding classroom discussions with students, asking them what they think they want to study after high school, discussing what the profession entails, and having them write a brief narrative on what a day would be like in that profession. Students then need to list nontraditional careers based on gender and identify people who are in those careers breaking the stereotype, for example, astronauts, nurses, politicians, and mechanics.

Counselor A enters her classroom with a definitive controlling air. As the authoritarian figure in the classroom, she uses a loud and commanding voice in the room, sets standards for the classroom without taking the time to explain to the students, and works hard on retaining control of the classroom. Although the classroom appears controlled, students are anxious and do not respond immediately to her questions. When a student acts in an inappropriate manner, she focuses on ending the disciplinary issue and ignores the students who are actually on task.

Counselor B decides that his classroom environment will be warm and supportive. Unfortunately, he does not set limits and seems to focus more on the student's perceived "good" behavior which deemphasizes the quality of the discussion. When a student challenges his authority in the classroom, he chooses to ignore the behavior which encourages others in the class to act out. And while the students think he is a nice guy, the classroom environment is at times chaotic and many students stress over his inability to control the classroom setting.

Counselor C is very uncomfortable entering an environment that is foreign to his usual one-on-one counseling. He deals with the new situation by remaining behind the desk, which appears to the students as his being aloof. This results in half the class withdrawing from the activity while the other half acts out to get his attention or because there is no apparent sense of control or order in the classroom.

Counselor D decides that the best way for students to respond to her task is to take the time to build some community in the classroom and get to know the students. She starts by explaining to the students they will be discussing their feelings on their future and places them in a circle for the activity. Next, she asks the students to participate in establishing the guidelines for the discussion—how it is decided who talks, how long they can speak for, rules when someone is speaking—and then asks the students to engage in a conversation that is meaningful and productive by allowing for all voices in the classroom to be heard. As a result, the students feel a sense of safety and believe their opinions are validated and respected. Disruptions are minimal, and the classroom environment is productive and supportive.

Counselor D in the aforementioned scenario uses a classroom management technique referred to as *restorative practice*. The restorative practice model for classroom management and discussion is not a new concept. The practice is based on the structure of restorative justice movement often used in American penal system. Where restorative justice places an emphasis on building critical relationships of young offenders rather than punishing them, restorative practice is an instructional framework that focuses on achieving discipline through collaborative discussion and decision-making (Zehr, 1990). Where restorative justice is a reactive process—addressing issues surrounding a crime, or harm, after it has taken place, restorative practice works to proactively build community in a classroom setting as a means to prevent disciplinary issues. International Institute for Restorative Practices founder and CEO Ted Wachtel states that, "The fundamental premise of restorative practices is that people are happier, more cooperative and productive, and more likely to make positive changes when those in authority do things with them, rather than to them or for them" (2013b).

• RESTORATIVE PRACTICE—A PRIMER

Restorative practice first took root during the 1970s as an experimental disciplinary program. Buxmont Academy, a small charter school in southeastern Pennsylvania, created a structure for at-risk youth to mediate and discuss disciplinary problems as an alternative to suspension and expulsion. News of the program's success spread, sparking similar programs throughout the state. In 1994, The International

Institute for Restorative Practices (IIRP) was founded, creating a unique framework for collaborative practice that expanded beyond the process used in the criminal justice system (McCold & Wachtel, 2001, 2003). The IIRP trains professionals around the world in restorative practices not only in education, but the fields of criminal justice, social work, counseling, and law to name a few (Wachtel, 2013).

Considered a new social science, restorative practices examine how to build social capital and achieve discipline through community building and participatory decision-making. In the classroom context, social capital refers to the interconnection of social groups to come together for a common cause. The community, in this case the classroom, benefits through the building of trust, a reciprocity of shared information, and the cooperative nature of decision-making (Putnam & Helliwell, 2007). The supporting framework of the restorative practice model rests on six guiding principles: the social discipline window, restorative justice typology, nine affects, compass of shame, fair process, and the restorative practices continuum. Regarding classroom management, the social discipline window outlines different approaches to establishing behavioral boundaries and maintaining the classroom social environment. It was also the model for outlines in the counselor scenario described at the beginning of the chapter.

Students are more responsive to a classroom activity when people in authority are willing to work with them instead of working at them—in essence telling them what to do. Based on the writing of Australian criminologist John Braithwaite and social psychologist Diane Baumrind, the paradigm maintains that the punitive authoritarian *to* mode and the neglectful/irresponsible and paternalistic *for* modes are not as effective for classroom control as the restorative participatory *with* mode (Baumrind, 1964; Braithwaite, 1989) (Figure 1). To achieve this level of community participation with a high level of control and support, counselors can engage in a spectrum of activities ranging from the informal (affective statements and questions, impromptu conferencing) to formal (circles and formal conferences).

The issue of power is at the heart of classroom management. For a class to be responsive to a counselor's activity, one cannot underestimate the importance of building community. Twenty-first century education demands that students be at a certain place academically to succeed. Counselors must take the time to get to know the students they work with in order to understand where they are coming from both socially and emotionally. For this to happen effectively, students must be given a voice and everyone's story needs to be part of the community. One of the most effective ways to maintain classroom control during instruction is with restorative circles.

Figure 1 Social Discipline Window

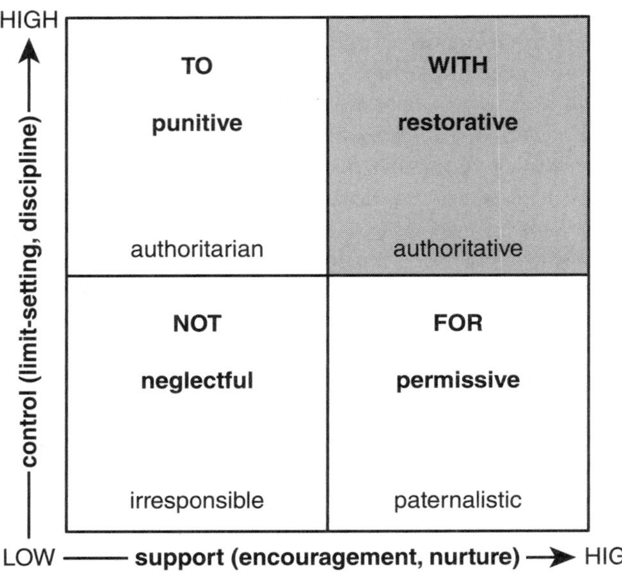

• CIRCLES

Restorative circles can minimize conflict and anxiety by giving all in the classroom the opportunity to speak and listen in a safe environment. Counselors often walk into a classroom situation feeling powerless—they might not know the students and are not the center of authority in the classroom. The good thing about a circle is that everyone's got your back because no one's back is exposed. It is a safe place for students to express their thoughts and feelings in a controlled environment.

Restorative circles are loosely based on the stages of group development first introduced by Bruce Tuckman in a 1965 article titled, "Developmental Sequence in Small Groups." Tuckman argued there are a series of necessary steps to working effectively in a collaborative group/circle: forming, storming, norm, performing, and adjourning. The first step, forming, initiates the circle and establishes why the participants are there, allowing for interpersonal relationships to be formed and roles to be established. The following step, storming, is when participants negotiate their role in the circle and vie for power and possible control. This bid for power, according to Tuckman, is a crucial element for a circle to reach its optimal health. It is in this stage that participants offer and explore communication parameters. Once the circle dynamic is established, participants move into the norm stage where a solid group feeling and cohesiveness develop, new standards evolve, and new roles are adopted. Once this happens and a safe environment is created, personal opinions can be expressed. At this point, ideas can be discussed and tasks can be delegated. This stage, known as perform, is where the group can focus their energy on the task at hand. Tuckman's final stage, adjourning, was added in 1977 to the original model, a fifth stage where participants can deconstruct what was decided and affirm the work they performed as a collaborative group (Tuckman, 1979).

There are a variety of purposes for conducting a class dialogue in circles. Minimizing classroom conflict, support, decision-making, community-building, and exchanging information are to name a few (Wachtel, 2013). To achieve this type of environment in class, two types of circles can be used: community-building circles and responsive circles. These types of circles are dependent upon each other—community in the classroom must be formed to best facilitate dialogue in the responsive circle. Community-building circles focus on giving students the chance to get to know one another and establish connections, particularly with regard to how they should treat one another. Community-building activities should take precedence before other types of circles are formed. Responsive circles use questioning to explore issues that arise in class and allow for a dialogue to make things right. The questions posed in a responsive circle must focus on issues relevant to the student to be dynamic and interactive (Clifford, 2015).

Three circles are presented in this chapter that help facilitate building connections in the classroom and managing potentially difficult class content. A check- in circle to build community helps students to connect with one another and allows them to be seen and be heard in the classroom. The objectives for this circle are for student opinions to be recognized and respected by their peers. On a daily basis, students are examining their relationships with their peers, both testing and refining their place in the social order of schools. Misbehavior often occurs when students feels excluded from the group, often leaving them to question their place in the social structure. Circles can be used to minimize this disconnect by facilitating a dialogue that requires each student voice to be heard. Responsive check- in circles ask questions that deal with conflict and are designed to address an issue or concern in the class. They are best used when there is a disruption in class: bullying, cheating, personal conflict, or racial/cultural tensions. The purpose of a responsive circle is to open dialogue and address these issues with full student participation in the process for conflict resolution.

The third type of activity, the fishbowl circle, is used to maintain stronger order in the classroom while discussing potentially disruptive content. Fishbowls are organized around a specific group of students—the inner circle—to be active participants, while the rest of students act as observers. A fishbowl circle is a completely student-centered activity—students take ownership of the questions being discussed and actively work together to formulate solutions to questions posed. When the counselor shares the task of problem solving, students are asked to be equal partners in classroom discussions, which leads to a feeling of empowerment. Responsive fishbowl circles diminish classroom disruptions through enlisting all in the class to have their voices heard.

● CONCLUSION

The International Institute for Restorative Practices argues that circles are one of the best strategies for minimizing conflict and building community in the classroom. As a tool for classroom management, circles can help the counselor maintain disciplinary control by addressing three areas of focus:

1. Think about what was happening in the class that wasn't working and have people take responsibility for what they were doing to contribute to that behavior.
2. Ask what type of atmosphere students and teachers ideally want in the classroom.
3. Reflect and think about what each person is going to do to help attain that ideal. (Costello, Wachtel, & Wachtel, 2010)

Circles present a new way of approaching dialogue and present an alternative to the authoritative classroom model. Through the creation of a cooperative and inclusive classroom environment, students are asked to take ownership of their thoughts and actions. By taking the time to build community, establishing guidelines for inclusive dialogue, and allowing students to speak their mind, counselors can minimize class conflict through proactive restorative techniques.

Activity 1: The Check-In Process—Building Community

1. Have students sit in a circle. Make sure that the circle is well defined and everyone can see each other's face without having to lean forward or turn in their seats.
2. As part of the democratic process, agree on a time the group would like to devote to the activity. As facilitator, you want to make sure that people hold to the designated time.
3. The circle facilitator poses a question to the group for discussion. This question should be a solid prompt that allows the group to focus. A high-quality prompt should be simple, open ended, and above all relevant to the students' experiences.
4. Once the question is posed, take 2 to 3 minutes to "center." Have participants sit comfortably, in silence, breathing deeply while they become aware of their own thoughts on the question posed. This wait time is important—students' need to have time to reflect on the prompt and form their own frame of reference. Otherwise, they often end up repeating what the person speaking before has said.
5. Someone volunteers to start the process. The order that participants speak can be random or go around the circle. Some facilitators like to use a "talking piece"—it is an object that is easily passed from one student to another. Examples of a talking piece are feathers, small objects, or balls. However, a talking piece is not necessary to hold a circle.
6. The speaker takes some time to say whatever he or she wants with no constraints other than the designated time. If someone in the group does not want to speak, he or she can just say "I pass," reserving the right to speak at the end of the circle or not speak at all if he or she chooses.
7. While the speaker is talking, no one interrupts or responds to his or her statements. This is known as the principle of "non-interference." In a community-building circle, this concept

allows for participants to express themselves freely without the fear of criticism from classmates. Someone may, however, chose to say something related to what has been already said when it is his or her turn.

8. When the speaker is done, another student simply says, "I'm in." The purpose of the statement is two-fold: practically, it keeps the flow of dialogue moving around the circle. Cognitively, the words signify that the participants are personally part of the conversation and by being "in" they have joined the community.
9. The process is repeated until everyone has had a chance to speak.
10. To close the circle, ask for a two-word checkout: "Say two words that sum up your thoughts on the circle today."

Activity 2: The Check-In Process—Responsive Circles

Responsive circles are organized in the same format as a community-building circle; however, the purpose is different. Responsive circles are best used for responding to misbehavior and harm and can be an effective tool for classroom management. Responsive circles work best in classrooms where community has been established.

Follow the directions for the community-building circle with the following alterations:

- The prompt uses specific questions to explore challenging circumstances and move toward making things right. Choosing questions that are "real" for the students and relevant to the issue being presented is imperative.
- It is important to clearly name the issue to be discussed. The issue must be student centered, meaning it either needs to come from the students or can be named by the facilitator as long as it is directed at student issues.

Question Prompt Guidelines	
For Building Community	*For Conflict Discussion*
• Noncontroversial subjects • Easy to answer without introspection • Wide range of choice in answers that are honest • Fun and fast, meant to open dialogue • No "edgy" questions	• Subject is controversial • In response to a situation • Harder to answer because of personal connection • Increased wait time • Questions are edgy—invite students to get out of their comfort zone

Source: Adapted from Center for Restorative Process (2015).

Activity 3: Fishbowl Activity

Fishbowl activities are best used when trying to solve a problem or manage a disruptive issue in class. While all students participate in a fishbowl circle, some are active participants while others are observers. At the end of a fishbowl activity, all students respond to a quick prompt to share final thoughts on the topic covered.

1. Discuss with the class the issue that is going to be addressed in the circle. Often, this is a class infraction or a behavioral issue that is causing disruption.
2. Form a large circle on the outside and then have a group of students form a smaller circle on the inside. The students who participate in the inner circle can either volunteer, or the facilitator can choose a selected group. The circle in the center should consist of roughly a quarter of the classroom. For example, in a class of 28 students, invite or choose six or seven into the center.
3. The facilitator sits in the inner circle and acts as the circle leader. That role is to guide the discussion but the facilitator does not contribute to the context of the discussion.
4. The students who are in the outer circle are required to act in a "witness" role. They are directed to sit quietly and observe the action taking place in the center of the circle. Explain that their role is crucial in that it removes them from the dialogue and because of this distance, they will often have a different perspective on what is taking place in the conversation. Guidelines for the outside circle may include listening quietly, taking notes on the main points in the discussions, or observing nonverbal cues. If a student "witness" wants to volunteer a comment on the discussion, he or she can raise his or her hand; however, it is up to the inner circle to decide on outside participation.
5. A variation on the inner circle is to put an empty chair in the mix. Someone from the outer group may join the inner circle on one round of the questioning. After he or she participates, that student returns to the outer circle and another may join.
6. All dialogue is conducted by the students in the center. The facilitator raises the issue that has occurred in class. Students in the inner circle are then prompted to talk about the issue using the restorative practice prompts:
   - From your point of view, what happened?
   - What were you thinking at the time?

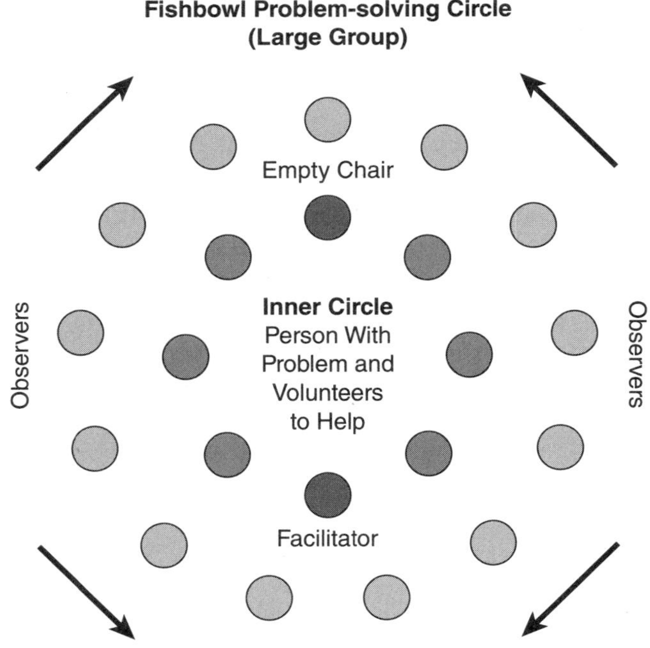

Source: From Building Community (December, 2014).

- How have you been affected? How have others been affected?
- What do you think should happen to make things right?

7. There are rules for the inner circle: only one person may speak at a time and all in the inner circle must speak once before anyone speaks a second time.

8. After the discussion, students need to form one circle and debrief on the discussion. A brief check-in can be conducted where students need to give a one-sentence explanation of what they think was the most positive outcome of the activity or what they observed.

REFERENCES

Baumrind, D. (1964). Some thoughts on ethics of research: After reading Milgram's "Behavioral Study of Obedience." *American Psychologist 19*(6), 421–423.

Braithwaite, J. (1989). *Crime, shame and reintegration*. New York, NY: Cambridge University Press.

Clifford, A. (2015). *Teaching restorative practices with classroom circles*. San Francisco, CA: Center for Restorative Process.

Costello, B., Wachtel, J., & Wachtel, T. (2010). *Restorative circles in schools: Building community and enhancing learning*. Bethlehem, PA: International Institute for Restorative Practices.

McCold, P., & Wachtel, T. (2001). Restorative justice in everyday life. In J. Braithwaite & H. Strang (Eds.), *Restorative justice and civil society* (pp. 114–129). Cambridge, England: Cambridge University Press.

McCold, P., & Wachtel, T. (2003). *In pursuit of paradigm: A theory of restorative justice*. Paper presented at the XIII World Congress of Criminology, Rio de Janeiro, Brazil. Retrieved from http://www.iirp.edu/article_detail.php?article_id=NDI0

Mstowerp. (2014). Fishbowls, solution-focused circles [Web log post]. Retrieved from https://mstowerp.wordpress.com/2014/12/31/fishbowls-solution-focused-circles

PBS Newshour. (2014). *To curb conflict, a Colorado high school replaces punishment with conversation*. Retrieved from http://www.pbs.org/newshour/bb/new-approach-discipline-school/

Putnam, R. D., & Helliwell, J. (2007). Education and social capital. *Eastern Economics Journal, 33,* 1–19.

Reach higher: Complete your education, claim your future. Retrieved from https://www.whitehouse.gov/reach-higher

Tuckman, B. W. (1965). Developmental sequence in small groups. *Psychological Bulletin (63)*, 384–399.

Tuckman, B. W. (1979). *Evaluating instructional programs*. Boston, MA: Allyn & Bacon.

Wachtel, T. (2013a). *Defining restorative*. Retrieved from http://www.iirp.edu/pdf/Defining-Restorative.pdf

Wachtel, T. (2013b). *Dreaming of a new reality: How restorative practices reduce crime and violence, improve relationships and strengthen civil society*. Bethlehem, PA: The Piper's Press.

Zehr, H. (1990). *Changing lenses: A new focus for crime and justice*. Scottsdale, PA: Herald Press.

Lesson 19

ADVISING, SCHEDULING, AND THEN ADD IN THE NCAA REGULATIONS

"2.3 or take a knee. . ."

Real Life

Mitch, a junior in high school, has a GPA of 2.7; he is the star of the basketball team and overall is well liked by peers and teachers. Mrs. Evergreen, the school counselor, calls Mitch to the office for his junior year postsecondary transition meeting. The counselor asks Mitch if he has thought about what he would like to do after high school. Mitch answers "Oh yeah, I'm playin' ball. I'm going to the pros." Mrs. Evergreen asks if he is going to apply to colleges with the hopes of playing college basketball. Mitch responds that he "won't need college ball"—he's "the Kobe of now."

Lesson Nineteen

Advising, Scheduling, and Then Add In the NCAA Regulations

"2.3 or take a knee. . ."

Essential Question: How do I best meet the needs of all students through advising and scheduling? How do I best serve the student-athletes in our school?

Objectives

Students will

- demonstrate an understanding of the school counselor's roles in advising and scheduling.
- demonstrate a familiarity with various types of scheduling.
- demonstrate an understanding of the impact advisement can have on a student's college and career readiness.
- demonstrate an understanding of the NCAA regulations and resources available to remain current for working with college-bound student-athletes.
- demonstrate knowledge of career, college, and educational paths as they intersect with college sports and the NCAA.

CACREP Standards

- school counselor roles in relation to college and career readiness (5.G.2.c)
- school counselor roles in school leadership and multidisciplinary team (5.G.2.d)
- interventions to promote academic development (5.G.3.d)
- use of developmentally appropriate career counseling interventions and assessments (5.G.3.e)
- approaches to increase promotion and graduation rates (5.G.3.j)
- strategies to promote equity in student achievement and college access (5.G.3.k)
- techniques to foster collaboration and teamwork within schools (5.G.3.l)

MPCAC Standards

- human development and wellness across the life span
- career and life development
- counseling, consultation, and social-justice advocacy theories and skills
- ecological, contextual, multicultural, social-justice foundation of human development

Video Spark

www.ncaa.org

Inside the NCAA (monthly video)

INTRODUCTION

Advisement and Scheduling

The American School Counseling Association identifies ***individual planning or academic advising*** as an appropriate activity for school counselors (American School Counselor Association [ASCA], 2012). Individual planning includes assisting students in course selection and scheduling; personal/social and career development; identification of strengths and interests; identification of areas in need of development; developing strategies to facilitate academic, personal and social growth; provides support for students in transitions (e.g., grade level, school transitions); and assists students with postsecondary transition planning. The specific role of the school counselor in advisement and scheduling varies from school to school based on the tasks assigned to the counselors in each school and the grade level of the students.

Academic advising not only requires the school counselors' time, but it also requires their close attention to detail. It is essential to be knowledgeable about the graduation requirements for the school district. Although there are state requirements for high school graduation, schools districts have the flexibility to offer a variety of courses and use credit systems (e.g., .5 credit) according to the needs of the students. For example, within the same state (requiring 21 credits for graduation), two school districts may have different graduation requirements as illustrated below. Both school districts are meeting the state requirements; however, the school districts have requirements specific to their district. Always carefully check the requirements prior to advising students. Receiving mentoring can be very helpful when new to the advising/scheduling system of a school.

School District #1	
Subject	*Credits*
English	4.0
Social Science	4.0
Science	4.0
Mathematics	4.0
Electives	6.5
High School 101	.05
Physical Education	2.0
Technology	1.5
Health	0.5
Career Development	0.5
Total	**27.5 Credits**

School District #2	
Subject	*Credits*
English	4.0
Social Science	4.0
Science	3.0
Mathematics	3.0
Art & Humanities	2.0
Electives	4.0
Health and Physical Education	1.5
World Language	2.0
Total	**23.5 Credits**

Academic advising and scheduling go hand in hand. Careful consideration of the advisement sheet is done while working with the scheduling system. As academic courses are selected, the counselor will then work with the scheduling program to register the student.

Scheduling involves two components. One is knowledge based; the other is skill based. The first component is to determine what type of schedule the school district uses. Each school district identifies the type of schedule that is optimal for meeting their students' needs. It is important to be knowledgeable about the types of scheduling and what schedule the school district uses. The following table provides examples of the various types of schedules for the school day.

Scheduling Models	
Traditional self-contained classrooms	Often seen in elementary schools
Traditional six, seven, or eight 45- to 50- minute class periods	Each class meets daily
Block scheduling—4 x 4 blocks	Four 90- to 120-minute classes a day
A/B block scheduling	Take six courses: three on "A" day/three on "B" day
Other block schedule options	Block scheduling can be designed specific to the school's needs

Once again, each school district will have identified the optimal schedule for its community. Inquire about the schedule and listen carefully. When the scheduling decision is presented, it may also provide information on what is important to the stakeholders and what the needs of the community are.

The second component of scheduling is acquiring the computer skills to competently work with the scheduling platform used by the school district. There are many and, once again, will be specific to the school. Learning the system does not take long and can be accomplished while you work with your site supervisor.

Academic Advising, the National Collegiate Athletic Association (NCAA) and the Role of the School Counselor

The National Collegiate Athletic Association (NCAA) is a nonprofit association that regulates collegiate athletic programs in the United States and Canada. NCAA regulations can greatly impact a high school student's path to college, college sports, and scholarship funding. The NCAA is one area where school counselor needs to be very detail oriented and knowledgeable about the NCAA requirements. Although there may be fewer student athletes than traditional high school students, as school counselors, we have responsibilities to provide them with the correct resources and materials needed throughout their high school experience. Specifically, we have a responsibility to provide students with accurate information or provide them with resources to acquire that information. In 2001, in *Sain vs. Cedar Rapids Community School District*, a student brought a lawsuit against the school district due to academic advising and NCAA eligibility. Carolyn Stone (2014) reported that "Bruce Sain was awarded a five-year basketball scholarship to Northern Illinois University, but lost his NCAA eligibility to play when his senior English class was changed to technical communication, a course not on the list of class his high school submitted to the NCAA for eligibility." Sain lost his scholarship. The suit cited the school counselor and the school district as guilty of negligence during the academic advising process because the counselor did not submit the technical communication course to NCAA for approval. This suit was settled out of court. However, my point in bringing this to your attention is multifaceted. As a school counselor, my first thought is "I don't ever want to be in that situation"—so how can it be avoided.

In essence, know what you know and what you don't know and consult, refer, and collaborate. Collaborate with the physical education department. Reach out to the student's parents. Reach out to NCAA. Consult other school counselors.

For additional information on the legal aspects of academic advising, please access the Stone (2014) article in *ASCA Schoolcounselor*, "The Courts and Academic Advising."

Currently, there are more than 450,000 student-athletes competing in over 1,100 colleges and universities while offering 23 different sports. As school counselors, we need to be aware of the NCAA eligibility requirements as well as the eligibility requirements of the three separate divisions (Division I, Division II, and Division III). There are approximately 350 schools in Division I, 300 schools in Division II, and 444 schools in Division III. Of the three, only Division I, which is the highest division, and Division II can offer students athletic scholarships to help pay for the cost of college.

For those students interested in participating in either Division I or Division II, they will need to register with the NCAA Eligibility Center (www.eligibilitycenter.org) to enroll as NCAA college-bound student-athlete. To be considered eligible for the NCAA, the students have to have completed different "core courses" as well as scored high enough on either the SAT or the ACT. The School Counselor 2016 Guide to NCAA is available at www.ncaapublications.com/productdownloads/COUNSELORS16.pdf. This guide provides information on the following topics:

- What Is the NCAA?
- NCAA Sports
- High School Review by the NCAA—What is it?
- Initial-Eligibility Process
- The Role of the High School
- What Are Core Courses?
- Nontraditional Courses
- Credit Recovery Programs
- Sending Transcripts
- Division I Standards
- Division II Standards
- Division III Standards
- Grade-Point Average
- Home School Students
- International Students
- NAA Student Registration
- Scholarships
- National Letter of Intent

The NCAA plays a very important role in student's access to scholarships. More than $2.7 billion in athletic scholarships is distributed each year along with access to medical care, academic support services, and first-class training opportunities. Nearly 1,100 colleges are members of NCAA, and there are more than 460,000 NCAA student-athletes. Being knowledgeable about the NCAA is an important aspect of a school counselor's toolbox when working with student-athletes on their postsecondary transitions.

While supporting student-athletes through the NCAA process, the postsecondary transition for these students goes beyond the athletics and has a significant focus on the academics. As noted above, 460,000 students participate in the NCAA program; however, of that 460,000 fewer than 2% will go pro in their sports. The student-athlete will go through the postsecondary transition process (e.g., career assessments, college search process, vocational interest inventories) as other high school students. This postsecondary transition process was comprehensive previously and is wholly relevant to student-athletes.

REFERENCES

American School Counselor Association. (2012). *The ASCA National Model: A framework for school counseling programs* (3rd ed.). Alexandria, VA: Author.

Council for Accreditation for Counseling and Related Program. (2014). *2016 standards.* Retrieved from http://www.cacrep.org

Masters in Psychology and Counseling Accreditation Council. (2015). *Accreditation manual.* Retrieved from http://www.mpcacaccreditation.org/about/accreditation-manual

National Collegiate Athletic Association. (2016). *School counselor 2016 guide to NCAA.* Retrieved from http://www.ncaapublications.com/productdownloads/COUNSELORS16.pdf

Stone, C. (2006). *College advising and the courts.* Retrieved from https://www.schoolcounselor.org/magazine/blogs/may-june-2006/college-advising-and-the-courts

LESSON 20

SOLUTION-FOCUSED COUNSELING APPROACHES

"There's not enough time."

Brian Wlazelek
Kutztown University of Pennsylvania

Real Life

A student in academic jeopardy was referred for counseling/advising services in an attempt to salvage failing efforts in several courses. If the problem was study skills rather than mastery of course content, the typical process, which the student knew and avoided, was an exploration of academic deficits and then referral to study skills resources. The student candidly stated that he didn't care about learning new ways to study and couldn't see how it would help him dig out of the academic "hole" that he was in.

Instead of conducting an inventory of problems, we looked at those instances when he was most successful recently in classes and on tests. There were areas of relative success in his current schedule and in recent years. Exploration of his successes revealed some important differences in the way he approached homework, course material, and test preparation for the courses he was passing. These differences became recipes for improvement in the courses he was failing and an existing skill set that could be "tweaked" rather than overhauled in addressing his current needs. He was more willing to pay attention to what already worked and to accept suggestions for improving these skills rather than starting from scratch with methods that he did not know or trust.

Exploring problems and deficits can amplify a student's sense of failure whereas searching for problem exceptions affirms existing resources and strengths. This approach doesn't prevent a counselor from digging into the problem history or considering new strategies for students to use if they make sense when considering all factors. Focusing on problems is not the starting point or presumed to be the only option. Choosing problems or solutions—what's a good fit for you and your setting?

Lesson Twenty

Solution-Focused Counseling Approaches

"There's not enough time."

Brian Wlazelek
Kutztown University of Pennsylvania

Essential Question: How can I meet the student's needs given the time constraints of a school day?

Objectives

Students will

- demonstrate an understanding of brief solution-focused counseling in a school setting.
- demonstrate a working knowledge of how to implement brief solution-focused counseling in a school setting.

CACREP Standards

- interventions to promote academic development (5.G.3.d)
- techniques of personal/social counseling in school settings (5.G.2.f)

MPCAC Standards

- human development and wellness across the life span
- counseling, consultation, and social-justice advocacy theories and skills
- ecological, contextual, multicultural, social-justice foundation of human development

Video Spark

https://www.cornerstoneondemand.com/blog/ted-talk-tuesday-power-yet#.VpwKyEuvv8s

TED Talk Tuesday: The Power of Yet

● INTRODUCTION

When first training to be a counselor, it is hard to imagine working with anyone without gathering extensive information about the problem and the past. Curiosity, empathy, and our perception of the counseling process lead us in that direction. We have come to believe that the details of the problem and the student's life provide a necessary foundation for the case conceptualization that guides our work. However, in some settings, a comprehensive exploration of problem details is impractical because of time or circumstance and yet we still are expected to provide services and to find ways to be helpful.

Aside from myriad obstacles (large caseloads, scheduling conflicts, limited opportunities for face-to-face meeting) that may prevent gathering detailed life information, models such as solution-focused counseling call into question the necessity of collecting this information in order to facilitate change. This is not to say that it is wrong to gather information or that it might not be necessary for other reasons such as meeting documentation requirements or discharging professional responsibilities related to risk assessment or referral. However, it is possible to help students move in the direction of desired outcomes by shifting attention to the resources, strengths, and past successes that they can access when faced with current life concerns.

Deborah L. Mostert, Erin Johnson, and Mark P. Mostert, (1997) noted that the training of school counselors often does not prepare them for the realities of providing counseling services in a school setting when faced with large caseloads and limited resources. The authors, in a small qualitative study exploring the benefits of training school counselors in a solution-focused approach, found that the counselors in the study viewed the solution-focused model as efficacious with both parents and students. Since that time, solution-focused approaches have been examined and supported as helpful with a variety of concerns in schools such as enhancing academic performance (Fearrington, McCallum, & Skinner, 2011), addressing social and behavioral issues (Newsome, 2005), helping teachers manage classroom behavior (Brown, Powell, & Clark, 2012), and reducing truancy (Enea & Dafinoiu, 2009). Camille Jones and colleagues (2009) caution that solution-focused approaches require certain minimum cognitive abilities, such as abstraction and language skills, but can be used with wide age range in a school setting with some adaptations.

Johnny Kim and Cynthia Franklin (2009) reviewed outcome studies examining the use of solution-focused brief therapy in school settings. Although mixed results were reported in the small number of studies reviewed, the authors cautiously supported the value of solution-focused approaches for a variety of problems in a school setting. Gerald Sklare (2014) also noted that solution-focused methods are well suited for counseling in schools and may buoy the spirits of school counselors by providing a model for counseling that can be used despite typical limitations and constraints.

Solution-focused models appear to be familiar to and accepted by school counselors. John Littrel and Laurie Carlson (2009) surveyed school counselors regarding their use of brief counseling approaches and found that 87% of the 175 school counselor respondents reported familiarity and skill in brief counseling. Additionally, 85% of respondents reported that they used brief counseling approaches at least occasionally in their work in schools, although most did not describe themselves as particularly knowledgeable or skillful in its use. Dawnette Cigrand, Susannah Wood, and David Duys (2014), citing the familiarity of school counselors with solution-focused approaches, suggested that they also may be a useful model for supervision in schools.

Solution-Focused Assumptions

Sklare (2014), based on the work of John L. Walter and Jane E. Peller (1992), outlined five basic assumptions of solution-focused counseling that help organize the work of counselors. First, to create solutions, counselors should focus on successes rather than problems. Second, all problems have exceptions that can become the basis for a solution. Third, only small changes are needed since they amplify over time. Fourth, clients are the experts on their own behavior and have the resources needed to handle the difficulties that brought them to counseling. Finally, client goals should be a statement of what they want in their lives rather than what they don't want in order to facilitate change.

As mentioned earlier, it can be a struggle for some counselors to let go of the notion that problems must be the focus of counseling for a successful outcome. For many who seek help, thoughts about "the problem" have been all-consuming. They may dwell on difficulties, and ongoing circumstances keep struggles in the foreground, or those around them remind them regularly of problems and failures. It seems consistent with the way we approach medical concerns to study the problem and to determine the underlying cause in order to select an appropriate intervention. It is possible that you have resolved difficulties without ever determining the underlying cause?

Reflect: *In your own life, have you ever successfully resolved difficulties without detailed examination or consideration of the problem and its presumed underlying cause(s)?*

The second assumption Sklare (2014) noted is that all problems have exceptions. Admittedly, when in the midst of a distressing experience, it can feel like there is no possibility of relief and never a time when the problem didn't exist. This perception often falls away under closer examination and challenge. "There's never a single moment when your mom is around that the two of you aren't arguing?" "Not even when you're out for dinner? Shopping?" or "The course is always boring?" "There has never been even a single minute when something interesting was discussed?" Although the extremes of exceptions may seem absurd, it helps to illustrate that problems are typically not constant and unwavering and that the circumstances under which a problem changes for the better can be a clue to producing desired changes.

Reflect: *Think about a current difficulty in your life—are there times when it is less of a problem or even absent completely in a given day or week?*

The third assumption described by Sklare (2014) is that small changes lead to bigger changes. It is easy to think in absolute terms about change—nothing short of things being exactly as wanted is acceptable. This perspective can affect both counselors and their clients/students. Rarely, if ever, can we begin where we want to end when it comes to change. Change is change no matter the dimensions and, generally, some change is an improvement over things remaining the same. An important step in starting the process of change process is some movement in a desired direction. If small changes take a person in the direction of desired outcomes, the idea is that the changes are likely to aggregate and amplify over time. We have heard this advice in many ways in life—"walk before you run" and the idea that a journey of any length begins with the first step. Change can be overwhelming and reaching a desired endpoint can seem overwhelming or impossible at times. For some, regular exercise or a healthy diet seems elusive. These goals may remain aspirations rather than possibilities given fluctuating motivation, busy schedules, and a host of other perceived obstacles. However, small changes in activity level and diet are better than none and may pave the way for more substantial change once benefits are recognized or a habit is established. When circumstances don't permit regular counseling contact or long-term involvement, "getting the ball rolling" may be the most reasonable expectation within a brief framework.

Reflect: *Consider any current life concern. What would be a small step in the direction of the change you want that actually seems possible? If that seems too big right now, can you make the step even smaller?*

Fourth on a list of assumptions underlying solution-focused models is the notion that clients/students are the experts on their own experience and have resources that they can bring to bear on the problems they currently face (Sklare, 2014). Peter DeJong and Insoo Kim Berg (2013) refer to this as "not knowing" and "leading from one step behind" (p. 20). Students are experts on their own experience, and the job of the counselor is to be curious and to learn as much as possible about a student's perceptions of the problem and strategies for change rather than imposing perspectives or solutions. This requires that you see your student as capable of change and possessing resources that can be used for meaningful change, which is a challenge for some counselors with some students.

But why would students ask for help if they already have the expertise needed to solve the problems? Counseling, as a process, is not typically defined as giving answers and advice. This means that we facilitate rather than force, which recognizes that clients/students bring resources of value to the process. Our job is help students recognize and make use of these resources in meeting personal goals. This is not to say that school counselors are without useful expertise, techniques, or perspectives that may help cultivate or fine tune the skills and resources that students bring. There may be times when students ask for this input or when using these counselor resources is appropriate given the needs of the student.

Reflect: *When you ask for help, are you usually asking someone to tell what to do? What is your typical reaction when someone offers you unsolicited advice?*

The last point mentioned by Sklare (2014) is that clients should state goals in terms of what they want in their lives. This is a foundation for setting useful goals since it is easier to move in the direction of something you want in your life rather than away from things you do not want. Helping students clearly define how they want their lives to be when the problem is solved provides direction and can be motivating when this picture of the future is clearly articulated.

CO: *How are you hoping I can be helpful?*

CT: *I don't want to feel like this anymore . . . down on myself.*

CO: *Ok . . . tell me more. What do you want to feel and do instead?*

CT: *Um . . . I don't know . . . I guess I don't want to question or doubt everything I do.*

CO: *So . . . what would you be doing or feeling if you weren't questioning and doubting yourself?*

CT: *I think I'd have more confidence in myself. Instead of worrying if I was going to mess up, I'd just do it . . . whatever . . . and do my best and be OK with that . . .*

Reflect: *Picture a change you want in your life. Try to visualize the change in two ways—as the absence of something you don't want* ***and*** *as the presence of something you do want in its place. Which was easier or more useful?*

● STAGES IN BEING SOLUTION FOCUSED

There are various ways to conceptualize the process of working from a solution-focused perspective. DeJong and Berg (2013) present the stages of building solutions as describing the problem, developing well-formed goals, exploring for exceptions, end-of-session feedback, and evaluating client progress (pp. 17–18).

Describing the Problem

As in most counseling models, the start of counseling begins with a description of the problem. Students are usually ready for this and have practiced how to say what is bothering them or how to explain or defend behavior that has been identified as a problem. The focus from a solution-focused perspective is the student's perception of the problem and what makes the problem a concern at the moment. It also can be useful to find out what the student has done so far to resolve the difficulty and how attempted solutions have turned out. It may be a longstanding problem so past solutions are also of interest. Past attempts at resolving problems or coping can shine a light on strategies to consider or to avoid when actively exploring options.

At times, counseling is initiated at the request of someone other than the student, so opinions may differ about whether there is a problem or, if present, how it is described.

CO: *How were you hoping I could be helpful?*

CT: *I don't know . . . Mrs. Smith is the one who sent me, ask her.*

CO: *Ok, so you're annoyed at being here—you see it all differently than she does.*

CT: *I think she has a problem. She's been on back for weeks about everything in class. I don't think it's fair.*

The challenge is to elicit the student's description of the problem and then to develop a "contract" for change based on the results that the student desires. The student's view of the problem also may differ from yours, but it represents something that the student may be willing to address. It can be unsettling when you feel caught between the wishes of colleagues and administrators at school and those of your student.

CO: *So . . . the way you see it, Mrs. Smith has been on your back for a while about your behavior in class and you'd like to see it stop.*

CT: *Yeah, that would be nice, but I don't see it happening. She just doesn't like me.*

With students who reach out for help on their own, the process is not unlike starting any other counseling relationship. Find out what brought the student for services and gather information about the student's experience of the problem. A key difference from other approaches is that the focus is on exploring solutions rather digging for possible causes of the problem.

CO: *Hello. I'm glad you came in. So what were you hoping to get from our talking together?*

CT: *I don't know; it's been so frustrating with my friends lately. Everybody is fighting and I'm getting blamed.*

CO: *I'm sorry to hear that. These weeks have been tough I imagine. What were you hoping we might do that would be helpful?*

CT: *I think I just need someone to talk to since they won't talk. Maybe figure out a way to get things back the way they were . . . or at least get them to hear my side of things.*

It is important to be empathic and understanding of the student's concerns, but usually there isn't need to gather as much information about the problem as you might do in traditional counseling approaches. There are a few exceptions to consider. When there is evidence of risk of harm to self or others or the suggestion of child abuse or neglect, it is important to gather the details necessary to adequately assess risk and to address legal and ethical responsibilities to protect those involved.

The initial exploration of the problem is an opportunity to acknowledge the student's concerns, to establish a relationship, and to define what changes the student would like to see as a result of counseling. When time is limited, aiming at desired changes or solutions rather than a detailed exploration of the problem and possible underlying causes can expedite the process. This is not a suggestion to ignore or dismiss concerns that are important to the students who seek your help. Instead, it is a recommended shift in attention from the details surrounding current difficulties to those associated with desired outcomes.

CT: *My friends argue with me about everything. All of a sudden everything I do is wrong. I said hello to a girl in the hall and they jumped on me for talking to her. I couldn't believe it, but then they asked me to hang out with them last weekend.*

CO: *It seems like things suddenly changed for the worse and it's been confusing. So it was a real surprise when they invited you out. What happened to make that possible?*

In this brief exchange, the counselor could be interested in the kinds of things the student and her friends fight about or why talking with another girl became an issue. Both of those issues may be interesting, but potentially a distraction from moving in the direction of the student's goal.

Goal Setting

Goals are an essential part of counseling relationships and goal setting is a basic counseling skill. Solution-focused approaches tend to be future oriented, and defining life without the problem is the aim of establishing goals. This stage often involves work and patience. What matters most is what your student wants to work on, and it may require restraint to resist imposing goals when students struggle with this step or choose a goal that you might not find important or relevant.

CO: *What do you want to be different in your life as a result of our work together?*

CT: *I just want all this to go away!*

Students often need assistance with taking vague, impressionistic goals and turning them into clear statements that can be used to guide and measure counseling efforts. As mentioned previously, it can be tempting to help the process along by feeding the student a goal or the language for the goal rather than exploring and clarifying.

CT: *I guess . . . I'm just tired of feeling this way . . .*

CO: *Ok, so can we say that your goal is to increase your self-esteem?*

CT: *Um . . . well . . . I guess so . . .*

There are some psychological constructs that we often find relevant when conceptualizing problems, but they may not be particularly meaningful to students and may not provide enough specific information to inform the counseling process.

CT: *I don't know; I'm just tired of feeling this way . . .*

CO: *How do you want it to be different?*

CT: *It would be nice to actually be happy sometimes, to go into a new situation and say "you can do this" rather than being afraid something bad is going to happen.*

CO: *So instead of avoiding things or doubting yourself you'd be more confident and the way that this would show is that you would be more likely to try new things. How else would you be different if this was no longer a problem?*

Similar to Sklare (2014), DeJong and Berg (2013) note that it tends to be easier for people to accomplish things that they view as positive so they recommend that goals describe the presence rather than the absence of something.

CT: *I want to stop fighting with my friends all the time.*

CO: *What will you being doing instead?*

CT: *I don't know—the stuff we used to do.*

CO: *Such as?*

CT: *We'd talk about school, music, friends, parents. . . . If we didn't agree, we just let it go.*

It is also useful to make sure that goals are realistic and can be accomplished with the time, energy, and resources available. Related to this is focusing on the first steps toward accomplishing a goal rather than the end point, especially if it seems overwhelming or out of reach at the moment. Breaking goals down into manageable steps can make it easier to commit to action and to realize positive change (DeJong & Berg, 2013).

One particular question that is often associated with solution-focused approaches is referred to as the "miracle question" (O'Connell, 2012). Although it is commonly associated with solution-focused counseling, practitioners may not fully understand its value or use this strategy correctly. The miracle question is primarily a tool to help clients visualize the future and to clarify specifically what they want life to look like after the problem is resolved, including the impact on significant others (Hanton, 2011; O'Connell, 2012).

The basic phrasing of the miracle question is often credited to de Shazer (1988): "Suppose that one night, while you were asleep, there was a miracle and this problem was solved. How would you know?

What would be different?" (p. 5). The presentation of the miracle question varies by practitioner and some solution-focused counselors may choose not to use it with some or all clients. The task for the student is to paint a clear picture of the future without the problem. As with goals in general, this may require helping the student to state what will be present and different rather than absent in life. If you choose to use this question, it is important to take time to develop a full picture of the change—the process may not be simple or quick.

CO: *So, let me ask you a question that may seem odd. Suppose you went home tonight and something happened when you were asleep and when you woke up this particular problem was gone, but you didn't know it because you were asleep. How would you know it was gone? What would be the first thing you would notice?*

CT: *Hmmm . . . the problem was just gone? I'd be happier . . . um . . . I wouldn't be afraid to go to school that day.*

CO: *OK . . . what would be feeling instead of fear?*

CT: *Well, I'd be excited to go to classes because I'd have homework done and I'd be ready to answer questions and talk to friends.*

CO: And what else would you notice? (What would others notice was different?)

Responses to the miracle question can be the beginning of exploring exceptions to the problem because some part of the change that students describe may already be occurring at times. The search for exceptions will be discussed in more detail in the next section.

CO: *Are there times now when you go to school and notice even a little bit of that miracle? Times when you feel more excited about classes or more confident?*

CT: *Well . . . yes . . . I have my days . . .*

CO: *What is different about those days—when you wake up and feel more confident?*

CT: *I don't know, sometimes I just say to myself—this is stupid, you are no different than anyone else. Just go and be yourself. Stop worrying what everyone thinks—as if I knew anyway.*

Searching for Exceptions

A key step in constructing solutions with students is exploring exceptions to problems. As discussed previously, typically problems are not always present in a person's life or vary in intensity during any particular day or week. Rather than hunting for root causes of problems, which can be difficult to determine with any degree of certainty, the task is to search for recent examples of exceptions to problems that can guide students in the direction of desired changes. At times, problems are so consuming that people fail to notice instances when the problem is better or absent.

CT: *I never get along with Ms. Smith. She always has it in for me and I never get a break. She's got her mind made up; I don't see how this will help. . .*

CO: *So . . . there is never been a time in class with her when you don't feel picked on?*

CT: *Not really. Well . . . I mean, when she's teaching she's not arguing with me or when she's talking with others in the class . . . times like that I guess.*

CO: *Was there a time this week when things were like that—when you two weren't arguing or getting into it?*

CT: *Um . . . sure. We discussed a book we were reading in class and everybody was into it and talking so she really wasn't paying attention to me.*

CO: *So what were you doing that made that possible—for her not to pay attention to you?*

CT: *Ah . . . I'm not sure . . . I guess I just was listening to everybody talking about the book. The book was OK, so I read most of it and had some of the same ideas as other kids.*

The challenge is to closely examine the times when a problem isn't present for clues to what was different at those times that helped. There are likely to be instances when the difference may not seem to be something your student said or did that can be repeated. While changes in context and circumstance can make a difference (e.g., I notice I can focus better on math if the TV is off.), identifying the events or differences that can be influenced intentionally by your student is also useful.

CO: *OK . . . so Ms. Smith and others in the class were busy with the book discussion. What were you doing that was different . . . that made it possible for Ms. Smith not to focus on you in the ways that you don't want?*

CT: *I'm not sure . . . I mostly just sat back and listened. I was tired that day too. I actually did answer a question she asked, but I raised my hand.*

CO: *It was different that you sat back and listened—what made that possible for you? (OR Wow—how did you decide to raise your hand that time?)*

At times, it is difficult to identify recent exceptions to the problem or any exceptions at all. An alternative is to search for times when the problem was less of a problem rather than completely absent.

CO: *So, there hasn't been a single week when you completed all of your assigned homework, but was there time recently when you completed some of it? What was different when you were able to complete some of the work?*

If no exceptions are identifiable, another option is to ask about times when the problem could have occurred but did not or times when the student was able to keep the problem from getting worse.

CO: *Feeling sad has been tough to shake over these last weeks from what you've said. You can't remember a time when it wasn't there and pretty intense. I'm curious about what happened after the fight with your friend. It seems like you didn't feel any sadder than before—how did you manage to not feel any worse?*

OR

CO: *You got into it again with your teacher, but this time you weren't sent to the office—what was different this time that it didn't get to that point?*

Given that problems garner so much attention, it's possible that exceptions are missed. Assigning the task of paying attention to one's experiences surrounding the problem may be useful in increasing awareness of changes in intensity and periods of reprieve. Between-session tasks such as this will be discussed later.

Activity: Experiment With the Model Yourself

Identify a current life concern (e.g., completing work on time, building confidence, practicing regular self-care, spending too much time on social media, etc.) that you would like to be different.

Consider—Is this problem always a problem? Every day? Every minute of every day? (If the answer isn't obvious, take some time over the next days to pay attention to the problem and its pattern in your life.)

If "no," (the problem is not always a problem) describe below when the **problem is not present.** In particular, note what is different about those times when the problem is not a problem. What do you do differently that makes the problem not a problem?

Exceptions to the problem:

____

____

____

____

If you said that the problem is always present, is the problem always at the same intensity or level of severity? If the **problem fluctuates** and is better at times, list below what you notice about the times when the problem is less severe/intense that may account for the difference.

____

____

____

____

If you noted that the problem is **always present** and does not fluctuate in intensity/severity, think about what have you done to keep the problem from getting worse? List below, the things that may not reduce or eliminate the problem, but have kept things from escalating.

____

____

____

____

Based on what you observed, what suggestions can you offer to yourself about factors that make a difference in your experience of the problem that could be used to achieve the change you want?

____

____

____

____

End-of-Session Feedback

The next step in working with students from a solution-focused perspective is providing end-of-session feedback. DeJong and Berg (2013) clarify that feedback is provided to help pull together information that can be useful in constructing solutions. They organize the process of providing end-of-session feedback into three components including compliments, a bridge, and a task or suggestion (p. 123).

Compliments show that you have listened to what matters to your student and that you recognize his or her strengths and resources. Compliments encourage and affirm those qualities and actions of your student that may contribute to positive change (Sklare, 2014).

CO: *It takes courage to tackle the academic struggles you've had, especially when you have doubts that anything will help.*

OR

CO: *It's impressive that you have made it to school every day, even though you've been feeling down and discouraged. School seems to really matter to you.*

DeJong and Berg (2013) characterize a *bridge* as a tool that ties compliments to the suggestions you offer at the end.

CO: *Because school matters so much, one thing I suggest over the next days is . . .*

OR

CO: *Because you've decided it's important to you to do something about your grades, until we get together again what I suggest is . . .*

A bridge uses your student's words, ideas, or qualities as the basis for doing something to address the concern that resulted in a counseling contact.

The final step in this process is offering suggestions. This can seem intimidating if you mistakenly view suggestions as advice or strategies for solving the problem. As a reminder, *solution focused* does not mean that the responsibility for solving the student's problem falls on the shoulders of the counselor. Offering an end-of-session suggestion does not require that you construct a brilliant, clever, complex task that resolves the problem by the next meeting. DeJong and Berg (2013) broadly categorize this step as either suggesting that the student observe something in his or her life or do something different until the next meeting. Which type of suggestion you provide is linked to what you have learned about your student. Sklare (2014) offers that for individuals who have clear goals and can identify exceptions to the problems in their lives, the primary suggestion is that they continue to do whatever worked before to produce the desired outcome (do something).

CO: *Because school matters so much and talking to yourself the way you suggested helps you feel more confident about going to school, I suggest that you continue to say those helpful things to yourself in the morning. Also notice which comments have the biggest effect on boosting your confidence.*

If students are not at the point of articulating specific goals or have not been able to identify exceptions to the problem, Sklare (2014) recommends that the end-of-session suggestions directing the student to pay attention to changes in the experience of the problem that could be a sign of an exception (observe something). As discussed previously, these include times when the problem is absent, less intense, or did not occur when normally it would.

CO: *As you said, you are tired of feeling this way, but you're not sure what to do. I appreciate that you really want it to change . . . so until we get together again, I'd like to suggest that you pay attention to any time when things are even a little better. Notice what's different whenever things are more like the way you want them. Pay attention to what is different that allows things to be even a little better.*

Finally, there are students who may not agree that there is a problem or they are not ready to develop a specific goal for meeting in counseling. With these individuals, since there is no "contract" yet for counseling, it does not make sense to assign tasks that involve anything active. Instead, the counselor is advised to simply provide compliments as possible (Sklare, 2014).

CO: *I get that it's difficult to be here today when it wasn't your idea and it's not something you're sure will be useful right now. I'm impressed that even though you feel that way, you decided to come anyway.*

Evaluating Progress

DeJong and Berg (2013) stress the importance of evaluating client progress on a regular basis by using a process of client self-rating called *scaling* (p. 18). Jeffrey Guterman (2013) notes that scaling helps clients pay attention to exceptions to problems and translate subjective experiences into numerical ratings.

Often counselors ask students to rate some aspect of their experience using a 0 to 10 scale. To facilitate understanding of the rating, it is helpful to define what the anchors of the scale mean.

CO: *So, on a scale of 0 to 10 scale—with 10 representing the most confident you have felt about yourself at school and 0 being the least confident—where are you today?*

The first use of scaling may occur in the initial meeting to gauge your student's assessment of the severity of the problem. Subsequent applications of scaling may be used in later sessions to mark progress to hunt for differences that could be explored to identify resources for change.

CT: *Last week I was a 3. But, Tuesday I would say it was maybe 5 or even 6.*

CO: *Wow, Tuesday was much better. What was different that made it a 5?*

CT: *It was what we talked about before. I got up and thought "I'm sick of this—I'm just as good as everyone else. I'm going to have a good day." It wasn't perfect, but it was better and it started out good. I guess I was more determined.*

CO: *Yeah, it sounds like it. What helped you feel more determined?*

Scaling also can be used to help construct plans for future change and even to decide when counseling has been successful.

CO: *Tuesday was a 5 . . . where do you want to be on that scale?*

CT: *Well, 10 would be great, but I don't really see that happening. I don't think anyone is really a 10 anyway. I was happy with a 5! Wednesday wasn't as good. I guess if I could be somewhere between 5 and 7 every day that would be some much better. I'd be happy with that.*

CO: *Going from 3 to 5 was a big jump. What could you do differently that would help you be more consistently at a 3.5 or even a 4 to start?*

OR

CO: *How will things be different when you are consistently a 6 or 7? What will you notice? What will others notice about you?*

As discussed previously, small changes are the focus, so small increases on the scale become part of planning. Realistically, change isn't always positive and in the desired direction, but the scaling technique still allows a student to pay attention to differences and to discern strategies for managing problems.

CT: *Today is a 2, if that. I just really started doubting myself. I don't do well when I have to present in front of the class. I think about messing up and looking stupid.*

CO: *OK . . . so being up in front of classmates is something you can get really worried about. How did you keep it from getting worse, like a 1? Somehow, you were able to get yourself to come in for the presentation even though you were feeling pretty unsure about it.*

Scaling questions can be used to assess and track a variety of aspects of a student's experience such as motivation and confidence as well as progress on specific goals. Given the value of scaling and its ease of use, it is important to guard against overuse in sessions. It is one important tool, but exclusive reliance on scaling in sessions may turn off students.

Subsequent Meetings

At times, you may have only one opportunity to meet with a student to address a current concern. In that meeting you will explore the student's perception of the problem, clarify a specific goal, identify exceptions to the problem that can be used to reach desired outcomes, and provide suggestions at the end of the meeting clarifying a process of change. If you have the opportunity to meet again, it is helpful to think about how to structure the next meetings. In subsequent meetings, the process becomes one of asking about change and inquiring about differences that may account for the changes noted. DeJong and Berg's (2013, p. 149) acronym *EARS* is a way to think about how to structure future meetings.

E – elicit the exceptions

A – amplify the exception

R – reinforce

S – start again

Using this model, the counselor asks about changes that have occurred since the last meeting related to the problem. When an exception is identified, it is explored in detail to gather specific information about what made the change possible. Successes are reinforced, and the process is recycled in the session to identify other changes that may yield exceptions and clues for change (DeJong & Berg, 2013). This process may include self-assessment (scaling) and then end with suggestions using the format described previously. When students have achieved goals, the focus becomes identifying strategies to successfully maintain the progress made and to summarize what changes made a difference.

CO: *It seems like you have been able to stay in that 5 to 7 range on confidence that you were hoping for. What have you learned that made a difference? What will you continue to do to keep yourself in that range or even move higher?*

● WHAT SOLUTION-FOCUSED COUNSELING IS AND IS NOT

A solution focus is not an avoidance of problems, but rather a choice about what to explore and emphasize in the helping process. Solution-focused counselors do not ignore concerns and look only at the "bright" side of life. The goal is not to find a quick fix, to provide false hope, or to bypass critical steps in relationship building or prudent counseling fundamentals in favor of supplying solutions (advice). When faced with the choice of digging into a problem or exploring an individual's existing resources as a path to change, the latter is chosen.

Solution-focused approaches tend to be pragmatic and do not involve the construction of problem explanations that involve complex models of psychological functioning or human development. However, pragmatic and straightforward should not be confused with simple. Becoming proficient as a solution-focused counselor requires dedication and supervised practice. Aside from learning strategies for exploring and identifying useful client resources, becoming solution focused may involve a reexamination of basic beliefs about the counseling process. For some, this model will "fit" and become a primary way of working with students. Others may choose to develop skills with this approach so that it can be combined with other models or available as an option depending on a student's needs and circumstances.

Ongoing professional reading, training, and supervision in solution-focused methods are critical in developing your skills. The following are a sample of the many resources available to assist with learning the model.

Watch: Online Resources

http://www.youtube.com/watch?v=tjdJhdA9mE4 (first sessions/substance users)

http://www.youtube.com/watch?v=n-G6KD1Dn3U (setting goals)

http://www.youtube.com/watch?v=6Fe8D0hAQh0 (defining goals)

http://www.youtube.com/watch?v=S5MPg0hhm4I (miracle question)

http://www.youtube.com/watch?v=ezK92jtu-c0 (goal-setting/differences)

http://www.youtube.com/watch?v=fQBZlgmebwY (exploring an exception)

http://www.youtube.com/watch?v=EtfFMiz5vKY (focusing on strengths/finding exceptions)

http://www.youtube.com/watch?v=U0Igt-cmUHM (scaling questions/prioritizing)

http://www.youtube.com/watch?v=EBuE5kjTmKw (scaling questions)

Resources: Organizations

Solution-Focused Brief Therapy Association: http://www.sfbta.org/
The Institute for Solution-Focused Therapy: http://www.solutionfocused.net
BRIEF: http://www.brief.org.uk/

• CLASSROOM ACTIVITIES

Listening for Exceptions

Of the basic steps in working from a solution-focused perspective in counseling, "listening for exceptions" can be particularly challenging. Students and counselors tend to be drawn to problems and intensely interested in what is going wrong and causing difficulties in life. The purpose of this activity is to help you make a deliberate decision to listen for strengths, resources, and exceptions to problems.

In a group of three, designate one member as counselor, the second as client, and the third as a process observer. For 10 minutes, invite the client to talk about a concern for which he or she wants help. The counselor's task is to be empathic while listening specifically for

- times when the problem was less of a problem or did not occur.
- strategies the student spontaneously uses to manage the concern.
- strategies the student deliberately used to handle the concern.

Remember that the goal is not to ignore or dismiss the concerns raised by your "student," but rather to be intentional about listening for the building blocks of change. Allow yourself to be naturally curious about past successes and times when the problem was absent or better.

The role of the observer is to stop the exercise if it becomes consistently problem focused. The counselor and observer can confer about possible exceptions and resources and return to the role-play when ready. The observer also can independently record exceptions, strengths, and resources for later discussion.

At the completion of the time period, discuss the following:

Counselor

- What was your experience listening for exceptions and resources rather than problems?
- At the times when you were better able to do this, what made it possible?
- What will help you be even more proficient in attending to exceptions and opportunities for change?

Student/Client

- Even though you were aware of the purpose of the exercise, what was your experience of this approach? Did you believe the counselor was ignoring your concerns?
- What did you find most helpful? Was it difficult to not talk about the problem?
- If you could coach the counselor in this role-play, what was missed or overlooked?

Observer

- What is your impression of the flow and focus of the role-play?
- What strengths, resources, and exceptions did you notice that were not mentioned by the counselor?
- What was different about the times when the role-play was solution versus problem focused?

Class/Group

- What fears or concerns did you have about applying this model? What will help you to be more proficient?
- What can you do if a student says there are no exceptions to the problem?

Case Example

Anita is a 16-year-old high school junior who was referred to the school counselor by her field hockey coach because of difficulty controlling her anger with teammates and opponents. Anita is a good player and, at times, a leader on the team, but she loses her temper with teammates when they make mistakes or fail to follow her directions. Recently, she was ejected from a game for inappropriate language directed at an opposing player and a referee. She has had conversations with her coach about her leadership role and the effect she has on teammates. Classroom teachers also have commented about Anita's "short fuse" and have had concerns about her behavior in competitive situations with peers.

Anita recognizes that she can be impatient and intolerant, but she sees it as stemming from her passion for sports and strong desire to do her best in situations. She acknowledged that she would like to have better control of her temper. Early in their work together, the school counselor asked Anita about exceptions to the problem: "Are there times when you could get angry about something, but don't?" "Are there times when you might feel annoyed or a little angry, but you can keep it in check and it doesn't cause any problems?"

With this line of exploration, Anita noted that she has a stressful part-time job, but never seems to lose her cool. Anita and her counselor explored this exception to the problem in detail. Anita described how she is able to "distance" herself from the behavior of customers and coworkers and gave several reasons why their behavior and comments do not affect her as much. The counselor became curious about Anita's success in managing reactions on her job ("I tell myself that what they think doesn't matter." "I'm polite, but I tell myself that their complaints aren't really about me." "I figure they can do it however they want—it's their life.") and invited her to consider how these same strategies might be useful in sports or the classroom. Anita admitted that she wasn't aware that she was doing anything in particular to manage her anger and paid closer attention to her successful anger management at work. The counselor complimented Anita's desire to do what is best for her team and to avoid hassles at school. Since Anita was indicating an awareness of the problem and a specific goal for change, she and her counselor constructed a task that involved using what already helps with anger at her job in other arenas of her life. Subsequent meetings with Anita tracked her experience of moving toward her goal of better anger management and her growing awareness of what made a difference in her emotional control.

Discussion

- How did a solution-focused approach differ from a traditional problem-focused model with this student?
- What advantages and disadvantages do you see with using a solution-focused approach in this case?

• REFERENCES

Brown, E. L., Powell, E., & Clark, A. (2012). Working on what works: Working with teachers to improve classroom behavior and relationships. *Educational Psychology in Practice, 28*(1), 19–30.

Cigrand, D., Wood, S. M., & Duys, D. (2014). School counselors' use of solution-focused tenets and techniques in school-based site supervision. *Journal of School Counseling, 12*, 1–33.

DeJong, P., & Berg, I. K. (2013). *Interviewing for solutions* (4th ed.). Belmont, CA: Brooks/Cole.

de Shazer, S. (1988). *Clues: Investigating solutions in brief therapy.* New York, NY: Norton.

Enea, V., & Dafinoiu, I. (2009). Motivational/solution-focused intervention for reducing school truancy among adolescents. *Journal of Cognitive and Behavioral Psychotherapies, 9*, 185–198.

Kim, J. S., & Franklin, C. (2009). Solution-focused brief therapy in schools: A review of the outcome literature. *Children & Youth Services Review, 31*, 464–470.

Fearrington, J. Y., McCallum, R. S., & Skinner, C. H. (2011). Increasing math assignment completion using solution-focused brief counseling. *Education and Treatment of Children, 34*(1), 61–80.

Guterman, J. T. (2013). *Mastering the art of solution-focused counseling* (2nd ed.). Alexandria, VA: American Counseling Association.

Hanton, P. (2011). *Skills in solution focused brief counselling & psychotherapy.* Thousand Oaks, CA: Sage.

Jones, C. N., Hart, S. R., Jimerson, S. R., Dowdy, E., Earhart, J., Renshaw, T. L., . . . & Anderson, D. (2009). Solution-focused brief counseling: Guidelines, considerations, and implications for school psychologists. *California School Psychologist, 14,* 111–122.

Littrell, J. M., & Carlson, L. (2009). School counselors' adoption of brief counseling: The diffusion of an innovative practice. *Journal of School Counseling, 7*(20), 20.

Mostert, D. L., Johnson, E., & Mostert, M. P. (1997). The utility of solution-focused, brief counseling in schools: Potential from and initial study. *Professional School Counseling, 1,* 21–24.

Newsome, W. S. (2005). The impact of solution-focused brief therapy with at-risk junior high school students. *Children & Schools, 27*(2), 83–90.

O'Connell, B. (2012). *Solution-focused therapy* (3rd ed.). Thousand Oaks, CA: Sage.

Sklare, G. B. (2014). *Brief counseling that works: A solution-focused therapy approach for school counselors and other mental health professionals* (3rd ed.). Thousand Oaks, CA: Corwin.

Walter, J. L., & Peller, J. E. (1992). *Becoming solution-focused in brief therapy.* New York, NY: Brunner/Mazel.

Lesson 21

GROUPS IN SCHOOLS

Sarah Springer
Monmouth University

Heidi Roselle
Professional School Counselor and Counselor Educator

"Am I the Only Person Worried About This Test?"

Real Life

Student: "Am I the only person worried about this test?"

Counselor-in-Training: "No—many of your peers are feeling very similarly about the upcoming state tests. With a lot of discussion in our community about what these scores mean, several students have expressed concerns about their performance. For instance, some of your classmates in Healthy Students' School District have shared worries about how this test might affect their academic placement in school, their abilities to get into a good college and have successful careers, and how their parents or friends might react toward them if they do not do well. This puts a lot of pressure on students just like you to feel like this upcoming state test can determine many things about your future academic, career, and social/emotional life.

"Fortunately, an important part of a school counselor's job is to support your academic, career, and social and emotional development (American School Counselor Association [ASCA], 2014a). Small-group counseling is one way that we can help you to know that you are not alone with these feelings and support you in recognizing that you can build strength and confidence in learning how to manage these feelings successfully. Your school counselor, Mrs. Saunders, and I would love for you to consider joining our upcoming small group, *Eyes on the Prize*."

Lesson Twenty-One

Groups in Schools

Sarah Springer
Monmouth University

Heidi Roselle
Professional School Counselor and Counselor Educator

"Am I the Only Person Worried About This Test?"

Essential Question: How can I learn to be a better test taker and put less pressure on myself?

Objectives

Students will

- demonstrate developmental knowledge of elementary school students.
- demonstrate an understanding of psychoeducation groups, including the infusion of content and process-oriented discussions.
- demonstrate an understanding of the stages of group process, therapeutic factors, and ethical and cultural considerations surrounding a diverse group of elementary-age students.

CACREP Standards

- Understand dynamics associated with group process and development. (II.6.b)
- Understand therapeutic factors and how they contribute to group effectiveness. (II.6.c)
- Understand approaches to group formation, including recruiting, screening, and selecting members. (II.6.e)
- Understand types of groups and other considerations that affect conducting groups in varied settings. (II.6.f)
- Understand ethical and culturally relevant strategies for designing and facilitating groups. (II.6.g)
- Understand school counselor roles as leaders, advocates, and systems change agents in P–12 schools. (V.2.a)

MPCAC Standards

- group theory, practice, and social-justice advocacy
- human development and wellness across the life span
- ecological, contextual, and social-justice foundations of human development
- counseling, consultation, and social-justice advocacy theories and skills

Video Spark

https://www.ted.com/talks/kelly_mcgonigal_how_to_make_stress_your_friend

How to make stress your friend (Kelly McGonigal)

GROUP COUNSELING IN THE SCHOOLS

Over the years, as our understanding of group counseling has continued to evolve, counselors have considered its application with a variety of populations. Research has suggested that group counseling represents a microcosm of children and adolescents' natural social environments (Gladding, 2012; Kulic, Dagley, & Horne, 2001; Pérusee, Goodnough, & Lee, 2009). With children and adolescents spending the better portions of their weekdays in the school setting and emotional projections or displacement of feelings likely to manifest themselves within this social context (Shillingford & Edwards, 2008), the school environment represents an opportunity for emotional expression skills and self-regulation to be effectively addressed through meaningful feedback exchanges in the small-group setting.

Embedded in the Delivery quadrant of the ASCA National Model (2012), group counseling is recognized as an essential intervention used to help address the academic, career, and social/emotional needs of children and adolescents in the school environment (Akos, Goodnough, & Milsom, 2004; Bore, Armstrong, & Womack, 2010; Sink, Edwards, & Eppler, 2012). In an effort to garner support and advocacy for group counseling interventions, stakeholder input is often sought through needs assessments to assist in the design, planning, and overall organization of each group. Data collected throughout this process can be used to further advocate for future group counseling interventions.

Accountability and Group Counseling Advocacy

Accountability represents another integral component of a successful comprehensive school counseling program (ASCA, 2012). Within this quadrant, school counselors use data-informed practice to advocate for the appropriate definition and usage of their roles and the interventions they provide to students on a daily basis (Stone & Dahir, 2011). Carolyn Stone and Carol Dahir's (2011) *MEASURE of Student Success* outlines an accountability tool used by many practicing school counselors to present sequential data demonstrating student outcomes. Using the acronym *MEASURE* (Mission, Elements, Analyze, Stakeholders Unite, Results, and Educate), school counselors can systematically collect data to support the development, design, and advocacy for their counseling programs.

This chapter walks readers through each of the six steps of *MEASURE* to illustrate how a school counselor can implement a data-driven approach to group counseling advocacy in the schools; these steps and their accompanying group counseling interventions reflect movement toward the Accountability quadrant embedded in the ASCA National Model. The example described in this chapter depicts collaborative decision-making between a preservice school counseling intern and her site supervisor. As the group counseling program is outlined, readers are encouraged to consider the following background information provided to help contextualize the specific priorities of the school district and surrounding community.

SCHOOL DISTRICT BACKGROUND

Healthy Students' School District is embedded in a high-achieving community. Individual schools within this district consistently win honors recognized within and among surrounding communities based on their academic, athletic, and musical achievements. Average students in this school district score above national norms on standardized assessments. Both gifted and talented and remedial programs are offered to support the individual academic needs of each student. The response to intervention (RTI) model is embedded throughout the curriculum and serves as a way to monitor the progress for struggling students. Likewise, project-based learning is embedded throughout the curriculum to serve as additive enrichment opportunity provided to all students. The secondary schools within this district are well respected across the region and are known to graduate students who attend prestigious universities and colleges throughout the country.

Each of the six steps of *MEASURE* is outlined below in relation to the priorities of this particular school district. The description of this program is based on the experience of school counselor "Mrs. Saunders" and preservice school counseling intern "Ms. Rogers." Sample surveys, letters, lesson plans, and group outlines are included under each heading to illustrate various group counseling interventions used to support students and collect data for future group counseling advocacy.

● STEP 1: MISSION

> "Connect the design, implementation, and management of the school counseling program to the mission of the school . . ."
>
> (Stone & Dahir, 2011, p. 29)

In connection with the mission of the school district, Mrs. Saunders and Ms. Rogers prepare parent/guardian and student surveys to further clarify student needs previously discussed in individual meetings with district and community stakeholders. Parent/guardian surveys are distributed during parent–teacher conferences. Families who are unable to attend these meetings are provided surveys in a sealed envelope given to their child to take home. Student surveys are provided during monthly developmental counseling groups following parent–teacher conferences. At this time, Mrs. Saunders and Ms. Rogers take the opportunity to answer any additional questions about the survey items. Examples of these surveys are provided below.

Sample Parent/Guardian Survey

Dear families,

As you gather to meet your child's teacher at parent–teacher conferences, we would like to take this opportunity to tell you that the school counseling department is looking for your feedback as we initiate small counseling groups for your children. Group counseling can be beneficial for all students. Each of our groups promises to incorporate social skill development, healthy communication skills, peer support, and self-awareness. Please check off as many of the areas below that you think may pertain to your child's needs. Depending on the results of this survey as well as one given to your children directly, we will begin to organize small groups specific to these topics. At this time, you will be contacted with more details to determine your interest level. Please note that checking off these boxes neither guarantees nor obligates your child to participate in any future group counseling interventions. If you have any questions about these topics, please do not hesitate to contact us.

Sincerely,

Mrs. Saunders, School Counselor & Ms. Rogers, School Counseling Intern

Parent/Guardian Survey

Your name: ______________________ Child's name: ______________________

Please feel free to elaborate on any of the experiences you check off below. This information will be stored in a confidential place in the school counseling office.

(Continued)

(Continued)

I wish my child knew someone else . . .

- whose parents have gone through or are going through a divorce.
- who struggles with academic stress.
- who struggles to make and keep good friends.
- who has lost a family or friend close.
- who often worries about tests and grades.
- who struggles with anger management.
- whose family speaks a different language other than English.
- who often experiences stress.
- who struggles to communicate their needs appropriately.
- who also (fill in) ____.

If there is any additional information you would like us to know about your child, such as any significant life events that have happened over the summer (e.g., death of a family member or pet, birth of a new sibling, change in dwelling or family structure, etc.), changes in behavior or emotional state, recent accomplishments, or anything else you feel is significant, please feel free to share on the lines provided below. Having this type of information will help us to better work with your child in the upcoming school year. If you'd like, you can also set up a time to meet with a counselor to discuss in person. We would love to hear from you!

____

____

____

____

Please return back to the school counseling office by (Date)

Sample Student Survey

Dear Upper Elementary Students,

The school counseling department is looking to hear from you! We have some exciting small groups that we would like to offer and want to know what topics are most important to you. If you are interested in possibly joining a group with Mrs. Saunders and Ms. Rogers, you may check off <u>up to THREE</u> topics below to complete this sentence.

Name:________________ Grade:__________________ Teacher:______________________

I wish I knew someone else . . .

- whose parents got a divorce.
- who sometimes worries about the way they look.
- who also wishes they had a good friend.
- who knows what it feels like to be the new kid at school.

- who has lost someone special in their life.
- whose family lives in two different houses.
- whose family speaks a different language other than English.
- who finds it hard to control their choices when they get angry.
- who also feels worried about taking tests and getting good grades.
- who also feels stressed out in school.
- who also feels pressure to get into a good college.
- who also likes to read and wants to learn how to become a leader in our school.
- who also ____.

Please return to the school counseling office by (Date)

● STEP 2: ELEMENT

"Identify and examine the critical data elements in your school district."

(Stone & Dahir, 2011, p. 29)

Data from the student and parent surveys suggest a need to further understand students' experiences with stress specific to standardized test-taking. In addition, many students expressed a desire to make more friends, and several families highlighted a need for their children to learn healthy coping strategies for managing anger and friendship conflict. These areas are targeted in the following two group interventions:

1. Developmental Large-Group Counseling Lesson

The following classroom lesson served as psychoeducation for students as well as additional sources of data for school counselors. Mrs. Saunders and Ms. Rogers used this group to identify additional themes in which to address in future small-group counseling interventions.

Classroom Developmental Counseling Lesson: Stress and Anger Management

Lesson Plan Title: "How to STOP before you POP."
Grade Level: Upper elementary school students
Learning Objectives Students will • identify situations that cause stress/anger in their personal lives and identify their unique physical/emotional stress and/or anger cues. • learn strategies to control and de-escalate physical/emotional reactions to stressful and/or anger-inducing situations. • recognize commonalities in their peers' experiences.

(Continued)

(Continued)

ASCA Mindsets and Behaviors for Student Success

Mindset Standards

- belief in development of whole self, including a healthy balance of mental, social/emotional, and physical well-being
- self-confidence in ability to succeed
- sense of belonging in the school environment
- belief in using abilities to their fullest to achieve high-quality results and outcomes
- positive attitude toward work and learning

Behavior Standards

- Demonstrate critical-thinking skills to make informed decisions.
- Demonstrate ability to assume responsibility.
- Demonstrate self-discipline and self-control.
- Demonstrate ability to overcome barriers to learning.
- Demonstrate effective coping skills when faced with a problem.
- Demonstrate personal safety skills.
- Demonstrate empathy.
- Demonstrate social maturity and behaviors appropriate to the situation and environment.

Duration of Lesson: 45 Minutes

Required Materials

- book: *Soda Pop Head* by Julia Cook
- copies of Body/Bottle Handout (one per student)
- writing implements for each student

Introduction to Lesson

Facilitator introduces the topic of stress/anger management. This lesson is used as a baseline assessment to determine students' abilities to recognize when they are starting to feel stressed or angry and any adaptive (and maladaptive) coping strategies already in place.

Facilitator instructs the class:

- Raise your hand if you have ever felt stressed or angry. (Remind students to look around the room to see whose hands are raised; facilitator notes shared experiences.)
- Next, raise your hand if you have noticed your body giving you warning signs that you are starting to feel stressed or angry? (Ask students with raised hands to provide examples of the warning signs. Highlight connections between physical symptoms—going to the nurse—and stress.)
- Finally, raise your hand if you know any ways to calm your mind and body down when you start to feel stressed or angry? (Ask students with raised hands to provide examples of coping strategies.)

Facilitator explains:

Today we are going to read a book about a little boy named Lester who struggles to control his anger and stress. As we read this book together, pay attention to what happens to Lester when he begins to feel stressed and angry. Notice what Lester's body looks like and how he describes his feelings. Also, see if you can listen for ways that Lester helps himself to feel better when he realizes that he is stressed or angry.

Step-by-Step Procedures

1) Story Time: Read the book aloud to the students, pausing periodically to check for understanding and to ask students to make text-to-self connections.

2) Class Discussion: After finishing the book, lead the class in a discussion using any of the following suggested prompts:

   - What were some things that made Lester feel like he might explode or POP in the book? *(e.g., being teased by other students, having to redo his school assignment, or when his sister played his video game without asking)*
   - How could Lester tell that he was starting to feel stressed or angry? *(e.g., his ears got hot, his head started to "fizz")*
   - What were some things that made Lester's feelings of stress or anger get WORSE? *(e.g., when someone sang the Soda Pop Head song, when he felt he was being treated unfairly)*
   - What were some things that helped make Lester's feelings of stress or anger get BETTER? *(e., taking 5 deep breaths, finding a quiet place, Push Pull Dangle, punching his pillow)*

1) Activity: Have the students return to their seats and provide the Body/Bottle Handout.

Facilitator explains the directions:

On this worksheet, I would like you to first write something in the soda bottle that makes you feel like you are going to pop. Next, I'd like you to look at the diagram of the person, and place an *X* on the areas in your body where you feel anger or stress.

2) Class Discussion/Evaluation: After finishing the worksheet, invite the students to share what they wrote.

   - Discuss common themes and bridge student's ideas.
   - Say, "In the beginning of class today, I asked you to raise your hands if you know any ways to calm your mind and body when you start to feel stressed or angry; only some of you raised your hands. I am wondering if I were to ask that question again now, after reading *Soda Pop Head,* how many of you would raise your hands?" *(note the number of students raising their hands)*
   - Ask the students for examples of things that might help them the next time they feel stressed or angry. *(e.g., taking 5 deep breaths, finding a quiet place, Push Pull Dangle, punching your pillow)*

Assessment

Observation of students' verbal (and physical) responses to the book, classroom discussions, and the handout each provides the facilitator with additional data about various stressors faced by students at home and in school. Results of this baseline assessment and evaluation provide the facilitator with valuable data about students' social/emotional states (e.g., who is feeling stressed or angry and what causes those feelings), and their understanding and abilities to implement successful coping strategies (who knows ways to de-stress and what are they). Such data will be useful in designing follow-up activities, classroom lessons, and small groups to meet the needs of students in your setting.

Accommodations

Each classroom is comprised of members from many different academic and social circles. It is important to accommodate for different learning styles (e.g., verbal/kinesthetic), language differences, as well as personality styles. To this effect, activities are differentiated in the following ways:

Facilitator pauses frequently when reading the book to check for student understanding and clarify challenging themes/topics.

Students are supported with written expression during the Body/Bottle exercise.

Students are not required to respond to any prompt and are provided additional clarification if needed.

Students are given additional time to process questions and supported with verbal praise for positive peer interactions.

Body/Bottle Handout

Name:____

#1: Inside the bottle, write one example of something that can make you feel angry or stressed!

#2: Using the person diagram, place an *X* in the place or places in your body where you can feel yourself get angry or stressed.

2. Pilot Lunch Group

The purpose of this "pilot" lunch small group is for the facilitator to use group process (bringing out the therapeutic factors) to further understand students' experiences with stress and to identify their accompanying coping strategies. Prior to organizing this group, school counselors met with each upper elementary school teacher to discuss emerging themes and to select students that might continue to help the school counseling department reflect on the needs of the student population. Following these meetings, a variety of upper elementary students were recommended by their teachers to participate based on their abilities to effectively communicate their feelings in class. Goals for this one-session group included highlighting shared experiences and learning more about students' struggles with stress specific to testing within the academic environment.

<table>
<tr><th>"LUNCH BUNCH" PILOT GROUP PLAN</th></tr>
<tr><td>Group Plan Title: "Really? Me, too!"</td></tr>
<tr><td>Grade Level: Eight selected upper elementary school students</td></tr>
<tr><td>Learning Objectives
Students will
• recall and further process their understanding of the strategies discussed in the classroom development lesson, Soda Pop Head.
• recognize commonalities in their peers' school experiences.
• express their feelings about the upcoming state testing.
• provide their peers with support and encouragement.</td></tr>
<tr><td>ASCA Mindsets & Behaviors for Student Success
<u>Mindset Standards</u>
• sense of belonging in the school environment
• belief in using abilities to their fullest to achieve high-quality results and outcomes
<u>Behavior Standards</u>
• Use time-management, organizational, and study skills.
• Apply self-motivation and self-direction to learning.
• Demonstrate effective coping skills when faced with a problem.
• Use effective oral and written communication skills and listening skills.
• Create positive and support relationships with other students.</td></tr>
<tr><td>Duration of Lesson: 30–40 minutes</td></tr>
<tr><td>Required Materials
• table for students to eat their lunches
• sitting area for group process
• blank paper and pencils</td></tr>
<tr><td>Introduction to Lesson: "Flying Thoughts"
Privately and anonymously students will write their answers to the following questions on a sheet of white paper:</td></tr>
</table>

(Continued)

(Continued)

1) My favorite subject in school is . . .
2) After school, I enjoy . . .
3) If I could choose NOT to do one thing in school, it would be . . .
4) I feel ____________________ about the state tests coming up.

Group leaders then help students to create a paper airplane out of this paper. Next, students line up in the room holding their paper airplanes. On the count of three, students are then asked to throw their airplanes across the room, and retrieve one that was not originally theirs.

As the students then sit down to eat lunch, they are asked to introduce themselves by sharing their

- name
- grade/teacher

They are then asked to unfold their airplanes, read the answers, and guess which group member wrote the answers on that airplane. Students continue eating lunch while engaging in this activity.

Step-by-Step Procedures

As students continue to eat . . .

1) *Brief overview of the group*
   - We formed this group after reading the results of the surveys and after hearing some of the feedback from the *Soda Pop* lesson. Does everyone remember that lesson? We were hoping we could all have lunch together to talk about some of the common themes we heard from many third- and fourth-grade students.

2) *Confidentiality talk*
   - Who knows what *confidentiality* means? (*It means that what we say inside the school counseling office stays here.*)
     - We want to keep our group private.
     - We want everyone to feel safe.
     - It's OK to share what happened with your mom and dad. No grown up should ever tell you to keep something from mom or dad.
   - Group is a closed group that will only meet one time.
   - No one new will join our group.
   - How are people feeling about coming?

Activity → "Step In"

- Children stand in a circle. As the facilitator reads questions aloud, children are instructed to "step in" to the circle if they have ever experienced this in their lives or can relate to the given example. This is a form of passive participation in which the students share their experiences nonverbally.

Sample "Step In" Questions:

- I have friends in school.
- Some days, we have a lot of homework.
- I love to read.

- There are some subjects in school that are hard for me.
- I enjoy art class.
- When I grow up, I might want to pick a career that involves math.
- I hear many people talk about the upcoming state testing.
- When I hear people talking about these tests, I feel a little stressed.
- Sometimes I feel pressure from my family to do well in school.
- When I am worried about something, I tend to think about it all day.

Processing "Step In"

- Students sit in a circle and discuss what they learned about themselves and each other throughout the game.
- Students are asked questions such as "What things did they notice in common with others? What things surprised them? How did it feel to learn that other students may be experiencing the same things?"

Assessment

Throughout the group, students' verbal (and physical) responses to discussions and the "Step-In" activity provide group leaders with additional data about various experiences in school. Follow-up questions during group process are likely to elicit additional themes to be used in preparing the small-group *Eyes on the Prize*.

Accommodations

Due to the nature of this lunch group, it is important to accommodate for any food allergies. Accommodations such as providing a separate table within the room, frequent handwashing, and cleaning supplies may be necessary. Additionally, this group is comprised of members from many different academic and social circles. It is important to accommodate for different learning styles (e.g., verbal/kinesthetic), language differences, as well as personality styles. To this effect, activities are differentiated in the following ways:

Students are supported with written expression during the airplane exercise.

Students are not required to respond to any prompt and provided additional clarification if needed.

Students are given additional time to process questions and supported with verbal praise for positive peer interactions.

Follow-up: Group Discussion

Talk about common themes:

- Many students spoke about their concerns specific to state testing. Students are then asked to describe how they feel before, during, and after taking tests in class. Some students have already taken the state test in previous years. Ask these students to describe what this experience was like for them.
- How would students feel about joining a consistent group aimed at targeting stress management, helping them to become more confident in their test-taking, and preparing them for the future?

Counselor Notes to Self re: Future Changes in Lesson Plan:

Notes are provided following the "Lunch Bunch" that include specific dialogue and themes from students' suggestions. The following themes were noted:

Majority of students feel some level of stress specific to test-taking.

Students enjoyed getting to know peers they did not know as well.

Students appreciated when peers shared their own experiences and strategies for managing stress.

● STEP 3: ANALYZE

"Analyze the critical data elements to determine which areas pose problems."

(Stone & Dahir, 2011, p. 30)

Qualitative data captured through the large-group developmental counseling lesson and the small, pilot lunch group are discussed and analyzed. An emergent theme common in students' discussions throughout both of these groups included concerns with the upcoming state test; school counselors' observations also noted students' lack of healthy coping strategies related to stress management. Analyzing each of these data points (individual student discussions, student/parent surveys, teacher meetings, classroom lessons for all upper elementary students, and a one-time small-group "lunch bunch" intervention), school counselors decided to design and advocate for a small-group counseling initiative that would service a larger number of elementary school students.

● STEP 4: STAKEHOLDERS-UNITE

"Identify stakeholders to involve in strategies to improve the data element."

(Stone & Dahir, 2011, p. 31)

According to the American School Counselor Association, school counselors have the responsibility of serving all students in the school building. Given the high student-to-counselor ratio in most school districts (Akos, Hamm, Mack, & Dunaway, 2007), group counseling appears to be an important way to accomplish this task. Sam Steen, Sheri Bauman, and Julie Smith (2007) suggest that time, logistics, and funding represent barriers to group counseling implementation. One way to overcome these barriers is to use data to show accountability for student outcomes (Stone & Dahir, 2011). Two letters, one to the board of education and administrators highlighting data points across the school counseling program, and one to families of potential group members are included below. After the school counseling department received administrative approval, the letter to families was sent to all upper elementary school students.

Sample Letter to the Board

Dear Board of Education and District Administrators,

As a member of the district school counseling department, I am writing to share with you some important data collected from stakeholders across our school community. Several data points have been gathered over the last few months reflecting the experiences of elementary school students, their families, and the community of educators interacting with our children and families on a regular basis. In an effort to address the many voices of students, families, and educators, we would like to ask for your support as we seek to develop some new small-group interventions that we believe will address common themes expressed by our community. According to the American School Counselor Association's (ASCA) position statement, "Group counseling . . . is an efficient, effective and positive way of providing direct services to students with academic, career, and social/emotional developmental issues and situational concerns." Based on community data presented below, we believe that providing additional targeted opportunities for small-group counseling will help to further support students' academic, career, and social/emotional success.

After surveying our upper elementary students and their families independently, we learned that (%) of students wished to know other children who are experiencing academic stress in the school environment. When asked more specifically about academic stress, (%) of students commented about feeling worried or nervous related to taking the upcoming state tests; (%) of students cited that they felt most stressed about having these conversations with their families at home. (%) of students also indicated that they would like to meet new friends in the school. Similarly, results of a parent survey provided at fall parent–teacher conferences indicated that (%) of parents/guardians expressed a desire to create more support around their children specific to standardized test-taking.

This initial data helped our department to create developmental school counseling classroom lessons geared toward further understanding students' knowledge and awareness of healthy academic and emotional coping strategies. In an effort to use a strengths-based approach, we hoped to use this large-group counseling setting to understand and celebrate students' current healthy approaches to managing stress and cultivate an environment of safety and shared experience talking through additional areas in which they may need some support. During the classroom lesson, a common theme emerged, as many of our students from each classroom expressed that they wished they knew more strategies to manage stress and anxiety.

After offering additional healthy coping strategies in the classroom environment, a pilot small-group "Lunch Bunch" was formed to further identify areas in which to target future small-group counseling interventions. A group of eight upper elementary students from diverse racial/cultural, academic, and socioeconomic backgrounds were chosen, with the input of classroom teachers, to participate in a one-session process-oriented group. Students were asked about their experiences and feelings leading up to, during, and immediately following state testing. Much of these discussions included students expressing academic isolation as the topic of state testing came up in the classroom and concerns that the test might hold them back in their current grade level, or worse yet, keep them from getting into college. Furthermore, students expressed feeling pressure (both internal and external) to do well to ensure that our community maintains its reputation.

Based on this data, the school counseling department believes that we can address each of the main themes: academic test-taking strategies, test implications (e.g., school and career focused), healthy emotional coping strategies, and friendship by organizing small psychoeducation counseling groups that will target each of these areas. The department is asking for your support to run these groups outside of class time to mitigate interference with the academic curriculum. Each group will address healthy test-taking strategies, mindfulness-anxiety reduction activities, and healthy peer communication and connection. Classroom teachers will be consulted throughout the process and families whose children are selected for these groups will receive weekly updates with strategies they can reinforce with their children at home.

As expressed by the American School Counseling Association, we believe that "by allowing individuals to develop insights into themselves and others, group counseling makes it possible for more students to achieve healthier personal adjustment, cope with the stress of a rapidly changing and complex environment and learn to communicate and cooperate with others." Furthermore, in alignment with Common Core State Standards, these groups will directly reflect movement toward college and career readiness by targeting interpersonal skills, organizational academic skill development, and emotional self-regulation.

Thank you in advance for considering your support for these interventions. We hope to have an opportunity to further discuss these opportunities and, if possible, present outcome student and community data reflecting student progress.

Sincerely,

Mrs. Saunders, School Counselor &
Ms. Rogers, School Counseling Intern

Sample Letter to Parents/Guardians

Dear Parents and Guardians,

With state testing nearing, we write to invite your **3rd and/or 4th grader(s)** to participate in a small-group program focused on test-taking skills called *Eyes on the Prize*. This six-week group has been designed to teach your child simple, easy-to-use strategies that can reduce test-taking anxiety and promote increased academic achievement and self-efficacy. By the end of the group, participants will learn to approach a test with a positive attitude; position himself or herself with confidence; control anxiety; read, think, and work through a test carefully; and double-check their work. Although each lesson reviews test-taking strategies, *Eyes on the Prize* is ultimately about improving your child's academic self-concept, building his or her skills for learning, and preparing each child to become a successful, confident, lifelong learner.

Throughout the group, we will be using the word *F.O.C.U.S.*, which is an acronym for each of the areas that we will cover in this group: **F**ace it, **O**rganize it, **C**onquer it, **U**nderstand it, and **S**can it. **This group will meet before school in the school counseling office from 7:45 a.m. to 8:45 a.m. for a total of six morning sessions. Sessions of this group will be offered at four times to accommodate morning schedules. Please see session dates below:**

Session 1 will be the following **WEDNESDAYS: 1/22, 1/29, 2/12, 2/19, 2/26, and 3/5.**

Session 2 will be the following **THURSDAYS: 1/23, 1/30, 2/13, 2/20, 2/27, and 3/6.**

Session 3 will be on the following **WEDNESDAYS: 3/26, 4/2, 4/9, 4/23, 4/30, and 5/7.**

Session 4 will be on the following **THURSDAYS: 3/27, 4/3, 4/10, 4/24, 5/1, and 5/8.**

Although we understand that mornings can be hectic, we strongly encourage group participants to be on time and present for each session, since group cohesiveness and interpersonal learning depends on the participation of all members.

Group work has been shown to successfully boost participants' self-concept, to increase individual's personal insights, to improve communication skills, and to create a feeling of trust, belonging, and togetherness, all factors linked to self-esteem and success. With many academic and social/emotional challenges ahead, including your child's upcoming transition to middle school, we believe that participation in *Eyes on the Prize* can help your child to succeed in life's many anxious situations

If you are interested in your child participating in *Eyes on the Prize*, please fill out the permission form below and send it back to the school counseling office no later than (Date).

- **After permission forms have been received, you will be contacted to confirm your first day of group. Please let us know if you are aware of a session in which your child CANNOT participate in all meetings.**

Sincerely,

Mrs. Saunders, School Counselor, and Ms. Rogers,
School Counseling Intern

Eyes on the Prize Permission Slip

___ I give permission for my child, ________________________, to participate in the test-taking skills morning group with Mrs. Saunders and School Counseling Intern, Ms. Rogers.

____________________________ ________________________ (Parent/Guardian Signature) (Date)

My preferred sessions are ranked in the following order from most to least desired:

___ ___ ___ ___

Sample Group Acceptance Letter to Parents/Caregivers

Dear Parents/Guardians
Congratulations, your child _______________has been selected for the group *Eyes on the Prize*.

THURSDAY MORNING GROUP

Our group will meet on the following dates:

THURSDAYS: 3/27, 4/3, 4/10, 4/24, 5/1, and 5/8.

Please note that we have had over (#) inquiries for this group and have tried to give you a preferable time, while making every effort to ensure that we create a healthy dynamic in each group. If you realize that your child is unable to attend every session, please let us know at your earliest convenience.

As a friendly reminder—

Although we understand that mornings can be hectic, we strongly encourage group participants to be on time and present for each session, since group cohesiveness and interpersonal learning depends on the participation of all members. The group will meet in Mrs. Saunders's office. PLEASE ENSURE THAT YOUR CHILD IS AT SCHOOL NO LATER THAN 7:40. Because of the amount of interest, we have a greater number of students in each group and will need every second of our time to get the most out of group!

We are looking forward to working with your child.

Sincerely,

Mrs. Saunders, School Counselor, and Ms. Rogers,
School Counseling Intern

After collecting all permission forms, in conjunction with stakeholder discussions, the following screening procedures were initiated to support the productivity of each group.

Screening

***Eyes on the Prize* Group Screening Procedures**

1. Permission slips were sent to all upper elementary school families with the group outline and benefits. Families were encouraged to inquire about any additional questions through e-mail, phone, and in-person meetings with group leaders.
2. After receiving permission slips, informal meetings were set up with teachers to discuss students' academic, social/emotional, and behavioral needs and overall appropriateness for group. Counselors also used their own observations, data from response to intervention (RTI) and 504 meetings, and consultation with case managers of students who had Individualized Education Plans (IEPs).

(Continued)

(Continued)

- For students who were determined not to be appropriate for this particular initiative due to prior behavioral/social struggles with peers or cognitive abilities, school counselors contacted families to provide alternative options (e.g., individualized support) and outside resource referrals.

3. During group session number one, group rules, including confidentiality and appropriate communication and feedback, were discussed. Students were aware that if rules were violated, their group membership privilege could be compromised. Rules and expectations for participants were continually addressed throughout the duration of each six-week group.

After screening all potential members, Mrs. Saunders and Ms. Rogers initiated the following group outlined below. This group was adapted from a small-group text, *F.O.C.U.S. on the Test,* written by Mary Pat McCartney (2009). Based on the unique needs of the students in the district, which included a desire to learn academic test-taking strategies, an outlet to share worries about test implications, and a desire to learn healthy emotional coping strategies and build friendships, each small group was customized to incorporate additional supplemental activities and discussion topics. Supplemental materials are included for each group session.

● SMALL-GROUP INTERVENTION: *EYES ON THE PRIZE*

Six-Week Group Outline

Week 1 Group Title: "Welcome to Group: Let's beat test stress together!"

Grade Level: Eight to 10 upper elementary school students

Learning Objectives

Students will

- understand the unique characteristics of group work and experience working together to develop goals for their group.
- recognize and respect that each group member has a unique perspective, which adds to the group experience.
- recognize commonalities in their peers' school experiences.
- express their feelings about the upcoming state testing.
- provide their peers with support and encouragement.

ASCA Mindsets & Behaviors for Student Success

Mindset Standards

- sense of belonging in the school environment
- self-confidence in ability to succeed
- belief in using abilities to their fullest to achieve high-quality results and outcomes

Behavior Standards

- Use time-management, organizational, and study skills.
- Apply self-motivation and self-direction to learning.
- Demonstrate effective coping skills when faced with a problem.
- Use effective oral and written communication skills and listening skills.
- Create positive and support relationships with other students.

Duration of Group Session: 1 Hour

Required Materials

- table for students to write
- name tags for each student
- Welcome Worksheet (for each student)
- pens or pencils (for each student)
- large poster for group rules
- marker for writing on group rules poster
- copies of opening assessment (for each student)
- duck/rabbit image (for each student)

Additional Suggested Materials

- Apples to Apples Jr. (board game)

Introduction to Lesson: "What is group and why am I here?"

1) *Welcome Worksheet & Introductory Processing Exercise*

   As the students begin to enter the classroom, invite them to pick out their name tags and take a seat around the table.

   - Distribute the Welcome Worksheet and ask the students to work independently to answer the questions.
   - Instruct students NOT to write their names on the paper.
   - After the students finish writing, ask them to fold their papers in quarters and collect the worksheets.
   - Shuffle the papers and redistribute so that each student receives someone else's answers.
   - Direct the students NOT to share if they happen to get their own paper back.

2) *Processing Activity*

   - Ask students to raise their hands and share answers written on the paper they received.
   - Encourage the remaining students to raise their hands if the paper in front of them says something similar to what was just shared.
   - Point out common themes, bridge ideas, and encourage students to comment on the experience.

Step-by-Step Procedure

Brief overview of the group.

- Welcome to "*Eyes on the Prize*!"
- We formed this group after learning that many students in our school feel stressed about taking tests! We collected student and parent surveys, heard your feedback from the *Soda Pop Head* lesson, and even talked to teachers about what they thought might benefit their students, and many people agreed that a group about reducing testing anxiety would be really helpful at our school.

(Continued)

(Continued)

- We thought it would be a good idea to form a group so that we can talk about our feelings around testing, learn some strategies to reduce stress, and even learn some test-taking tips that might help us feel more confident during testing!
- It might sound somewhat boring, but we promise there will be games and fun activities mixed in!
- First though, before the fun part, we need to talk some business.

Confidentiality talk.

- Who knows what *confidentiality* means? It means that what we say inside Mrs. Saunders's room stays here.
  - We want to keep our group private.
  - We want everyone to feel safe.
  - It's OK to share what happened with your mom and dad. No grown up should ever tell you to keep something from mom or dad.
  - This group is a closed group that will meet a total of six times on (dates/times).
  - A closed group means that no one new will join our group.
  - This is YOUR group, so it is really important that everyone comes on time and tries to be here every time we meet. It really won't be the same without you.

3) *Activity → "Every Perspective Matters"*
   - Now we have a fun activity to o demonstrate the unique perspective that each member brings to group and to highlight why it is so important to have each member come to group each week!
   - Before you start, check that students understand the definition of *perspective* or *point-of-view*.
   - Distribute the duck/rabbit optical illusion and ask each student to take a moment to look at the image.
   - Ask the students to raise their hand and invite them to share what they see.
   - After the first person shares what she or he sees, ask if anyone sees anything different?
   - If students are having trouble seeing one image or both, invite other students to help their groupmates locate the duck or rabbit.
4) *Process "Every Perspective Matters"*
   - Ask the group to raise their hands if they saw the rabbit first.
   - Next ask who saw the duck first.
   - Which group was right about what they saw? (the answer is BOTH)
   - Explain that every person in the group has a unique and valuable perspective and each group member brings something special to our group when they share that perspective.
5) *Activity → Group Rules Poster*
   - Now that students understand the importance of contributing to the group and sharing their unique perspectives, encourage the group to develop a set of rules and talk about how members might encourage people to stick to the rules if they start to deviate.
   - You might ask the group, "What does everyone need to feel safe in group?" to get things started.
   - Write down the rules on a poster and display the poster during group each week.
6) *Optional Additional Activity → Apples to Apples, Jr.*
   - The game Apples to Apples Jr. is a fun way to end the first group if time permits. Group leaders can use Apples to Apples Jr. to reinforce the idea that everyone has a unique perspective in our group. What is a funny, "winning" card to one person may not have been the choice of their neighbor.

Assessment

Throughout the group, students' verbal (and physical) responses to discussions and activities provide group leaders with additional information about student's feelings about group work. Follow-up questions during group process are likely to elicit additional themes to be used in preparing future agendas for upcoming group meetings.

Accommodations

This group is comprised of members from many different academic and social circles. Not only is it important to provide name tags to accommodate for the fact that not everyone knows each other, it is important to accommodate for different learning styles (e.g. verbal/kinesthetic), language differences, as well as personality styles. To this effect, group leaders differentiate activities in the following ways:

Students are supported with written expression during the opening exercise.

Students are not required to respond to any prompt and provided additional clarification if needed.

Students are given additional time to process questions and supported with verbal praise for positive peer interactions.

Follow-up: Group discussion

Talk about common themes:

- You might say, "In the beginning of group, we asked everyone to share their feelings about joining group. I am wondering if anyone's perspective has changed now that we have finished our first session."
- Invite students to share how they feel and discuss common themes.

Counselor Notes to Self re: Future Changes in Lesson Plan—

Notes are provided following the first meeting of *Eyes on the Prize* that include specific dialogue and themes from students' suggestions. The following themes were noted:

Majority of students were not very excited about coming to group because they thought they would just be taking a lot of tests.

Students enjoyed getting to know other members of the group.

Students where excited to play games even if they were "learning games."

Many students said their perspective about group had changed from the start of group to the end.

Welcome Worksheet

1) How do you feel about coming to group? (BE HONEST!)

____

____

____

____

____

(Continued)

(Continued)

2) What do you think this group is all about?

____

____

____

____

____

3) What do you hope to learn from this group?

____

____

____

____

____

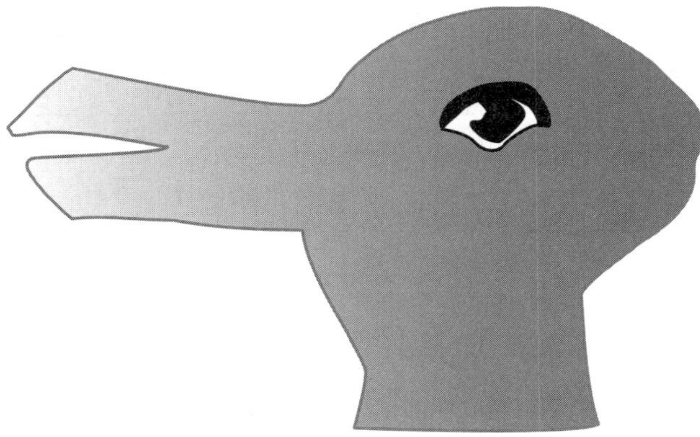

Source: Optical Illusions—Free Picture Illusions. Retrieved from http://www.123opticalillusions.com/pages/opticalillusions5.php.

Week 2 Group Title: *"F stands for Face It!"*

Grade Level: Eight to 10 upper elementary school students

Learning Objectives

Students will

- understand the definition of *acronym* and how acronyms can help us remember information.
- recognize how their internal dialogue or "self-talk" can affect them during a test.
- learn the importance of attitude during testing and how their body positions can help or hinder them during a test.
- recognize commonalities in their peers' school experiences.
- express their feelings about the upcoming state testing.
- provide their peers with support and encouragement.

ASCA Mindsets & Behaviors for Student Success

Mindset Standards

- sense of belonging in the school environment
- self-confidence in ability to succeed
- belief in using abilities to their fullest to achieve high-quality results and outcomes

Behavior Standards

- Use time-management, organizational, and study skills.
- Apply self-motivation and self-direction to learning.
- Demonstrate effective coping skills when faced with a problem.
- Use effective oral and written communication skills and listening skills.
- Create positive and support relationships with other students.

Duration of Group Session: 1 Hour

Required Materials

- table for students to write
- blackboard, whiteboard, or large paper to write on so the group can see
- name tags for each student
- pens or pencils (for each student)
- timer or stopwatch
- Group Rules poster
- *F.O.C.U.S. on the Test* (book) by Mary Pat McCartney, 2009
- Print-out of Face It poster (p. 18)
- Copies of *F.O.C.U.S. on the Test* pre-test (p. 15) (for each student)

Introduction to Lesson: "Why F.O.C.U.S. Is so Important"

Brief review of last week and introduction to the acronym F.O.C.U.S.

As the students begin to enter the classroom, invite them to pick out their name tag and take a seat around the table.

- Begin the group by inviting students to share their feelings about the prior group and discussing what went on during the first group.
- Review confidentiality and point out where their Group Rules poster is displayed in the room.

Introduction to acronyms

- Standing in front of the blackboard, whiteboard, or large paper, write the word *acronym* on the board and ask students to raise their hands if they know what an acronym is.
- Explain that an acronym is a word formed from the first letters of each one of the words in a phrase. An acronym is a shorter word that can help you to remember a series of longer words.
- Write *R.O.Y.G.B.I.V.* on the board.
- For instance, does anyone know what the acronym *R.O.Y.G.B.I.V* stands for and what it helps us to remember?
- Explain that *R.O.Y.G.B.I.V* is an acronym that can help you remember the colors of the rainbow in order. "R.O.Y.G.B.I.V. stands for red, orange, yellow, green, blue, indigo, violet." You may wish to point to the letters in the acronym as you name the colors to help students to understand how the first letter of each color forms R.O.Y.G.B.I.V.
- Invite students to provide additional examples of acronyms (e.g., FBI = Federal Bureau of Investigation, LOL= Laughing Out Loud, etc.).

(Continued)

(Continued)

Introduction to the acronym F.O.C.U.S.

- Write *F.O.C.U.S.* on the board.
- Explain to students that over the remaining 5 weeks of group, we will be discussing the components of the acronym F.O.C.U.S.
- As we introduce what each letter in *F.O.C.U.S.* stands for, you will be learning a new tip or strategy to help reduce testing anxiety.
- Today, we will be talking about the letter *F* and what it stands for, but before we get to that, we have an activity for you.

Step-by-Step Procedure

1) *Activity → F.O.C.U.S. on the Test Pretest*

   - Switch the tone of your voice to a more serious tone and inform the students "today we are going to be taking a very important test."
   - Pass out the pretest face down and a writing implement for each student.
   - Create an intentionally stressful environment for the students as you let them know that they will have "only five minutes to get as many answers right as possible."
   - Without answering any questions about what is on the test, instruct the students to begin, and start your stopwatch.
   - As the students take the test, continue to create a stressful environment by making noise sharpening pencils, reminding the students, "this test is very important so please do your best," "two minutes left," and "don't leave any blanks," for example. The goal is to simulate an actual "real-world" testing environment that the students may face in a classroom.
   - At the end of the 5 minutes, call "time is up, pencils down."

Processing the Pretest

   - Ask students to flip over their papers and to write on the back of the paper how it felt to take the test.
   - Explain that *self-talk* is the words we say to ourselves that no one else can hear.
   - Ask students to write down what their self-talk was like as the tests were handed out and as they were taking the test. (Most students should express such feelings as stressed out, worried, etc.)
   - Invite students to share what they wrote and process feelings together.
   - Inform the students that they can all take a deep breath because the answers they wrote on test that the just took do not count for anything. However, the self-talk we just discussed is what is really important to today's lesson.

*Learning Exercise—*F *stands for "Face It!"*

   - Hang the Face It poster and explain to the students that the *F* in F.O.C.U.S. stands for "Face It," which actually means a couple of things when it comes to taking a test.
     - o Face the fact that it's important for me to try hard on tests.
   - Say "Let's face it, tests are part of life and no one can avoid them; however the attitude you chose to use when facing the test is really important!" Explain "our attitude is like our self-talk, and it makes a difference how we feel when we face a test. If you face the test with a negative attitude like your self-talk during the pretest we just finished, chances are you'll have a negative outcome on the test."

- "Face it" also reminds us that our faces can actually help us focus during a test.
- For example, when the teacher is talking and giving directions, where do you think your face should be pointed? Should you be looking at the ground, looking at what your neighbor wore to school today, or looking at the teacher to ensure that you are hearing what she is telling you?"
- How about when you are taking the actual test? Where should your face be pointing? Should you be looking at the clock as the minutes tick by, starring at that weird scuff mark on the floor, or looking at the actual test questions and answer key? What is most likely to help you succeed on the test?

Assessment

Throughout the group, students' verbal (and physical) responses to discussions and activities provide group leaders with additional information about students' feelings about group work. Follow-up questions during group process are likely to elicit additional themes to be used in preparing future agendas for upcoming group meetings.

Accommodations

This group is comprised of members from many different academic and social circles. Not only is it important to provide nametags to accommodate for the fact that not everyone knows each other, it is important to accommodate for different learning styles (e.g. verbal/kinesthetic), language differences, as well as personality styles. To this effect, group leaders differentiate activities in the following ways:

Students are supported with written expression during the pretest.

Students are not required to respond to any prompt and provided additional clarification if needed.

Students are given additional time to process questions and supported with verbal praise for positive peer interactions.

Follow-up: Group Discussion/Review

Review the lessons of the day:

- Ask the students to discuss what they learned today.
- Review the definition of an *acronym* and how acronyms can be helpful tools.
- Discuss the idea of self-talk and how negative self-talk can hurt your chances for success on a test.
- Review the meaning of "Face It" and how this can help us during a test.
- Invite students to share how they feel and discuss common themes.

Counselor Notes to Self re: Future Changes in Lesson Plan:

Notes are provided following the second meeting of *Eyes on the Prize* that include specific dialogue and themes from students' suggestions. The following themes were noted:

Majority of students had very negative self-talk during the pretest activity,

Students shared that they had "trouble focusing" and "felt like I was going to fail."

Students expressed relief in the group setting in realizing that a lot of people share their same feelings.

Week 3 Group Title: *"O stands for Organize It"*

Grade Level: Eight to 10 upper elementary school students

Learning Objectives

Students will

- understand different ways to get organized before and during a test, including organizing their thoughts, organizing their space, organizing their positions, organizing their answers, and organizing their speed.
- recognize how internal dialogue or self-talk can affect them during a test.
- recognize commonalities in their peers' school experiences.
- express their feelings about the upcoming state testing.
- provide their peers with support and encouragement.

ASCA Mindsets & Behaviors for Student Success

Mindset Standards

- sense of belonging in the school environment
- self-confidence in ability to succeed
- belief in using abilities to their fullest to achieve high-quality results and outcomes

Behavior Standards

- Use time-management, organizational, and study skills.
- Apply self-motivation and self-direction to learning.
- Demonstrate effective coping skills when faced with a problem.
- Use effective oral and written communication skills and listening skills.
- Create positive and support relationships with other students.

Duration of Group Session: 1 Hour

Required Materials

- one messy and one organized sample backpack (see instructions below)
- table for students to write
- blackboard, whiteboard, or large paper to write on so the group can see
- name tags for each student
- pens or pencils (for each student)
- plain paper (for each student)
- timer or stopwatch
- Group Rules poster
- *F.O.C.U.S. on the Test* (book) by Mary Pat McCartney, 2009.
- print-out of "Organize It" poster (p.19)

How to Make the Messy and Organized Backpacks

For this lesson, you will need to prepare two sample backpacks, one organized and one messy, in advance of the group meeting. Here is a step-by-step guide to make the backpacks.

Step 1: Take eight pieces of plain paper. Using large lettering, on two sheets write *Math Homework*, on two more sheets write *Science Homework*, on two more sheets write *Language Arts Homework*, and on the last two sheets write *Social Studies Homework*. In addition, take eight folders and label two each with the subjects *Math, Science, Language Arts*, and *Social Studies* respectively. (*Note:* You will use one set of each folder and one set of each homework sheet in each backpack.)

Step 2: Prepare the organized backpack. Fill this bag with books, folders, and a pencil case—only the essential items that you would need for school. Take one set of the homework papers you created in Step 1 and place them neatly in the corresponding folder. You can use a real textbook, or you may wish to make some "textbooks" by wrapping a magazine in brown paper and writing *textbook* on the cover. Use your imagination. The idea is to have a very organized backpack with each homework type appearing in the appropriate, corresponding folder.

Step 3: Prepare the messy backpack. Fill this backpack with books, folders, crumpled papers, toys, an old gym shoe, and some empty water bottles, for example. The goal is to make everything seem very disorganized in this backpack. Include homework folders, but put the wrong homework sheet in the wrong folder (e.g., language arts homework in the science folder) and put <u>nothing</u> in the math folder. Crumple up the paper labeled *Math Homework* and shove it someplace strange in the backpack, for example inside the old gym shoe. The math homework will be what the student is looking for during the demonstration, so make it difficult to find. If you include a textbook in the messy backpack, you can also have homework sticking out of the top of the textbook.

Introduction to Lesson: "Ahh! I Can't Find My Homework!"

1) *Brief review of last week—"*F *stands for Face It!"*

   As the students begin to enter the classroom, invite them to pick out their name tag and take a seat around the table.

   - Begin discussion by inviting students to share their feelings about the prior group and by briefly reviewing the letter *F* in the acronym *F.O.C.U.S.*
   - Point to the Face It poster to help jog their memories if they have trouble remembering the prior group discussion.

2) *Activity → Backpack Demonstration*

   - Let the students know that you have prepared a special demonstration to introduce them to what the second letter in our acronym, *O*, stands for.
   - Ask for two student volunteers and split the remainder of the students into two cheer teams. Assign one team to cheer for volunteer #1 and the other team to cheer for volunteer #2.
   - Move two chairs to the front of the group where the cheer team students can see the volunteers in the "hot seats."
   - Explain that in a moment you will hand out backpacks to each volunteer in the hot seats. When you say go, the volunteers will then race to turn in their math homework to you. The first person who hands you their math homework wins.
   - Let the cheer teams know that their jobs are to encourage their volunteer in the hot seat and also to make suggestions of where that person should look.
   - The only rule in the game is that you cannot dump the backpacks.
   - Start the race.

Note: Ideally, the person with the organized backpack should have no trouble locating his or her math homework in the neatly labeled math folder, while the person with the messy backpack will have more of a struggle.

3) *Process the Backpack Demonstration*

   - Start by asking the students in the hot seats how it felt to look for their math homework in their respective backpacks.
   - For the person with the messy backpack—how was your self-talk during this exercise?

(Continued)

(Continued)

- Ask the cheer teams if they noticed anything about the person looking in the messy backpack verses the organized backpack.
- Ask the group if they have any idea what *O* might stand for today?

4) *Optional Additional Activity*

- As a second or additional part of this activity, you can ask the students to search for their math homework in their own backpacks and process what this is like. This will allow them to critique their own organizational skills.

Step-by-Step Procedure

Discussion—How does it feel to be organized versus disorganized?

- Open the discussion by asking students to share some ways they can be organized *right* ***before*** *they take a test.*
- After students share their thoughts, say, "Some examples of how you might get organized right before the test are to organize your thoughts, organize your space, and your position."
- How do you think you might organize your thoughts right before you take a test? Remember, we talked about self-talk last week. What kind of self-talk might help you prepare for a test?
  (Examples: I studied and now I am prepared to do my best, I am capable, Thanks to Mrs. Saunders and Ms. Rogers's group, I can face the test with confidence.)
- How might you organize your space on your desk?
  (Examples: Remove everything off your desk, Have your pencil and eraser ready.)
- How might you organize your positions? Hint: This is similar to one of the "Face It" facts we talked about last week.
  (Examples: Sit in a comfortable position with your feet on the floor. Position your body so that you are facing the teacher.)
- Next ask, "What are some ways that you can be organized ***during*** *the test?"*
- After students share their thoughts, say, "Some examples of how you might get organized during the test are to organize your thoughts, organize your answers, and organize your speed."
- How might you organize your thoughts during the test? This question is about self-talk, but also about what happens to some of us when our minds start to wander . . .
  (Examples: Remind yourself that you can do it. If your mind starts to wander, refocus by taking a deep breath and putting your eyes back on the paper.)
- How might you organize your answers during the test?
  (Examples: On a multiple choice test, cross out the answers that you know are wrong, Make sure you transfer your answers to the answer key and bubble in the correct answer thoroughly.)
- Say, "Instead of just talking about how you might organize your speed, let's do a fun activity to show the best way to organize your speed."

5) *Activity → Organize Your Speed*

- Hand out a sheet of plain paper and a writing implement to each student.
- Instruct the students to fold the paper in half so that they have four different boxes for the activity.
- Explain the activity.
- What we are going to do now are some speed challenges.
- For the first challenge I will give you 30 seconds, and in that time I want you to **QUICKLY** write the alphabet as many times as you can in the first box on your piece of paper.
- Remember, this is a challenge about a **QUICK** speed.
- Instruct the students to "go" and start your stopwatch.
- As soon as the 30 seconds are over, go into the next challenge.
- For the second speed challenge, please move to the second box on your paper.

- In this box, I want you to use your **SLOWEST** speed to write the alphabet as many times as you can.
- Remember, this is a challenge about having a **SLOW** speed.
- Instruct the students to "go" and start your stopwatch.
- As soon as the 30 seconds are over, go into the final challenge.
- For the final speed challenge, I want you to use a **MEDIUM** speed to write the alphabet as many times as you can.
- Remember, this is a challenge about having a **MEDIUM** speed.
- Instruct the students to "go" and start your stopwatch.

After they have completed all three speed challenges, ask the students to process the activity. Questions might include

- Which speed felt best?
- What was your self-talk like during each challenge?
- Which speed allowed for the neatest and most easily readable writing?
- When did you feel most likely to make a mistake?
- When did you feel most likely to run out of time?

Assessment

Throughout the group, students' verbal (and physical) responses to discussions and activities provide group leaders with additional information about students' feelings about group work. Follow-up questions during group process are likely to elicit additional themes to be used in preparing future agendas for upcoming group meetings.

Accommodations

This group is comprised of members from many different academic and social circles. Not only is it important to provide name tags to accommodate for the fact that not everyone knows each other, it is important to accommodate for different learning styles (e.g., verbal/kinesthetic), language differences, as well as personality styles. To this effect, group leaders differentiate activities in the following ways:

Students are supported with written expression during the speed challenges.

Students are not required to respond to any prompt and provided additional clarification if needed.

Students are given additional time to process questions and supported with verbal praise for positive peer interactions.

Follow-up: Group Discussion/Review

Review the lessons of the day:

- Hang the Organize It poster and remind the students that the *O* in F.O.C.U.S. stands for "Organize It," which actually means a couple of things when it comes to taking a test and for being a student in general.
- Ask the students to review what they learned about being organized today.
- Invite students to share how they feel and discuss common themes.

Counselor Notes to Self re: Future Changes in Lesson Plan:

Notes are provided following the third meeting of *Eyes on the Prize* that include specific dialogue and themes from students' suggestions. The following themes were noted:

All students agreed that the student with the organized backpack had an easier time finding their homework.

Majority of students felt that using a medium speed would help them to answer questions correctly and organize their time so that they would not run out of time.

Students reported that having "good self-talk" helped to keep them calm.

Counselor noted that students were forgetting some of the rules they established and may need a little refresher.

Week 4 Group Title: *"C stands for Conquer It."*

Grade Level: Eight to 10 upper elementary school students

Learning Objectives

Students will

- understand different ways to overcome stress or nervousness before and during tests, and practice different techniques (deep breathing, squeeze and release, and positive self-talk) to beat stress.
- develop a list of positive study techniques to help build their brain power and conquer test questions.
- recognize how internal dialogue or self-talk can affect them during a test.
- recognize commonalities in their peers' school experiences.
- express their feelings about the upcoming state testing.
- provide their peers with support and encouragement.

ASCA Mindsets & Behaviors for Student Success

Mindset Standards

- sense of belonging in the school environment
- self-confidence in ability to succeed
- belief in using abilities to their fullest to achieve high-quality results and outcomes

Behavior Standards

- Use time-management, organizational, and study skills.
- Apply self-motivation and self-direction to learning.
- Demonstrate effective coping skills when faced with a problem.
- Use effective oral and written communication skills and listening skills.
- Create positive and support relationships with other students.

Duration of Group Session: 1 Hour

Required Materials

- table for students to write
- blackboard, whiteboard, or large paper to write on so the group can see
- name tags for each student
- pens or pencils (for each student)
- Group Rules poster
- *F.O.C.U.S. on the Test* (book) by Mary Pat McCartney, 2009
- print-out of Conquer It poster (p. 20)

Introduction to Lesson: "C Stands for Conquer It!"

1) *Brief review of last week—"O stands for Organize It!"*

   As the students begin to enter the classroom, invite them to pick out their name tag and take a seat around the table.

   - Begin discussion by inviting students to share their feelings about the prior group and by briefly reviewing the letter **O** in the acronym F.O.C.U.S.
   - Point to the Organize It poster to help jog their memories if they have trouble remembering the prior group discussion.

1) *Discussion—What does it mean to conquer something?*

    - Ask the students if they know what it means to conquer something? *(To conquer is to defeat [someone or something] through the use of force, or to gain control of [a problem or difficulty] through great effort).*
    - How do you think the word *conquer* might apply to taking a test?

Step-by-Step Procedure

2) *Check-In, Discussion, and Introduction to Termination*

    - Group has now met three times. How is everyone feeling about being part of this group?
    - After today, we will only have two sessions left. What are some reactions to that?
    - How will it feel to stop coming here every week?
    - Is there anything that we can do as a group that might make it easier to end our group?

3) *Optional Discussion—Quick Review of Group Rules*

    - Remind students of the rules they created as a group during the first week and point out the poster in the room.
    - Does the group feel like we need to make any changes to better follow the rules?
    - What are some things the group might change?
    - What are some things the group might keep the same?

4) *Activity → How to Conquer Nervous Feelings (or Stress) Through Relaxation!*

One of the ways we can conquer tests is to conquer our stress or those feelings of nervousness. Today we are going to learn a few techniques to do this.

- Ask students to sit in a circle on the floor in a comfortable position and introduce and have students practice the following relaxation techniques:
- **Deep Breathing**

  Practice 3, 4, 5 breathing.

  Breathe in through your nose for 3 seconds.

  Hold your breath for 4 seconds.

  Breathe out through your mouth for 5 seconds.

  And repeat.
- **Squeeze and Release**

  Practice tightening different body parts, holding for 3 seconds, and then releasing.

  Hint: Ask students to share where in their body they feel stress. Have them practice squeezing or tightening that body part and then releasing.

  Repeat this together as a group, targeting different body parts.
- **Positive Self-Talk**

  Practice saying calming and kind things to yourself when you feel the negative thoughts come on.

  Ask students for examples of affirming things they can say to themselves that will help calm their nerves during a test.

(Continued)

(Continued)

Process Relaxation Techniques

- Ask the students if they feel like the breathing, squeeze and release, and positive self-talk techniques they just learned might be helpful in conquering their stress.
- Let them know that the neat thing about those techniques is that no one else needs to know they are doing it.
- These are "tools" to conquer stress that they always have with them no matter where they are or who they are with!

1) *Learning Exercise—How to Conquer the Questions*

    - Explain that a conqueror must use brain power to study and beat the questions.
    - Ask the students for examples of ways they can build up their brain power before a test and write their examples on the board. (*Examples: study, make flash cards, review your notes from class, rewrite your notes if that helps, make up silly rhymes to help you memorize, try making acronyms like R.O.Y G. B.I.V. or F.O.C.U.S.)*
    - Explain that the more you build up your brain power before the test, the better you'll be able to conquer the questions during the test!
    - Hang the Conquer It poster and transition into follow up activity.

Assessment

Throughout the group, students' verbal (and physical) responses to discussions and activities provide group leaders with additional information about students' feelings about group work. Follow-up questions during group process are likely to elicit additional themes to be used in preparing future agendas for upcoming group meetings.

Accommodations

This group is comprised of members from many different academic and social circles. Not only is it important to provide name tags to accommodate for the fact that not everyone knows each other, it is important to accommodate for different learning styles (e.g., verbal/kinesthetic), language differences, as well as personality styles. To this effect, group leaders differentiate activities in the following ways:

Students are not required to respond to any prompt and provided additional clarification if needed.

Students are given additional time to process questions and supported with verbal praise for positive peer interactions.

Follow-up: Group Discussion/Review

Review the lessons of the day:

- Hang the Conquer It poster and remind the students that the *C* in F.O.C.U.S. stands for "Conquer It," which actually means a couple of things when it comes to taking a test and for being a student in general.
- Ask the students to review what they learned about being conquering stress and conquering the questions.
- Invite students to share how they feel and discuss common themes.

Counselor Notes to Self re: Future Changes in Lesson Plan:

Notes are provided following the fourth meeting of *Eyes on the Prize* that include specific dialogue and themes from students' suggestions. The following themes were noted:

Most students shared that they were somewhat sad that group will be ending.

Some students expressed "relief" that group is ending because it is "one more thing" on their plate.

Students appeared to physically relax during the relaxation exercises; students expressed excitement that they now had "tools" to help them relax.

Week 5 Group Title: *"U* stands for Understand It and *S* stands for Scan It"

Grade Level: Eight to 10 upper elementary school students

Learning Objectives

Students will

- understand the importance of knowing what the question is asking in order to be able to answer it properly.
- learn to scan and understand directions, scan, and double-check their answers on all tests.
- recognize how internal dialogue or self-talk can affect them during a test.
- recognize commonalities in their peers' school experiences.
- express their feelings about the upcoming state testing.
- provide their peers with support and encouragement.

ASCA Mindsets & Behaviors for Student Success

Mindset Standards

- sense of belonging in the school environment
- self-confidence in ability to succeed
- belief in using abilities to their fullest to achieve high-quality results and outcomes

Behavior Standards

- Use time-management, organizational, and study skills.
- Apply self-motivation and self-direction to learning.
- Demonstrate effective coping skills when faced with a problem.
- Use effective oral and written communication skills and listening skills.
- Create positive and support relationships with other students.

Duration of Group Session: 1 Hour

Required Materials

- table for students to write
- blackboard, whiteboard, or large paper to write so the group can see
- name tags for each student
- pens or pencils (for each student)
- Group Rules poster
- Following Directions quiz
- *F.O.C.U.S. on the Test* (book) by Mary Pat McCartney, 2009
- print-out of Understand It and Scan It posters (pp. 21, 22)
- copies of Practice Test 2 (p. 46) (for each student)

Introduction to Lesson: "Understanding and Scanning Is Everything."

1) *Brief review of last week—"C Stands for Conquer It!"*

   As the students begin to enter the classroom, invite them to pick out their name tag and take a seat around the table.

   - Begin discussion by inviting students to share their feelings about the prior group and by briefly reviewing the letter *C* in the acronym F.O.C.U.S.
   - Point to the Conquer It poster to help jog their memories if they have trouble remembering the prior group discussion.

(Continued)

(Continued)

1) *Activity → Following Directions Quiz*
   - Tell the students that we are now going to take a quiz to introduce our next topics.
   - If you notice moaning in discontent or worried facial expressions, take a moment to process in the moment what the groups self-talk is like.
   - Hand out the Following Directions Quiz face down and a pencil to each student.
   - **Important**: Remind the students to read the directions carefully before they get started. *Note: The quiz instructs students to read everything before do anything. If the students do not read all of the questions before getting started, they will take part in a series of silly activities before reaching the final question which tells them only to do questions 1 and 2.*
   - Instruct the students to get started and start the timer.
2) *Process the Following Directions Quiz*
   - Start by asking the students why they think we took this silly quiz today.
   - Why is it so important to understand the directions *before* you get started on a test?
   - How can understanding the directions help you to be more successful?

Step-by-Step Procedure

1) *Learning Exercise—How to be sure you understand the directions and the questions*
   - Hang the Understand It poster and explain that we are now going to practice some tricks that can help make sure you understand what the question is asking you.
   - Hand out Practice Test #2 and pencil and explain that today we are going to work on the test together to practice tricks for understanding.
   - Explain, "Today we are not focused on the answers, but rather on the questions."
   - Use the blackboard to teach the following techniques:

Key Words

- Key words are the words in the question or the directions that help us to identify the most important parts of the question.
- Looking at question #2 on the test in front of you and take a moment to underline all of the key words in the sentence.
- "Remember: I don't want you to choose an answer. I want you to look closely at the question only and underline key words in question #2."
- *Hint: In question #2 "what is the name of the 4th planet from the sun?" students should underline the following words:* name, 4th planet, from, and sun.
- Ask why the students underlined the words that they chose?
- What would have happened if they missed a key word like the word *planet*?
- Repeat this activity of underlining key words in question #3 "Which of these is not a verb."
- What could happen if you missed the key word *not*?

Absolute Words

- Absolute words are a special kind of key word that can help you narrow down the correct answer or trick you if you're not paying close attention.
- Examples of absolute words are *all, none, always, never*.
- If you see an absolute word in a sentence, such as *none* or *never,* you can immediately eliminate any answers that happen sometimes or all the time.

Likewise, if you see an absolute word like *all* or *always*, you can immediately eliminate any answers that never happen or happen only sometimes.

- Ask the students to circle the absolute word in question #4.

  Hint: In question #4 "Plants never need _________ to grow," students should circle never.

- What does the word *never* tell us about the answers?
- What would happen if you missed the absolute word *never*?

Key Words AND Absolute Words

- Ask the students to practice what they have just learned by first circling the absolute word in question #5 and then underlying all of the key words.
  Hint: In question #5, "All of these are names of original colonies except," the word all *is the absolute word, which should be circled, and the words* names, original colonies, *and* except *are key words which should be underlined.*

  - Point to the absolute word *all* and ask the students what this tells us.
  - Next point to the key word *except* and ask the students how this switches what the question is asking?
  - What would happen if they read quickly and missed the word *except* or the word *all*?
  - Review the importance of understanding the directions and the question. Point to the Understand It poster if they need help jogging their minds about what we just learned.

Learning Exercise—Don't forget to scan it before you turn it in!

- Explain that the *S* in F.O.C.U.S. reminds us of the importance of scanning the entire test before we start and scanning the answers before we turn in the test.
- Ask the students how the Following Directions Quiz might have turned out differently if they had taken the time to scan over (and actually read) the entire test before they got started?
- **Scan the test <u>before</u> you get started**

  - Scanning the test before you get started allows you to make sure that you are not missing any directions.
  - Scanning the test gives you an idea of how many questions you will need to answer so that you can organize your speed.

- **Scanning your answers <u>after you are done</u> but <u>before you turn it in</u>**

  - Scanning your answers allows you to ensure that you remembered to answer all of the questions.
  - Scanning your answers allows you to check that you colored in all bubbles on the answer key thoroughly.
  - Scanning your answers is a way to proofread. You can gain back valuable points by making sure that you have spelled words correctly, used proper punctuation, and started sentences with a capital letter for example.

Even if you are tired after taking a test, if you have any time left, use that time to scan over your answers. You will not be sorry!

Assessment

Throughout the group, students' verbal (and physical) responses to discussions and activities provide group leaders with additional information about students' feelings about group work. Follow-up questions during group process are likely to elicit additional themes to be used in preparing future agendas for upcoming group meetings.

(Continued)

(Continued)

Accommodations

This group is comprised of members from many different academic and social circles. Not only is it important to provide name tags to accommodate for the fact that not everyone knows each other, it is important to accommodate for different learning styles (e.g. verbal/kinesthetic), language differences, as well as personality styles. To this effect, group leaders differentiate activities in the following ways:

Students are not required to respond to any prompt and provided additional clarification if needed.

Students are given additional time to process questions and supported with verbal praise for positive peer interactions.

Follow-up: Group Discussion/Review

Review the lessons of the day:

- Point to the Understand It and Scan It posters and ask students to share what they learned about scanning and understanding.
- Invite students to share how they feel and discuss common themes.

Counselor Notes to Self re: Future Changes in Lesson Plan:

Notes are provided following the fifth meeting of *Eyes on the Prize* that include specific dialogue and themes from students' suggestions. The following themes were noted:

Most students felt like the facilitators "tricked" them with the Following Directions Quiz.

Students shared that it is really a challenge to rescan their work by the time they are done taking a test.

Students found the practicing of underline and circling key and absolute words to be "helpful."

Can You Follow Directions?

Directions: This is a timed activity. You will have 3 minutes to complete this quiz. First, read everything on this page before doing anything so that you will know exactly what to do.

4. Write your full name in the upper left-hand corner of the paper.
5. Underline your first name and put an *X* through your last name.
6. Loudly call out your school counselor's name.
7. Draw five small squares in the upper right-hand corner of the paper.
8. Put a circle in the middle square and a triangle in the fifth square.
9. Turn to your neighbor and shake hands.
10. Ask your neighbor if they would like to participate in a whistling contest. See who can whistle the tune of "Row, row, row your boat" the fastest.
11. Underline all of the even numbers on the left side of this paper and put circles around the odd numbers.

12. Stand up, flap your wings, and cluck like a chicken three times, then sit back down.
13. On the back of this paper, add 5855 and 2321.
14. Loudly call out "I am nearly finished! I have followed the directions."
15. Underline the third sentence in the directions.
16. Draw a smiley face next to the directions at the top of the page.
17. Now that you have finished reading everything carefully, do only test questions 1 and 2!

Week 6 Group Title: *"Put it all together to F.O.C.U.S. on the Test!"*

Grade Level: *Eight to 10 upper elementary school students*

Learning Objectives

Students will

- demonstrate mastery of the acronym F.O.C.U.S. and each of its key components.
- recognize how internal dialogue or self-talk can affect them during a test.
- recognize commonalities in their peers' school experiences.
- express their feelings about the upcoming state testing.
- provide their peers with support and encouragement.

ASCA Mindsets & Behaviors for Student Success

Mindset Standards

- sense of belonging in the school environment
- self-confidence in ability to succeed
- belief in using abilities to their fullest to achieve high-quality results and outcomes

Behavior Standards

- Use time-management, organizational, and study skills.
- Apply self-motivation and self-direction to learning.
- Demonstrate effective coping skills when faced with a problem.
- Use effective oral and written communication skills and listening skills.
- Create positive and support relationships with other students.

Duration of Group Session: 1 Hour

Required Materials

Important: Prior to the lesson, the facilitator will need to premake F.O.C.U.S. Bingo boards for each student. (Instructions below)

- table for students to write
- name tags for each student
- Group Rules poster
- small plastic bingo chips, boxes of paperclips, or other small items to use to cover letters once they are called in F.O.C.U.S. Bingo

(Continued)

(Continued)

- *F.O.C.U.S. on the Test* (book) by Mary Pat McCartney, 2009
- F.O.C.U.S. Bingo boards (p. 42) (premade for each student. Instructions below)
- F.O.C.U.S. calling cards (p. 40) cut and placed in a box or hat.
- copies of Test Taking Tips from A–Z (p. 48) (for each student)
- copies of My F.O.C.U.S. Plan For Every Test (p. 27) (for each student)

How to make F.O.C.U.S. Bingo boards

Print 10 sets of the F.O.C.U.S. calling cards (p. 40) and 10 sets of the F.O.C.U.S. Bingo boards (p. 42). One at a time, cut out a sheet of calling cards and paste the boxes on a F.O.C.U.S. Bingo board according to the corresponding column. Note: All of the *F* clues in the *F* column should be glued in random order, all of the *O* clues in random order in the *O* column and so on. Repeat this step for all of the boards until you have made 10 randomly ordered F.O.C.U.S. Bingo boards. *Hint: You may want to laminate the boards after they are finished so that you can use them with future groups.*

Introduction to Lesson: "Put it all together and what do you get? F.O.C.U.S."

1) *Activity → Post Test*

As the students begin to enter the classroom, invite them to pick out their name tag and take a seat around the table.

- Begin the group by reminding students that today will be our final meeting of *Eyes on the Prize*.
- Remind them of how far they have come and how much they have learned.
- Tell them that you'd like them to take one more quick test to demonstrate all that they have learned.
- Hand out My Focus Plan for Every Test and ask the students to fill out the worksheet by indicating how they will use different tools and strategies from each of the letters in the acronym F.O.C.U.S. to help them with the test.
- There are no wrong answers.
- Give them 10 minutes to complete this task.

Step-by-Step Procedure

1) *Activity → F.O.C.U.S. Bingo*

   - As a reward for all of their hard work during the past 6 weeks and as a way to review what the group has learned, spend the majority of group time playing F.O.C.U.S. Bingo.
   - Hand out the F.O.C.U.S. Bingo bards and chips, paperclips, or small covering objects to students.
   - Pick a F.O.C.U.S. Bingo calling card from a hat or box and <u>without reading the letter of the acronym F.O.C.U.S.</u>, read the clue aloud.
   - Ask the students to guess which letter the clue corresponds with and cover that clue on their board, or, for a harder game have students determine independently which letter on the board the clue corresponds with.
   - To win the game, the student must spell out FOCUS either across or diagonally.
   - Just like in the game bingo, when a student feels s/he has won, she or he must call out FOCUS!

Assessment

Throughout the group, students' verbal (and physical) responses to discussions and activities provide group leaders with additional information about students' feelings about group work. Follow-up questions during group process are likely to elicit additional themes to be used in preparing future agendas for upcoming group meetings on the same subject matter.

Accommodations

This group is comprised of members from many different academic and social circles. Not only is it important to provide name tags to accommodate for the fact that not everyone knows each other, it is important to accommodate for different learning styles (e.g. verbal/kinesthetic), language differences, as well as personality styles. To this effect, group leaders differentiate activities in the following ways:

Students are not required to respond to any prompt and provided additional clarification if needed.

Students are given additional time to process questions and supported with verbal praise for positive peer interactions.

Follow-up: Group Discussion and Summation

Review the lessons learned during six sessions of *Eyes on the Prize*:

- How did it feel to be part of this group?
- What surprised you about this group?
- What are some of your favorite lessons you learned?
- What was something you did not enjoy or wish you could have changed about group?
- Would you be interested in participating in future groups with Mrs. Saunders and Ms. Rogers?

Before students depart, hand out Test Taking Tips from A–Z for the students to take home as a reminder of what we learned during group!

Counselor Notes to Self re: Future Changes in Lesson Plan:

Notes are provided following the sixth meeting of *Eyes on the Prize* that include specific dialogue and themes from students' suggestions. The following themes were noted:

Today was the "most fun."

Students reported feeling "more confident" and "more prepared" to take tests.

Students felt they made new friends through the group; students felt like being in group was a positive thing.

The following are weekly communication letters to parents/guardians to help reinforce strategies and attendance.

Sample Reminder E-mail— GROUP STARTS SOON.

Good Afternoon.

We are excited to welcome your student to *Eyes on the Prize* beginning (Date) at 7:45 a.m. in the school counselor's office.

Ms. Rogers and I are very excited to begin group with your students. Please make sure that your child arrives in my office promptly.

The schedule for this group was sent home with your child last week and has also been attached to this e-mail. Please do not hesitate to contact us with any questions.

(Continued)

(Continued)

In the event that school is canceled OR we have any other weather-related delay on a day when your child is scheduled to attend, please be advised that we will be rescheduling your child's group. I will let you know as soon as possible about the date change when that situation arises.

We are looking forward to working with your child.

Sincerely,

Mrs. Saunders, School Counselor, and
Ms. Rogers, School Counselor Intern

****

SESSION 1: (Introductions)

Dear Parents,

At this point, your child has taken part in the first session of our 6-week group, *Eyes on the Prize*. During our first meeting, students introduced themselves, worked together to establish group rules and goals, and started to share some feelings surrounding test-taking anxiety and what it feels like to be in this group. We also played a few fun games together and (like we always do in our room) had some good laughs. It was a pleasure to work with your students, and we look forward to our next meeting together.

Next week, we will introduce the students to the word *F.O.C.U.S.*, which is an acronym for each of the areas that we will cover in this group, and we will devote time to the letter *F* which stands for "**F**ace It."

As a reminder, please do your best get your child to school by 7:45 a.m., so that they do not miss a minute of all of the fun activities we have in store!

Feel free to contact us if you have any questions or concerns.

Sincerely,

Mrs. Saunders, School Counselor, and
Ms. Rogers, School Counselor Intern

****

SESSION 2: (*F* stands for "Face it")

Dear Parents,

We had another fun and exciting session with your students today. During our group, the students learned about the acronym *F.O.C.U.S.* and discussed different ways to apply the phrase "Face It" to taking a test. We talked about how "attitude is everything," so even though taking a test may not be one's favorite thing to do, we need to face the fact that tests are a part of life. We also discussed the importance of facing the teacher when she or he is providing instructions before a test so that we know what to do! For our next session we will move on to *O* which stands for "Organize It!"

Thank you for your continued efforts to get your students here on time! As always, feel free to contact us if you have any questions, comments, or concerns.

Sincerely,

Mrs. Saunders, School Counselor, and
Ms. Rogers, School Counselor Intern

****

SESSION 3: (*O* stands for "Organize It")

Dear Parents,

The conclusion of today's group marks the halfway point! Today we had a crash course in organizational skills, and how our ability to get organized can be so helpful in reducing test-related anxiety. The group took part in a very fun activity to demonstrate why organization is key! We then processed how it feels to be organized on the day of a test versus disorganized. We also talked about organizing our speed when we take a test (so that we have enough time to finish) and organizing our answers (so that we don't accidently forget to transfer something to the answer key). Next session, we will discuss how to *Conquer* the test, including how to conquer stress and how to conquer the questions.

Please keep up the good work in getting your students here on time. We have so many fun activities planned each week, so even a few minutes delay can really hurt our ability to get to everything.

Feel free to contact us if you have any questions or concerns.

Sincerely,

Mrs. Saunders, School Counselor, and
Ms. Rogers, School Counselor Intern

****

SESSION 4: (*C* stands for "Conquer It")

Dear Parents,

Our group topic today was all about conquering the test. This is one of my favorite letters in the *F.O.C.U.S.* acronym because it really gets to the heart of what people need to be able to be successful on a test. The students learned that in order to be able to conquer the questions, they must first learn to conquer stress so that they will be in their best mental state during testing. We talked about a few breathing and relaxation techniques that your child can do to de stress. We also talked about some ways they can use their brain power to "beat the test." Next week, we will introduce the group to letter *U* which stands for "Understand It" and the letter *S* which stands for "Scan It."

We look forward to seeing your child again next week at 7:45 a.m.!

Please feel free to reach out to us with questions.

Sincerely,

Mrs. Saunders, School Counselor, and
Ms. Rogers, School Counselor Intern

****

SESSION 5: (*U* stands for "Understand It" and *S* stands for "Scan It")

Dear Parents,

Today marked our second to last meeting of *Eyes on the Prize*. Please remind your child that our next meeting will be our last session. During group today, we discussed the importance of understanding the test! We discussed how key words and absolute words can help us to understand what the question is asking us. We also discussed the importance of scanning over the test before you submit your final answers to ensure that everything was answered completely and correctly. The students took part in a very silly following directions quiz, which highlighted the importance of understanding what to do *before* you start answering the questions and the importance of scanning their work.

(Continued)

(Continued)

Only one more early morning drop off to go! Thanks for continuing to ensure your child gets here promptly at 7:45 a.m.

Looking forward to our last meeting together.

Sincerely,

Mrs. Saunders, School Counselor, and
Ms. Rogers, School Counselor Intern

****

SESSION 6: FINAL EMAIL TO PARENTS

Dear Parents,

I am writing to let you know that the first 6-week session of *Eyes on the Prize* has concluded this week. We wanted to take a moment to thank you for your patience as we navigated scheduling issues and for your ongoing efforts to get your child to group on time. It was an absolute pleasure to work with each student in this group. For your reference, and so that you can hopefully continue to reinforce these themes at home, below we are providing a small synopsis of our weekly sessions.

1. During our first meeting, students introduced themselves, worked together to establish group rules and goals, and started to share some feelings surrounding test-taking anxiety and what it feels like to be in this group. We also played a few fun games together and had some good laughs.
2. During week two, the students learned about the acronym *F.O.C.U.S.* and discussed different ways to apply the phrase "**F**ace It" to taking a test. We talked about how "attitude is everything," so even though taking a test may not be one's favorite thing to do, we need to face the fact that tests are a part of life. We also discussed the importance of facing the teacher when she or he is providing instructions before a test so that we know what to do!
3. For our third session, we had a crash course in **O**rganizational skills and how our ability to get organized can be so helpful in reducing test-related anxiety. The group took part in a very fun activity to demonstrate why organization is key! We also talked about organizing our speed when we take a test (so that we have enough time to finish) and organizing our answers (so that we don't accidently forget to transfer something to the answer key).
4. Our fourth session was all about **C**onquering the test. This is one of our favorite letters in the *F.O.C.U.S.* acronym because it really gets to the heart of what students need in order to be successful on a test. The students learned that in order to be able to conquer the questions, they must first learn to conquer stress so that they will be in their best mental state during testing. We tried a few breathing and relaxation techniques that your child can do to de-stress. We also talked about some ways they can use their brain power to "beat the test."
5. During our fifth group, we discussed the importance of **U**nderstanding the test! We discussed how key words and absolute words can help us to understand what the question is asking us. We also discussed the importance of **S**canning over the test before you submit your final answers to ensure that everything was answered completely and correctly. The students also took part in a very silly following directions quiz, which highlighted the importance of understanding what to do *before* you start answering the questions and the importance of scanning over the test.
6. During the final meeting of our test-taking skills group, we played a fun game of F.O.C.U.S Bingo to review all of the lessons from previous weeks. The students had so much fun playing together, and they impressed us with how much information they had retained from weeks prior.

Thank you for allowing your child to participate in this group. We hope they have shared with you what they have learned and that you can continue to reinforce these ideas throughout their school-age years and beyond.

If you have any questions, comments, or concerns, please do not hesitate to contact us!

Sincerely,
Mrs. Saunders, School Counselor, and
Ms. Rogers, School Counselor Intern

● STEPS 5 AND 6: RESULTS AND EDUCATE

"Did the results of everyone's efforts show that the interventions and strategies successfully moved the critical data elements in a positive direction?"

"Disseminate to internal and external stakeholders the changes in the targeted data elements."

(Stone & Dahir, 2011, p. 35)

Several pieces of data were collected throughout each 6-week group to show student growth. The following letter to board members and administrators demonstrates the results and implications of these data and one of the ways this information was disseminate to internal and external stakeholders.

Sample Data Communication Letter to Board Members and Administrators

Dear Board of Education and District Administrators,

Thank you for supporting the school counseling department's small-group counseling initiative. With your support, we were able to run 10 sections of *Eyes on the Prize* and service a total of 80 upper elementary school students. I believe that our students benefited in a number of ways as evidenced by their verbal, behavioral, and academic responses. It is with pride that I share with you some of the positive outcomes shared by students, families, and teachers.

First and foremost, I am excited to report that students' national percentile ranking from the previous year was compared to their national percentile ranking in the current year, after participating in an *Eyes on the Prize* group. (%) of students increased in their national percentile ranking. While we cannot confirm that this increase was caused by participation in this small-group opportunity, as there are many additional factors to consider, it does appear that there is a positive correlation between participation in this group and an increase in national percentile ranking. Moreover, when examining students who had not participated in these groups in terms of their percentile ranking from year to year, an overall lower percentage of these students increased in percentile ranking from one year to the next. This information leads us to believe that these groups may have been influential in students' success.

More specific to the group itself, after analyzing the pre- and posttest data, we found that students increased their knowledge of test-taking strategies by (%). They also reported, as demonstrated by a Likert scale, a decrease in stress thinking about taking the upcoming state test. Qualitatively, the majority of students (%) mentioned that knowing they were not alone in feeling stressed about these tests was one of the main reasons for their decrease in stress. Many students also talked about how the group helped them

(Continued)

(Continued)

to develop ideas and strategies in which to talk with their parents specific to the academic and career pressures experienced throughout the year. Furthermore, students appreciated opportunities to learn mindfulness activities that they could implement before and during the test if they felt anxious in the moment.

Qualitative feedback was also gathered from families and teachers. With confidentiality in mind, families and teachers were provided weekly reports about the specific skills discussed each week. During the initial screening process, teachers' feedback provided helpful information in terms of determining students' appropriateness for these groups. Teachers identified specific areas of need and then were asked to provide follow-up feedback a month after the group had ended. (%) of teachers reported at least some noticeable areas of improvement as far as students' overt anxiety, organizational skills, and knowledge and usage of test-taking strategies during in-class assessments. Likewise, during the screening process, families were asked to provide group leaders with some areas related to test-taking in which they felt their children could grow. As evidenced by email responses (such as the one highlighted below) families appreciated the opportunity to reinforce mindfulness practices and emotional expression skills specific to test-taking at home.

As suggested by this outcome data, students appeared to gain a number of valuable skills and connect more deeply with their peers around a common theme of test-taking stress. Thank you again for supporting this initiative.

Sincerely,

Mrs. Saunders, School Counselor, and
Ms. Rogers, School Counseling Intern

Example Parent E-mail

Dear Mrs. Saunders and Ms. Rogers,

Thank you for updating us with weekly strategies presented in your *Eyes on the Prize* group. As you know, my son is in the Gifted and Talented program at school, and I never thought he would need additional help taking tests. It turns out that your group has helped him to speak with us more about his concerns about this test and what it means for his future. In fact, we had no idea that he was worried that not getting 100% would keep him from getting into Harvard! As a parent of an elementary school student, I appreciate that you provide these groups to our children at such a young age, so that they can feel validated in their experiences and be better prepared to manage test-taking anxiety.

Thank you again.

Mrs. Happy Parent

● CONCLUSION

School counselors are trained to facilitate many types of groups in the school setting. This chapter focused on several of these groups as they supported student growth and provided data in which the department could use to further advocate for interventions that contribute to a comprehensive school counseling program. Using Stone and Dahir's acronym *MEASURE*, data were sequentially collected through several group interventions and stakeholder discussions; ultimately the presentation of this data to district administrators and community stakeholders supported the implementation of a small-group counseling initiative that addressed the mission of the school district while specifically targeting upper elementary school students struggling with stress and standardized test-taking.

● REFERENCES

Akos, P., Goodnough, G. E., & Milsom, A. S. (2004). Preparing school counselors for group work. *The Journal for Specialists in Group Work, 29*(1), 127–136.

Akos, P., Hamm, J. V., Mack, S. G., & Dunaway, M. (2007). Utilizing the developmental influence of peers in middle school groups. *The Journal for Specialists in Group Work, 32*, 51–60.

American School Counselor Association. (2012). *The ASCA National Model: A framework for school counseling programs* (3rd ed.). Alexandria, VA: Author.

American School Counselor Association. (2014a). *ASCA mindsets & behaviors for student success: K–12 college- and career-readiness standards for every student*. Retrieved from https://search.yahoo.com/search;_ylc=X3oDMTFiN-25laTRvBF9TAzIwMjM1MzgwNzUEaXRjAzEEc2VjA3NyY2hfcWEEc2xrA3NyY2h3ZWI-?p=ASCA+Mindsets&fr=yfp-t&fp=1&toggle=1&cop=mss&ei=UTF-8

American School Counselor Association. (2014b). *The school counselor and group counseling* [Position statement]. Alexandria, VA: Author.

Bore, S. K., Armstrong, S. A., & Womack, A. (2010). School counselors' experiential training in group work. *Journal of School Counseling, 8*(26). Retrieved from http://www.jsc.montana.edu/articles/v8n25.pdf

Cook, J. (2011). *Soda Pop Head*. Chattanooga, TN: National Center for Youth Issues.

Gladding, S. T. (2012). *Groups: A counseling specialty* (6th ed). Upper Saddle River, NJ: Pearson.

Kulic, K. R., Dagley, J. C., & Horne, A. M. (2001). Prevention groups with children and adolescents. *The Journal for Specialists in Group Work, 26*(3), 211–218.

McCartney, M. P. (2009). *FOCUS on the Test*. New Bern, NC: Marco Products. Optical Illusion. (2015). Retrieved from http://www.123opticalillusions.com/pages/opticalillusions5.php

Pérusse, R., Goodnough, G. E., & Lee, V. V. (2009). Group counseling in the schools. *Psychology in the Schools, 46*(3), 225–231.

Shillingford, M. A., & Edwards, O. W. (2008). Application of choice theory with a student whose parent is incarcerated: A qualitative case study. *International Journal of Reality Therapy, 28*(1), 41–44.

Sink, C. A., Edwards, C. N., & Eppler, C. (2012). *School based group counseling*. Belmont, CA: Brooks/Cole.

Steen, S., Bauman, S., & Smith, J. (2007). Professional school counselors and the practice of group work. *Professional School Counseling, 11*(2), 72–80.

Stone, C. B., & Dahir, C. A. (2011). *School counselor accountability: A MEASURE of student success* (3rd ed.). Upper Saddle River, NJ: Pearson Education.

LESSON 22

MENTAL HEALTH IN SCHOOLS

"I could use some help with this student."

Margaret Herrick
Kutztown University of Pennsylvania

Helen Hamlet

Real Life

Counselor-in-Training: I met with John today. He was sent to the counseling office this morning because he fell asleep in history class again today. When we talked about what is going on in his life, he said nothing. He just was tired and didn't feel like doing anything. John said he was tired because "he never really sleeps." He didn't really want to talk about it because he felt that "what is, is." I touched base with John's teachers and they definitely have noticed a change in his behavior. Previously he was pretty lively and was always considered the class clown. Last semester, he was always making jokes with his friends at lunch and having a good time. Academically his grades have slipped slightly, but he is a very strong student. How can I best support John at this point?

Supervisor: Sounds like you know John pretty well. And—great job gathering information and consulting with his teacher. It's very helpful to know that this is a change in behavior and not the John teachers observed last year. Next time you meet with John, I recommend continuing to develop rapport with him and begin to gather information on what is going on in his life right now and if there have been any changes in this world. You'll meet with him on Monday? Great—let's meet right after the meeting for supervision.

Lesson Twenty-Two

Mental Health in Schools

"I could use some help with this student."

Margaret Herrick
Kutztown University of Pennsylvania

Helen Hamlet

Essential Question: What is the role as a school counselor when working with students with mental health issues?

Objectives

Students will

- demonstrate an understanding of possible causes and current data regarding mental health.
- describe and illustrate the characteristics of different types of mental health disabilities.
- describe current approaches to understanding the social and academic experience of individuals with mental health disabilities.
- identify reliable and valid assessment procedures.
- consult with parents, teachers, and agency staff to identify the various community-based services, associations, and resources available to children and adolescents with mental health disabilities.
- outline key issues and evidence-based counseling interventions, adaptations, and accommodations in working with children and adolescents with mental health disabilities.
- integrate developmental life-span issues and typical behavioral milestones into working with children and adolescents with mental health disabilities.
- research public health policies, ethical issues, and laws in working with children and adolescents with mental health disabilities.
- develop formative and summative outcome methods to assess the effectiveness of their intervention.

CACREP 2016 Standards

- Demonstrate knowledge about the characteristics, risk factors, and warning signs of students at risk for mental health and behavioral disorders (5.G.2.g)
- Demonstrate knowledge about the common medications that affect learning, behavior, and mood in children and adolescents (5.G.2.h)
- Demonstrate knowledge of community resources and referral sources (5.G.2.j)
- Demonstrate ability to critically examine the connections between social, familial, emotional, and behavior problems and academic achievement (5.G.3.h)

MPCAC Standards

- Neuroscientific, physical, and biological foundations of human development and wellness
- Human development and wellness across the life span
- Assessment of human behavior and organizational/community/institutional systems
- Counseling, consultation, and social-justice advocacy theories and skills

Video Spark

http://www.nimh.nih.gov/health/topics/child-and-adolescent-mental-health/index.shtml

What goes on in the adolescent brain?

INTRODUCTION

According to the National Institute of Mental Health (NIMH, 2014), 20% of our nation's children and adolescents are diagnosed with a mental health disability at some point in their young lives. As these individuals present for counseling services, certified school counselors and licensed professional counselors are increasingly called upon to develop effective counseling interventions. It is essential for counselors-in-training to (a) understand the role of the school counselor; (b) understand the developmental nature of mental health; and (c) acquire the skills, knowledge, and dispositions necessary to work with children and adolescents suffering from the conditions most noted by the NIMH. Included will be the top four conditions identified by NIMH: attention–deficit/hyperactivity disorder, disruptive behavior disabilities, depression, and anxiety disabilities. Additional disabilities, as they complicate the top four conditions, will be addressed.

THE ROLE OF THE SCHOOL COUNSELOR AND STUDENT MENTAL HEALTH

Working with students with mental health issues can be a quagmire for the school counselor. The counselor can be pulled in multiple directions by multiple stakeholders—some realistic, some unrealistic. For example, parents often want us to be therapists to their child; administrators want us to meet the students' needs in order to facilitate academic success; and the public or popular press always want to know "where was the school counselor" when a tragedy occurs in the school community. Hence, it is very important to have a strong commitment to our role and a true clarity as to what that role is.

To provide a guideline for the profession, the American School Counselor Association's (ASCA) position statement (2015) on The School Counselor and Student Mental Health (Appendix A) is

> School counselors recognize and respond to the need for mental health and behavioral prevention, early intervention and crisis services that promote psychosocial wellness and development for all students. School counselors are prepared to address barriers and to assess ways to maximize students' success in schools communities and their family structure by offering education, prevention, and crisis and short-term intervention until the student is connected with available community resources.

Specifically, ASCA identifies the role of the school counselor in terms of education, prevention, and crisis and short-term intervention.

In practice, parents and teachers often turn to the school counselor for help in identifying the cause(s) of student's concerning behaviors. School counselors gather information regarding student behaviors through classroom observations, behavior rating scales, collaborating with teachers, reviewing the records, and interviews with the student's parents or guardians. These data are then shared with the parents, school psychologist, or other appropriate (on a need to know basis) professional educator in the school district. At this point, further assessment may be indicated. This assessment normally occurs outside of the school setting. Most mental health disorders are diagnosed by outside physicians or mental health professionals, not the school counselor. If a student is diagnosed, a 504 Plan is generated. Based on the

504 plan, interventions will be implemented to support the student. The school counselor in the role of advocate will provide information, resources, and support to the student, family, and teachers. School counselors also provide direct services through individual counseling and small-group counseling.

● DEVELOPMENTAL MODEL OF MENTAL HEALTH

The Centers for Disease Control and Prevention (CDC, 2016) writes that "mental health in childhood means reaching developmental and emotional milestones, and learning healthy social skills and how to cope when there are problems. Mentally healthy children have a positive quality of life and can function well at home, in school, and in their communities." The CDC continues that the "symptoms of mental disorders change over time as a child grows, and may include difficulties with how a child plays, learns, speaks and acts or how the child handles their emotions. Symptoms often start in early childhood, although some disorders may develop throughout the teenage years. The diagnosis is often made in the school years and sometimes earlier. However, some children with a mental disorder may not be recognized or diagnosed as having one."

The model below illustrates several potential factors that could lead to a child or adolescent developing a mental health disability and gives the school counselor or mental health counselor areas to investigate when doing an initial interview.

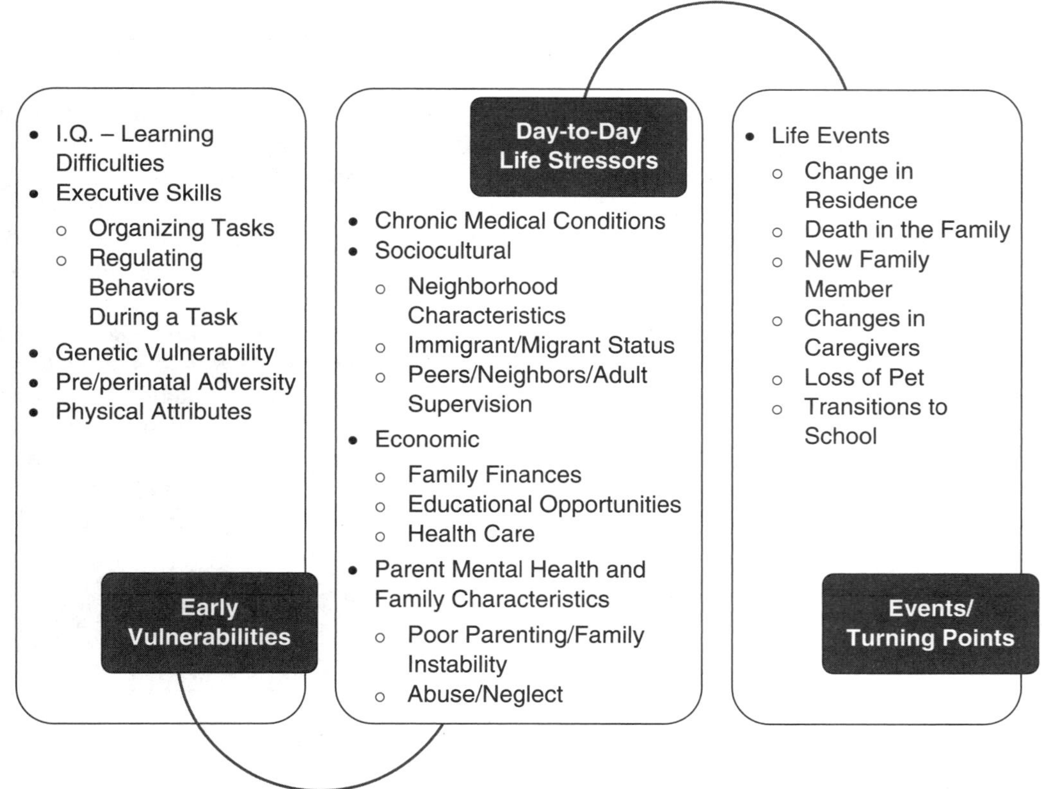

<u>Early Vulnerabilities:</u> These include predisposing factors toward mental illness. For example, a child with a learning disability or executive skill difficulty can be continually frustrated in school if accommodations are not made for him or her. In addition, that child could have parents with genetic

predispositions to mental illness (e.g., bipolar disorder). Also, if mom did not have good prenatal care, a problem could compromise healthy development. Lastly, children with physical attributes that result in being made fun of or bullying present additional early vulnerabilities.

Day-to-Day Stressors: These include all the daily challenges that a child might encounter and are fairly self-explanatory. We don't often recognize the external stressors on children, such as poverty, inadequate access to health care, parents who don't have good parenting skills, for example.

Events/Turning Points: A child with early vulnerabilities and day-to-day stressors may have a difficult time with a major change in her or his life. Even what adults perceive as a small change can trigger a mental health disability in a child. Asking "When did the behaviors start?" or "Was there something going on that might upset him or her at that time?" are key questions to investigating this factor.

● MENTAL HEALTH ISSUES FREQUENTLY IDENTIFIED IN CHILDHOOD AND ADOLESCENCE

Attention–Deficit/Hyperactivity Disorder

The National Institute of Mental Health (2014) indicates that "Attention deficit hyperactivity disorder (ADHD) is one of the most common childhood disorders and can continue through adolescence and adulthood. Symptoms include difficulty staying focused and paying attention, difficulty controlling behavior, and hyperactivity (over-activity)." *The Diagnostic and Statistical Manual of Mental Disorders*, 5th edition (DSM-V) (American Psychiatric Association, 2013) identifies three subtypes of ADHD: combined presentation (both inattention and hyperactive-impulsivity behaviors), predominantly inattentive, and predominantly hyperactive/impulsive presentation and is classified as a neurodevelopmental disorder. Individuals with ADHD may also face challenges due to comorbidity. Commonly occurring comorbid conditions are substance use disorders, mood disorders, medical conditions (i.e., chronic illness, etc.), anxiety disorders, speech language disorders, and learning disorders (Gathright & Tyler, 2014). As the school counselor plans to support and accommodate the student with ADHD, it is also important to remain cognizant of possible concerns due to other factors.

Treatment for ADHD is multifaceted. Strategies include behavioral interventions, cognitive-behavioral interventions, parent education, medication, and parent–school collaboration. School counselors support students with ADHD through collaboration with parents, collaboration with teachers, development of behavioral intervention plans, cognitive-behavioral counseling, and individual and small-group counseling. The LD OnLine website has developed a list of ADHD interventions (Appendix A). This resource list is at the end of the chapter. If deemed necessary, physicians prescribe medication. Stimulants, such as Adderall (amphetamine and dextroamphetamine), are often used to treat ADHD. However, it is important to remain current on ADHD interventions through professional development.

● ACTIVITY 1

ADHD Case Study (DSM-V: Neurodevelopmental Disorder)

Ten-year-old Julio is in constant motion. He has difficulty concentrating on what the teacher is saying or watching a film with his classmates. Rather, Julio will get up from his seat and try to get others to pay attention to him. Julio will often raise his hand to answer a question even before the teacher finishes talking. When given a pencil and paper task, he will rush through it, often leaving parts of it incomplete.

He prefers word games and seems to be better able to concentrate on learning activities that involve flash cards. Julio has pushed other children aside just to be first in line. At home, Julio will start a simple chore—like taking out the garbage—but become distracted and end up in another activity. His mother reports that he cannot sit at the table through a family meal without getting up several times or watch his favorite television show without "flipping through" the channels several times.

Julio is in good physical health and has met all developmental milestones to date. He has some difficulty with motor coordination and has been described as "clumsy." He does not experience problems with sleep onset or sleep maintenance. His appetite is good. Julio plays cooperatively with peers. His overall mood is described as "happy."

Case Study Discussion Questions

- What more do you need to know to help Julio? How will you get this information?
- Which of Julio's behaviors are suggestive of ADHD?
- What general approaches would be appropriate for helping Julio?
- What specific steps will you take to assist him? What priority should each of these steps have?

● ACTIVITY 2

Read the following book:

ADHD & me: what i learned from lighting fires at the dinner table **by blake e. s. taylor**

Disability Experience. The purpose of this assignment is to provide the counselor-in-training with some sense of the narrative and cognitive process of a child with a mental health disability.

ADHD Book Discussion Questions

Instructions: Using what you have learned in the reading, respond to the following questions in your own words and in a way that someone not familiar with ADHD can understand. Put yourself in a real-world not a graduate-student setting.

1. What did Mr. Taylor's life experiences teach you about living with ADHD?
2. What were his coping resources and skills when he felt overwhelmed?

● DISRUPTIVE BEHAVIOR DISORDERS

NIMH identifies disruptive behavior disorders as one of the top four mental health issues impacting children and adolescents. This section addresses oppositional defiant disorder, conduct disorders, and unspecified disruptive behavior disorder. These three disorders are classified in the disruptive, impulsive control and conduct disorders category. The DSM 5 groups the symptoms of Disruptive Behavior Disorders into three categories: angry/irritable mood, argumentative/defiant behavior, and vindictiveness. The American Psychiatric Association (APA, 2013) notes that the symptoms of these disorders "are unique in that these problems are manifested in behaviors that violate the rights of others (e.g., aggression, destruction of property) and/or that bring the individual into significant conflict with societal norms or authority figures. The underlying causes of the problems in the self-control of emotions and behaviors can vary greatly across the disorders in this chapter and among individuals within a given diagnostic category." The Substance Abuse and Mental Health Services Administration (SAMSHA, 2015) reports that the prevalence rate of oppositional defiant disorders is 3.3% among children and adolescents, while the average prevalence rate of children and adolescents who have met the criteria for conduct disorder at some point in their lifetime is 8.5%. With these high prevalence statistics, the probability of a school counselor working with children with these disorders is probable if not likely.

The following case studies provide information on the key symptoms of disruptive behavior disorders, oppositional defiant disorder, and conduct disorder. Treatment resources are in Appendix B at the end of this chapter.

● ACTIVITY: CASE STUDIES

Disruptive Behavior Disorder Case Study: (DSM-V—Disruptive, Impulsive-Control, and Conduct Disorders)

Eight-year-old Jimmy will erupt into temper outbursts, even over what might be considered minor annoyances. For example, he will cry, kick, and scream if he drops something by accident, if other children bump into him, or if he has to share his favorite toy. He is also easily frustrated and discouraged when play does not go his way or when he is bored. These outbursts can occur three to five times per day. In addition, Jimmy needs several prompts to get him to do simple tasks, such as hanging up his coat or getting his book and pencils ready to a lesson. His typical response to adult requests is "No" followed by either "I don't care" or "You are being mean to me." Behaviors observed by his teachers include refusing to follow directions, hitting other children, climbing tables and shelves, name-calling and using foul language, and calling out or speaking over the teacher. On the playground, Jimmy frequently instigates fights with other children and will take their toys and refuse to share. Overall, Jimmy's mother describes his general demeanor as "cranky" and says that "nothing" seems to soothe him or make him happy.

Jimmy has no reported health problems and has met all developmental milestones. He has no difficulty with sleep onset or nightmares. He can be cheerful when things are "going his way." His appetite is good, and he enjoys a variety of foods. Jimmy has no difficulty concentrating on homework or attending to a conversation. He shows no sensory sensitivities and responds to verbal and nonverbal cues for reciprocal social interaction.

Case Study Discussion Questions

- What more do you need to know to help Jimmy? How will you get this information?
- Which of Jimmy's behaviors are suggestive of disruptive behavior disorder?
- What general approaches would be appropriate for helping Jimmy?
- What specific steps will you take to assist him? What priority should each of these steps have?

Oppositional Defiant Disorder (ODD) Case Study: (DSM-V—Disruptive, Impulsive-Control, and Conduct Disorders)

Fourteen-year-old Amy refuses to take prescribed medication, perform assigned household chores, or complete in-school and homework assignments. When her father says "This is the fourth time I've told you to come to the dinner table," Amy will respond with "This is the fourth time I've told you I am not going to do it." When she is angered, Amy will swear and use profanity, regardless of the setting or others in her presence. She has punched her mother and gotten into a fistfight with her younger brother. She has destroyed furniture and, just last week, threw a rock through a window of the family home. These behaviors carry over into the school setting. Amy has shoved her teacher, thrown books, and toppled desks in the classroom. On one occasion, she stole a classmate's purse and emptied the contents in the toilet. When confronted with her aggressive behaviors, Amy will say "Well, they made me do it." Most of the time, these behaviors occur when Amy is denied something that she wants or when limits are set on her behaviors. At other times, she seeks purposeful revenge upon those who she perceives to have wronged her. For example, in an attempt to get a classmate in trouble, Amy lied to the school nurse, saying that a classmate cut her with a knife.

Case Study Discussion Questions

- What more do you need to know to help Amy? How will you get this information?
- Which of Amy's behaviors are suggestive of ODD?
- What general approaches would be appropriate for helping Amy?
- What specific steps will you take to assist her? What priority should each of these steps have?

Conduct Disorder Case Study: (DSM-V—Disruptive, Impulsive-Control, and Conduct Disorders)

Sixteen-year-old Seth has a history of purposeful oppositional and vengeful behaviors. Family, peers, and school officials know him as a bully who is verbally and physically aggressive to anyone he perceives as "weak." Seth also torments the family dog by throwing firecrackers at him. In the last year, Seth has stolen cigarettes and money from his mother's purse, a video camera from the school IT room, and cigarettes and candy from a local grocery store. When he is caught with the stolen goods, Seth will deny his actions and say "It wasn't me." Seth has also set fires, first in a trashcan in his bedroom and then to the bathroom shower curtain. Recently, he activated the smoke alarm at school after setting some papers on fire and holding them against the alarm. Twice, Seth sneaked out of the family home in the middle of the night to join his group of teens to "fight" another group of teens. Both times, the police escorted Seth back to his home. Recently, Seth's teacher found a journal in his desk. One of the entries included a detailed description of how Seth and two friends were going to obtain a gun and rob a grocery store.

Case Study Discussion Questions

- What more do you need to know to help Seth? How will you get this information?
- Which of Seth's behaviors are suggestive of conduct disorder?
- What general approaches would be appropriate for helping Seth?
- What specific steps will you take to assist him? What priority should each of these steps have?

● ANXIETY, DEPRESSIVE, AND TRAUMA- AND STRESSOR-RELATED DISORDERS

Working with children and adolescents requires an expertise in child development. The professional school counselor is charged with identifying what is developmentally normal, what is a "phase," what behaviors require "watching," and what needs intervention. Symptoms of internalizing behavior disorders, such as depression and anxiety, are present in normal development. It is not uncommon for adolescents to be irritable, have poor self-esteem, or have problems completing their schoolwork. It's also not uncommon for an individual to feel anxious about taking a test or giving a presentation. However, when these feelings begin to impair an individual's functioning and everyday life, intervention is required. The number of students challenged by anxiety, depression, and trauma- and stress-related disorders are seen in school counseling centers all of the country. Specifically, let's look at the lifetime prevalence of these disorders. "Lifetime prevalence is the proportion of a population who, at some point in life up to the time of assessment, has ever had the characteristic" (National Institute of Mental Health [NIMH], 2014b). The National Institute of Mental Health reports the lifetime prevalence of *anxiety disorders* among children is 25.1% for 13 to 18 year olds. The lifetime prevalence of *mood disorders* in children and adolescents is 14% for 13 to 18 year olds; 2.8% for 8 to 11 year olds; and 5.8% for 12 to 15 year olds (NIMH, 2014a).

The prevalence of *posttraumatic stress disorder* (PTSD) for children and adolescents is studied by the U.S. Department of Veterans Affairs. The results are as follows: "The National Comorbidity Survey Replication—Adolescent Supplement is a nationally representative sample of over 10,000 adolescents ages 13 to 18. Results indicate that 5% of adolescents have met criteria for PTSD in their lifetime. Prevalence is higher for girls than boys (8.0% vs. 2.3%) and increase with age (4). Current rates (in the past month) are 3.9% overall (5). There are no definitive studies on prevalence rates of PTSD in younger children in the general population" (Hamblen & Barnett, 2014).

The prevalence of *reactive attachment disorder* (RAD) for children and adolescents tends to be studied within specific populations. In a study done by Stine Lehmann, Odd E. Havik, Toril Havik, and Einar Heiervang (2013), information on the prevalence of RAD in children eligible for foster care was gathered. The results of that study are "Diagnostic information was obtained about 279 (70.5%) of 396 eligible foster children. In total, 50.9% of the children met the criteria for one or more DSM-IV disorders. The most common disorders were grouped into 3 main diagnostic groups: Emotional disorders (24.0%), ADHD (19.0%), and Behavioral disorders (21.5%). The comorbidity rates among these 3 main groups were high: 30.4% had disorders in 2 of these 3 diagnostic groups, and 13.0% had disorders in all 3 groups. In addition, Reactive attachment disorder (RAD) was diagnosed in 19.4% of the children, of whom 58.5% had comorbid disorders in the main diagnostic groups. Exposure to violence, serious neglect, and the number of prior placements increased the risk for mental disorders."

The following case studies provide information on the key symptoms of social phobia, depression, posttraumatic stress disorder, and reactive attachment disorder. Treatment resources are in Appendix C at the end of this chapter.

• ACTIVITY 1: CASE STUDIES

Social Phobia Case Study: (DSM-V—Anxiety Disorders)

Twelve-year-old Maggie shows high levels of anxiety when faced with having to go to school or community activities. She constantly worries about what others think of her. When she hears peers whispering, she believes that they are talking negatively about her. As a result, Maggie refuses to cooperate with the accommodations specified in her individualized educational program (IEP) because she fears that peers will find out that she has a learning disability. At times, Maggie will sit with her head on her desk and her feet tucked up under her legs. She has complained about having stomachaches prior to having to walk to the front of the class to participate in a group activity or turn in her homework. As a result, she does not get credit for completing these activities and her grades have fallen. Maggie is constantly asking to see the school nurse. On one occasion, she cut herself with a metal eraser so that she could go home. Maggie's mother said that her avoidant behaviors are worse on Mondays. However, on a daily basis, she struggles to get Maggie out of bed in the morning and get her dressed and ready for school.

Maggie responds to this by yelling, "I can't do this," screaming, swearing, and throwing her school books. Maggie also has "meltdowns" after returning home from school. These generally involve crying and or angry outbursts that can last for up to an hour. Overall, Maggie's avoidance behaviors interfere with her routine at home, school grades, social activities, and peer relationships.

Maggie is in good health and does not use tobacco products, drugs, or alcohol. On weekends and during the summer months, especially when she can spend time at home with her mother, her mood is described as "content and happy." When Maggie started school, she would cry, cling to her mother, and refuse to go into the school building. However, these behaviors subsided during the second grade. Maggie's mother was unaware of any bullying toward Maggie, and Maggie also denied this.

Case Study Discussion Questions

- What more do you need to know to help Maggie? How will you get this information?
- Which of Maggie's behaviors are suggestive of social phobia?
- What general approaches would be appropriate for helping Maggie?
- What specific steps will you take to assist her? What priority should each of these steps have?

Major Depression Case Study

Eleven-year-old Marla started showing behavioral changes midway through the school year. She started spending less time with friends and more time alone on the playground. At home, she complained about being tired and, at least three times per week, would go to bed right after coming home from school. Marla does not eat breakfast. She carries her lunch to school but generally ends up throwing it away or giving it to another classmate. As a result, she has lost about eight pounds in the last 3 weeks. Marla's parents and teachers report that she seems moody, mostly sad. Marla is easily irritated with friends, teachers, and family members. She will burst into tears over "little things" like breaking a shoelace or dropping a pencil. At the last marking period, Marla's grades fell from her usual A average to little better than a C average. She no longer takes pride in her schoolwork. Nor does she seem to enjoy her favorite food, music, or television shows. Last week, her teacher found a sketchbook of dark images and poetry that included themes of death and hopelessness.

Case Study Discussion Questions

- What more do you need to know to help Marla? How will you get this information?
- Which of Marla's behaviors are suggestive of major depression?
- What general approaches would be appropriate for helping Marla?
- What specific steps will you take to assist her? What priority should each of these steps have?

PTSD Case Study: (DSM-V—Trauma- and Stressor-Related Disorders)

Nine-year-old Penny witness a shooting in her neighborhood two years ago. In the last month, another shooting occurred and one of the bullets lodged in the porch of her home. Penny now has reoccurring nightmares of monsters harming her. The nightmares prevent Penny from getting enough sleep. As a result she is unable to focus on schoolwork and her grades are suffering. Penny is also vigilant during the school day and "jumpy" when there are loud noises in the hallway. She worries constantly, and her appetite has decreased. She is easily irritated and will lash out at teachers and peers. At home,

Penny insists on sleeping in her older sister's room and wants the television and lights on. The other night, a car backfired and Penny became hysterical. She curled herself into a ball and cried for an hour. She had the same reaction when a classmate dropped a metal tray in the cafeteria.

Case Study Discussion Questions

- What more do you need to know to help Penny? How will you get this information?
- Which of Penny's behaviors are suggestive of PTSD?
- What general approaches would be appropriate for helping Penny?
- What specific steps will you take to assist her? What priority should each of these steps have?

Reactive Attachment Disorder Case Study: (DSM-V—Trauma- and Stressor-Related Disorders)

Nine-year-old Adam came to live with his adoptive parents when he was 4 years old. Prior to that time, he lived in an orphanage in Europe. His adoptive parents note that he has always been resistant to physical contact from others (e.g., hugging and touching) and has difficulty making eye contact. The only "being" in the family home that Adam is attached to is the family dog. Adam does not ask for what he wants but will try to get his needs met by acting cute and charming. He then gets upset if others do not "read his mind" and give him what he wants. Adam is prone to temper outbursts and arguing with his parents, teachers, and peers. He will lash out at them verbally and physically and then laugh when they express hurt. At other times, Adam does not recognize or respond to others' feelings. Adam tends to try to dominate his classmates, taking their toys and insisting they are his or actually destroying the toys. He also hoards food in his room and will lie about having done so when confronted with evidence of his actions.

Little is known about Adam's early medical or family history. He has no reported current health problems. He does not show signs of having been physically or sexually abused. There are no issues with sleep, appetite, concentration, or mood.

Case Study Discussion Questions

- What more do you need to know to help Adam? How will you get this information?
- Which of Adam's behaviors are suggestive of reactive attachment disorder?
- What general approaches would be appropriate for helping Adam?
- What specific steps will you take to assist him? What priority should each of these steps have?

• ACTIVITY 2

Read the following book

What You Must Think of Me: A Firsthand Account of One Teenager's Experience with Social Anxiety Disorder **by Emily Ford**

Disability Experience. The purpose of this assignment is to provide the counselor-in-training with some sense of the narrative and cognitive process of a child with a mental health disability.

Social Anxiety Book Discussion Questions

Instructions: Using what you have learned in the reading, respond to the following questions in your own words and in a way that someone not familiar with social anxiety can understand. Put yourself in a real world not a graduate-student setting.

1. What did Ms. Ford's life experiences teach you about living with social anxiety disorder?
2. What were her coping resources and skills when she felt overwhelmed?

● REFERENCES

American Psychiatric Association. (2013). *Diagnostic Criteria from DSM-5*. Washington, DC: Author.

American School Counselor Association. (2015). *The school counselor and student mental health* [Position Statement]. Retrieved from https://www.schoolcounselor.org/asca/media/asca/PositionStatements/PS_StudentMentalHealth.pdf

Centers for Disease Control and Prevention. (2016, March). *Children's mental health: Basics*. Retrieved from http://www.cdc.gov/childrensmentalhealth/basics.html

Council for Accreditation for Counseling and Related Program. (2014). *2016 standards*. Retrieved from www.cacrep.org

Eyberg, S. M., Nelson, M. M., & Boggs, S. R. (2008). Evidence-based psychosocial treatments for children and adolescents with disruptive behavior. *Journal of Clinical Child & Adolescent Psychology, 37*(1), 215–237.

Gathright, M. M., & Tyler, L. H. (2014). *Disruptive behaviors in children and adolescents*. Little Rock: University of Arkansas for Medical Services. Retrieved from http://psychiatry.uams.edu/files/2015/02/disruptive.pdf

Hamblen, J., & Barnett, E. (2014). *PTSD in children and adolescents*. Washington, DC: U.S. Department of Veterans Affairs, National Center for PTSD. Retrieved from http://www.ptsd.va.gov/professional/treatment/children/ptsd_in_children_and_adolescents_overview_for_professionals.asp

Health Central. (2015). *20 Classroom interventions for children with anxiety disorders*. Retrieved from http://www.healthcentral.com/anxiety/school-258065-5.html

Lehmann, S., Havik, O. E., Havik, T., & Heiervang, E. R. (2013, November). Mental disorders in foster children: A study of prevalence, comorbidity and risk factors. *Child Adolescent Psychiatry Mental Health, 21,* 7(1). Retrieved from https://capmh.biomedcentral.com/articles/10.1186/1753-2000-7-39

Masters in Psychology and Counseling Accreditation Council. (2015). *Accreditation manual*. Retrieved from http://www.mpcacaccreditation.org/about/accreditation-manual

National Institute of Mental Health. (2014). *Child and adolescent mental health*. Retrieved from http://www.nimh.nih.gov/health/index.shtml

● APPENDIX A

The School Counselor and Student Mental Health

(Adopted 2009, Revised 2015)

The American School Counselor Association (ASCA) Position

School counselors recognize and respond to the need for mental health and behavioral prevention, early intervention, and crisis services that promote psychosocial wellness and development for all students. School counselors are prepared to address barriers and to assess ways to maximize students' success in schools, communities, and their family structure by offering education, prevention, and crisis and short-term intervention until the student is connected with available community resources.

The Rationale

Students' unmet mental health needs can be a significant obstacle to student academic, career and social/emotional development and even compromise school safety. Schools are often one of the first places where mental health crises and needs of students are recognized and initially addressed (Froeschle & Moyer, 2004). Most students in need do not receive adequate mental health supports (Centers for Disease Control and Prevention [CDC], 2013). Research indicates 20% of students are in need of mental health services, yet only one out of five of these students receive the necessary services (Kaffenberger & Seligman, 2007).

Furthermore, students of color and those from families with low income are at greater risk for mental health needs but are even less likely to receive the appropriate services (Panigua, 2005; Vera, Buhin, & Shin, 2006) despite increased national attention to these inequities (Alegria, Vallas, & Pumariega, 2010). Of school-age children who receive any behavioral and mental health services, 70–80% receive them at school (Atkins, Hoagwood, Kutash, & Seidman, 2010). Preventive school-based mental health and behavioral services are essential. Without planned intervention for students exhibiting early-warning signs, setbacks in educational, social, and career development during later school years and adulthood can result. The ASCA Mindsets & Behaviors (American School Counselor Association [ASCA], 2014) identify and prioritize the specific attitudes, knowledge, and skills students should be able to demonstrate as a result of a school counseling program. School counselors use the standards to assess student growth and development, guide the development of strategies and activities and create a program that helps students achieve their highest potential. This includes offering education, prevention, and short-term intervention services designed to promote positive mental health and to remove any barriers.

The School Counselor's Role

School counselors focus their efforts on designing and implementing comprehensive programs that promote academic, career, and social/emotional success for all students. School counselors acknowledge they may be the only counseling professional available to students and their families. While implementing a comprehensive program, school counselors:

- Deliver the school counseling core curriculum that proactively enhances awareness of mental health; promotes positive, healthy behaviors; and seeks to remove the stigma associated with mental health issues
- Provide responsive services including internal and external referral procedures, short-term counseling or crisis intervention focused on mental health or situational (e.g., grief, difficult transitions) concerns with the intent of helping the student return to the classroom and removing barriers to learning
- Recognize warning signs: changes in school performance (changes in grades, attendance), mood changes, complaining of illness before school, increased disciplinary problems at school, experiencing problems at home or family situation (stress, trauma, divorce, substance abuse, exposure to poverty conditions, domestic violence), communication from teachers about problems at school, and dealing with existing mental health concerns

- Provide school-based prevention and universal interventions and targeted interventions for students with mental health and behavioral health concerns
- Provide students with individual planning addressing their academic, career, and social/emotional (including mental health) needs
- Educate teachers, administrators, parents/guardians, and community stakeholders about the mental health concerns of students, including recognition of the role environmental factors have in causing or exacerbating mental health issues and provide resources and information
- Advocate, collaborate, and coordinate with school and community stakeholders to ensure that students and their families have access to mental health services
- Recognize and address barriers to access mental health services and the associated stigma, including cultural and linguistic impediments
- Adhere to appropriate guidelines regarding confidentiality, the distinction between public and private information, and consultation
- Direct students and parents to school and/or community resources for additional assistance through referrals that treat mental health issues (suicidal ideation, violence, abuse, and depression)
- Help identify and address students' mental health issues while working within the ASCA's Ethical Standards; Competencies for School Counselors; and national, state and local legislation (Family Educational Rights and Privacy Act and Health Insurance Portability and Accountability Act), which guide school counselors' informed decision-making and standardize professional practice to protect both the student and school counselor
- Seek to continually update their professional knowledge regarding the students' social/emotional needs

● SUMMARY

Students' unmet mental health needs pose barriers to learning and development. Because of school counselors' training and position, they are uniquely qualified to provide education, prevention, intervention, and referral services to students and their families. Although school counselors do not provide long-term mental health therapy in schools, they provide a comprehensive school counseling program designed to meet the developmental needs of all students. As a component of this program, school counselors collaborate with other educational professionals and community service providers.

● REFERENCES

Alegria, M., Vallas, M., & Pumariega, A. J. (2010). Racial and ethnic disparities in pediatric mental health. *Child and Adolescent Psychiatric Clinics of North America, 19*(4), 759–774. doi:10.1016/j.chc.2010.07.001

American School Counselor Association. (2012). *The ASCA National Model: A framework for school counseling programs* (3rd ed.). Alexandria, VA: Author.

American School Counselor Association. (2014). *Mindsets & behaviors for student success: K–12 college- and career-readiness standards for every student.* Alexandria, VA: Author.

Atkins, M., Hoagwood, K. E., Kutash, K., & Seidman, E. (2010). Toward the integration of education and mental health in schools. *Administration and Policy in Mental Health, 37*, 40–47.

Centers for Disease Control and Prevention. (2010). *Mental health surveillance among children—United States, 2005–2011.* Retrieved from http://www.cdc.gov/features/childrensmentalhealth

Froeschle, J., & Moyer, M. (2004). Just cut it out: Legal and ethical challenges in counseling students who self-mutilate. *Professional School Counseling, 7*, 231–235.

Kaffenberger, C., & Seligman, L. (2007). Helping students with mental and emotional disorders. In B. T. Erford (Ed.), *Transforming the school counseling profession* (2nd ed., pp. 351–383). Upper Saddle River, NJ: Pearson.

Panigua, F. A. (2005). *Assessing and treating culturally diverse clients: A practical guide* (3rd ed.). Thousand Oaks, CA: Sage.

Vera, E. M., Buhin, L., & Shin, R. Q. (2006). The pursuit of social justice and the elimination of racism. In M. G. Constantine & D. W. Sue (Eds.), *Addressing racism: Facilitating cultural competence in mental health and educational settings* (pp. 271–287). Hoboken, NJ: Wiley.

APPENDIX B

Teaching Children With Attention-Deficit/Hyperactivity Disorder: Instructional Strategies and Practices

***Source:* U.S. Department of Education (2008)**

INTRODUCTION

Inattention, hyperactivity, and impulsivity are the core symptoms of attention–deficit/hyperactivity disorder (ADHD). A child's academic success is often dependent on his or her ability to attend to tasks and teacher and classroom expectations with minimal distraction. Such skill enables a student to acquire necessary information, complete assignments, and participate in classroom activities and discussions. When a child exhibits behaviors associated with ADHD, consequences may include difficulties with academics and with forming relationships with his or her peers if appropriate instructional methodologies and interventions are not implemented.

IDENTIFYING CHILDREN WITH ADHD

"ADHD is one of the more common mental disorders diagnosed among children. Data from the 2011 National Health Interview Survey (NHIS) indicate that parents of 8.4% of children aged 3 to 17 years had been informed that their child had ADHD. For youth ages 13 to 18, the prevalence rate is 9%. The disorder occurs four times as often among boys than girls. It is estimated that the prevalence of ADHD among adults is 2.5%" (NIMH, 2014a). Although for years it was assumed to be a childhood disorder that became visible as early as age 3 and then disappeared with the advent of adolescence, the condition is not limited to children. It is now known that while the symptoms of the disorders may change as a child ages, many children with ADHD do not grow out of it.

The behaviors associated with ADHD change as children grow older. For example, a preschool child may show gross motor overactivity—always running or climbing and frequently shifting from one activity to another. Older children may be restless and fidget in their seats or play with their chairs and desks. They frequently fail to finish their schoolwork, or they work carelessly. Adolescents with ADHD tend to be more withdrawn and less communicative. They are often impulsive, reacting spontaneously without regard to previous plans or necessary tasks and homework.

According to the fifth edition of the *Diagnostic Statistical Manual of Mental Disorders* (DSM-V) of the American Psychiatric Association (APA, 2013), ADHD can be defined by behaviors exhibited. Individuals with ADHD exhibit combinations of the following behaviors:

Inattention

- often fails to give close attention to details or makes careless mistakes in schoolwork, at work, or during other activities
- often has difficulty sustaining attention in tasks or play activities
- often does not seem to listen when spoken to directly
- often does not follow through on instructions and failure to finish schoolwork, chores, or duties in the workplace
- often has difficulty organizing tasks and activities
- often avoids, dislikes, or is reluctant to engage in tasks that require sustained mental effort
- often loses things necessary for tasks and activities
- is often easily distracted by extraneous stimuli
- is often forgetful in daily activities

Hyperactivity and impulsivity

- often fidgets and taps hands or feet or squirms in seat
- often leaves seat in situations when remaining in seat is expected
- often runs about or climbs in situations where it is inappropriate
- often unable to play or engage in leisure activities quietly
- is often "on the go," acting as if "driven by a motor"
- often talks excessively
- often blurts out an answer before a question has been completed
- often has difficulty waiting his or her turn
- often interrupts or intrudes on others

Children with ADHD show different combinations of these behaviors and typically exhibit behavior that is classified into two main categories: poor sustained attention and hyperactivity-impulsiveness. Three subtypes of the disorder have been described in the *DSM-V*: combined presentation, predominantly inattentive presentation, and predominantly hyperactive/impulsive presentation (APA, 2013). For instance, children with ADHD, without hyperactivity and impulsivity, do not show excessive activity or fidgeting but instead may daydream, act lethargic or restless, and frequently do not finish their academic work. Not all of these behaviors appear in all situations. A child with ADHD may be able to focus when he or she is receiving frequent reinforcement or is under very strict control. The ability to focus is also common in new settings or while interacting one on one. While other children may occasionally show some signs of these behaviors, in children with ADHD, the symptoms are more frequent and more severe than in other children of the same age.

Although many children have only ADHD, others have additional academic or behavioral diagnoses. The National Comorbidity Study-Adolescent Supplement (NCS-A) is a nationally representative, face-to-face survey of more than 10,000 teens ages 13 to 18. They used standard diagnostic criteria set by the APA's *Diagnostic and Statistical Manual* (DSM-IV) to determine lifetime prevalence of mental disorders among the teens. To follow up on the teens' responses, they also collected data via mailed questionnaires completed by one parent or guardian of each teen surveyed.

Results of the Study indicate that nearly half of the sample reported having met diagnostic criteria for at least one disorder over a lifetime, and about 20% reported that they suffered from a mental disorder with symptoms severe enough to impair their daily lives. In addition,

11% reported being severely impaired by a mood disorder (e.g., depression or bipolar disorder),

10% reported being severely impaired by a behavior disorder such as attention deficit hyperactivity disorder or conduct disorder,

8% reported being severely impaired by at least one type of anxiety disorder.

In addition, about 40% of those who reported having a disorder also met criteria for having at least one additional disorder. Those with a mood disorder were more likely than others to report having a coexisting disorder. Underscoring the notion that mental disorders manifest early in life, the researchers also found that symptoms of anxiety disorders tended to emerge by age 6, behavior disorders by age 11, mood disorders by age 13, and substance use disorders by age 15 (NIMH, 2010).

When selecting and implementing successful instructional strategies and practices, it is imperative to understand the characteristics of the child, including those pertaining to disabilities or diagnoses. This knowledge will be useful in the evaluation and implementation of successful practices, which are often the same practices that benefit students without ADHD.

AN OVERALL STRATEGY FOR THE SUCCESSFUL INSTRUCTION OF CHILDREN WITH ADHD

Teachers who are successful in educating children with ADHD use a three-pronged strategy. They begin by identifying the unique needs of the child. For example, the teacher determines how, when, and why the child is inattentive, impulsive, and hyperactive. The teacher then selects different educational practices associated with academic instruction, behavioral interventions, and classroom accommodations that are appropriate to meet that child's needs. Finally, the teacher combines these practices into an individualized educational program (IEP) or other individualized plan and integrates this program with educational activities provided to other children in the class. The three-pronged strategy, in summary, is as follows:

- **Evaluate the child's individual needs and strengths.** Assess the unique educational needs and strengths of a child with ADHD in the class. Working with a multidisciplinary team and the child's parents, consider both academic and behavioral needs, using formal diagnostic assessments and informal classroom observations. Assessments, such as learning style inventories, can be used to determine children's strengths and enable instruction to build on their existing abilities. The settings and contexts in which challenging behaviors occur should be considered in the evaluation.
- **Select appropriate instructional practices.** Determine which instructional practices will meet the academic and behavioral needs identified for the child. Select practices that fit the content, are age appropriate, and gain the attention of the child.
- **For children receiving special education services, integrate appropriate practices within an IEP.** In consultation with other educators and parents, an IEP should be created to reflect annual goals and the special education-related services, along with supplementary aids and services necessary for attaining those goals. Plan how to integrate the educational activities provided to other children in your class with those selected for the child with ADHD.

Because no two children with ADHD are alike, it is important to keep in mind that no single educational program, practice, or setting will be best for all children.

HOW TO IMPLEMENT THE STRATEGY: THREE COMPONENTS OF SUCCESSFUL PROGRAMS FOR CHILDREN WITH ADHD

Successful programs for children with ADHD integrate the following three components:

- academic instruction
- behavioral interventions
- classroom accommodations

The remainder of this document describes how to integrate a program using these three components and provides suggestions for practices that can help children with ADHD in a classroom setting. It should be emphasized that many of the techniques suggested have the additional benefit of enhancing the learning of other children in the classroom who *do not have* ADHD. In addition, while they have been used most widely with children at the elementary level, the following practices are useful for older students as well.

Academic Instruction

The first major component of the most effective instruction for children with ADHD is effective academic instruction. Teachers can help prepare their students with ADHD to achieve by applying the principles of effective teaching when they introduce, conduct, and conclude each lesson. The discussion and techniques that follow pertain to the instructional process in general (across subject areas); strategies for specific subject areas appear in the subsequent subsection "Individualizing Instructional Practices."

Introducing Lessons

Students with ADHD learn best with a carefully structured academic lesson—one where the teacher explains what he or she wants children to learn in the current lesson and places these skills and knowledge in the context of previous lessons. Effective teachers preview their expectations about what students will learn and how they should behave during the lesson. A number of teaching-related practices have been found especially useful in facilitating this process:

- **Provide an advance organizer.** Prepare students for the day's lesson by quickly summarizing the order of various activities planned. Explain, for example, that a review of the previous lesson will be followed by new information and that both group and independent work will be expected.
- **Review previous lessons.** Review information about previous lessons on this topic. For example, remind children that yesterday's lesson focused on learning how to regroup in subtraction. Review several problems before describing the current lesson.
- **Set learning expectations.** State what students are expected to learn during the lesson. For example, explain to students that a language arts lesson will involve reading a story about Paul Bunyan and identifying new vocabulary words in the story.
- **Set behavioral expectations.** Describe how students are expected to behave during the lesson. For example, tell children that they may talk quietly to their neighbors as they do their seatwork or they may raise their hands to get your attention.
- **State needed materials.** Identify all materials that the children will need during the lesson, rather than leaving them to figure out on their own the materials required. For example, specify that children need their journals and pencils for journal writing or their crayons, scissors, and colored paper for an art project.
- **Explain additional resources.** Tell students how to obtain help in mastering the lesson. For example, refer children to a particular page in the textbook for guidance on completing a worksheet.
- **Simplify instructions, choices, and scheduling.** The simpler the expectations communicated to an ADHD student, the more likely it is that he or she will comprehend and complete them in a timely and productive manner.

Conducting Lessons

In order to conduct the most productive lessons for children with ADHD, effective teachers periodically question children's understanding of the material, probe for correct answers before calling on other students, and identify which students need additional assistance. Teachers should keep in mind that transitions from one lesson or class to another are particularly difficult for students with ADHD. When they are prepared for transitions, these children are more likely to respond and to stay on task. The following set of strategies may assist teachers in conducting effective lessons:

- **Be predictable.** Structure and consistency are very important for children with ADHD; many do not deal well with change. Minimal rules and minimal choices are best for these children. They need to understand clearly what is expected of them, as well as the consequences for not adhering to expectations.
- **Support the students' participation in the classroom.** Provide students with ADHD with private, discreet cues to stay on task and advance warning that they will be called upon shortly. Avoid bringing attention to differences between ADHD students and their classmates. At all times, avoid the use of sarcasm and criticism.
- **Use audiovisual materials.** Use a variety of audiovisual materials to present academic lessons. For example, use an overhead projector to demonstrate how to solve an addition problem requiring regrouping. The students can work on the problem at their desks while you manipulate counters on the projector screen.
- **Check student performance.** Question individual students to assess their mastery of the lesson. For example, you can ask students doing seatwork (i.e., lessons completed by students at their desks in the classroom) to demonstrate how they arrived at the answer to a problem, or you can ask individual students to state, in their own words, how the main character felt at the end of the story.
- **Ask probing questions.** Probe for the correct answer after allowing a child sufficient time to work out the answer to a question. Count at least 15 seconds before giving the answer or calling on another student. Ask follow-up questions that give children an opportunity to demonstrate what they know.
- **Perform ongoing student evaluation.** Identify students who need additional assistance. Watch for signs of lack of comprehension, such as daydreaming or visual or verbal indications of frustration. Provide these children with extra explanations, or ask another student to serve as a peer tutor for the lesson.
- **Help students correct their own mistakes.** Describe how students can identify and correct their own mistakes. For example, remind students that they should check their calculations in math problems and reiterate how they can check their calculations; remind students of particularly difficult spelling rules and how students can watch out for easy-to-make errors.
- **Help students focus.** Remind students to keep working and to focus on their assigned task. For example, you can provide follow-up directions or assign learning partners. These practices can be directed at individual children or at the entire class.
- **Follow-up directions.** Effective teachers of children with ADHD also guide them with follow-up directions:
    - *Oral directions.* After giving directions to the class as a whole, provide additional oral directions for a child with ADHD. For example, ask the child if he or she understood the directions and repeat the directions together.
    - *Written directions.* Provide follow-up directions in writing. For example, write the page number for an assignment on the chalkboard and remind the child to look at the chalkboard if he or she forgets the assignment.
- **Lower noise level.** Monitor the noise level in the classroom, and provide corrective feedback, as needed. If the noise level exceeds the level appropriate for the type of lesson, remind all students—or individual students—about the behavioral rules stated at the beginning of the lesson.

- **Divide work into smaller units.** Break down assignments into smaller, less complex tasks. For example, allow students to complete five math problems before presenting them with the remaining five problems.
- **Highlight key points.** Highlight key words in the instructions on worksheets to help the child with ADHD focus on the directions. Prepare the worksheet before the lesson begins, or underline key words as you and the child read the directions together. When reading, show children how to identify and highlight a key sentence, or have them write it on a separate piece of paper, before asking for a summary of the entire book. In math, show children how to underline the important facts and operations; in "Mary has two apples, and John has three," underline *two*, *and*, and *three*.
- **Eliminate or reduce frequency of timed tests.** Tests that are timed may not allow children with ADHD to demonstrate what they truly know due to their potential preoccupation with elapsed time. Allow students with ADHD more time to complete quizzes and tests in order to eliminate test anxiety and provide them with other opportunities, methods, or test formats to demonstrate their knowledge.
- **Use cooperative learning strategies.** Have students work together in small groups to maximize their own and each other's learning. Use strategies such as think-pair-share where teachers ask students to think about a topic, pair with a partner to discuss it, and share ideas with the group (Slavin, 2002).
- **Use assistive technology.** All students, and those with ADHD in particular, can benefit from the use of technology (such as computers and projector screens), which makes instruction more visual and allows students to participate actively.

• CONCLUDING LESSONS

Effective teachers conclude their lessons by providing advance warning that the lesson is about to end, checking the completed assignments of at least some of the students with ADHD, and instructing students how to begin preparing for the next activity.

- **Provide advance warnings.** Provide advance warning that a lesson is about to end. Announce 5 or 10 minutes before the end of the lesson (particularly for seatwork and group projects) how much time remains. You may also want to tell students at the beginning of the lesson how much time they will have to complete it.
- **Check assignments.** Check completed assignments for at least some students. Review what they have learned during the lesson to get a sense of how ready the class was for the lesson and how to plan the next lesson.
- **Preview the next lesson.** Instruct students on how to begin preparing for the next lesson. For example, inform children that they need to put away their textbooks and come to the front of the room for a large-group spelling lesson.

Individualizing Instructional Practices

In addition to the general strategies listed above for introducing, conducting, and concluding their lessons, effective teachers of students with ADHD also individualize their instructional practices in accordance with different academic subjects and the needs of their students within each area. This is because children with ADHD have different ways of learning and retaining information, not all of which involve traditional reading and listening. Effective teachers first identify areas in which each child requires extra assistance and then use special strategies to provide structured opportunities for the child to review and master an academic lesson that was previously presented to the entire class. Strategies that may help facilitate this goal include the following (grouped by subject area):

Language Arts and Reading Comprehension

To help children with ADHD who are poor readers improve their reading comprehension skills, try the following instructional practices:

- **Silent reading time.** Establish a fixed time each day for silent reading (e.g., D.E.A.R.: Drop Everything and Read and Sustained Silent Reading [Holt & O'Tuel, 1989; Manzo & Zehr, 1998]).
- **Follow-along reading.** Ask the child to read a story silently while listening to other students or the teacher read the story aloud to the entire class.
- **Partner reading activities.** Pair the child with ADHD with another student partner who is a strong reader. The partners take turns reading orally and listening to each other.
- **Storyboards.** Ask the child to make storyboards that illustrate the sequence of main events in a story.
- **Storytelling.** Schedule storytelling sessions where the child can retell a story that he or she has read recently.
- **Playacting.** Schedule playacting sessions where the child can role-play different characters in a favorite story.
- **Word bank.** Keep a word bank or dictionary of new or "hard-to-read" sight-vocabulary words.
- **Board games for reading comprehension.** Play board games that provide practice with target reading-comprehension skills or sight-vocabulary words.
- **Computer games for reading comprehension.** Schedule computer time for the child to have drill and practice with sight vocabulary words.
- **Recorded books.** These materials, available from many libraries, can stimulate interest in traditional reading and can be used to reinforce and complement reading lessons.
- **"Backup" materials for home use.** Make available to students a second set of books and materials that they can use at home.
- **Summary materials.** Allow and encourage students to use published book summaries, synopses, and digests of major reading assignments to review (not replace) reading assignments.

Phonics

To help children with ADHD master rules of phonics, the following are effective:

- **Mnemonics for phonics.** Teach the child mnemonics that provide reminders about hard-to-learn phonics rules (e.g., "when two vowels go walking, the first does the talking") (Scruggs & Mastropieri, 2000).
- **Word families.** Teach the child to recognize and read word families that illustrate particular phonetic concepts (e.g., "ph" sounds, "at-bat-cat").
- **Board games for phonics.** Have students play board games, such as bingo, that allow them to practice phonetically irregular words.
- **Computer games for phonics.** Use a computer to provide opportunities for students to drill and practice with phonics or grammar lessons.
- **Picture-letter charts.** Use these for children who know sounds but do not know the letters that go with them.

Writing

In composing stories or other writing assignments, children with ADHD benefit from the following practices:

- **Standards for writing assignments.** Identify and teach the child classroom standards for acceptable written work, such as format and style.
- **Recognizing parts of a story.** Teach the student how to describe the major parts of a story (e.g., plot, main characters, setting, conflict, and resolution). Use a storyboard with parts listed for this purpose.
- **Post office.** Establish a post office in the classroom and provide students with opportunities to write, mail, and receive letters to and from their classmates and teacher.
- **Visualize compositions.** Ask the child to close his or her eyes and visualize a paragraph that the teacher reads aloud. Another variation of this technique is to ask a student to describe a recent event while the other students close their eyes and visualize what is being said as a written paragraph.
- **Proofread compositions.** Require that the child proofread his or her work before turning in written assignments. Provide the child with a list of items to check when proofreading his or her own work.
- **Tape recorders.** Ask the student to dictate writing assignments into a tape recorder, as an alternative to writing them.
- **Dictate writing assignments.** Have the teacher or another student write down a story told by a child with ADHD.

Spelling

To help children with ADHD who are poor spellers, the following techniques have been found to be helpful:

- **Everyday examples of hard-to-spell words.** Take advantage of everyday events to teach difficult spelling words in context. For example, ask a child eating a cheese sandwich to spell *sandwich*.
- **Frequently used words.** Assign spelling words that the child routinely uses in his or her speech each day.
- **Dictionary of misspelled words.** Ask the child to keep a personal dictionary of frequently misspelled words.
- **Partner spelling activities.** Pair the child with another student. Ask the partners to quiz each other on the spelling of new words. Encourage both students to guess the correct spelling.
- **Manipulatives.** Use cutout letters or other manipulatives to spell out hard-to-learn words.
- **Color-coded letters.** Color code different letters in hard-to-spell words (e.g., *receipt*).
- **Movement activities.** Combine movement activities with spelling lessons (e.g., jump rope while spelling words aloud).
- **Word banks.** Use 3" x 5" index cards of frequently misspelled words sorted alphabetically.

Handwriting

Students with ADHD who have difficulty with manuscript or cursive writing may well benefit from their teacher's use of the following instructional practices:

- **Individual chalkboards.** Ask the child to practice copying and erasing the target words on a small, individual chalkboard. Two children can be paired to practice their target words together.

- **Quiet places for handwriting.** Provide the child with a special "quiet place" (e.g., a table outside the classroom) to complete his or her handwriting assignments.
- **Spacing words on a page.** Teach the child to use his or her finger to measure how much space to leave between each word in a written assignment.
- **Special writing paper.** Ask the child to use special paper with vertical lines to learn to space letters and words on a page.
- **Structured programs for handwriting.** Teach handwriting skills through a structured program, such as Jan Olsen's (2003) Handwriting Without Tears program.

Math Computation

Numerous individualized instructional practices can help children with ADHD improve their basic computation skills. The following are just a few:

- **Patterns in math.** Teach the student to recognize patterns when adding, subtracting, multiplying, or dividing whole numbers (e.g., the digits of numbers which are multiples of 9 [18, 27, 36 . . .] add up to 9).
- **Partnering for math activities.** Pair a child with ADHD with another student and provide opportunities for the partners to quiz each other about basic computation skills.
- **Mastery of math symbols.** If children do not understand the symbols used in math, they will not be able to do the work. For instance, do they understand that the *plus* in 1 + 3 means to add and that the *minus* in 5 – 3 means to take away?
- **Mnemonics for basic computation.** Teach the child mnemonics that describe basic steps in computing whole numbers. For example, "Don't Miss Susie's Boat" can be used to help the student recall the basic steps in long division (i.e., divide, multiply, subtract, and bring down).
- **Real-life examples of money skills.** Provide the child with real-life opportunities to practice target money skills. For example, ask the child to calculate his or her change when paying for lunch in the school cafeteria, or set up a class store where children can practice calculating change.
- **Color coding arithmetic symbols.** Color code basic arithmetic symbols, such as +, –, and =, to provide visual cues for children when they are computing whole numbers.
- **Calculators to check basic computation.** Ask the child to use a calculator to check addition, subtraction, multiplication, or division.
- **Board games for basic computation.** Ask the child to play board games to practice adding, subtracting, multiplying, and dividing whole numbers.
- **Computer games for basic computation.** Schedule computer time for the child to drill and practice basic computations, using appropriate games.
- **"Magic minute" drills.** Have students perform a quick (60-second) drill every day to practice basic computation of math facts and have children track their own performance.

Solving Math Word Problems

To help children with ADHD improve their skill in solving word problems in mathematics, try the following:

- **Reread the problem.** Teach the child to read a word problem *two times* before beginning to compute the answer.
- **Clue words.** Teach the child clue words that identify which operation to use when solving word problems. For example, words such as *sum*, *total*, or *all together* may indicate an addition operation.

- **Guiding questions for word problems.** Teach students to ask guiding questions in solving word problems. For example, "What is the question asked in the problem?" "What information do you need to figure out the answer?" "What operation should you use to compute the answer?"
- **Real-life examples of word problems.** Ask the student to create and solve word problems that provide practice with specific target operations, such as addition, subtraction, multiplication, or division. These problems can be based on recent, real-life events in the child's life.
- **Calculators to check word problems.** Ask the student to use a calculator to check computations made in answering assigned word problems.

Use of Special Materials in Math

- Some children with ADHD benefit from using special materials to help them complete their math assignments, including:
    - **Number lines.** Provide number lines for the child to use when computing whole numbers.
    - **Manipulatives.** Use manipulatives to help students gain basic computation skills, such as counting poker chips when adding single-digit numbers.
    - **Graph paper.** Ask the child to use graph paper to help organize columns when adding, subtracting, multiplying, or dividing whole numbers.

ORGANIZATIONAL AND STUDY SKILLS USEFUL FOR ACADEMIC INSTRUCTION OF CHILDREN WITH ADHD

Many students with ADHD are easily distracted and have difficulty focusing their attention on assigned tasks. However, the following practices can help children with ADHD improve their organization of homework and other daily assignments:

- **Designate one teacher as the student's advisor or coordinator.** This teacher will regularly review the student's progress through progress reports submitted by other teachers and will act as the liaison between home and school. Permit the student to meet with this advisor on a regular basis (e.g., Monday morning) to plan and organize for the week and to review progress and problems from the past week.
- **Assignment notebooks.** Provide the child with an assignment notebook to help organize homework and other seatwork.
- **Color-coded folders.** Provide the child with color-coded folders to help organize assignments for different academic subjects (e.g., reading, mathematics, social science, and science).
- **Work with a homework partner.** Assign the child a partner to help record homework and other seatwork in the assignment notebook and file work sheets and other papers in the proper folders.
- **Clean out desks and book bags.** Ask the child to periodically sort through and clean out his or her desk, book bag, and other special places where written assignments are stored.
- **Visual aids as reminders of subject material.** Use banners, charts, lists, pie graphs, and diagrams situated throughout the classroom to remind students of the subject material being learned.

Assisting Students With ADHD With Time Management

Children with ADHD often have difficulty finishing their assignments on time and can thus benefit from special materials and practices that help them to improve their time management skills, including the following:

- **Use a clock or wristwatch.** Teach the child how to read and use a clock or wristwatch to manage time when completing assigned work.
- **Use a calendar.** Teach the child how to read and use a calendar to schedule assignments.
- **Practice sequencing activities.** Provide the child with supervised opportunities to break down a long assignment into a sequence of short, interrelated activities.
- **Create a daily activity schedule.** Tape a schedule of planned daily activities to the child's desk.

Helpful Study Skills for Students With ADHD

Children with ADHD often have difficulty in learning how to study effectively on their own. The following strategies may assist ADHD students in developing the study skills necessary for academic success:

- **Adapt worksheets.** Teach a child how to adapt instructional worksheets. For example, help a child fold his or her reading worksheet to reveal only one question at a time. The child can also use a blank piece of paper to cover the other questions on the page.
- **Venn diagrams.** Teach a child how to use Venn diagrams to help illustrate and organize key concepts in reading, mathematics, or other academic subjects.
- **Note-taking skills.** Teach a child with ADHD how to take notes when organizing key academic concepts that he or she has learned, perhaps with the use of a program such as Anita Archer's *Skills for School Success* (Archer & Gleason, 2002).
- **Checklist of frequent mistakes.** Provide the child with a checklist of mistakes that he or she frequently makes in written assignments (e.g., punctuation or capitalization errors), mathematics (e.g., addition or subtraction errors), or other academic subjects. Teach the child how to use this list when proofreading his or her work at home and school.
- **Checklist of homework supplies.** Provide the child with a checklist that identifies categories of items needed for homework assignments (e.g., books, pencils, and homework assignment sheets).
- **Uncluttered workspace.** Teach a child with ADHD how to prepare an uncluttered workspace to complete assignments. For example, instruct the child to clear away unnecessary books or other materials *before* beginning his or her seatwork.
- **Monitor homework assignments.** Keep track of how well your students with ADHD complete their assigned homework. Discuss and resolve with them and their parents any problems in completing these assignments. For example, evaluate the difficulty of the assignments and how long the children spend on their homework each night. Keep in mind that the *quality*, rather than the *quantity*, of homework assigned is the most important issue. While doing homework is an important part of developing study skills, it should be used to reinforce skills and to review material learned in class, rather than to present, in advance, large amounts of material that is new to the student.

● HOW TO IMPLEMENT THE STRATEGY: BEHAVIORAL INTERVENTIONS

The second major component of effective instruction for children with ADHD involves the use of *behavioral interventions*. Exhibiting behavior that resembles that of younger children, children with ADHD often act immaturely and have difficulty learning how to control their impulsiveness and hyperactivity. They may have problems forming friendships with other children in the class and may have difficulty thinking through the social consequences of their actions.

The purpose of behavioral interventions is to assist students in displaying the behaviors that are most conducive to their own learning and that of classmates. Well-managed classrooms prevent many disciplinary problems and provide an environment that is most favorable for learning. When a teacher's time must be spent interacting with students whose behaviors are not focused on the lesson being presented, less time is available for assisting other students. Behavioral interventions should be viewed as an opportunity for teaching in the most effective and efficient manner, rather than as an opportunity for punishment.

Effective Behavioral Intervention Techniques

Effective teachers use a number of behavioral intervention techniques to help students learn how to control their behavior. Perhaps the most important and effective of these is **verbal reinforcement** of appropriate behavior. The most common form of verbal reinforcement is **praise** given to a student when he or she begins and completes an activity or exhibits a particular desired behavior. Simple phrases such as "good job" encourage a child to act appropriately. Effective teachers praise children with ADHD frequently and look for a behavior to praise before, and not after, a child gets off task. The following strategies provide some guidance regarding the use of praise:

- **Define the appropriate behavior while giving praise.** Praise should be specific for the positive behavior displayed by the student: The comments should focus on what the student did right and should include exactly what part(s) of the student's behavior was desirable. Rather than praising a student for not disturbing the class, for example, a teacher should praise him or her for quietly completing a math lesson on time.
- **Give praise immediately.** The sooner that approval is given regarding appropriate behavior, the more likely the student will repeat it.
- **Vary the statements given as praise.** The comments used by teachers to praise appropriate behavior should vary; when students hear the same praise statement repeated over and over, it may lose its value.
- **Be consistent and sincere with praise.** Appropriate behavior should receive consistent praise. Consistency among teachers with respect to desired behavior is important in order to avoid confusion on the part of students with ADHD. Similarly, students will notice when teachers give insincere praise, and this insincerity will make praise less effective.

It is important to keep in mind that the most effective teachers focus their behavioral intervention strategies on *praise* rather than on *punishment*. Negative consequences may temporarily change behavior, but they rarely change attitudes and may actually increase the frequency and intensity of inappropriate behavior by rewarding misbehaving students with attention. Moreover, punishment may only teach children what not to do; it does not provide children with the skills that they need to do what is expected. Positive reinforcement produces the changes in attitudes that will shape a student's behavior over the long term.

In addition to verbal reinforcement, the following set of generalized behavioral intervention techniques has proven helpful with students with ADHD as well:

- **Selectively ignore inappropriate behavior.** It is sometimes helpful for teachers to selectively ignore inappropriate behavior. This technique is particularly useful when the behavior is unintentional or unlikely to recur or is intended solely to gain the attention of teachers or classmates without disrupting the classroom or interfering with the learning of others.
- **Remove nuisance items.** Teachers often find that certain objects (such as rubber bands and toys) distract the attention of students with ADHD in the classroom. The removal of nuisance items is generally most effective after the student has been given the choice of putting it away immediately and then fails to do so.
- **Provide calming manipulatives.** While some toys and other objects can be distracting for both the students with ADHD and peers in the classroom, some children with ADHD can benefit from

having access to objects that can be manipulated quietly. Manipulatives may help children gain some needed sensory input while still attending to the lesson.

- **Allow for "escape valve" outlets.** Permitting students with ADHD to leave class for a moment, perhaps on an errand (such as returning a book to the library), can be an effective means of settling them down and allowing them to return to the room ready to concentrate.
- **Activity reinforcement.** Students receive activity reinforcement when they are encouraged to perform a less desirable behavior before a preferred one.
- **Hurdle helping.** Teachers can offer encouragement, support, and assistance to prevent students from becoming frustrated with an assignment. This help can take many forms, from enlisting a peer for support to supplying additional materials or information.
- **Parent conferences.** Parents have a critical role in the education of students, and this axiom may be particularly true for those with ADHD. As such, parents must be included as partners in planning for the student's success. Partnering with parents entails including parental input in behavioral intervention strategies, maintaining frequent communication between parents and teachers, and collaborating in monitoring the student's progress.
- **Peer mediation.** Members of a student's peer group can positively impact the behavior of students with ADHD. Many schools now have formalized peer mediation programs, in which students receive training in order to manage disputes involving their classmates.

Effective teachers also use *behavioral prompts* with their students. These prompts help remind students about expectations for their learning and behavior in the classroom. Three, which may be particularly helpful, are the following:

- **Visual cues.** Establish simple, nonintrusive visual cues to remind the child to remain on task. For example, you can point at the child while looking him or her in the eye, or you can hold out your hand, palm down, near the child.
- **Proximity control.** When talking to a child, move to where the child is standing or sitting. Your physical proximity to the child will help the child to focus and pay attention to what you are saying.
- **Hand gestures.** Use hand signals to communicate privately with a child with ADHD. For example, ask the child to raise his or her hand every time you ask a question. A closed fist can signal that the child knows the answer; an open palm can signal that he or she does not know the answer. You would call on the child to answer only when he or she makes a fist.

In some instances, children with ADHD benefit from instruction designed to help students learn how to manage their own behavior:

- **Social skills classes.** Teach children with ADHD appropriate social skills using a structured class. For example, you can ask the children to role-play and model different solutions to common social problems. It is critical to provide for the generalization of these skills, including structured opportunities for the children to use the social skills that they learn. Offering such classes, or experiences, to the general school population can positively affect the school climate.
- **Problem-solving sessions.** Discuss how to resolve social conflicts. Conduct impromptu discussions with one student or with a small group of students where the conflict arises. In this setting, ask two children who are arguing about a game to discuss how to settle their differences. Encourage the children to resolve their problem by talking to each other in a supervised setting.

For many children with ADHD, *functional behavioral assessments* and *positive behavioral interventions and supports*, including behavioral contracts and management plans, tangible rewards, or token economy systems, are helpful in teaching them how to manage their own behavior. Because students' individual needs are different, it is important for teachers, along with the family and other involved professionals, to evaluate whether these practices are appropriate for their classrooms. Examples of these techniques, along with steps to follow when using them, include the following:

- **Functional Behavioral Assessment (FBA).** FBA is a systematic process for describing problem behavior and identifying the environmental factors and surrounding events associated with problem behavior. The team that works closely with the child exhibiting problem behavior (1) observes the behavior and identifies and defines its problematic characteristics, (2) identifies which actions or events precede and follow the behavior, and (3) determines how often the behavior occurs. The results of the FBA should be used to develop an effective and efficient intervention and support plan (Gable et al., 1997).
- **Positive Behavioral Interventions and Supports (PBIS).** This method is an application of a behavior-based systems approach that is grounded in research regarding behavior in the context of the settings in which it occurs. Using this method, schools, families, and communities work to design effective environments to improve behavior. The goal of PBIS is to eliminate problem behavior, to replace it with more appropriate behavior, and to increase a person's skills and opportunities for an enhanced quality of life (Todd, Horner, Sugai, & Sprague, 1999).
- **Behavioral contracts and management plans.** Identify specific academic or behavioral goals for the child with ADHD, along with behavior that needs to change and strategies for responding to inappropriate behavior. Work with the child to cooperatively identify appropriate goals, such as completing homework assignments on time and obeying safety rules on the school playground. Take the time to ensure that the child agrees that his or her goals are important to master. Behavioral contracts and management plans are typically used with individual children, as opposed to entire classes, and should be prepared with input from parents.
- **Tangible rewards.** Use tangible rewards to reinforce appropriate behavior. These rewards can include stickers, such as "happy faces" or sports team emblems, or privileges, such as extra time on the computer or lunch with the teacher. Children should be involved in the selection of the reward. If children are invested in the reward, they are more likely to work for it.
- **Token economy systems.** Use token economy systems to motivate a child to achieve a goal identified in a behavioral contract (Barkley, 1990). For example, a child can earn points for each homework assignment completed on time. In some cases, students also lose points for each homework assignment not completed on time. After earning a specified number of points, the student receives a tangible reward, such as extra time on a computer or a "free" period on Friday afternoon. Token economy systems are often used for entire classrooms, as opposed to solely for individual students.
- **Self-management systems.** Train students to monitor and evaluate their own behavior without constant feedback from the teacher. In a typical self-management system, the teacher identifies behaviors that will be managed by a student and provides a written rating scale that includes the performance criteria for each rating. The teacher and student separately rate student behavior during an activity and compare ratings. The student earns points if the ratings match or are within one point and receives no points if ratings are more than one point apart; points are exchanged for privileges. With time, the teacher involvement is removed, and the student becomes responsible for self-monitoring (DuPaul & Stoner as cited in Shinn, Walker, & Stoner, 2002).

HOW TO IMPLEMENT THE STRATEGY: CLASSROOM ACCOMMODATIONS

The third component of a strategy for effectively educating children with ADHD involves physical *classroom accommodations*. Children with ADHD often have difficulty adjusting to the structured environment of a classroom, determining what is important, and focusing on their assigned work. They are easily distracted by other children or by nearby activities in the classroom. As a result, many children with ADHD benefit from accommodations that reduce distractions in the classroom environment and help them to stay on task and learn. Certain accommodations within the physical and learning environments of the classroom can benefit children with ADHD.

Special Classroom Seating Arrangements for ADHD Students

One of the most common accommodations that can be made to the physical environment of the classroom involves determining where a child with ADHD will sit. Three special seating assignments may be especially useful:

- **Seat the child near the teacher.** Assign the child a seat near your desk or the front of the room. This seating assignment provides opportunities for you to monitor and reinforce the child's on-task behavior.
- **Seat the child near a student role model.** Assign the child a seat near a student role model. This seat arrangement provides opportunity for children to work cooperatively and to learn from their peers in the class.
- **Provide low-distraction work areas.** As space permits, teachers should make available a quiet, distraction-free room or area for quiet study time and test-taking. Students should be directed to this room or area privately and discreetly in order to avoid the appearance of punishment.

● INSTRUCTIONAL TOOLS AND THE PHYSICAL LEARNING ENVIRONMENT

Skilled teachers use special instructional tools to modify the classroom learning environment and accommodate the special needs of their students with ADHD. They also monitor the physical environment, keeping in mind the needs of these children. The following tools and techniques may be helpful:

- **Pointers.** Teach the child to use a pointer to help visually track written words on a page. For example, provide the child with a bookmark to help him or her follow along when students are taking turns reading aloud.
- **Egg timers.** Note for the children the time at which the lesson is starting and the time at which it will conclude. Set a timer to indicate to children how much time remains in the lesson and place the timer at the front of the classroom; the children can check the timer to see how much time remains. Interim prompts can be used as well. For instance, children can monitor their own progress during a 30-minute lesson if the timer is set for 10 minutes three times.
- **Classroom lights.** Turning the classroom lights on and off prompts children that the noise level in the room is too high and they should be quiet. This practice can also be used to signal that it is time to begin preparing for the next lesson.
- **Music.** Play music on a tape recorder or chords on a piano to prompt children that they are too noisy. In addition, playing different types of music on a tape recorder communicates to children what level of activity is appropriate for a particular lesson. For example, play quiet classical music for quiet activities done independently and jazz for active group activities.
- **Proper use of furniture.** The desk and chair used by children with ADHD need to be the right size; if they are not, the child will be more inclined to squirm and fidget. A general rule of thumb is that a child should be able to put his or her elbows on the surface of the desk and have his or her chin fit comfortably in the palm of the hand.

CONCLUSION

This guide has outlined a series of instructional strategies that have proven to be successful in educating children with ADHD. However, it should be emphasized again that these techniques are also highly useful for *all* children. The three main components of a successful strategy for educating children with ADHD are *academic instruction*, *behavioral interventions*, and *classroom accommodations*. By incorporating techniques from these three areas into their everyday instructional and classroom management practices, teachers will be empowered to improve both the academic performance and the behavior of their students with ADHD. In doing so, teachers will create an enhanced learning environment for all students.

REFERENCES

American Psychiatric Association. (2013). *Diagnostic and statistical manual of mental disorders* (5th ed.). Washington, DC: Author.

Archer, A., & Gleason, M. (2002). *Skills for school success: Book 5*. North Billerica, MA: Curriculum Associates.

Barkley, R. A. (1990). *Attention deficit hyperactivity disorder: A handbook for diagnosis and treatment*. New York, NY: Guilford Press.

DuPaul, G. J., & Stoner, G. (2002). Interventions for attention problems. In M. R. Shinn, H. M. Walker, & G. Stoner (Eds.), *Interventions for academic and behavior problems II: Preventive and remedial approaches* (pp. 913–938). Bethesda, MD: National Association of School Psychologists.

Gable, R. A., Sugai, G. M., Lewis, T. J., Nelson, J. R., Cheney, D., Safran, S. P., & Safran, J. S. (1997). *Individual and systemic approaches to collaboration and consultation*. Reston, VA: Council for Children with Behavioral Disorders.

Holt, S. B., & O'Tuel, F. S. (1989). The effect of sustained silent reading and writing on achievement and attitudes of seventh and eighth grade students reading two years below grade level. *Reading Improvement, 26*, 290–297.

Manzo, K. K., & Zehr, M. A. (1998). Take note. *Education Week, 18*(3), 3.

National Institute of Mental Health. (2014a). *Any anxiety disorder among children*. Retrieved from http://www.nimh.nih.gov/health/statistics/prevalence/any-anxiety-disorder-among-children.shtml

National Institute of Mental Health. (2014b). *What is prevalence?* Retrieved from http://www.nimh.nih.gov/health/statistics/prevalence/index.shtml

Olsen, J. (2003). *Handwriting without tears*. Retrieved from http://hwtears.com

Scruggs, T. E., & Mastropieri, M. A. (2000). The effectiveness of mnemonic instruction for students with learning and behavior problems: An update and research synthesis. *Journal of Behavioral Education, 10*(2/3), 163–173.

Slavin, R. E. (2002). *Education psychology: Theory into practice*. Boston, MA: Allyn & Bacon.

Substance Abuse and Mental Health Services Administration. (2015, October 27). *Mental disorders: Oppositional defiant disorder*. Retrieved from http://www.samhsa.gov/disorders/mental

Todd, A. W., Horner, R. H., Sugai, G., & Sprague, J. R. (1999). Effective behavior support: Strengthening school-wide systems through a team-based approach. *Effective School Practices, 17*(4), 23–37.

APPENDIX C

Disruptive Behavior Disorders Strategy Resources

The following interventions were identified as evidence-based treatments by Sheila Eyberg, Melanie Nelson, and Stephen Boggs (2008):

Anger Control Training

Group Assertive Training

Helping the Noncompliant Child

Incredible Years (IY)

Incredible Years Parent Training

Incredible Years Child Training

Multidimensional Treatment Foster Care

Multisystemic Therapy

Parent–Child Interaction Therapy

Parent Management Training—Oregon Model

Positive Parenting Program

Triple P Standard Individual Treatment

Triple P Enhanced Treatment

Problem-Solving Skills Training

PSST + Practice

PSST + Parent Management Training

Rational-Emotive Mental Health Program

● APPENDIX D

Anxiety Disorders Strategy Web Resources

WorryWiseKids, Sample Accommodations for Anxious Kids: http://www.worrywisekids.org/node/40

Anxiety and Depression Association of America: http://www.adaa.org/living-with-anxiety/children/childhood-anxiety-disorders

Massachusetts General Hospital, School Psychiatry Program and MADI Resource Center: http://www2.massgeneral.org/schoolpsychiatry/info_anxiety.asp

Child Mind Institute: http://childmind.org/article/what-to-do-and-not-do-when-children-are-anxious/

Health Central: http://www.healthcentral.com/anxiety/school-258065-5.html

TeensHealth: http://kidshealth.org/en/teens/center/stress-center.html?WT.ac=t-ra

● TRAUMA- AND STRESSOR-RELATED DISORDERS

Resources available to educators can be found at Child Trauma Toolkit for Educators, The National Child Trauma Stress Network: http://www.nctsn.org/resources/audiences/school-personnel/trauma-toolkit

PART V

SPECIAL EDUCATION

Lesson 23

THE ROLE OF THE SCHOOL COUNSELOR IN SPECIAL EDUCATION

"I was never top of the class at school, but my classmates must have seen potential in me, because my nickname was 'Einstein.'"

—Stephen Hawking

Real Life

You notice that your on-site supervisor often supports the needs of students with special needs by attending IEP meetings, conducting classroom behavioral observations, meeting with small groups of students due to behavioral challenges, and writing 504 medical accommodation plans. Upon attending a recent IEP meeting, the special education teacher facilitating the meeting asks all attendees to sign the IEP form to document their attendance. When the form comes your way, you notice that your on-site supervisor has signed in as the "LEA." Although you pay attention during the meeting, you keep wondering about the terminology, so you ask you supervisor about it after the meeting.

Counselor-in-Training: "I noticed at the IEP meeting that you signed your name on the line marked 'LEA' instead of 'School counselor.' Would you mind explaining what that means?"

Site Supervisor: "Sure! It can be a bit confusing, but overall the *LEA* stands for 'Local Education Agency.' It basically means that the school system has determined I am capable of overseeing how we provide special education services here at our school in addition to being knowledgeable about the general education curriculum. Because of those capabilities, I am charged with making decisions in the IEP meeting about the available resources of the school."

Counselor-in-Training: "Wow, I don't know if I will ever feel comfortable making those types of decisions. Will I be required to do that?"

Lesson Twenty-Three

The Role of the School Counselor in Special Education

"I was never top of the class at school, but my classmates must have seen potential in me, because my nickname was 'Einstein.'"

—Stephen Hawking

Essential Question: What are the special education laws? What is the role of the school counselor in the special education process? What is the difference between an IEP and a 504 Plan? What is the difference between an accommodation and a modification?

Objectives

Students will

- demonstrate understanding of the special education laws.
- demonstrate understanding of the ethical and legal mandates for working with students with special needs.
- demonstrate knowledge about the role of the school counselor in these processes.
- demonstrate understanding of the difference between an IEP and a Section 504 plan.
- demonstrate knowledge of the difference between an accommodation and a modification.

CACREP 2016 Standards

- Demonstrate appropriate school counselor roles in consultation with families, P–12 and post-secondary school personnel, and community agencies (5.G.2.b)
- Demonstrate knowledge about legislation and government policy relevant to school counseling (5.G.2.m)
- Demonstrate knowledge of legal and ethical considerations specific to school counseling (5.G.2.n)
- Implements strategies to promote equity in student achievement and college access (5.G.3.j)

MPCAC Standards

- Human development and wellness across the life span
- Neuroscientific, physical, and biological foundations of human development and wellness
- Ecological, contextual, multicultural, and social-justice foundations of human development

Video Spark

http://6abc.com/education/school-counselor--uses-rap-to-reach-students/557252/

School Counselor in Wynnefield Uses Rap to Reach Students

INTRODUCTION

School counselors have an active role in supporting students with special needs. This role ranges from providing emotional support for the student to doing classroom observations to participating in the special education or ADA Plan 504 process. School counselors should know laws that protect students with special needs, the role of the school counselor in special education and the Section 504 process, how to read a psychoeducational evaluation, how to read an IEP, and how to relate psychoeducational evaluations to IEPs. They should also know the difference between an accommodation and a modification and how to write a 504 Plan. This lesson addresses the laws that impact students with special needs, the role of the school counselor, the difference between an IEP and a 504 Plan, and the difference between an accommodation and a modification.

LAWS PROTECTING STUDENTS WITH SPECIAL NEEDS

Section 504 of the Rehabilitation Act of 1973 is a civil rights statute prohibiting discrimination on the basis of disability in programs and activities that receive Federal funding from the U.S. Department of Education. Section 504 ensures that students with disabilities have ***access*** to a free appropriate public education (FAPE).

Individuals with Disabilities Education Act (IDEA) ensures that children with disabilities receive a free appropriate public education.

Americans with Disabilities of 1990 (ADA) is a civil rights statute prohibiting discrimination on the basis of disability. ADA extends Section 504 protections into organizations that do not receive federal funding.

Americans with Disabilities Act Amendments Act of 2008 (ADAAA) broadens the original ADA terms by expanding the definition of major life activities and redefining who is regarded as having a disability. The ADAAA includes impairments that are episodic or in remission if these impairments would limit a major life activity; modifies the regulatory definition of "substantially limits," and prohibits consideration of the ameliorative effects of "mitigating measures" when assessing whether an impairment substantially limits a person's major life activities with one exception. For example, the use of a medication cannot be considered when assessing the impact of an individual's disability; however, the exception to this rule is the use of eyeglasses or contacts (U.S. Department of Labor, 2009).

THE ROLE OF THE SCHOOL COUNSELOR IN THE SPECIAL EDUCATION PROCESS

The American School Counselor Association (ASCA, 2013) in its position statement on the role of the school counselor and students with disabilities states

> School counselors work with students individually, in group settings, in special education class settings and in the regular classroom. School counselor responsibilities may include but are not limited to:
>
> - providing school counseling curriculum lessons, individual and/or group counseling to students with special needs within the scope of the comprehensive school counseling program
> - providing short-term, goal-focused counseling in instances where it is appropriate to include these strategies in the individual educational program (IEP)
> - encouraging family involvement in the educational process
> - consulting and collaborating with staff and families to understand the special needs of a student and understanding the adaptations and modifications needed to assist the student
> - advocating for students with special needs in the school and in the community

- contributing to the school's multidisciplinary team within the scope and practice of the comprehensive school counseling program to identify students who may need to be assessed to determine special education eligibility
- collaborating with related student support professionals (e.g., school psychologists, physical therapists, occupational therapists, special education staff, speech and language pathologists, teachers of deaf and hearing impaired) in the delivery of services providing assistance with developing academic and transition plans for students in the IEP as appropriate

● SPECIAL EDUCATION AND INDIVIDUAL EDUCATION PLANS (IEPS)

When a student is having difficulty learning, a process to support the child is triggered. Each school district will have its own specific process and may have different names for the teams; however, the goal of the overall process is to support the student, identify if the student needs additional assistance, and, if appropriate, refer the student for assessment to determine eligibility for special education services. The process begins with the teacher. If a student is struggling, the teacher implements strategies to support the student's academic progress. If these strategies are not providing the support the child needs to be academically successful, the concern about the student will move forward to a student support team. School counselors are often part of this team. The team will generate additional strategies that may facilitate the student's academic success. If those strategies do not work, the student will be referred for a comprehensive assessment to identify areas for intervention and to determine student eligibility for special education services.

The assessment process and timeline for the special education evaluation process is strictly regulated. The school administrators and special education faculty will implement this process. The results of this comprehensive assessment indicate whether a student is eligible for special education services. A student eligible for special education services fits into one of IDEA's categories and is in need of services. The categories of disabilities as identified by IDEA are mental retardation (now referred to as *developmental delay*), a hearing impairment (including deafness), a speech or language impairment, a visual impairment (including blindness), a serious emotional disturbance (referred to in this part as "emotional disturbance"), an orthopedic impairment, autism, traumatic brain injury, other health impairment, a specific learning disability, deaf-blindness, or multiple disabilities (U.S. Department of Education, 2004). Following this comprehensive assessment process and identification, an Individualized Education Plan (IEP) will be developed to create a plan that will document the student's needs and services needed.

The role of the school counselor in the IEP process varies according to the state and school district. In general, the role of the counselor in the IEP process is to provide information regarding the student's social/emotional status, to develop short-term, goal-focused strategies to be included in the IEP, to provide observations (e.g., classroom, recess, lunch room), and to serve as a school representative as well as an advocate for the student.

● 504 PLANS: STUDENTS WITH SPECIAL NEEDS WHO DO NOT REQUIRE SPECIAL EDUCATION

A student who is not eligible for and does not require special education may be eligible for services in order to ***access*** and fully participate in the educational system. This access is guaranteed under the student's right to a free and appropriate public education (FAPE). The student's needs and the accommodations required are documented in a 504 Plan. In order to be eligible for a 504 Plan, a student must be determined to (1) have a physical or mental impairment that substantially limits one or more major life activities, (2) have a record of such an impairment, and (3) be regarded as having such an impairment. *Major life activities* as defined in the Section 504 regulations include functions such as eating, standing, self-care, walking, hearing, and concentrating (U.S. Department of Education, 2008). The assessment process varies depending on the student's disability. However, a comprehensive evaluation must be done and include multiple sources of information. The assessment process for some students may include a full psychoeducational evaluation to determine if special education is appropriate. Determination for other students may require information from a medical professional and sources documenting that the student has a substantial impairment that limits one or more major life activity.

The role of the school counselor in the 504 Plan process again varies according to state and school district. The variation is much greater than in the IEP process—one reason is because the IEP process is implemented by special education professionals. In the 504 Plan process, the role of the counselor has expanded considerably. School counselors are now writing 504 Plans, communicating the appropriate information to those who need to know, and monitoring the 504 process.

• HOW DO IEPS AND 504 PLANS DIFFER?

Individualized education plans are developed for students who are eligible for special education services under IDEA. IEPs may provide both accommodation and modification and alter the educational requirements for the student. A Section 504 Plan will provide accommodations that provide the student with access to a FAPE. "The primary purpose of IDEA is to guide assessment, planning, and the provision of education and related services to students with disabilities and to provide funding to states for this purpose. The primary purpose of Section 504 is to prevent discriminatory practices against children with disabilities in public schools, but it does not provide any type of federal funding for this purpose" (Skalski & Stanke, 2010).

• WHAT IS THE DIFFERENCE BETWEEN A MODIFICATION AND AN ACCOMMODATION?

The terms *modification* and *accommodation* are often used interchangeably in schools. They are not the same, and the difference is important to understanding the appropriate strategies or interventions to be used in IEPs and Section 504 plans. An accommodation changes *how* a student learns. Accommodations do not alter the content or academic expectation; they provide support to level the playing field of learning. Accommodations are support services designed to help students access the general education curriculum. For example, taking tests in a quiet room may be an appropriate accommodation to support a student with attention-deficit/hyperactivity disorder.

A modification changes *what* a student learns. A modification is a change to the curriculum or content a student learns and also to the performance expectations or requirements. Modifications are more often seen in an IEP as compared to a Section 504 plan. For example, the performance output of a student with a specific learning disorder in written expression may be modified and the expectation for writing assignments may be altered (e.g., shorter, chunked). As the role of the school counselor increases in the area of special education, knowledge of accommodation and modifications is fundamental.

Activity: Complete the worksheet (Appendix A). Small group—discuss why you labeled the intervention as a modification or an accommodation. Discuss what type of student would benefit from the different interventions.

REFERENCES

American School Counselor Association. (2013). *The school counselor and students with disabilities* [Position Statement]. Retrieved from https://www.schoolcounselor.org/asca/media/asca/PositionStatements/PS_Disabilities.pdf

Council for Accreditation for Counseling and Related Program. (2014). *2016 standards*. Retrieved from www.cacrep.org

Masters in Psychology and Counseling Accreditation Council. (2015). *Accreditation manual*. Retrieved from http://www.mpcacaccreditation.org/about/accreditation-manual

Skalski, A., & Standek, J. (2010). *Section 504: A guide for parents and educators*. Retrieved from https://www.nasponline.org/Documents/Research%20and%20Policy/Advocacy%20Resources/35-1_S8-35_section_504.pdf

U.S. Department of Education. (2004). *Individuals with Disabilities Act*. Retrieved from http://findit.ed.gov/search?utf8=%E2%9C%93&affiliate=ed.gov&query=IDEA

U.S. Department of Labor. (2009). *Americans with Disabilities Act Amendments Act of 2008*. Retrieved from http://www.access-board.gov/the-board/laws/americans-with-disabilities-act-intro

APPENDIX A

Modification vs Accommodations—Worksheet

Identify each item as a modification or an accommodation.

1. Listening to audio recordings instead of reading the book. _____
2. Have fewer items on each page or have materials in a larger font. _____
3. Answer fewer or different test questions. _____
4. Take tests in a separate quiet room. _____
5. Reduce the quantity of work assigned. _____
6. Consider effort when assigning grades. _____
7. Use a different standard for grading. _____
8. Write shorter papers. _____
9. Allow use of computer. _____
10. Do not take points off for spelling. _____
11. Allow open book or open note tests. _____
12. Have student repeat directions. _____
13. Use behavioral management techniques. _____
14. Provide word bank on tests. _____
15. Provide visual organizer prior to class. _____

Lesson 24

UNDERSTANDING PSYCHOEDUCATIONAL ASSESSMENTS

"I'm looking forward to learning more about this process."

Real Life

While sitting in a relatively contentious IEP meeting with a student's parents, the principal, the Director of Student Support Services, the special education teacher, and the regular education teacher, the parents ask the school counselor, ***"What is the counselor's input and interpretation of the social-emotional assessment results of the psychoeducational assessment?"***

Faculty Supervisor: "This scenario happens all the time. For every IEP meeting, there is a psychoeducational assessment. Now—all eyes are on the school counselor. The ethical responsibility of the school counselor is to be prepared for these meetings and these questions. Saying 'I haven't read it' or 'I don't know' is unacceptable. Additionally, this is a leadership opportunity. Make the most of it!"

Lesson Twenty-Four

Understanding Psychoeducational Assessments

"I'm looking forward to learning more about this process."

Essential Question: Can I read and understand a psychoeducational assessment?

Objectives

Students will

- demonstrate an understanding of a psychoeducational assessment.
- demonstrate an understanding of the assessments specific to P–12 education.
- demonstrate knowledge of the school counselor's role in multidisciplinary teams.

CACREP 2016 Standards

- Knowledge of assessments specific to P–12 education (5.G.1.e)
- Understands the school counselor's roles in leadership and multidisciplinary teams (5.G.2.d)
- Knowledge of the legal and ethical considerations specific to school counseling (5.G.2.n)
- Knowledge of interventions to promote academic development (5.G.3.d)
- Skills to critically examine the connections between social, familial, emotional, and behavior problems and academic achievement (5.G.2.h)

MPCAC Standards

- Assessment of human behavior and organizational/community/institutional systems
- Tests and measurements
- Traditional and social-justice-oriented research and evaluations

Video Spark

https://www.youtube.com/watch?v=kOLwDBcgSjs&feature=em-share_video_user

Standardized Testing—The Simpsons

● INTRODUCTION

The role of the school counselor in the special education process varies greatly from school district to school district. What doesn't vary is that school counselors work with students who have psychoeducational assessments in their file. It is the responsibility of the school counselor to be competent in addressing the needs of these students. In order to do that, school counselor must know how to read a psychoeducational assessment and have at least a rudimentary knowledge of the implications of the information in the report. These reports to a great extent determine whether or not a student receives accommodations and also identifies what accommodations best meet the student's needs.

The following is an annotated psychoeducational assessment. This assessment is designed to introduce you to the multiple sections of this complex report and provides descriptions of each section.

Educational Specialist, PhD

Licensed Psychologist

Certified School Psychologist

Sweet School District

Savory, USA

• CONFIDENTIAL PSYCHOEDUCATIONAL ASSESSMENT

NAME: Patricia Peppermint

REPORT DATE: 1/5/0000

AGE: 8 years, 5 months

EXAMINER: Educational Specialist, PhD

DATE OF BIRTH: 0/00/0000

GENDER: Female

Reason for Referral

Patty was referred for evaluation by her parents and the Chocolate Charter School to clarify the nature of her strengths and weaknesses with respect to intellectual ability and learning. She is an interested and motivated student who is having difficulty staying on task and keeping pace academically. Concerns have been raised regarding a slower than expected rate of skill acquisition, possible attentional concerns, and Patty's overall academic progress.

> The **"Reason for Referral"** provides the rationale for the evaluation. It is important to get as much specific information from the referral source(s) as possible. If the referral source is an educator, the referral information may be detailed and behavioral. However, if the referral source is not an educator, the referral source may have difficulty putting his or her thoughts into behavioral terms. Hence, it is important to take the time to interview the referral source with the goal of clarifying all information provided.

Background Information and Parent Interview

Patty is a second-grade student at the Chocolate Charter School, Milky Way, Pennsylvania. She lives with her parents, Mr. and Mrs. Kit K. Peppermint. Patty's parents have been married for 15 years. Patty's maternal grandparents are an important part of her life. Mrs. Peppermint stated that Patty likes school, is happy, responsible, and has good friends.

Mrs. Peppermint completed the Structured Developmental History (SDH) providing information about Patty's growth and development. Patty was a product of a 38-week pregnancy and was healthy at birth. All developmental milestones were met within the normal age ranges. Although her mother did indicate that she rode a bike much earlier than her peers, Patty's health as a child was good and she had no difficulty in developing both fine and gross motor skills. It was reported that Patty is an athlete, always loves to be on the move, and is quite good at sports.

Background Information and Parent Interview: This section provides a comprehensive developmental history of the student. Information on the child's birth history, medical history, developmental history, family history, and social-emotional history is documented here.

Academic Background (Review of Records)

Patty has attended Chocolate Charter School since prekindergarten. Mrs. Crayola, Patty's prekindergarten teacher noted that Patty is an enthusiastic learner, consistently applies her advanced fine motor skills to all projects, and shows pride in the work she has done. Mrs. Crayola met with Mrs. Peppermint at the spring conference and noted that Patty was demonstrating a bit more impulsive behavior both academically and socially. In addition, Mrs. Peppermint contacted Ms. Caring, the counselor, to help Patty develop coping skills that will help her in the classroom and with her peers.

Mrs. Legos, Patty's kindergarten teacher, noted in the March progress report that Patty never ceases to amaze me with her capabilities and eye for detail. Patty is independently completing her sentences; however, she often like to play it safe by writing words she knows she can complete successfully. Staying focused during writing time is a challenge for Patty. She is often busy checking out what her peers are doing all around her instead of focusing on her own work. At times, she needs to be moved so she is not distracting her peers from their work as well. With numerous reminders she gets her work completed. She is very capable and has demonstrated this through all she has accomplished so far.

Mrs. Reading, Patty's first-grade teacher, noted in the spring, 2009 progress report that "Patty is working hard to strengthen her reading skills. Now we have moved to a higher level, and we have read *The Dragon's Scale*. Recently, she is showing a hesitation to sound out words, even ones that I know she knows. I feel confident that her comprehension skills are fine. She is able to discuss the story with knowledge. We will keep an eye on Patty's progress in the next two and a half months."

Academic Background (Review of Records): This section provides insight into the student's academic history. It also includes information from the teachers as the child progressed through school. If a child were identified with a concern of any type, it would be documented in this section. Accommodations or modifications would also be included. Reviewing the history of teacher feedback on the student provides a wealth of information.

Classroom Observation

Two school classroom and behavioral observations were done. Patty was observed at the Chocolate Charter School. Patty was observed during a mathematics lesson taught by Ms. Pencils with Mrs. Pens assisting. Initially, Patty was facing the front of the classroom looking at the math problem being done on the board. The students and teachers interacted in a relaxed, active exchange of information. The students asked questions and participated in solving the problem. A few minutes into the lesson, Patty began to tie and untie the scarf to her dress. The teacher called on Patty to reengage her in the classroom activity, and Patty correctly answered the question. Patty, however, continued to tie and untie her scarf. Patty then took her scarf off and put it in her desk. Back on task, Patty began to work on the problem the teacher was doing on the board and started to write information on her paper.

The children were independently and quietly working on the problems at their desks. After a couple of minutes, Patty initiated conversation with the student at the desk next to her. She had not completed the assignment. When Ms. Pencils and Mrs. Pens began to go around the room and work individually with students, Patty quickly completed the problem. Ms. Pencils worked with Patty on her math problem in order to get the correct answer. When she got the correct answer, she smiled and laughed. When Ms. Pencils had the class begin another math problem, Patty was the only student who loudly verbalized the problem, 77 + 6. Patty then announced with pride that she "never got a carrying problem wrong yet!"

Manipulatives were then used to illustrate a mathematical concept. The students were to follow Ms. Pencils's use of the manipulatives to illustrate the carrying of "tens" into the "hundreds" column. The students were actively engaged in this demonstration and were asking questions throughout the process. During a timed observation, Patty was off-task for 3 minutes out of a period of 4 minutes. Mrs. Pens went over to Patty's desk to help her refocus and engage in the classroom activity.

Patty was observed during a transition from Ms. Pencils's language arts class to Mrs. Rain's science class. Patty was very social and enjoyed walking and chatting with her friends from one class to the other. When it was time to line up outside of the science room and wait for the other class to finish, Patty got out of line twice. The rest of the class stayed in line for this short period of time. Ms. Pencils asked her to get back in line with the other students and Patty very respectfully got back in line. Ms. Pencils thanked Patty and complimented her prior to her entering the science class.

Classroom Observation: Classroom observations are usually done by the school counselor or the school psychologist. Classroom observations should be behavioral and provide information on the context in which the observation takes place. Observing a student in multiple settings is best practice.

Teacher Interview/Reports

Ms. Pencils expressed concerns regarding Patty's attentional skills and her ability to maintain focus in the classroom. She noted that one of Patty's strengths is her verbal ability and vocabulary. Ms. Pencils said that Patty is a joy to have in the classroom, but that she can distract other children with her calling out. Ms. Pencils reported that Patty has a great deal of difficulty completing written assignments. One of Ms. Pencils's concerns is that Patty's challenge with staying on task is impeding her ability to reach her academic potential.

Fall, 2009 Progress report—Teacher comments: "Patty is an intelligent, engaging, happy and spirited member of our class. It is obvious she wants to succeed and she tries to do her best. Unfortunately, she easily loses focus and this affects the consistency in both her work approach and her productivity. At this time, when asked to complete written tasks, Patty is not an independent worker. She has difficulty interpreting both oral and written directions, beginning work, staying focused and completing assignments within a reasonable time frame. In the same vein, she seems to grasp only bits and pieces of lessons and has difficulty applying them independently. This is evidenced through her written assignments. She requires additional explanations and teacher demonstration in order to be successful. Interestingly, in contrast, during discussion times, or games such as Jeopardy where verbal recall of information is required, Patty shines! I'm sure this dichotomy is frustrating to her. Another goal for Patty is to garner more self-control. Patty's smile and determination contributes to the joy of having her in class. I will continue to support her, but as the lessons increase and become more varied and complex, I worry about Patty feeling overwhelmed. Socially she enjoys peer interaction, but frequently she can quickly find fault with her friends and this leads to misunderstandings and hurt feelings. We are working on being flexible. I look forward to helping Patty reach her full potential" (Ms. Pencils, 2009).

Current Teacher Interview/Reports: Building on the history previously provided, interviews with the student's teachers are essential. It provides information on what is happening in the context of the grade level, academic subjects, and classroom environment and provides the teachers' perspective of the student.

Testing Observation

Testing was completed over three sessions with Patty. These three sessions took place over a 3-week period, and the times were varied from morning to midafternoon. Patty is an engaging, outgoing, and friendly child. She demonstrated strong social skills and was interactive and conversant. Patty spoke about her plans for the upcoming winter break from school. She was interested in the assessment process and liked to discuss the tasks and expound on the questions asked. Patty was motivated and actively engaged throughout the testing process; however, when she decided she was finished—she was finished. In response to Patty's stamina and ability to remain on task, the testing was ended as soon as Patty became fatigued. This evaluation can be considered representative of her cognitive ability and achievement.

Testing Observation: The school counselor or school psychologist provides her or his observations of the student during the testing sessions. These observations provide information about the student in a one-on-one setting and provide additional insight into the student's learning profile.

Tests Administered

Classroom Observations

Parent Interview

Teacher Interview

Review of the Records

Wechsler Intelligence Scale for Children—Fourth Edition (WISC-IV)

Wechsler Individual Achievement Test for Children—Second Edition (WIAT-II)

Woodcock-Johnson III Tests of Achievement Fluency Subtests (WJ-III)

Behavioral Assessment System for Children—Second Edition (BASC-2)

Conners 3—Behavior Rating Scale: Parent

Conners 3—Behavior Rating Scale: Teacher

● PART 1: COGNITIVE ABILITY

Wechsler Intelligence Scale for Children—Fourth Edition (WISC-IV)

	Index Scores	Percentile	Classification
Verbal Comprehension	136	99	Very Superior
Perceptual Reasoning	125	95	Superior
Working Memory	107	68	Average
Processing Speed	83	13	Low Average
Full Scale	**120**	**91**	**Superior**

Patty was administered ten subtests of the Wechsler Intelligence Scale for Children—Fourth Edition (WISC-IV) from which the composite scores are derived. The Full Scale IQ (FSIQ) is derived from a combination of ten subtest scores and is considered the most representative estimate of global intellectual functioning. Composite scores range from 40 to 160; a score of 100 represents the strict average. Scaled scores range from 1 to 19; a score of 10 represents the strict average. The Full Scale IQ represents an overall general level of cognitive ability and is considered the most representative estimate of global intellectual functioning. Patty's FSIQ is 120 which is in the 91st percentile when compared with individuals her age.

Verbal Comprehension	**Scaled Score**	**Percentile**
Similarities	19	99.9
Vocabulary	16	98
Comprehension	13	84

Verbal Comprehension Index (VCI): measures verbal ability utilizing reasoning, comprehension, and conceptualization.

Patty's verbal reasoning abilities as measured by the Verbal Comprehension Index are in the Very Superior range and above those of approximately 99% of her peers (VCI = 136; 95% confidence interval = 127–141). The Verbal Comprehension Index is designed to measure verbal reasoning and concept formation. Patty's performance on the verbal subtests presents a diverse set of verbal abilities, performing much better on some verbal skills than others. The VCI consists of three required subtests:

1. <u>Similarities</u> measures verbal reasoning, conceptual formation, memory, and auditory comprehension. Patty scored in the 99.9th percentile on the Similarities subtest. This test requires the student to identify the similarity between two seemingly dissimilar items, such as, "flood and drought." The words are presented auditorily to the student.
2. <u>Vocabulary</u> measures word knowledge and verbal concept formation. The student is required to give definitions for words the examiner reads aloud. Patty's vocabulary score was in the 98th percentile. She is confident in her word knowledge and easily defined words such as *mimic* and *fable*.
3. <u>Comprehension</u> measures verbal reasoning and conceptualization and the ability to demonstrate practical information. This test requires the student to answer questions based on his or her understanding of general principles and social situations. Patty confidentally answered the question, "Why is it important for people to keep their promise?" Patty's score on the Comprehension subtest was in the 84th percentile.

Perceptual Reasoning	**Scaled Score**	**Percentile**
Block Design	14	91
Picture Concepts	15	95
Matrix Reasoning	13	84

Perceptual Reasoning Index (PRI): measures fluid reasoning in the perceptual domain with tasks that assess nonverbal concept formation, visual perception and organization, simultaneous processing, visual-motor coordination, learning, and the ability to separate figure and ground in visual stimuli.

The tasks require fluid reasoning involving the process of manipulating abstractions, rules, generalization, and logical relationships. Patty's nonverbal reasoning abilities as measured by the Perceptual Reasoning Index are in the Superior range and above those of approximately 95% of her peers (PRI = 125; 95% confidence interval = 115–131). Patty performed comparably on the perceptual reasoning subtests contributing to the PRI, suggesting that her visual-spatial reasoning and perceptual-organizational skills are similarly developed. PRI has three subtests—Block Design, Picture Concepts, and Matrix Reasoning:

1. Block Design measures the ability to analyze and synthesize abstract visual stimuli, nonverbal concept formation, and visual perception and organization. This test requires the student to view a constructed model or a picture in the stimulus book, and use red-and-white blocks to re-create the design within a specified time limit. Patty's score was in the 91st percentile when compared with individuals her age. Patty reported that she enjoyed working on this task and wished there were more design for her to make.
2. The Picture Concepts subtest measures fluid reasoning and abstract categorical reasoning ability. The task invokes verbal concepts, but does not require verbal responses. This subtest also focuses on information that is found in everyday life. The student is presented with two or three rows of pictures and chooses one picture from each row to form a group with a common characteristic. Patty's score was in the 95th percentile on the Picture Concepts subtest.
3. Matrix Reasoning measures fluid intelligence, general intellectual ability, and pattern completion and classification. This test requires the student to view an incomplete matrix and select the missing portion from five response options. Patty's score was in the 84th percentile on the Matrix Reasoning subtest.

Working Memory	**Scaled Score**	**Percentile**
Digit Span	11	63
Letter–Number Sequencing	12	75

Working Memory Index (WMI): measures attention, concentration, and working memory. The WMI has an increased emphasis on working memory—an essential component of fluid reasoning and other higher order cognitive processes. Working memory is the ability to actively maintain information in conscious awareness, perform some operation or manipulation with it, and produce a result. Patty's ability to sustain attention, concentrate, and exert mental control is in the Average range. She performed better than approximately 68% of her age-mates in this area (Working Memory Index = 107; 95% confidence interval 99–114). Patty's abilities to sustain attention, concentrate, and exert mental control are a weakness relative to her verbal reasoning abilities. A relative weakness in mental control may make the processing of complex information more time consuming for Patty and perhaps result in more frequent errors on a variety of learning tasks. WMI has two subtests: Digit Span and Letter–Number Sequencing.

- Digit Span measures auditory short-term memory, auditory processing, and sequencing skills. The student is read a series of numbers and is required to repeat them verbatim as stated by the examiner; there are two parts of this subtest: Digit Span Forward and Digit Span Backward. Patty's score was in the 63rd percentile on the Digit Span subtest.
- Letter–Number Sequencing measures mental manipulation, attention, and short-term auditory memory. A number and letter sequence are read, and the student is required to recall numbers in ascending order and letters in alphabetical order. Patty's score on this subtest was in the 75th percentile.

Processing Speed	**Scaled Score**	**Percentile**
Coding	5	5
Symbol Search	9	37

Processing Speed Index (PSI): measures speed of mental and graphomotor processing. PSI requires visual perception and organization, and visual scanning. Patty's ability in processing simple or routine visual material without making errors is in the Low Average range when compared to her peers. She performed better than approximately 13% of her peers on the processing speed tasks (Processing Speed Index = 83; 95% confidence interval 76–94). Patty's performance on the subtests that comprise the PSI is quite variable; therefore, the PSI score should be interpreted with caution. She performed much better on Symbol Search (Scaled Score = 9), which is more demanding of attention to detail and mental control, than on Coding (Scaled Score = 5), which is more demanding of fine-motor skills, short-term memory, and learning. Processing visual material quickly is an ability that Patty performs poorly as compared to her verbal and nonverbal reasoning ability. Processing speed is an indication of the rapidity with which Patty can mentally process simple or routine information without making errors. PRI has two subtests: Coding and Symbol Search.

- Coding measures short-term memory, learning ability, visual perception, visual-motor coordination, visual scanning ability, cognitive flexibility, attention, and motivation. It requires the student to copy symbols that are paired with simple geometric shapes or numbers. Patty's score on this subtest was in the 5th percentile.
- Symbol Search measures processing speed, short-term visual memory, visual-motor coordination, cognitive flexibility, visual discrimination, and concentration. This test requires the student to scan a search group and indicate whether the target symbol(s) matches any of the symbols in the search group within a specified time limit. Patty's score on the Symbol Search subtest was in the 37th percentile.

Part 1: Cognitive Ability Cognitive Ability tests provide scores that represent intellectual or cognitive functioning as compared with the general population. Cognitive ability tests measure an individual's potential ability. Specifically, cognitive tests are designed to measure an individual's general ability to solve problems, understand concepts, and use reasoning skills, memory, and processing. These specific cognitive domains are then combined to generate an overall IQ (Intellectual Quotient) score.

PART 2: ACADEMIC ACHIEVEMENT

Wechsler Individual Achievement Test—II (WIAT-II)

Reading	**Percentile**
Word Reading	39
Reading Comprehension	75
Pseudoword Decoding	55
Overall Reading	**50**

Patty presents a diverse set of skills on different aspects of reading. She performed much better on tasks that assessed her capability to read sentences and paragraphs and answer questions about what was read (Reading Comprehension standard score = 110) than on tasks that required her to name alphabet letters, identify and generate letter sounds and rhyming words, and match and read a series of printed words (Word Reading standard score = 96). For this reason, the Reading Composite score may not be the most accurate manner in which to summarize her reading skills. Her Reading Comprehension subtest score is higher than approximately 75% of her peers, placing these skills in the High Average range. Patty's performance on Word Reading is within the Average range and exceeds that of approximately 39% of students her age.

Mathematics	**Percentile**
Numerical Operations	53
Arithmetic	70
Overall Mathematics	**63**

In overall mathematics skills, Patty performed in the Average range, as indicated by her Mathematics Composite standard score (105). Her skills in this area exceed that of approximately 63% of students her age. Patty's performance on tasks that required her to add and subtract numbers up to three digits (Numerical Operations standard score = 101) is comparable to her performance on tasks that require her to understand basic number concepts, including unit and geometric measurement, and solve one-step word problems (Math Reasoning standard score = 108).

Oral Language	**Percentile**
Listening Comprehension	84

Patty performed in the High Average range on tasks that required her to identify the picture that best represents an orally presented descriptor or generate a word that matches the picture as indicated by her Listening Comprehension standard score (115). Her skills in this area exceed that of approximately 84% of students her age.

Written Language	**Percentile**
Spelling	18
Written Expression	22

In overall written language skills, Patty performed below Average range, as indicated by her Written Language Composite standard score. Her achievement in this area is in the 18th percentile when compared with students her age. Patty's skill level of written expression is below grade level.

Woodcock-Johnson III Tests of Achievement

Academic Fluency Cluster: The Academic Fluency cluster is a combination of Test 2: Reading Fluency, Test 6: Math Fluency, and Test 8: Writing Fluency and provides an overall index of academic fluency. Patty's overall Academic Fluency is in the Limited to Average range and 9th percentile when compared with others her age.

Reading Fluency measures the person's ability to quickly read simple sentences in the subject response booklet, decide if the statement is true, and then circle Yes or No. The difficulty level of the sentences gradually increases to a moderate level. The individual attempts to complete as many items as possible within a 3-minute time limit. Patty scored in the 10th percentile which is in the Limited range on the Reading Fluency subtest.

Math Fluency measures the ability to solve simple addition, subtraction, and multiplication facts quickly. The person is presented a series of simple arithmetic problems in the subject response booklet. This test has a 3-minute time limit. Patty scored in the 19th percentile, which is in the Average range on the Math Fluency subtest.

Writing Fluency measures skill in formulating and writing simple sentences quickly. Each sentence must relate to a given stimulus picture in the subject response booklet and include a given set of three words. This test has a 7-minute time limit. Patty scored in the 21st percentile which is in the Limited to Average range on the Writing Fluency subtest.

Part 2: Academic Achievement Achievement tests provide scores that represent acquired learning in specific subject areas such as reading and mathematics. Achievement tests are standardized tests that provide a comparison of an individual's knowledge to the performance of a group of peers who have previously taken the same test. An example of a frequently used standardized achievement test would be the SATs.

PART 3: BEHAVIORAL, SOCIAL, AND EMOTIONAL MEASURES

Behavioral Assessment System for Children—Second Edition (BASC-2)

The Behavioral Assessment System for Children—Second Edition (BASC-2) is an integrated system designed to facilitate the differential diagnosis and classification of a variety of emotional and behavioral disorders of children and to aid in the design of treatment plans. There are three forms of the BASC-2: the teacher form, the parent form, and a self-report form. Any score in the Clinically Significant range suggests a high level of maladjustment. Scores in the At-risk range identify either a significant problem that may not be severe enough to require formal treatment or a potential of developing a problem that needs careful monitoring.

BASC-2 Teacher Report: There are two scales: Clinical Scales and Adaptive Scales. The Clinical Scales include Externalizing Behavior (hyperactivity, aggression, conduct problems), Internalizing Behavior (anxiety, depression, somatization), and School Problems (attention problems, learning problems), which combine to provide a composite score called the Behavioral Symptoms Index. Also measured in the Behavioral Symptom Index are Atypicality and Withdrawal. The Adaptive Scales include adaptability, social skills, leadership, activities of daily living, and functional communication. Areas of concern noted on the BASC-2 Teacher forms were attention, hyperactivity, school problems, learning problems, adaptability, social skills, leadership, study skills, communication, emotional self-control, and executive functioning. Please see attached results table for additional information.

BASC-2 Parent Report: There are two scales: Clinical Scales and Adaptive Scales. The Clinical Scales include Externalizing Behavior (hyperactivity, aggression, conduct problems) and Internalizing Behavior (anxiety, depression, somatization), which combine to provide a composite score called the Behavioral Symptoms Index. Also measured in the Behavioral Symptom Index are Atypicality and Withdrawal. The Adaptive Scales include adaptability, social skills, leadership, activities of daily living, and functional communication. No areas of concern were noted on the BASC-2 Parent form. Please see attached results table for additional information.

BASC-2 Self-Report: The Self-Report of Personality form measures the areas of School Problems (attitude to school, attitude to teachers and sensation seeking), Internalizing Problems (atypicality, locus of control, social stress, anxiety, depression, sense of inadequacy, and somatization), Attention/Hyperactivity (attention problems and hyperactivity), Emotional Symptoms Index, and Personal Adjustment. Areas of concern noted on the BASC-2 Self-Report form were Attention Problems and Hyperactivity. Please see attached results table for additional information.

Conners 3 Parent Rating Scale

The Conners Rating Scales are specifically constructed to help identify students at-risk for attention deficit disorder (ADD) or attention–deficit/hyperactivity disorder (ADHD). The Conners 3 parent form was completed by Patty's mother, Mrs. Peppermint. This behavior rating scale has six subscales: Inattention, Hyperactivity/Impulsivity, Learning Problems, Executive Functioning, Defiance/Aggression, and Peer Relations. Areas of concern noted were Learning Problems and Executive Functioning. The ADHD Predominantly Inattentive Type Scale was considered elevated with a t-score of 68. Please see attached results table for additional information.

Conners 3 Teacher Rating Scale

The Conners Rating Scales are specifically constructed to help identify students at-risk for attention deficit disorder (ADD) or attention–deficit/hyperactivity disorder (ADHD). The Conners 3 teacher form was completed by three of Patty's teachers. This behavior rating scale has seven subscales: Inattention, Hyperactivity/Impulsivity, Learning Problems/Executive Functioning, Learning Problems, Executive Functioning, Defiance/Aggression, and Peer Relations. Areas of concern noted were Inattention, Hyperactivity/Impulsivity, Learning Problems/Executive Functioning, Learning Problems, and Executive Functioning. The ADHD Predominantly Inattentive Type Scale and the ADHD Predominantly Hyperactive-Impulsive Type Scale were considered elevated. Please see attached results table for additional information.

Part 3: Behavioral, Social, and Emotional Measures Behavior rating scales provide information about particular aspects of a student's behavior compared to other children of the same age and sometimes same gender. The rating scales may be global and focus on several areas or look more in depth at a specific behavior, emotional issue, or social issue. Rating scales are given to teachers, parents, and/or the student as a way to obtain standardized data about the severity of a concern. The rating scales have been standardized, by giving the scale to thousands of respondents. The makers of the rating scales, took those responses and developed a range of "normal", "at-risk," or "clinically significant," and assigned scores to those ranges.

PART 4: SUMMARY

Patty is an 8-year-old student at the Chocolate Charter School in Milky Way, Pennsylvania. She is an engaging, intelligent child who has begun to experience academic challenges. In addition, teachers have observed Patty having difficulty staying on task and focusing both in and out of the classroom. The results of this assessment indicate that Patty has the innate ability to be successful in a rigorous academic setting. However, there are weaknesses in her learning profile that seem to be barriers to her academic achievement.

- Patty's general cognitive ability, as estimated by the WISC-IV, is in the Superior range (FSIQ = 120). Patty's general verbal comprehension abilities were in the Very Superior range (VCI = 136), and general perceptual reasoning abilities were in the Superior range (PRI = 125). Patty performed exceptionally well on the cognitive ability tasks involving verbal knowledge, language comprehension, and fluency. Her verbal strength should be used to faciliate academic skill development.
- Learning is a complex interaction. Some factors which influence learning are an individual's innate potential, current academic level of achievement, processing skills, attentional and focusing abilities, and environment. This confluence of factors makes clarifying Patty's learning profile a multifaceted endeavor.
- The results of this assessment, the Conners 3, the BASC-2, and teacher reports and observations indicate that Mrs. Peppermint, three of Patty's teachers, and Patty herself endorse signficant concern regarding her ability to pay attention and stay focused. This difficulty with attention and focus was also observed during the assessment process and classroom observations. Patty was motivated and worked hard during the individual testing sessions; however, she was not able to sustain focus and attention on the tasks at hand. When Patty became fatigued, she would immediately stop working. Though a break would be taken from the testing process, Patty was very resistant to getting back on task. This behavior is consistent with the behavior observed by the teachers. Taken together, parent, teacher, self-ratings, behavioral observations in the classroom and during evaluation, and the profile of test results are consistent with a diagnosis of attention-deficit/hyperactivity disorder—hyperactive/impulsive type.
- Patty's scores on the WISC-IV Processing Speed Index are considered a relative weakness in her learning profile. However, it is not unusual for processing speed to be impacted by an individual's attention and focusing skills. This combination of factors is also reflected in her Academic Fluency scores on the Woodcock-Johnson Achievement test (Reading—10th percentile; Mathematics—19th percentile; Written—21st percentile).
- Patty's Reading scores on the WIAT-II were compared to the levels of achievement predicted for a student with her general cognitive ability, as indicated by her Full Scale IQ score of 120 on the WISC-IV. She scored in the 39th percentile in the achievement test measuring word reading and in the 23rd percentile in the achievement test measuring her written language skills. There is a significant discrepancy between Patty's cognitive abilities and educational achievement in Reading. However, because Patty's achievement in Reading is in the Average range when compared with her peers, her pattern of scores does not meet the State's Educational Code and the Diagnostic and Statistical Manual of Mental Disorders—Fifth Edition (DSM-V) criteria for a learning disability.
- Patty's scores on the WIAT-II were compared to the levels of achievement predicted for a student with her general cognitive ability, as indicated by her Full Scale IQ score of 120 on the WISC-IV. There is a significant discrepancy between Patty's cognitive abilities and educational achievement in Written Expression. Patty's academic achievement in Written Expression was below Average when compared with her peers and is below grade level. Patty's pattern of scores meets the State's Educational Code and the Diagnostic and Statistical Manual of Mental Disorders—Fifth Edition (DSM-V) criteria for a learning disability in Written Expression.

Diagnosis

314.01 Attention Deficit/Hyperactvitiy Disorder, Combined Type

315.2 Disorder of Written Expression

Part 4: Summary/Diagnosis This section summarizes, integrates, and interprets the information gathered during the assessment. Discussion of Patty's case will follow.

● PART 5: RECOMMENDATIONS

ADHD

- Counseling may help Patty learn strategies and techniques to address her difficulties with inattention and impulsivity.
- Patty's mother may want to explore resources available to parents of children with attentional issues, such as Children with Attention Deficit Disorder (CHADD at www.chadd.org).
- If behavioral interventions are not sufficient to support Patty, consultation with her pediatrician may be considered. The consultation should focus on determining whether Patty will benefit from medication treatment to help with her attentional difficulties.

Metacognition

- Introduce the concept of "thinking about how you think" to Patty.
- Explain the active nature of metacognition and its role in the learning process.
- Use techniques to capture Patty's attention (e.g., begin topic with a personal discussion in order to increase her connection and trigger active participation in processing).
- Tutoring or academic support can provide Patty foundational techniques and skills required to produce quality work. (Make certain directions are understood, consult with teachers as needed, check for errors, neatness, edit, etc.)
- Basic learning processes and skills should be taught and reviewed to facilitate academic progress. These processes and skills include focusing skills (defining problems, setting goals, etc.), information-gathering skills, organizational skills, and evaluation skills.
- Patty should be taught specific methods for encoding, storing, and retrieving information to strengthen her short-term and long-term memory. Specific interventions are
    - Chunking of information: present information in stages
    - Have Patty ask questions about directions or assignments to clarify and encode information
    - Teach Patty how to determine what is important to remember (use the Consequence/Sequence strategy of If . . . Then . . . processing).
    - Use of highlighter when reading; follow up with the teacher to determine Patty's accuracy in selection of important ideas and to further teach identification of important ideas
    - Writing in the margins as reading
    - Use of games, such as Concentration
- Use of notecard writing for memory encoding.
- Patty's strength was demonstrated in her oral verbal abilities. In the classroom, this strength can be maximized by allowing and encouraging her to use the process of subvocalization to facilitate learning new material. Subvocalization and active verbalization are one of the best memory approaches for Patty.

- Have Patty review her schoolwork with the teacher in order for her to become aware of the quality and completeness of her work.

Attention

- Patty may benefit from preferential seating near the teacher to help sustain focus and engagement in lesson.
- Break larger assignments into smaller tasks that can be completed in a shorter period of time.
- Establish a private signal that would cue Patty that she is "tuning out." A tap on the shoulder could be an effective method.
- Pair written instructions with oral instructions.
- Assist Patty in setting short-term goals leading to long-term goals for larger projects.
- Provide structure for successful task completion and teach Patty strategies to begin to implement this structure and organization system on her own.

Written Expression

- Receive academic support to facilitate the development of Patty's writing skills.
- Specific and enumerated instructions should be provided for written assignments to help develop fluency and output in writing. Patty should be encouraged to verbalize her thoughts as she proceeds through the writing process.
- Patty would benefit from verbalizing her thoughts on tape first, then proceeding with her assignment.
- Patty should use a structured format for written assignments.
- Have Patty read or review her written schoolwork with her parent or the teacher. Maximize on Patty's strength in the Oral Expression area may facilitate an awareness of what she has left "unsaid."
- Provide Patty with a sample of work, which may serve as models for her to follow.
- Provide Patty with the opportunity to have a preliminary evaluation of her work, requiring her to make necessary changes before final grading. Work jointly with Patty to identify the areas that should be targeted for improvement.
- Extend time on classroom and standardized testing. This accommodation would provide Patty with the time she requires to read and process the written word and use the strategies she is learning to accommodate her learning disorder. This accommodation would provide Patty with the time needed to focus and attend to the details of the questions and the test. In addition, this accommodation would provide Patty with the time needed to check on accuracy and also provide time to track between the question and the answer.
- Take standardized tests in a separate room. This accommodation would provide Patty with an environment that is free of distractions, which would faciliate her ability to perform.

Part 5: Recommendations This section provides strategies and accommodations that should be implemented in order to meet Patty's needs.

If you have any questions, please feel free to contact me. Thank you.

Respectfully submitted,

Licensed Psychologist

Certified School Psychologist

****

INTERPRETATION OF PATTY'S REPORT

Learning is a complex interaction. Some factors that influence learning are an individual's innate potential, current academic level of achievement, processing skills, attention and focusing abilities, and environment. This confluence of factors makes clarifying Patty's learning profile a multifaceted endeavor. As a school counselor, you will want to outline Patti's strengths, weaknesses, diagnoses, and recommended interventions. The Sample Information Sheet for School Counselors for IEP Meetings is provided for your use. When completing the form, make sure to include all the information you would want to know when you attend the IEP or multidisciplinary team meeting for this student.

Activity 1

At the beginning of the chapter is a "real-life" situation. Answer the real-life situation question.

Activity 2

Complete the Information sheet (Appendix A) for the case study of Patty Peppermint.

REFERENCES

Council for Accreditation for Counseling and Related Program. (2014). *2016 standards.* Retrieved from www.cacrep.org

Masters in Psychology and Counseling Accreditation Council. (2015). *Accreditation manual.* Retrieved from http://www.mpcacaccreditation.org/about/accreditation-manual

APPENDIX A

Information Sheet for School Counselors for IEP Meeting

IEP Meeting for: Student Name **Date:** 1/5/0000

Strengths:

Concerns:

Diagnosis:

Accommodations:

List the accommodations or modification in the Recommendation section of the report. It would be difficult to remember all of the recommendations, and it would be best to have them "in your pocket." All of the accommodations and modifications are important; however, it is important to remember that extended time for standardized and classroom tests (along with a separate room for testing) were recommended.

LESSON 25

HOW TO READ AN IEP

"I hear your concerns. Let me read the student's IEP and consult with my site supervisor."

Real Life

Counselor-in-Training: "When I was at my field experience, I took a phone message from a parent who was very upset. I took notes of the parent's concerns and gave them to my site supervisor. The parent believes that the school is not following her child's IEP. The parent shared that she believes that the school is the cause of the student's lack of academic achievement and also the student's low self-esteem. I accessed the student's file so that I would be informed when I spoke with my site supervisor. I am so confused—I don't really understand the Individualized Education Plan. What services are appropriate for this identified student?"

On-site Supervisor: "Thank you for taking this parent phone call. Your notes are informative and very helpful. Have you read the student's IEP yet?"

Lesson Twenty-Five

How to Read an IEP

""I hear your concerns. Let me read the student's IEP and consult with my site supervisor."

Essential Question: How do I read an IEP with full understanding of its content?

Objectives

Students will

- demonstrate an understanding of the special education process.
- demonstrate an understanding of the function of an IEP.
- demonstrate knowledge of the school counselor's role in the IEP process.
- demonstrate an understanding of assessments specific to P–12 education.

CACREP 2016 Standards

- Knowledge of assessments specific to P-12 education (5.G.1.e)
- Understanding the school counselors roles in leadership and multidisciplinary teams (5.G.2.d)
- Knowledge of the legal and ethical considerations specific to school counseling (5.G.2.n)
- Knowledge of interventions to promote academic development (5.G.3.d)
- Skills to critically examine the connections between social, familial, emotional, and behavior problems and academic achievement (5.G.2.h)

MPCAC Standards

- Assessment of human behavior and organizational/community/institutional systems
- Tests and measurements
- Traditional and social-justice-oriented research and evaluations

Video Spark

https://www.youtube.com/watch?v=q2XlAWcMAUk

What is an IEP? (The National Center for Learning Disabilities)

● INTRODUCTION

Although the role of the school counselor does not include writing IEPs, school counselors often provide information for these educational plans and participate in the IEP process. Hence, it is important for the school counselor to know how to read an IEP and understand the content and implications of the plan. The importance of this document cannot be stressed enough. An IEP is a legal document that documents a student's needs, the services to be provided, and how the student's progress will be monitored and measured. The IEP will document what modifications, accommodations, and services will be provided to the student. Development of an IEP is a process requiring team collaboration. Who is on an IEP team can vary; however, the team generally consists of the student, the student's parents/guardians, teachers, administrators, the school counselor, and any other relevant specialists. An IEP will identify the student's strengths, areas that need development and support, and the specific services that will be provided by the school district.

In most school districts, school counselors attend IEP meetings. The counselor may attend as a representative of the school district who is familiar with both regular education and special education or may attend IEP meetings that address the needs of students with whom they are working in the role of school counselor. In the IEP meeting, the school counselor may be asked to provide input on the student's social/emotional status and concerns. This is done in a professional manner and is consistent with the ethical and legal standards of confidentiality. For example, if a student is doing well overall but has a specific learning disorder in mathematics and the goal of the IEP meeting is to identify strategies to support the student's academic achievement in mathematics, the school counselor sharing information about the student's social life may not be appropriate. In general, information in schools is shared on a need-to-know basis. School counselors work to achieve a delicate balance between meeting the needs-of-the student while fully participating in the team collaboration and providing information on a need-to-know basis.

The role of the school counselor in the IEP process focuses on providing short-term, goal-focused counseling strategies; supporting the family in this process; collaboration and consultation with faculty, administration, staff, and families to facilitate an understanding of the child's needs and the adaptations and modifications in the IEP; and being part of the multidisciplinary IEP team (American School Counselor Association [ASCA], 2013). These responsibilities clearly require school counselors to be competent in fully understanding the IEP document. As you read the annotated IEP in this chapter, you will note that counseling services are considered a ***"Related Service"*** in an IEP.

Case Studies With Completed IEPs

Academic core standards, special education guidelines, and processes vary from state to state. Hence, the format for IEPs also varies dependent on the state or school district. The National Association of State Directors of Special Education's (NASDSE) Project Forum developed examples of standards-based IEPs. This format will be used to provide information on and gain familiarity with reading IEPs. The following is the process for writing an IEP and a case study with an accompanying IEP written by Marla Davis Holbrook (2007) as part of NASDSE's Project Forum. Project Forum at NASDE is a cooperative agreement funded by the Office of Special Education Programs of the U.S. Department of Education.

● STEPS TO CREATING A STANDARDS-BASED IEP

Step 1: Consider the grade-level content standards for the grade in which the student is enrolled or would be enrolled based on age.

Ask

- What is the intent of the content standard?
- What is the content standard saying that the student must know and be able to do?

Step 2: Examine classroom and student data to determine where the student is functioning in relation to the grade-level standards.

Ask

- Has the student been taught content aligned with grade-level standards?
- Has the student been provided appropriate instructional scaffolding to attain grade-level expectations?

- Were the lessons and teaching materials used to teach the student aligned with state grade-level standards?
- Was the instruction evidence based?

Step 3: Develop the present level of academic achievement and functional performance.

Describe the individual strengths and needs of the student in relation to accessing and mastering the general curriculum.

Ask

- What do we know about the student's response to academic instruction (e.g., progress monitoring data)?
- What programs, accommodations (i.e., classroom and testing), or interventions have been successful with the student?
- What have we learned from previous IEPs and student data that can inform decision-making?
- Are there assessment data (i.e., state, district, and/or classroom) that can provide useful information for making decisions about the student's strengths and needs (e.g., patterns in the data)?

Consider the factors related to the student's disability and how they affect how the student learns and demonstrates what he or she knows.

Ask

- How does the student's disability affect participation and progress in the general curriculum?
- What supports does the student need to learn the knowledge and attain the skills to progress in the general curriculum?
- Is the student on track to achieve grade-level proficiency within the year?

Step 4: Develop measurable annual goals aligned with grade-level academic content standards.

Ask

- What are the student's needs as identified in the present level of performance?
- Does the goal have a specific time frame?
- What can the student reasonably be expected to accomplish in one school year?
- Are the conditions for meeting the goal addressed?
- How will the outcome of the goal be measured?

Step 5: Assess and report the student's progress throughout the year.

Ask

- How does the student demonstrate what he or she knows on classroom, district, and state assessments?
- Are a variety of assessments used to measure progress?
- How will progress be reported to parents?

Step 6: Identify specially designed instruction including accommodations and/or modifications needed to access and progress in the general education curriculum.

Ask

- What accommodations are needed to enable the student to access the knowledge in the general education curriculum? What accommodations have been used with the student and were they effective?
- Has the complexity of the material been changed in such a way that the content has been modified?

Step 7: Determine the most appropriate assessment option.

Ask

- What types of assessments are offered in my state?
- What types of responses do different state assessments require?
- What are the administrative conditions of the assessment (i.e., setting, delivery of instructions, time allotted, etc.)?
- What accommodations are allowed on the assessment(s)?
- Are the accommodations approved for the assessment also used in the classroom?
- Has the student received standards-based, grade-level instruction?
- Was the instruction evidence based?
- What is the student's instructional level?
- How different is the student's instructional level from the level of typical peers?
- Can the student make progress toward grade-level standards in the same time frame as typical peers? (If no, consider modified academic achievement standards.)
- What can be learned from the student's previous state assessment results?
- Can the student demonstrate what he or she knows on the assessment option under consideration?

• APPLYING THE 6-STEP PROCESS TO A CASE STUDY

Applying Steps 1 and 2 for Kimi (Consider the grade-level content standards and examine classroom and student data.)

Steps 1 and 2 constitute the initial planning for the IEP. After completing the first two steps, the IEP team will have information that can be synthesized into a description of the student. Some states include student profiles as part of the IEP document, but such descriptions are not a requirement under IDEA. It is necessary, however, for the IEP team to develop a picture of grade-level expectations and know where each student is functioning in relation to those expectations.

Kimi: Grade 8

The IEP team, including Kimi's father, spent time reviewing their state's content standards. They were interested in learning specifically what Kimi was expected to know in each subject area (Step 1). The team recognized that it was important to compare what Kimi was expected to know in each content area with her present level of performance. So the team reviewed the methods by which Kimi had been taught and examined whether this content was aligned with state standards. It also was important for the team to examine the methods by which data were collected about Kimi's performance to determine whether these measures were good indicators of Kimi's progress (Step 2).

Student Profile: Kimi

Kimi is an eighth-grade student who was retained in the first grade due, in part, to the difficulties she was experiencing maintaining and using information she had been taught. Kimi was found to have significant auditory processing problems that negatively affected all academic areas, particularly early literacy. A review of Kimi's previous IEPs revealed that a variety of strategies and programs have been tried over the years. Kimi began receiving speech and language services in Grade 3. She began working with an auditory trainer in the fifth grade. Currently, the speech and language pathologist provides strategies to Kimi's general education teachers. She is currently receiving a research-based reading intervention curriculum from a highly qualified teacher and also is included in language arts class with her eighth-grade peers.

The auditory processing difficulties associated with Kimi's disability have widened the gap over the years between her academic levels and the levels of typical same-age peers. According to classroom and state assessment data, her reading comprehension skills are similar to typical students in the fourth grade. Her vocabulary and word recognition skills, however, are closer to a sixth-grade level.

Kimi's parents report that she gets frustrated when she has to listen attentively for a long period of time. Her mother states that Kimi continues to become anxious when homework assignments require a lot of reading and she is not sure that she remembers all of the teacher's directions. Her parents are concerned that Kimi often forgets things they have told her to do and would like some strategies to work on at home.

Mathematics data from classroom progress monitoring indicate relative strengths in the areas of numbers and operations. Kimi has difficulty, however, generalizing the skills she learns in math class to situations in daily life. For example, she may make a perfect score on a page of math problems but be unable to decide how much each person owes when a group orders lunch and is splitting the check. Kimi's difficulty generalizing skills is also apparent in applying math concepts to science investigations and in other classes when required to analyze data.

Kimi's disability affects the amount of auditory material that she can process within a designated time frame. She can master state content standards given additional time for instruction, but she is not achieving grade-level proficiency in the time frame designated for typical peers. Because language arts, science, and social studies classes are often in lecture format and require students to read lengthy narratives, her progress in these areas is slowed.

Kimi's need for additional time is accommodated on classroom assignments and on classroom and state assessments. Kimi has learned strategies to help her retain auditory information and practices the strategies during classroom lectures and when teachers are giving assignments.

Applying Step 3 for Kimi (Develop the present level of academic achievement and functional performance.)

Kimi: Grade 8 (Reading)

Kimi enjoys reading and often selects books from the classroom library. Kimi can respond to simple fact-based comprehension questions but needs more work on applying a variety of reading comprehension strategies. Kimi's scores on state assessments place her in the "Does Not Meet Standards" category on reading comprehension. On classroom assessments, Kimi answers simple "Who, What, When, and Where" questions with 80% accuracy but experiences difficulty with making inferences to determine bias or theme and making predictions for comprehension of eighth-grade reading materials.

Kimi: Grade 8 (Math)

Kimi's state and classroom assessment data indicate computational fluency with addition, subtraction, and multiplication of integers. She can solve one- and two-step algebraic expressions on worksheets and classroom assessments. Generalizing what she has learned in mathematics, however, to real-world situations is an area of need for Kimi. She can do the computations if the problems are written as numerals and presented as math problems. It is difficult for Kimi to apply what she knows about mathematics to situations that occur in daily life. Kimi needs to learn a process for applying what she knows about the operations of math to problem situations in other disciplines and in daily life.

Applying Step 4 for Kimi (Develop measurable annual goals.)

Kimi: Grade 8 (Reading)

One measurable annual goal related to meeting Kimi's needs and a corresponding content standard:

- At the end of the 36 weeks, Kimi will use prior knowledge and personal experience to make inferences to determine bias or theme to comprehend eighth-grade materials with an average of 80% accuracy on classroom assessments.
  (8th-Grade Reading Content Standard: Students will connect their own background knowledge and personal experience to make inferences presented in text.)

Kimi: Grade 8 (Math)

One measurable annual goal related to meeting Kimi's needs and a corresponding standard:

- At the end of the fourth grading period, Kimi will apply mathematics in problem situations outside of the discipline of mathematics with 100% accuracy on 8 out of 10 problem scenarios.
  (8th-Grade Math Content Standard: Students will recognize and apply mathematics concepts outside of "mathematics" classrooms.)

Applying Step 5 for Kimi (Assess and report the student's progress throughout the year.)

Kimi: Grade 8 (Reading)

All types of assessment and report formats were considered for Kimi in the area of reading. The following were chosen:

- curriculum-based assessment,
- teacher/text test,
- state assessment(s): Kimi will participate in the alternate assessment based on modified academic achievement standards.

Kimi: Grade 8 (Math)

All types of assessment and report formats were considered for Kimi in the area of math. The following were chosen:

- curriculum-based assessment,
- data collection,
- teacher observation,
- state assessment(s): Kimi will participate in the alternate assessment based on modified academic achievement standards.

Applying Step 6 for Kimi (Identify specially designed instruction.)

Kimi: Grade 8 (Reading)

Special education and related services were considered based on the questions for Step 6. The following were decided on for Kimi in the area of reading:

- Special education services: The special education teacher will provide intensive reading instruction using a research-based reading program.
- Supplementary aids and services: Kimi will be allowed additional time for classroom assignments.
- Related services: The speech and language pathologist will consult with the general education teacher and provide strategies for classroom use.
- Accommodations needed for assessment: Kimi will be allowed additional time for classroom and state assessments.

Kimi: Grade 8 (Math)

Special education and related services were considered. The following were decided on for Kimi in the area of math:

- Special education services: The special and general education teachers will collaborate on math strategies and assignments.
- Supplementary aids and services: Kimi will be allowed additional time for classroom assignments.
- Accommodations needed: Kimi will be allowed additional time for classroom and state assessments.

Applying Step 7 for Kimi (Determine the most appropriate assessment option.)

Kimi: Grade 8

Kimi's IEP team made an assessment decision based on a review of the data. Kimi will participate in the **alternate assessment based on modified academic achievement standards.** The IEP team selected the assessment option based on the following information:

- Kimi's assigned grade level and instructional levels are several years apart. Kimi is in the eighth grade and is working on reading comprehension at the fourth-grade level.
- Her history of persistent academic concerns resulting in large gaps between her knowledge and that of typical peers.
- The differences between Kimi's skills and those of typical peers increased each year.
- Her progress toward grade-level-content standards is slower than that of typical peers.
- She is unable to achieve grade-level standards in the same time frame as typical peers.

• CONCLUDING REMARKS

Kimi received instructional support, interventions, and classroom and assessment accommodations. Kimi requires modified academic achievement standards because her instructional levels are as many as 4 years behind her typical peers. Because she does not learn as quickly as other students, Kimi falls further behind with each year of schooling. The IEP team determined that Kimi needs an alternate assessment based on modified academic achievement standards to provide useful information regarding her academic progress.

Standards establish clear expectations about what students should know and be able to do at each grade level. Educators can use innovative instructional methods to engage students in academic content, while ensuring that students are taught appropriate grade-level academic content. IEP teams must know and be able to do. With greater clarity comes opportunities for special education teachers, general education teachers, parents, and other stakeholders to share common understandings that can result in improved access to learning and, ultimately, to improved student achievement.

• INDIVIDUALIZED EDUCATION PROGRAM

STUDENT'S NAME: Kimi

DOB 8/14/1993 **SCHOOL YEAR** 2006--2007 **GRADE 8**

IEP INITIATION/DURATION DATES FROM 08/10/06 **TO** 05/23/07

• THIS IEP WILL BE IMPLEMENTED DURING THE REGULAR SCHOOL TERM UNLESS NOTED IN EXTENDED SCHOOL YEAR SERVICES

Student Profile

Kimi is an eighth-grade student who was retained in the first grade due, in part, to the difficulties she was experiencing maintaining and using information she had been taught. Kimi was found to have significant auditory processing problems that negatively affected all academic areas, particularly early literacy. A review of Kimi's IEPs revealed a variety of strategies and programs that have been tried over the years. Kimi began receiving speech and language services in Grade 3. She began working with an auditory trainer in the fifth grade. Currently, the speech and language pathologist provides strategies to Kimi's general education teachers. She is currently receiving a research-based reading intervention curriculum from a highly qualified teacher and also included in language arts class with her eighth-grade peers.

The auditory processing difficulties associated with Kimi's disability have widened the gap over the years between her academic levels and the levels of typical same-age peers. According to classroom and state assessment data, her reading comprehension skills are similar to typical students in the fourth grade. Her vocabulary and word recognition skills, however, are closer to a sixth-grade level.

Kimi's parents report that she gets frustrated when she has to listen attentively for a long period of time. Her mother states that Kimi continues to become anxious when homework assignments require a lot of reading and she is not sure that she remembers all of the teacher's directions. Her parents are concerned that Kimi often forgets things they have told her to do and would like some strategies to work on at home.

Mathematics data from classroom progress monitoring indicate relative strengths in the areas of numbers and operations. Kimi has difficulty, however, generalizing the skills she learns in math class to situations in daily life. She may make a perfect score on a page of math problems but be unable to decide how much each person owes when a group orders lunch and is splitting the check.

Kimi's disability affects the amount of auditory material that she can process within a designated time frame. She can master state content standards given additional time for instruction, but she is not achieving grade-level proficiency in the time frame designated for typical peers. Because language arts, science, and social studies classes are often in lecture format and require that students read lengthy narratives, her progress in these areas is slowed.

Kimi's need for additional time is accommodated on classroom assignments and on classroom and state assessments. Kimi has learned strategies to help her retain auditory information and practices the strategies during classroom lectures and when teachers are giving assignments.

STUDENT'S NAME: Kimi

SPECIAL INSTRUCTIONAL FACTORS

Items checked "YES" will be addressed in this IEP:	**YES**	**NO**
• Does the student have behavior which impedes his/her learning or the learning of others?	☐	☒
• Does the student have limited English proficiency?	☐	☒
• Does the student need instruction in Braille and the use of Braille?	☐	☒
• Does the student have communication needs (deaf or hearing impaired only)?	☐	☒
• Does the student need assistive technology devices and/or services?	☐	☒
• Does the student require specially designed P.E.?	☐	☒
• Is the student working toward alternate achievement standards and participating in the Alternate Assessment? Are transition services addressed in this IEP?	☐	☒

TRANSPORTATION AS A RELATED SERVICE

Does the student require transportation as a related service?	YES ☐	NO ☒
Does the student need accommodations or modifications for transportation?	YES ☐	NO ☒

☐ If yes, check any transportation accommodations/modifications that are needed.

☐ Bus driver is aware of student's behavioral and/or medical concerns.

☐ Wheelchair lift Restraint system. Specify:

____

☐ Other. Specify:

____

NONACADEMIC AND EXTRACURRICULAR ACTIVITIES

Will the student have the opportunity to participate in nonacademic/extracurricular activities with his/her nondisabled peers?

☒ YES.

☐ YES, with supports. Describe:

____

☐ NO. Explanation must be provided:

____

METHOD/FREQUENCY FOR REPORTING PROGRESS OF ATTAINING GOALS TO PARENTS

Annual Goal Progress reports will be sent to parents each time report cards are issued (every 9.0 weeks)

STUDENT'S NAME: Kimi

AREA: Reading

• PRESENT LEVEL OF ACADEMIC ACHIEVEMENT AND FUNCTIONAL PERFORMANCE

Kimi enjoys reading and often selects books from the classroom library. Kimi can respond to simple fact-based comprehension questions but needs more work on applying a variety of reading comprehension strategies. Kimi's scores on state assessments place her in the "Does Not Meet Standards" category on reading comprehension. On classroom assessments, Kimi answers simple "Who, What, When, and Where" questions with 80% accuracy but experiences difficulty with making inferences to determine bias or theme and making predictions for comprehension of eighth-grade reading materials.

• MEASURABLE ANNUAL GOAL RELATED TO MEETING THE STUDENT'S NEEDS

At the end of 36 weeks, Kimi will use prior knowledge and personal experience to make inferences to determine bias or theme to comprehend eighth-grade reading materials with an average of 80% accuracy on classroom assessments.

(8th-Grade Reading Content Standard: Students will connect their own background knowledge and personal experience to make inferences presented in text.)

• TYPE(S) OF EVALUATION FOR ANNUAL GOAL

☒ Curriculum-Based Assessment ☒ Teacher/Text Test ☐ Teacher Observation ☐ Grades

☐ Data Collection ☒ State Assessment(s) ☐ Work Samples

Other: Kimi will participate in the alternate assessment based on modified academic achievement standards.

Other: ______________________________

• DATE OF MASTERY

BENCHMARKS:

1. Date of Mastery: ________
2. Date of Mastery: ________
3. Date of Mastery: ________
4. Date of Mastery: ________

SPECIAL EDUCATION AND RELATED SERVICE(S): (Special Education, Supplementary Aids and Services, Program Modifications, Accommodations Needed for Assessments, Related Services, Assistive Technology, and Support for Personnel.)

Type of Service(s)	*Anticipated Frequency of Service(s)*	*Amount of time*	*Beginning/ Ending Date*	*Location of Service(s)*
Special Education Special Education teacher will provide intensive reading instruction using a research-based reading program	Daily	40 mins.	08/10/06 to 05/23/07	Special Education Classroom
Supplementary Aids and Services Additional time for classroom assignments	Daily	55 mins.	08/10/06 to 05/23/07	Special and General Education Classrooms
Program Modifications			____to ____	
Accommodations Needed for Assessments Additional time for classroom and state assessment	Weekly in classrooms	55 mins.	08/10/06 to 05/23/07	Special and General Education Classrooms

Type of Service(s)	*Anticipated Frequency of Service(s)*	*Amount of time*	*Beginning/ Ending Date*	*Location of Service(s)*
Related Services Speech and Language Pathologist consults with general education teacher to provide strategies	Biweekly in classrooms	30 mins.	8/10/06 to 5/23/07	General Education Classrooms
Assistive Technology			____to __	
Support for Personnel			____to ____	

● INDIVIDUALIZED EDUCATION PROGRAM

STUDENT'S NAME: Kimi

AREA: Math

Present Level of Academic Achievement and Functional Performance

Kimi's state and classroom assessment data indicate computational fluency with addition, subtraction, and multiplication of integers. She can solve one- and two-step algebraic expressions on worksheets and classroom assessments. Generalizing what she has learned in mathematics, however, to real-world situations is an area of need for Kimi. She can do the computations if the problems are written as numerals and presented as math problems. It is difficult for Kimi to apply what she knows about mathematics to situations that occur in daily life. Kimi needs to learn a process for applying what she knows about the operations of math to problem situations in other disciplines and in daily life.

● MEASURABLE ANNUAL GOAL RELATED TO MEETING THE STUDENT'S NEEDS

At the end of the fourth grading period, Kimi will apply mathematics in problem situations outside of the discipline of mathematics with 100% accuracy on 8 out of 10 problem scenarios.

(8th-Grade Math Content Standard: Students will recognize and apply mathematics concepts outside of mathematics" classrooms.)

● TYPE(S) OF EVALUATION FOR ANNUAL GOAL

☒ Curriculum Based Assessment ☐ Teacher/Text Test ☒ Teacher Observation ☐ Grades

☒ Data Collection ☒ State Assessment(s) ☐ Work Samples

Other: Kimi will participate in the alternate assessment based on modified academic achievement standards.

Other: ______________________________

● DATE OF MASTERY

BENCHMARKS:

1. Date of Mastery: ________

2. Date of Mastery: ________

3. Date of Mastery: ________

4. Date of Mastery: ________

SPECIAL EDUCATION AND RELATED SERVICE(S): (Special Education, Supplementary Aids and Services, Program Modifications, Accommodations Needed for Assessments, Related Services, Assistive Technology, and Support for Personnel.)

Type of Service(s)	*Anticipated Frequency of Service(s)*	*Amount of time*	*Beginning/ Ending Date*	*Location of Service(s)*
Special Education Special and General Education teachers will collaborate on reading strategies and assignments	Weekly	15 mins.	08/10/06 to 05/23/07	General Education Classroom
Supplementary Aids and Services Additional time for classroom assignments	Daily	55 mins.	08/10/06 to 05/23/07	Special and General Education Classrooms
Program Modifications			___to___	
Accommodations Needed for Assessments Additional time for classroom and state assessments	Weekly for classrooms	55 mins.	08/10/06 to 05/23/07	Special and General Education Classrooms
Related Services Speech and Language Pathologist consults with general education teacher to provide strategies	Biweekly in classrooms	30 mins.	8/10/06 to 5/23/07	General Education Classrooms
Assistive Technology			___to___	
Support for Personnel			___to___	

● INDIVIDUALIZED EDUCATION PROGRAM

STUDENT'S NAME: Kimi

GENERAL FACTORS THE IEP TEAM HAS CONSIDERED:

	YES	NO
• The strengths of the child?	☒	☐
• The concerns of the parents for enhancing the education of the child?	☒	☐
• The results of the initial or most recent evaluations of the child?	☒	☐
• As appropriate, the results of performance on any state or districtwide assessments?	☒	☐
• The academic, developmental, and functional needs of the child?	☒	☐
• The need for extended school year services?	☒	☐

● LEAST RESTRICTIVE ENVIRONMENT

Does this student attend the school (or for a preschool-age student, participate in the environment) he/she would attend if nondisabled? Yes ☒ No ☐

If no, justify:

Does this student receive all special education services with nondisabled peers? Yes ☒ No ☐

If no, justify (justification may not be solely because of needed modifications in the general curriculum): Kimi requires modifications in the general curriculum.

6-21 YEARS OF AGE ☒ **3-5 YEARS OF AGE** ☐

(Select one from the drop-down box.)

02 99% to 80% of Day Inside the Gen Ed Environment

Secondary LRE (only if LRE above is Private School-Parent Placed)

COPY OF IEP

Was a copy of the IEP given to parent at the IEP meeting? ☒ **YES** ☐ **NO**

COPY OF SPECIAL EDUCATION RIGHTS

Was a copy of the *Special Education Rights* given to parent at the IEP meeting? ☒ Yes ☐ No

If no, date sent to parent: ________ If no, date sent to parent: ________

Date copy of **amended** IEP provided/sent to parent ________

THE FOLLOWING PEOPLE ATTENDED AND PARTICIPATED IN THE MEETING TO DEVELOP THIS IEP

Position	*Signature*	*Date*
Parent		
Parent		
LEA Representative		
Special Education Teacher		
General Education Teacher		
Student		
Career/Technical Education Rep		
Other Agency Representative		

INFORMATION FROM PEOPLE NOT IN ATTENDANCE

Position	*Name*	*Date*

Activity: At your field experience site, work with your site supervisor on reviewing IEPs for students on his/her caseload. Complete the IEP form used at your site.

REFERENCES

American School Counselor Association. (2013). *The school counselor and students with disabilities* [Position statement]. Retrieved from https://www.schoolcounselor.org/asca/media/asca/PositionStatements/PS_Disabilities.pdf

Council for Accreditation for Counseling and Related Program. (2014). *2016 standards.* Retrieved from www.cacrep.org

Holbrook, M. D. (2007, August). *Standards-based individualized education program examples.* Retrieved from http://www.nasdse.org/portals/0/standards-basediepexamples.pdf

Masters in Psychology and Counseling Accreditation Council. (2015). *Accreditation manual.* Retrieved from http://www.mpcacaccreditation.org/about/accreditation-manual

Lesson 26

HOW TO WRITE A 504 PLAN

"I have to actually write a 504?"

Parent Phone Call

"Joshua's diabetes is acting up and he is in the hospital. He'll probably be in the hospital for another day or two. He is worried because he doesn't want to fall behind in his schoolwork. You know how much he dreads having to make up missed work. Is there a way we can work with his teachers so that he won't have to do all the homework? Also, the doctors mentioned that his routine will have to change quite a bit in order to stabilize his numbers. How do I go about communicating that to all of his teachers?"

Counselor: "Hi, Joan. I'm sorry to hear about Josh. He is such a great kid and works so hard. We haven't discussed this before because he hasn't needed one, but it sounds like putting a plan into place would be helpful. There is a process to help students who have chronic conditions like diabetes. Let's meet and I can explain the 504 process to you. I know it will be very helpful to both of you."

Lesson Twenty-Six

How to Write a 504 Plan

"I have to actually write a 504?"

Essential Question: How do I write a comprehensive and accurate 504 Plan?

Objectives

Students will

- demonstrate the ability to write a 504 Plan.
- demonstrate knowledge of interventions to promote academic development and increase promotion and graduation rates.
- demonstrate use of collaboration in meeting students' needs.

CACREP 2016 Standards

- Core curriculum design, lesson plan development, classroom management strategies, and differentiated instructional strategies (5.G.3.c)
- Interventions to promote academic development (5.G.3.d)
- Approaches to increase promotion and graduation rates (5.G.3.i)
- Strategies to promote equity in student achievement and college access (5.G.3.k)
- Techniques to foster collaboration and teamwork within schools (5.G.3.l)
- Strategies for implementing and coordinating peer interventions programs (5.G.3.m)

MPCAC Standards

- Assessment of human behavior and organizational/community/institutional systems
- Ecological, contextual, multicultural, social-justice foundations of human development
- Tests and measurements
- Traditional and social-justice-oriented research and evaluations

Video Spark

https://www.youtube.com/watch?v=pMK6cab3LRM

Why It's Good to Have a 504 Plan

● INTRODUCTION

The role of the school counselor is gaining clarity through the efforts of American School Counselor Association (ASCA) and school counselors across the states and evolving with the needs of each school district. One responsibility not previous in the prevue of the school counselor was writing 504 Plans. However, current practice and research support the occurrence of this phenomenon (Hamlet, Gergar, & Schaeffer, 2011). The responsibility of writing and monitoring 504 Plans has become part of the role of the school counselor in many districts. In light of this shift, it is essential that counselor education programs prepare students for this task. This chapter will briefly review the purpose of the Section 504 regulation, address the prevalence and need for 504 Plans, and provide information on how to write a 504 Plan while keeping in mind that the requirements will vary from state to state.

● SECTION 504 OF THE REHABILITATION ACT OF 1973

Section 504 ensures that students with disabilities have ***access*** to a free appropriate public education (FAPE). The 504 Section of the Rehabilitation Act states "No otherwise qualified individual with a disability . . . shall solely by reason of her and his disability, be excluded from the participation in, be denied the benefits of, or be subjected to discrimination under any program or activity receiving Federal financial assistance" (29 U.S.C. § 794). The prevalence of students needing 504 Plans is high and increasing. The Department of Education's Office of Civil Rights reports that 433,908 students across the United States have 504 plans (U.S. Department of Education, 2013). To illustrate the need and complexities of students needing 504 Plans, this lesson will address students with chronic illness.

"Joshua is sick and in the hospital. They don't know what's wrong. He'll probably be in the hospital for another day or two. I'm worried and we don't want him to fall behind in his school work."

Although nothing about an initial contact with a parent or caregiver of an ill child is typical, these are often the words school counselors will first hear. This is a frightening situation for parents, as their child is now in the health care system, an unfamiliar system in which parents have little or no control. Reaching out to the school is an understandable effort to "do something" in a more familiar and accessible environment. Early parent–counselor communication can provide support to the parent while building the foundation for future collaboration.

Interactions of this nature are occurring with greater frequency. As professional school counselors, what is our role and how do we best meet the needs of these students and families? As the incidence rate of chronic illness in children rises, the responsibilities and complexities of the role of the school counselor must expand to include this growing population. Although the majority of children in the United States are considered healthy, approximately 31% of school-age children are living with chronic illness (Centers for Disease Control and Prevention [CDC], 2015). With advancements in health care and emphasis on having students return to their normal routine, children with chronic illness are increasingly coping with both the challenges of their illness and the demands of a typical school day (Van Cleave, Gortmaker, & Perrin, 2010). The difficulties incurred while coping with chronic illness impact students' academic, social, and emotional development, thereby making the role of the school counselor even more complex.

Support for children facing these issues is within the realm of the entire school community. Leading the effort within this community is the school counselor.

As community leaders, school counselors initiate the support process through collaboration with the various professionals in the student's life and by providing responsive services to the student, the student's family, and the community. The American School Counselor Association's (2012) National Model provides the framework for the role of school counselors that includes providing responsive services that support students' academic, career, and social-emotional development. These responsive services encompass consultation, individual and group counseling, crisis counseling, referrals, and peer facilitation (ASCA, 2012). Students with chronic illnesses such as asthma, diabetes, epilepsy, allergies, cardiac conditions, and Addison's disease are in need of many, if not all, of these services (Van Cleave et al., 2010). Additionally, due to the nature of chronic illness, the services required may change frequently and must therefore be evaluated continuously in order to keep current with the fluctuations in a student's health.

Meeting the changing needs of this diverse student population calls for the use of a holistic, developmental, and systemic approach. Using the developmental systems theory, counselors can address the life stage and development of these students within the context of the various systems in their world (Lerner, 2005). This approach is especially salient when working with students with chronic illness.

Once a student becomes chronically ill, the number of systems in his or her world can expand exponentially within a matter of days due in large part to the additional health care systems. Furthermore, individual student characteristics, the unique nature of the illness, the developmental stage of the child, the phase of the illness, and the interaction of these different variables top the long list of potential developmental, systemic, and contextual factors affecting student adjustment. Subsequently, addressing the needs of these students demands a significant degree of cooperation and collaboration among the systems in the student's life, with a keen awareness of and sensitivity to developmental factors (Powers, DuPaul, Shapiro, & Kazak, 2003).

Educating the whole child is a concept that emphasizes the need to provide students with an educational community that has the resources and personnel to meet their academic, social, emotional, and physical needs. The notion of educating the whole child has a substantial history in the field of American education and can be traced as far back as John Dewey in the early 20th century (Sidorsky, 1977). Support for this concept is evidenced through House Resolution 1093, currently before the United States Senate, that designates March as "National Whole Child Month." Educating the whole child, by definition, incorporates the expertise of multiple professionals involved in the student's life. Meeting the comprehensive needs of students with chronic illness takes this call for action to a higher standard.

The fields of education and health care embrace this holistic approach to meeting the complex needs of students with chronic illness. ASCA's position statement (2013) indicates the professional school counselor advocates for students with special needs, participates in the multidisciplinary team, and collaborates with the family and other professionals involved in the child's life. ASCA's statement clearly represents the importance of the counselor's role in supporting students with chronic illness while highlighting the team approach and need for collaboration among all members of the school community. Hence, the school counselor's role when working with students with chronic illness includes writing 504 Plans, coordinating appropriate services, and collaborating with other school, community, and health professionals.

This collaborative team determines whether a student is eligible for a 504 Plan. Specifically, an individual qualifies for a 504 Plan if the individual is diagnosed with a physical or mental disability, has a record or history of a disability, or is regarded as having a disability, **and** that disability ***substantially limits a major life activity***. The Americans with Disabilities Act Amendments Act of 2008 (ADAAA) Section 504 does not provide an exhaustive list of major life activities. However, examples of major life activities for a child in school are learning, sitting, standing, walking, talking, and self-care.

"Substantially limits a major life activity" means limiting an individual when compared with people in the general population. A major life activity does not have to be severely or significantly limited to be considered substantially limited. The United States Equal Opportunity Commission indicates that the concept of "substantially limited" should be construed broadly with the primary focus on avoiding discrimination of an individual with a disability.

Additionally, ADAAA prohibits consideration of the ameliorative effects of "mitigating measures" when assessing whether an impairment substantially limits a person's major life activities with one exception. For example, the use of a medication cannot be considered when assessing the impact of an individual's disability; however, the exception to this rule is the use of eye glasses or contacts (U.S. Department of Labor, 2009).

• 504 PLANS: STEPS IN THE PROCESS

Section 504 regulations require a multidisciplinary team approach to making a determination about eligibility for a 504 Plan. The team is made up of people who are familiar with the student and knowledgeable about the assessment process and services.

Step 1: The Referral. The referral may be generated by an educator, parent, or other appropriate individual (e.g., physician). Dependent on the state and local regulations, the referral may be sent to the school counselor (if they are overseeing the 504 process). If the referral is not from the parent, school districts should contact the parent to let them know that their child has been referred to the 504 Team. (See Appendix A.)

Step 2: Assessment. The multidisciplinary team gathers information on the student from a variety of sources (e.g., teachers, parents, doctor's notes, attendance records, state testing, and academic records). If additional information and assessments (that are not in the student's file) are needed to make an eligibility determination, parental consent is required.

Step 3: Written Notice. The school representation (e.g., school counselor, 504 coordinator) will send out a notification to the parents and the multidisciplinary team about the 504 meeting to be held in order to determine if the student is eligible for services under Section 504. (See Appendix B.)

Step 4: Parental rights. At this meeting, the parents will be given information on their rights in the 504 process.

Step 5: Determine eligibility. The team meets to determine if the student is eligible for services under Section 504. The team must determine if the student has a disability that is substantially limiting a major life activity (National Association of School Psychologists, www.nasponline.org).

Step 6: Write the 504 Plan. Once the student has been identified as eligible for a 504 Plan or an Individual Accommodation Plan (IAP), the team develops identified accommodations that will meet the student's needs. The accommodations are designed to provide the student with equal access to a free and appropriate education (FAPE) and extracurricular activities that the student is otherwise qualified to participate. (See Appendix C and Appendix D.)

Step 7: Disseminate information. If a child is identified as eligible for services under Section 504, the information regarding accommodations should be provided to the appropriate school personnel. Additionally, clarification of the accommodations should be provided as needed.

Step 8: Monitor and Revise. The school representative in charge of 504 plans will monitor the implementation of the plan. If revisions are needed, a 504 meeting will be held to review and determine how best to meet the student's needs.

Activity: The American Diabetes Association has comprehensively prepared a 504 Plan for a student with diabetes. Read this 504 Plan and develop one for a student at your site. Share this draft of a 504 Plan with your site supervisor. (See Appendix E.)

● REFERENCES

American Diabetes Association. (2012). *Written care plans: Section 504 plan*. Retrieved from http://www.diabetes.org/living-with-diabetes/parents-and-kids/diabetes-care-at-school/written-care-plans/section-504-plan.html

American School Counselor Association. (2012). *The ASCA National Model: A framework for school counseling programs* (3rd ed.). Alexandria, VA: Author.

American School Counselor Association. (2013). *The school counselor and students with disabilities* [Position statement]. Retrieved from https://www.schoolcounselor.org/asca/media/asca/PositionStatements/PS_Disabilities.pdf

Centers for Disease Control and Prevention. (2015). *Chronic conditions*. Retrieved from http://www.hhs.gov/ash/oah/adolescent-health-topics/physical-health-and-nutrition/chronic-conditions.html#

Council for Accreditation for Counseling and Related Program. (2014). *2016 standards*. Retrieved from http://www.cacrep.org

Hamlet, H., Gergar, P., & Schaeffer, B. (2011). Working with chronically ill children: The role of the school counselor. *Professional School Counselor, 14*(3), 202–210.

Lerner, R. M. (2005). *Promoting positive youth development: Theoretical and empirical bases* (White paper). Retrieved from http://ase.tufts.edu/iaryd/documents/pubpromotingpositive.pdf

Masters in Psychology and Counseling Accreditation Council. (2015). *Accreditation manual.* Retrieved from http://www.mpcacaccreditation.org/about/accreditation-manual

National Association of School Psychologists: https://www.nasponline.org/

Powers, T. J., DuPaul, G. J., Shapiro, E. S., & Kazak, A. E. (2003). *Promoting children's health: Integrating school, family and community.* New York, NY: Guilford Press.

Sidorsky, D. (Ed.). (1977). *John Dewey: The essential writings.* New York, NY: HarperCollins.

U.S. Department of Education. (2013). *High schools and career readiness: Strengthening the pipeline to the middle class.* Retrieved from http://www.ed.gov/highschool

U.S. Department of Labor. (2009). *Americans with Disabilities Act Amendments Act of 2008.* Retrieved from http://www.access-board.gov/the-board/laws/americans-with-disabilities-act-intro

Van Cleave, J., Gortmaker, S. L., & Perrin, J. M. (2010). Dynamics of obesity and chronic health conditions among children and youth. *Journal of the American Medical Association, 303,* 623–630.

APPENDIX A

SAMPLE: 504 Referral form

Student Name: ______________________________ **Grade:** ______________

Referral Source: ______________________________ **Date:** ______________

REFERRAL INFORMATION

In order to be referred for a 504 Plan, a student must be suspected of having a physical or mental impairment that may substantially limit a major life activity when compared to the average student.

Please specify the major life activity and suspected limitations:

____

____

____

____

____

____

____

Major life activity: The ADAAA Section 504 does not provide an exhaustive list of major life activities. However, examples of major life activities for a child in school are learning, sitting, standing, walking, talking, and self-care.

Substantially limits: "Substantially limits a major life activity" means limiting an individual when compared with people in the general population. A major life activity does not have to be severely or significantly limited to be considered substantially limited. The United States Equal Opportunity Commission indicates that the concept of "substantially limited" should be construed broadly with the primary focus on avoiding discrimination of an individual with a disability.

● APPENDIX B

SAMPLE 504 Determination of Eligibility Meeting Form

Student:____ **Grade:**______________

Date of Birth: ____

____ **Initial Meeting** ____ **Annual Review Date:** ____________________________________

A. Referral Information Summary:

____

____

____

____

____

____

B. Sources of evaluation information (check each one used):

Family interview		School health information	
Review of school records		Medical reports	
Standardized testing		Other	
Response to Intervention data		Other	
Teacher/Administrator/Staff reports		Other	
Disciplinary records		Other	

C. Mitigating measures: None______ Yes, described below _____

____

____

____

____

D. Indicate the ***major life activity*** that is being substantially limited: (e.g., walking, reading, learning, concentrating, breathing, eating, lifting)

____

____

____

____

E. Determination of Eligibility: Based on the analysis of the evaluation data, does the student have a disability that is substantially limiting a major life activity?

____ Yes, the student is eligible for services under Section 504.

____ No, the student is not eligible for services under Section 504.

Name/Signatures Position Date

● DEFINITIONS

Major life activity: The ADAAA Section 504 does not provide an exhaustive list of major life activities. However, examples of major life activities for a child in school are learning, sitting, standing, walking, talking, and self-care.

Substantially limits: Substantially limits a major life activity means limiting an individual when compared with people in the general population. A major life activity does not have to be severely or significantly limited to be considered substantially limited. The United States Equal Opportunity Commission indicates that the concept of "substantially limited" should be construed broadly with the primary focus on avoiding discrimination of an individual with a disability.

● APPENDIX C

SAMPLE 504 Plan

Student: ______________________________ **Grade:** ______________

Date of Birth: ______________________________

Strengths:

____

____

____

Weaknesses:

____

____

____

Accommodation	*Person Responsible*	*Notes*

● APPENDIX D

SAMPLE 504 Plan

DEVELOPED BY THE AMERICAN DIABETES ASSOCIATION (ADA) AND THE DISABILITY RIGHTS AND DEFENSE FUND, INC. (DREDF, 2015)

MODEL 504 PLAN FOR A STUDENT WITH DIABETES

[NOTE: This model 504 Plan lists a broad range of services and accommodations that might be needed by a child with diabetes in school. The plan should be individualized to meet the needs, abilities, and medical condition of each student and should *include only those items in the model that are relevant to that student*. Some students will need additional services and accommodations that have not been included in this model plan.]

Section 504 Plan for ______________________________

School ______________________________ School Year: ______________

TYPE ____ DIABETES (DISABILITY)

Student's Name ______________________ Birth Date ______________________ Grade ________________

Homeroom Teacher: __________________________ Bus Number: _________________________________

Objectives/Goals of This Plan

Diabetes can cause blood glucose (sugar) levels to be too high or too low, both of which affect the student's ability to learn as well as seriously endangering the student's health both immediately and in the long term. The goal of this plan is to provide the special education and/or related aids and services needed to maintain blood glucose within this student's target range and to respond appropriately to levels outside of this range in accordance with the instructions provided by the student's personal health care team.

REFERENCES

- School accommodations, diabetes care, and other services set out by this Plan will be consistent with the information and protocols contained in the National Diabetes Education Program *Helping the Student with Diabetes Succeed: A Guide for School Personnel*, June 2010.

DEFINITIONS USED IN THIS PLAN

1. ***Diabetes Medical Management Plan (DMMP)*:** A plan that describes the diabetes care regimen and identifies the health care needs of a student with diabetes. This plan is developed and approved by the student's personal health care team and family. Schools must do outreach to the parents and child's health care provider if a DMMP is not submitted by the family **[Note: School districts may have other names for the plan. If so, substitute the appropriate terminology throughout.]**
2. ***Quick Reference Emergency Plan:*** A plan that provides school personnel with essential information on how to recognize and treat hypoglycemia and hyperglycemia.
3. ***Trained Diabetes Personnel (TDP)*:** Non-medical school personnel who have been identified by the school nurse, school administrator, and parent who are willing to be trained in basic diabetes knowledge and have received training coordinated by the school nurse in diabetes care, including the performance of blood glucose monitoring, insulin and glucagon administration, recognition and treatment of hypoglycemia and hyperglycemia, and performance of ketone checks, and who will perform these diabetes care tasks in the absence of a school nurse.

1. PROVISION OF DIABETES CARE

1.1. At least _______ staff members will receive training to be Trained Diabetes Personnel (TDP), and either a school nurse or TDP will be available at the site where the student is **at all times** during school hours, during extracurricular activities, and on school sponsored field trips to provide diabetes care in accordance with this Plan and as directed in the DMMP, including performing or overseeing administration of insulin or other diabetes medications (which, for pump users includes programming and troubleshooting the student's insulin pump), blood glucose monitoring, ketone checks, and responding to hyperglycemia and hypoglycemia including administering glucagon.

1.2. Any staff member who is not a TDP and who has primary care for the student at any time during school hours, extracurricular activities, or during field trips shall receive training that will include a general overview of diabetes and typical health care needs of a student with diabetes, recognition of high and low blood glucose levels, and how and when to immediately contact either a school nurse or a TDP.

1.3. Any bus driver who transports the student must be informed of symptoms of high or low blood glucose levels and provided with a copy of the student's Quick Reference Emergency Plan and be prepared to act in accordance with that Plan.

● TRAINED DIABETES PERSONNEL

The following school staff members will be trained to become TDPs by ______________________ (date).

____

____

____

____

STUDENT'S LEVEL OF SELF-CARE AND LOCATION OF SUPPLIES AND EQUIPMENT

3.1 As stated in the attached DMMP:

(a) The student is able to perform the following diabetes care tasks without help or supervision:

____

____

____

and the student will be permitted to provide this self-care at any time and in any location at the school, at field trips, at sites of extracurricular activities, and on school buses.

(b) The student needs assistance or supervision with the following diabetes health care tasks:

____

____

____

(c) The student needs a school nurse or TDP to perform the following tasks:

____

____

____

3.2 The student will be permitted to carry the following diabetes supplies and equipment with him/her at all times and in all locations.

____

____

____

3.3 Diabetes supplies and equipment that are not kept on the student and additional supplies will be kept at:

____

____

____

____

4.1 The school nurse or TDP, if school nurse is not available, will work with the student and his/her parents/guardians to coordinate a meal and snack schedule in accordance with the attached DMMP that will coincide with the schedule of classmates to the closest extent possible. The student shall eat lunch at the same time each day or earlier if experiencing hypoglycemia. The student shall have enough time to finish lunch. A snack and quick-acting source of glucose must always be immediately available to the student.

4.2 The attached DMMP sets out the regular time(s) for snacks, what constitutes a snack, and when the student should have additional snacks. The student will be permitted to eat a snack no matter where the student is.

4.3 The parent/guardian will supply snacks needed in addition to or instead of any snacks supplied to all students.

4.4 The parent/guardian will provide carbohydrate content information for snacks and meals brought from home.

4.5 The school nurse or TDP will ensure that the student takes snacks and meals at the specified time(s) each day.

4.6 Adjustments to snack and meal times will be permitted in response to changes in schedule upon request of parent/guardian.

● EXERCISE AND PHYSICAL ACTIVITY

5.1 The student shall be permitted to participate fully in physical education classes and team sports except as set out in the student's DMMP.

5.2 Physical education instructors and sports coaches must have a copy of the emergency action plan and be able to recognize and assist with the treatment of low blood glucose levels.

5.3 Responsible school staff members will make sure that the student's blood glucose meter, a quick-acting source of glucose, and water are always available at the site of physical education class and team sports practices and games.

• WATER AND BATHROOM ACCESS

6.1 The student shall be permitted to have immediate access to water by keeping a water bottle in the student's possession and at the student's desk, and by permitting the student to use the drinking fountain without restriction.

6.2 The student shall be permitted to use the bathroom without restriction.

• 7. CHECKING BLOOD GLUCOSE LEVELS, INSULIN AND MEDICATION ADMININSTRATION, AND TREATING HIGH OR LOW BLOOD GLUCOSE LEVELS

7.1 The student's level of self-care is set out in Section 3 above including which tasks the student can do by himself/herself and which must be done with the assistance of, or wholly by, either a school nurse or a TDP.

7.2 Blood glucose monitoring will be done at the times designated in the student's DMMP, whenever the student feels her/his blood glucose level may be high or low, or when symptoms of high or low blood glucose levels are observed.

7.3 Insulin and/or other diabetes medication will be administered at the times and through the means (e.g., syringe, pen, or pump) designated in the student's DMMP for both scheduled doses and doses needed to correct for high blood glucose levels.

7.4 The student shall be provided with privacy for blood glucose monitoring and insulin administration if the student desires.

7.5 The student's usual symptoms of high and low blood glucose levels and how to respond to these levels are set out in the attached DMMP.

7.6 When the student asks for assistance or any staff member believes the student is showing signs of high or low blood glucose levels, the staff member will immediately seek assistance from the school nurse or TDP while making sure an adult stays with the student at all times. Never send a student with actual—or suspected—high or low blood glucose levels anywhere alone.

7.7 Any staff member who finds the student unconscious will immediately contact the school office. The office will immediately do the following in the order listed:

1. **Contact the school nurse or a TDP (if the school nurse is not on site and immediately available) who will confirm the blood glucose level with a monitor and immediately administer glucagon (glucagon should be administered if no monitor is available);**

2. **Call 911 (office staff will do this without waiting for the school nurse or TDP to administer glucagon); and**

3. **Contact the student's parent/guardian and physician at the emergency numbers provided below.**

7.8 School staff including physical education instructors and coaches will provide a safe location for the storage of the student's insulin pump if the student chooses not to wear it during physical activity or any other activity.

8. FIELD TRIPS AND EXTRACURRICULAR ACTIVITIES

8.1 The student will be permitted to participate in all school-sponsored field trips and extracurricular activities (such as sports, clubs, and enrichment programs) without restriction and with all of the accommodations and modifications, including necessary supervision by identified school personnel, set out in this Plan. The student's parent/guardian will not be required to accompany the student on field trips or any other school activity.

8.2 The school nurse or TDP will be available on site at all school-sponsored field trips and extracurricular activities, will provide all usual aspects of diabetes care (including, but not limited to, blood glucose monitoring, responding to hyperglycemia and hypoglycemia, providing snacks and access to water and the bathroom, and administering insulin and glucagon), and will make sure that the student's diabetes supplies travel with the student.

9. TESTS AND CLASSROOM WORK

9.1 If the student is affected by high or low blood glucose levels at the time of regular testing, the student will be permitted to take the test at another time without penalty.

9.2 If the student needs to take breaks to use the water fountain or bathroom, check blood glucose, or to treat hypoglycemia or hyperglycemia during a test or other activity, the student will be given extra time to finish the test or other activity without penalty.

9.3 The student shall be given instruction to help him/her make up any classroom instruction missed due to diabetes care without penalty.

9.4 The student shall not be penalized for absences required for medical appointments and/or for illness. The parent will provide documentation from the treating health care professional if otherwise required by school policy.

10. COMMUNICATION

10.1 The school nurse, TDP, and other staff will keep the student's diabetes confidential, except to the extent that the student decides to openly communicate about it with others.

10.2 Encouragement is essential. The student should be treated in a way that encourages the student to eat snacks on time and to progress toward self-care with his/her diabetes management skills.

10.3 The teacher, school nurse, or TDP will provide reasonable notice to parent/guardian when there will be a change in planned activities such as exercise, playground time, field trips, parties, or lunch schedule, so that the lunch, snack plan, and insulin dosage can be adjusted accordingly.

10.4 Each substitute teacher and substitute school nurse will be provided with written instructions regarding the student's diabetes care and a list of all school nurses and TDP at the school.

11. EMERGENCY EVACUATION AND SHELTER-IN-PLACE

11.1 In the event of emergency evacuation or shelter-in-place situation, the student's 504 Plan and DMMP will remain in full force and effect.

11.2 The school nurse or TDP will provide diabetes care to the student as outlined by this Plan and the student's DMMP, will be responsible for transporting the student's diabetes supplies and equipment, will attempt to establish contact with the student's parents/guardians and provide updates, and will receive information from parents/guardians regarding the student's diabetes care.

12. PARENTAL NOTIFICATION

12.1 ***NOTIFY PARENTS/GUARDIANS IMMEDIATELY IN THE FOLLOWING SITUATIONS:***

- Symptoms of severe low blood sugar such as continuous crying, extreme tiredness, seizure, or loss of consciousness.
- The student's blood glucose test results are below ________ or are below ________ 15 minutes after consuming juice or glucose tablets.
- Symptoms of severe high blood sugar such as frequent urination, presence of ketones, vomiting, or blood glucose level above ____________.
- The student refuses to eat or take insulin injection or bolus.
- Any injury.
- Insulin pump malfunctions cannot be remedied.
- Other:____

12.2 **EMERGENCY CONTACT INSTRUCTIONS**

Call parent/guardian at numbers listed below. If unable to reach parent/guardian, call the other emergency contacts or student's health care providers listed on next page.

EMERGENCY CONTACTS

______________________	____________	____________	____________
Parent's/Guardian's Name	Home Phone #	Work Phone #	Cell Phone #
______________________	____________	____________	____________
Parent's/Guardian's Name	Home Phone #	Work Phone #	Cell Phone #

Other emergency contacts:

______________________	____________	____________	____________
Name	Home Phone #	Work Phone #	Cell Phone #
______________________	____________	____________	____________
Name	Home Phone #	Work Phone #	Cell Phone #

Student's Health Care Provider(s)

______________________________	__________________
Name	Phone Number
______________________________	__________________
Name	Phone Number

This Plan shall be reviewed and amended at the beginning of each school year or more often if necessary.

Approved and received:

____	______________________
Parent/Guardian	Date

Approved and received:

____	______________________
School Administrator and Title	Date
____________________________________	______________________
School Nurse	Date

PART VI

POSTSECONDARY TRANSITIONS

Lesson 27

POSTSECONDARY TRANSITIONS

"I have no idea what I want to do after high school."

Real Life

Student: "I am starting my senior year and I still have no idea what I would like to do after high school. My parents are telling me that I should just go right to college, but I don't feel ready. I do all right in school, but I do not want to continue another 4 years; it is just too much. I have heard that some people go on to do a gap year when they take a year off before they go to college."

Counselor-in-Training: "It sounds like you are feeling uncertain of what your next step is, and you are afraid to tell you parents that you might not want to go to college right away. Why don't we look at what you are interested in and go from there. What do you think about exploring those options and when you feel ready, we can bring that discussion to your parents?"

Lesson Twenty-Seven

Postsecondary Transitions

"I have no idea what I want to do after high school."

Essential Question: What is postsecondary transitioning and how do I do it?

Objectives

Students will

- demonstrate an understanding of the multiple career and college options available to students.
- demonstrate knowledge of career, college, and educational paths.
- understand career development and related life factors.
- understand career, avocational, educational, occupational, and labor market information resources and career information systems.
- understand interrelationships among and between work, family, and other life roles and factors, including the role of multicultural issues in career development.
- demonstrate knowledge of career and educational planning, placement, follow-up, and evaluation.

CACREP 2016 Standards

- Implement interventions used to promote college and career readiness (5.G.3.j)
- Demonstrate knowledge of assessments specific to P–12 education (5.G.1.c)
- Implement strategies to promote equity in student achievement and college access (5.G.3.k)
- Demonstrate knowledge of school counselors' role in relation to college and career readiness (5.G.2.c)
- Implements interventions to promote academic development (5.G.3.d)
- Use developmentally appropriate career counseling interventions and assessments (5.G.3.e)
- Implement approaches to increase promotion and graduation rates (5.G.3.i)

MPCAC Standards

- Career and life development

Video Spark

https://www.youtube.com/watch?v=AcNSpKX8kVs

Success in the New Economy by Kevin Fleming (Brainpower Task Force)

INTRODUCTION

Reach Higher (2016), an initiative of the First Lady Michele Obama, highlights the need for students to understand and be prepared for the requirements of today's work world. This initiative is "the First Lady's effort to inspire every student in America to take charge of their future by completing their education past high school, whether at a professional training program, a community college, or a four-year college or university. In today's economy, a high school diploma just isn't enough. Students have to reach higher, which is why the first lady is working to rally the country around the President's 'North Star' goal—that by 2020, America will once again have the highest proportion of college graduates in the world." Reach Higher places great emphasis on the need for comprehensive postsecondary transition planning for students and highlights the role of school counselors in this process.

Importantly, the National College Access Network (2016) reports, "In today's economy, a postsecondary credential is in greater demand than ever before. By 2020, 65 percent of U.S. jobs will require some form of postsecondary education, but only 39 percent of U.S. working-age adults hold a postsecondary credential as of 2012. Postsecondary education is also increasingly the only route to upward mobility. The lowest income Americans who obtain a college degree are five times more likely than their peers to escape poverty."

According to the National Center for Educational Statistics (NCES), approximately 3.1 million students are expected to graduate from high school in 2014–2015 (NCES, 2015). Changes in the workplace are "requiring higher levels of achievement and preparation for the emerging workforce" (Association for Career and Technological Education, 2008). As students leave high school, they must be better informed and better educated about the possibilities in their future; they need to be college and career ready (Gysbers, 2013, p. 283). Counseling for postsecondary transitioning may focus on college counseling, career counseling, life-skills development, technical training, and various other paths open to students (e.g., a gap year). This lesson addresses the multiple and varied options for students as they graduate high school.

What does a college- and career-ready student look like? According to Norman C. Gysbers (2013), "they have the knowledge, skills, and dispositions to visualize and plan their futures . . . [and] know how to engage in various current and potential life roles, including being a learner and worker" (p. 284). College- and career-ready students are knowledgeable on a broad range of topics. From filing for financial assistance and writing essay papers to writing resumes and filling out job applications, college- and career-ready students are able to complete these tasks skillfully. They are skilled learners who are able to function both in the higher level classroom and as an employee.

Career counseling further helps students to accomplish readiness for real-world activities with the aid of guidelines. State standards and guidelines for career counseling often assist professional school counselors in defining processes and programs designed to help students recognize individual interests and abilities. Students are assisted in identifying changing societal roles and how these roles effect career choices and identify the training and education required to pursue specific career paths.

In addition to state standards, the National Career Development Association published the National Career Development Guidelines (NCDG) in 1989. The NCDG "were written . . . to specifically define the career development tasks most appropriate for elementary, middle, and high school students" (Anctil, Smith, Schenck, & Dahir, 2012, p. 110). These guidelines help to define career counseling goals and provide a framework for current career counseling standards. With these guidelines and goals in place, professional school counselors are able to tailor their curriculum to meet the needs of their students.

• THE POSTSECONDARY TRANSITION PROCESS

What Is It?

Postsecondary transition is the process of preparing students to leave the world of school and transition into the adult world of work. Assisting students in preparing for the future is a vital role of the professional school counselor. Best practice indicates that the postsecondary transition process should begin as early as in the elementary school. Postsecondary transition information should also be presented in a developmentally appropriate format. For example, a "Getting to know your neighborhood" approach of introducing the work done by different people in the community is age appropriate. Children interact with individuals doing their job every day. However, they often do not realize that the person they are observing may be performing the tasks of a job that may be of interest in their career development. An excellent website for this is Virginia Career VIEW (www.vacareerview.org/k5/). It is an interactive site that is colorful, entertaining, and a hit with the younger students. And—it is free. Many free resources and curricula are available online to professional school counselors.

As the students move into middle school, the postsecondary transition process continues through education and the start of self-exploration of the students' interests. For example, education can take the form of "Career Day." Inviting professionals from a wide range of work roles to visit class is an important feature of this event. I recommend inviting individuals who have jobs ranging from doctor and lawyer (which require many years of education) to plumbers, carpenters, and cosmetologists (which require postsecondary training and may require apprenticeships). One successful invite for a career day was having a train conductor and the individual who takes the tickets on the train explain their work roles. This experience provided students who have little or no exposure to trains insight into an unfamiliar career. These activities help to increase student awareness that most adults they interact with on a daily basis are employed and in a work role.

At the high school level, we tend to implement a "full court press" approach. Best practice (and mandated by many states) is to begin the postsecondary transition in 9th grade. Many school districts are using computer systems (e.g., Naviance, Career Cruising) to establish a "file" for the student. The student then completes assessments identifying their interests, skills, work values, and so on. The program will then help students explore postsecondary options consistent with their interests. By 11th grade, the rubber is meeting the road and counseling for postsecondary transitioning is being fully implemented. Depending on their school district (and state regulations), there may be mandated postsecondary transition meetings with the student and the school counselor. A school counselor's knowledge of all of the postsecondary options is now crucial.

School counselors not only must have a solid grasp on the college counseling information, but they also must have a comprehensive knowledge of the other multiple and varied career options. For example, science, technology, engineering, and math education (STEM) funds are available in a multitude of ways. Counselors will want to be up to date with funding available. Once current funding is identified, the next step is to work with the student to identify if it is a good match. Student familiarity with the problem-solving aspect of STEM education is a skill that is easily generalized to a wide variety of industries. In addition, investigation of alternate work and educational opportunities is beneficial to the students. For example, a woman who enjoys working outdoors may want to consider construction work, which pays quite a bit more than a stereotypical job for a woman. Importantly, postsecondary transition is not only college counseling. It is career counseling that may include college counseling. They are not mutually exclusive. Let's look at some of the postsecondary transition options.

Postsecondary Transition Options

Work Force

School counselors must have current information on the job market, skills required, and options available to students. This requires Internet exploration of government and employment websites, networking, community consultation, and collaboration with other relevant resources. For example, exploration of "green careers" has provided me with a great deal of information and insight into careers that focus on improving the environment. In 2010, the Department of Labor proposed spending $100 million in Energy Training Partnership Grants. These funds are for green-job training programs. Examples of green jobs that do not require a degree are solar panel installer, green carpenters, organic farmers, and organic food distributors.

Thus, school counselors must also work with and empower their students to investigate the career options in which they are interested. This collaborative effort of student and educator working together provides students with the support and encouragement needed in this life transition. Working with students as they plan for their future is a privilege and can reinforce your own career choice!

Activity: What resources are available in your area?

____

____

____

Career and Technical Education (CET)

The Carl Perkins Career and Technical Education Act (2006) transformed the traditional vocational technology programs into strong academic programs that are career focused and skill based. With this act, the federal government increased its commitment to vocational education by increasing federal resources. With the implementation of this act and the emphasis of CET programs preparing students for the school-to-career transitions, there has been an increase in the types of programs available. These educational programs teach students the skills required for professions such as electrician, plumber, auto mechanic, and culinary arts. "CET is delivered through various institutions, including comprehensive high schools, shared or part time technical high schools, regional technology centers, statewide institutes, and community colleges" (American Institutes for Research, 2015, p. 4).

Participation in CET programs can begin in high school. It is important for the school counselors not only to know the programs that are available in their school district but also to visit the CTE program sites. Visiting the program sites is important for multiple reasons. One reason is that the best information a school counselor can provide is firsthand knowledge, which goes beyond the written description of the program. Further, this professional site visit gives the school counselor an idea of how the programs meet student needs and gives the counselor a "feel" for which students may thrive there. Also, knowledge of postsecondary partnerships with employers is essential information for the counselor to be able to provide to the student. Postsecondary partnerships may facilitate work-based learning experiences, apprenticeships, and internships.

Postsecondary transition to a training program for a skilled trade requires familiarity with the options available and awareness of which trades are considered growth fields. Traditional professions, such as cosmetology and automotive repairs, continue to be sought-out professions. However, thinking outside of the box increases the potential effectiveness of a school counselor's work with students. For example, nanotechnology isn't normally the first career field that comes to mind when thinking of CET programs. However, nanotechnology is a growth profession with many opportunities for individuals who have attended technology schools or certification programs. Nano.gov (2015) reports that

> in a global economy where workers face new demands and opportunities every year, the need to acquire new skills and update existing ones is vital. Nanotechnology—which is estimated to need a worldwide workforce of 2 million by 2015—offers rewarding, cutting-edge employment that touches many different areas of research, technology, and manufacturing, among others. Nanotechnology will create many jobs, at levels requiring post graduate education, four and two year college degrees, as well as skills that can be acquired through training and vocational program.

Activity: What resources are available in your area?

____

____

____

Community College

Community college is a two-year educational institution that provides student with the opportunity to receive training (as discussed above) and confers skills training, certifications, and associate's degrees. Many community colleges have partnerships with local high schools. These partnerships are known as *dual enrollment*. Students will take a college-level course while still in high school resulting in credit toward their high school diploma as well as college credits. Community outreach to the community colleges is a win-win situation. The school counselor can develop a relationship with the community college admissions officers; the students benefit from that relationship (e.g., community college admissions officers come to the high school to facilitate application process). Students benefit from dual enrollment programs, and the college benefits by increasing community awareness of their programs.

A community college degree will transfer to a four-year college or university. Many four-year educational institutions have articulation relationships with community college. This provides a transparent process for what community college courses can be transferred and accepted at these universities. In addition, students can get a two-year associates degree that prepares them to work in a specific field.

Collegeboard (2015) reports:

> Community colleges offer students the opportunity to save money, prepare for transfer to a four-year college, get ready for a career, try out college and take advantage of a flexible schedule. According to the American Association of Community Colleges, 44 percent of all undergraduate college students are enrolled at a community college. Giving your students a reality check while still in high school will increase their chances of a successful outcome once they enroll in a community college.

Activity: What resources are available in your area?

____

____

____

____

____

College

Postsecondary transition to college is an important part of the 11th- or 12th-grade educational process. School counselors work with these students to identify their interests, skills, and personality style and investigate what colleges would be a "good fit" for the student. This can be accomplished through the curriculum in a traditional classroom setting or through the computer system provided by the school district (Naviance, Career Cruising, etc.) and then followed up by face-to-face meetings with the school counselor. These meetings will help students explore colleges and develop a list of colleges for application.

How many colleges should students apply to? There is no rule on how many colleges students can apply to; however, keep in mind most applications require an application fee. Carefully researching colleges and applying to colleges that are a good fit can be very important to students with limited financial resources. Financial constraints can impact many students who would not otherwise be eligible for financial assistance. "Application fee waivers" may be available for students who meet financial assistance requirements depending upon the policy of the college to which the student applies. This is dependent on what the university offers.

The Princeton Review (2014) recommends applying to a few colleges in each of the following categories: match schools, reach schools, and safety schools. A student's academic record is within or exceeds the college's admission requirements of a match school. A student's academic record is below the college's admission requirements of a reach school. And, a student's academic record exceeds the college's admission requirements of a safety school.

There are multiple options for admissions to college. The admissions options are dependent on the college's or university's policies. The major options are

> Regular decision: Colleges have a definite due date for the application. The majority of these dates fall between January 15 and February 1. It is important to carefully check the application deadline for each college and strictly adhere to this date.
>
> Rolling decision: Colleges with rolling decision do not have an admissions deadline. The college evaluates each of the applications as they are received. Decisions are then sent to the potential student in approximately 6 to 8 weeks.
>
> Early decision: If a student has an absolute favorite university and is committed to attending that college, early decision may be the option for them. Early decision allows students to apply early to one college. If they are accepted, they must attend that school. Early decision application deadlines (dependent on the college) tend to be November 1.
>
> Early Action: Similar to early decision, students apply early and receive decisions early. However with early action, students are not required to commit to attend a particular college until May 1.
>
> Single Early Action: This is a combination of early decision and early action. Students apply *early* to one (and only one) college. They may apply to other colleges through the regular decision application process. Single early action application deadlines (dependent on the college) are between November 1 and 15.

Other admissions options are available, but tend to be used for students with specific needs. These options are late admission, early admission, open admission, deferred admission, and early evaluation. These options are not available at all colleges or universities and should be explored as needed.

Activity: What resources are available in your area?

____

____

____

____

____

Military

Postsecondary transition options also include entry into the military. An introduction to the military may take place at the high school level. Some high schools have a Junior Reserves Officers' Training Corp (JROTC) Program. The United States Army's JROTC website (2014) indicates that

> the Army Junior Reserve Officer Training Corps (JROTC) is a program offered to high schools that teaches students character education, student achievement, wellness, leadership, and diversity. It is

a cooperative effort between the Army and the high schools to produce successful students and citizens, while fostering in each school a more constructive and disciplined learning environment.

If JRTOC is not available in your school district, postsecondary transition counseling regarding the military can be done in cooperation with the armed services. Recruiters are available to meet with the school counselor, parents, and the student. Recruiters are available for each of the branches of the armed services: Air Force and Air Force Reserve, Air National Guard, Army and Army Reserve, Army National Guard, Coast Guard and Coast Guard Reserve, Marine Corps and Marine Corps Reserve, and the Navy and Navy Reserve. Each branch of the armed forces has a specific role and function in the overall mission of U.S. peace and security (www.military.com, 2014). Collaboration between the school counselor and the recruiters provides students with comprehensive information regarding their options.

Another aspect of postsecondary transition planning through resources provided by the military is a widely used vocational assessment. More than one million military applicants, high school and postsecondary students, take the Armed Services Vocational Assessment Battery (ASVAB) (official-asvab.com, 2015). The ASVAB is another resource and assessment available to high school students and provides them with an opportunity to investigate their career interests and aptitudes. The ASVAB measures strengths and weaknesses in eight different areas.

Activity: What resources are available in your area?

____

____

____

____

The Gap Year

The gap year is when students take off the year between high school and college to explore their interests. It can provide time for personal growth. Choosing a gap year is a very personal decision and should be made by the parents and student. The school counselor's role is to support the students and family while providing information about gap year options. There are many paths to take during the gap year. Parents and students will have to determine which path is best for the student. There are formal gap programs that have an associated cost (some as high as $30,000). There are also volunteer programs, such as AmeriCorps or City Year, which pay the student's room and board. Some students work during this year; other students travel during this year. The possibilities are many and varied.

Activity: What resources are available in your area?

____

____

____

____

FINANCIAL AID

Professional school counselors need to be informed regarding financial aid available for post-high school education and training. My best recommendation is to attend a financial aid workshop or seek the most current resources online. The availability of funding changes annually and given that consistent change, there is a mandate for school counselors to remain current. Workshops are often offered by school districts and other organizations. One excellent resource is the Financial Aid Toolkit that was developed by the United States Department of Education. The Federal/Student Aid website (2015) also suggests the following resources:

- "In addition to hosting the National Training for Counselors and Mentors (NT4CM) Web pages, Federal Student Aid's Financial Aid Toolkit provides other resources and information to support your outreach and training needs. The Toolkit includes information on:
- Learn About Financial Aid: Provides information to help you learn about types of aid, student eligibility, the FAFSA, and loan repayment. It includes information on FAFSA updates and the FAFSA completion effort.
- Conduct Outreach: Provides tools and tips to support your outreach efforts including hosting an event, presentations, resources for target audiences, social media examples, and public service announcements.
- Search Financial Aid Tools and Resources: Provides tool for searching and filtering FSA resources by type, audience, topic, and time of year.
- Federal Student Aid's Publication Ordering System (FSAPubs) offers a variety of free publications on financial aid and college preparation. Visit www.fsapubs.gov to order items for middle school, high school, and/or college students, as well as other target audiences. The Order Federal Student Aid Forms and Publications fact sheet provides additional information on accessing and using FSAPubs.
- National Association of Student Financial Aid Administrators (NASFAA) includes information on college preparation, as well as a resource guide on how to increase awareness among students and families of the necessity of preparing financially for college early.
- National Council of Higher Education Resources (NCHER) offers a comprehensive and up to date library of information on the latest postsecondary financial aid issues.
- National Association for College Admission Counseling (NACAC) offers a variety of valuable resources, including publications and online resources, for anyone involved in the admission process.
- American School Counselor Association (ASCA) provides professional development, publications and other resources, research, and advocacy to more than 24,000 professional school counselors around the globe.
- National Association of State Student Grant and Aid Programs (NASSGAP) provides a library of research articles on topics such as preK–12 and postsecondary education, parent involvement, and financial aid and affordability.
- National College Access Network (NCAN) provides regular updates on trends in college admissions, financial aid, and career path development to help students and their families prepare for college or postsecondary education.
- Council for Opportunity in Education (COE) offers training, publications, and other resources to help further the expansion of educational opportunities throughout the United States."

Activity: Using the handout "The Academic Standards for Career Education and Work" "I" Statements for Curriculum Integration and Portfolio Development (Appendix A), discuss four ideas for lessons in the four grade-level areas.

REFERENCES

Anctil, T. M., Smith, C. K., Schenck, P., & Dahir, C. (2012). Professional school counselors' career development practices and continuing education needs. *Career Development Quarterly, 60,* 109–121.

American Institutes for Research. (2015). *AIR Index: The pay gap for workers with disabilities.* Retrieved from http://www.air.org/resource/air-index-pay-gap-workers-disabilities

Armed Services Vocational Aptitude Battery. (2015). *ASBAV home.* Retrieved from http://official-asvab.com

Association for Career and Technological Education. (2008). *Career and education's role in career guidance.* Retrieved from http://official-asvab.comhttp://nces.ed.gov/programs/coe/indicator_coi.asp

Bureau of Labor Statistics. (2010). *Measuring green jobs.* Retrieved from http://www.bls.gov/green/home.htm

Capital Region Partnership for Career Development. (2009). *Career education & work standards.* Retrieved from http://pcd.caiu.org/Resources/CareerPortfolio/Portfolio9_12.aspx

Collegeboard. (2015). *Community college.* Retrieved from https://www.collegeboard.org/search?tp=usearch&x=15&x1=t4&y=13&searchType=site&word=community+college

Council for Accreditation for Counseling and Related Program. (2014). *2016 standards.* Retrieved from www.cacrep.org

Gysbers, N. C. (2013). Career-ready students: A goal of comprehensive school counseling programs. *The Career Development Quarterly, 61*, 283–288. doi: 10.1002/j.2161-0045.2013.00057.x

Masters in Psychology and Counseling Accreditation Council. (2015). *Accreditation manual.* Retrieved from http://www.mpcacaccreditation.org/about/accreditation-manual

National Center for Educational Statistics. (2015). *Public school graduation rates.* Retrieved from http://nces.ed.gov/programs/coe/indicator_coi.asp

National College Access Network: http://www.collegeaccess.org/Why_College_Access_Success_

National Nanotechnology Initiative. (2015). *Nanotechnology 101.* Retrieved from http://www.nano.gov/node/1529

Princeton Review. (2014). *The K & W guide to college programs and services* (11th ed.). New York, NY: Random House.

Reach Higher. (2016). Retrieved from https://www.whitehouse.gov/reach-higher

U.S. Army Junior Reserve Officer Training Corps. (2014). *Program information.* Retrieved from http://www.usarmyjrotc.com/jrotc-program/jrotc-program-information

U.S. Department of Labor. (2010). *Americans with Disabilities Act Amendments Act of 2008.* Retrieved from http://www.access-board.gov/the-board/laws/americans-with-disabilities-act-intro

U.S. Department of Labor, Bureau of Labor Statistics. (2015). *Occupational outlook handbook: School and career counselors.* Retrieved from http://www.bls.gov/ooh/community-and-social-service/school-and-career-counselors.htm

APPENDIX A

The Academic Standards for Career Education and Work

"I" Statements for Curriculum Integration and Portfolio Development

© 2009 Capital Region Partnership for Career Development

Permission granted by PCD to use this handout/activity.

Grades K–3

13.1.3 Career Awareness and Preparation

I can list my interests and hobbies. **(A)**

I can name things that I don't like to do. **(A)**

I can name a friend's interests and hobbies. **(A, B)**

I can name the things that my parents or family members do during their week. **(C)**

I can name five (5) different jobs in my community. **(D)**

I have watched three (3) people in my school or community, and I can describe what they do in their jobs. **(E)**

I can name three (3) workers and tell you how they learned what they do on their jobs. **(H)**

I can explain how important school is for my future career. **(F, G)**

13.2.3 Career Acquisition

I have spoken in front of a small group of my friends in class. **(A)**

I have listened to others speak, and I can listen for important facts. **(A)**

I know that the Internet, newspapers and magazines are good places to look to learn about jobs. **(B)**

I have written a letter to a friend or relative. **(C)**

I have made a plan of activities that I want to do over the summer and next school year. **(D)**

I have worked on a team in class with my friends. **(D)**

I can use a computer to send messages to family and friends, to key and print a report for school, and to visit a website. **(B)**

I know how many times I have been absent from school this year. **(E)**

13.3.3 Career Retention and Advancement

I have talked to an adult about good work habits for success in school and at a job. **(A)**

I can name three (3) habits that I have that will make me successful in school. **(A, B)**

I can name one or more habits that I must change to be successful at school. **(A)**

I can give examples of how I complimented and encouraged a friend. **(C)**

I can name types of money and three (3) ways that money is used. **(D)**

I can plan a weekly schedule for home and school. **(E)**

I can tell you how my parents'/guardians' role at home is different from their role at work. **(F)**

I have talked to adults about what they learn at their jobs and how it helps them to do a good job. **(G)**

13.4.3 Entrepreneurship

I have met a business owner and I know what he/she does. **(A)**

I can describe work habits that help a business owner to be successful (flexibility, positive attitude, risk-taker, leader, etc.). **(B)**

I have set up my own business activity to earn real or fake money (i.e., lemonade stand, pet care, crafts). **(C)**

Grades 4–5

13.1.5 Career Awareness and Preparation

I can describe how my interests and skills will help me to choose a career. **(A)**

I can explain the difference between traditional and non-traditional careers. **(A, B)**

I have interviewed a person in a non-traditional career. **(C)**

I can list five (5) different types of career training programs. **(D)**

I have made a list of what is important to me in a career—working conditions, work schedule, salary, benefits, location, etc. **(E)**

I have interviewed three (3) adults to find out why they chose their careers and then reported their career stories. **(F)**

I have started to collect items for my career portfolio. **(G)**

I have made a list of my skills and interests and have begun to match them to careers. **(H)**

13.2.5 Career Acquisition

I am polite when talking with others and use proper English speaking skills. **(A)**

I have read an ad for a job both on the Internet and in a newspaper. **(B)**

I can state the difference between a personal and a business letter. **(C)**

I have written a letter to a business person. **(C)**

I have updated my career portfolio, including awards, special projects, and school work. **(D)**

I can give five (5) examples of good work habits that I demonstrate (Examples of good work habits are dependability, communication, initiative, time management, teamwork, and technical literacy). **(E)**

13.3.5 Career Retention and Advancement

I can describe five (5) attitudes and work habits that are important both at school and at home. **(A)**

I can describe a team and how the team members work together to achieve a goal. **(B)**

I have learned to accept others' opinions even when I don't agree with them. **(C)**

I can describe a budget and why it is necessary. **(D)**

I can define the following terms: gross pay, taxes, net pay, savings, expenses, contributions. **(D)**

I can describe my schedule both at school and at home. **(E)**

I can give an example of how a person's career changes (promotions, transfers, etc.) and why it's important to keep learning. **(F, G)**

13.4.5 Entrepreneurship

I can explain the term entrepreneurship. **(A)**

I have interviewed an entrepreneur to learn the good and bad aspects of his/her business. **(B)**

I have interviewed or researched an entrepreneur to learn about his/her work skills. **(B)**

I have interviewed or researched a business to find out how their goods or services are sold. **(C)**

Grades 6–8

13.1.8 Career Awareness and Preparation

_____ I can list ten (10) careers that match my interests and abilities. **(A, B)**

_____ I can list five (5) non-traditional careers for both boys and girls. **(C)**

_____ I have researched three (3) different types of career training programs and their related employment possibilities. **(D)**

_____ I can list five (5) careers in demand in the area where I live. **(E)**

_____ I understand how the global economy influences each person's job opportunities, earnings, and the rate of unemployment in our area. **(E)**

_____ I have made a list of my extracurricular activities and community experiences and can describe how they may influence my career development. **(F)**

_____ I have written a career plan with goals, assessments, interests, abilities, and postsecondary plans. **(G)**

_____ I have met with my 8th-grade counselor and my parents to list courses and extracurricular plans for high school, matched to my academic and career goals. **(H)**

13.2.8 Career Acquisition

_____ I have made a formal speech in front of others. **(A)**

_____ I can list five (5) effective listening skills and can demonstrate these skills in a role-play situation. **(A)**

_____ I have used three (3) different resources to research three (3) regional job openings linked to my interests and abilities. **(B)**

_____ I have completed a formal job application. **(C)**

_____ I have drafted a resume. **(C)**

_____ I have written a thank-you letter after an interview. **(C)**

_____ I have assembled my written career plan and goals in a portfolio along with my awards, achievements, school work, and projects. **(D)**

_____ I can describe five (5) workplace skills* that I will need in my future career. **(E)**

***Workplace skills include attitude, punctuality/attendance, commitment, communication, dependability, initiative, time management, teamwork, technical literacy, and getting along with others.**

13.3.8 Career Retention and Advancement

_____ I have interviewed a worker to find out what attitudes and work habits helped him/her to get promoted and to keep his/her job. **(A)**

_____ I have worked with others on a team and can state each person's contribution to the project. **(B)**

_____ I have discussed various conflict resolution skills in a group setting and can use them to solve a problem. **(C)**

_____ I have set up a sample budget with imaginary expenses and income to understand the importance of financial planning. **(D)**

_____ I have developed a weekly and a monthly time schedule and kept track of events in a daily/weekly planner. **(E)**

_____ I have interviewed a person with a disability and asked him/her how it affected his/her career planning and goals. **(F)**

_____ I have interviewed a person who has been retrained for a new career. **(G)**

13.4.8 Entrepreneurship

_____ I have interviewed both someone who works for a company and a business owner to learn about the difference in their job security, wages, costs, and benefits. **(A)**

_____ I have interviewed three (3) business owners to learn the entrepreneurial qualities needed to be successful. **(B)**

_____ I have started to develop a basic business plan after interviewing an entrepreneur. **(C)**

_____ I have discussed with my teacher or parent the basic components of a business plan (competition, daily operations, finances, marketing, and resource management) as applied to the creation of a new business. **(C)**

Grades 7–8

13.1.8 Career Awareness and Preparation

I can list ten (10) careers that match my interests and abilities. **(A, B)**

I can list five (5) non-traditional careers for both boys and girls. **(C)**

I have researched three (3) different types of career training programs and their related employment possibilities. **(D)**

I can list five (5) careers in demand in the area where I live. **(E)**

I understand how the global economy influences each person's job opportunities, earnings and the rate of unemployment in our area. **(E)**

I have made a list of my extracurricular activities and community experiences and can describe how they may influence my career development. **(F)**

I have written a career plan with goals, assessments, interests, abilities, and postsecondary plans. **(G)**

I have met with my 8th-grade counselor and my parents to list courses and extracurricular plans for high school, matched to my academic and career goals. **(H)**

13.2.8 Career Acquisition

I have made a formal speech in front of others. **(A)**

I can list five (5) effective listening skills and can demonstrate these skills in a role-play situation. **(A)**

I have used three (3) different resources to research three (3) regional job openings linked to my interests and abilities. **(B)**

I have completed a formal job application. **(C)**

I have drafted a resume. **(C)**

I have written a thank-you letter after an interview. **(C)**

I have assembled my written career plan and goals in a portfolio along with my awards, achievements, school work, and projects. **(D)**

I can describe five (5) workplace skills* that I will need in my future career. **(E)**

*** Workplace skills include attitude, punctuality/attendance, commitment, communication, dependability, initiative, time management, teamwork, technical literacy, and getting along with others.**

13.3.8 Career Retention and Advancement

I have interviewed a worker to find out what attitudes and work habits helped him/her to get promoted and to keep his/her job. **(A)**

I have worked with others on a team and can state each person's contribution to the project. **(B)**

I have discussed various conflict resolution skills in a group setting and can use them to solve a problem. **(C)**

I have set up a sample budget with imaginary expenses and income to understand importance of financial planning. **(D)**

I have developed a weekly and a monthly time schedule and kept track of events in a daily/weekly planner. **(E)**

I have interviewed a person with a disability and asked him/her how it affected his/her career planning and goals. **(F)**

I have interviewed a person who has been retrained for a new career. **(G)**

13.4.8 Entrepreneurship

I have interviewed both someone who works for a company and a business owner to learn about the difference in their job security, wages, costs, and benefits. **(A)**

I have interviewed three (3) business owners to learn the entrepreneurial qualities needed to be successful. **(B)**

I have started to develop a basic business plan after interviewing an entrepreneur. **(C)**

I have discussed with my teacher or parent the basic components of a business plan (competition, daily operations, finances, marketing, and resource management) as applied to the creation of a new business. **(C)**

Grades 9–12

13.1.12 Career Awareness and Preparation

I have completed at least two (2) self-assessments (interest, aptitude, personality, and values). **(A)**

I have reviewed my career options based on my self-assessments, experiences, and achievements. **(B)**

I have researched five (5) to ten (10) careers that match my interests and aptitudes. **(B, C)**

I have participated in three (3) of the following: **(D)**

- Community service
- Cooperative education/Internship
- Job shadowing and/or career-focused field trips
- Part-time employment
- School-based enterprise
- Industry-based career programs

Based on research, self-assessment, as well as school and work experiences, I can select my future career path. **(E)**

My career goals have influenced my high school course selection. **(E)**

I attended a college fair and researched postsecondary training programs, and I can determine the training needed for careers in my interest area. **(F)**

I understand postsecondary education and certification programs and the degrees awarded in those programs. **(F)**

I updated my career portfolio and I am looking at postsecondary options that relate to my career goals. **(G, H)**

13.2.12 Career Acquisition

I have participated in an interview and demonstrated effective speaking and listening skills. **(A)**

I have used Internet-based systems to research a career field in my area of interest. **(B)**

I have used newspapers and professional associations to research employment prospects in my career field. **(B)**

I have registered my resume on the Career Link system. **(C)**

I have completed a job application. **(C)**

I have completed a cover letter. **(C)**

I have an up-to-date resume. **(C)**

I use my career portfolio when making career decisions. **(D)**

I can demonstrate workplace skills* by citing specific examples from my academic and work history. **(E)**

***Workplace skills include attitude, punctuality/attendance, commitment, communication, dependability, initiative, time management, teamwork, technical literacy, and getting along with others.**

13.3.12 Career Retention and Advancement

Based on my school and work/volunteer experiences, I can describe what I need to do to get and to keep a job. **(A)**

I contributed to a project's successful outcome while working on a team. **(B)**

I have used listening techniques such as clarifying, encouraging, restating, and summarizing when working as part of the team. **(B)**

I can give examples of how I used mediation, negotiation, and problem solving in the workplace to diffuse and/or resolve conflict. **(C)**

I have estimated a personal budget based on an amount for a realistic income in my chosen career. **(D)**

I can give three (3) examples of time management strategies, which help me at school and/or on the job. **(E)**

I have evaluated how the global workplace affects my chosen career, and I can describe strategies needed to respond to change. **(F)**

I can give five (5) examples of people who have advanced in their careers through continued learning. **(G)**

13.4.12 Entrepreneurship

I have compared working in the corporate environment with starting my own business in order to achieve career goal. **(A)**

I can give three (3) examples of how entrepreneurial traits (adaptability, ethical behavior, leadership, positive attitude, and risk-taking) match—or don't match—my personality. **(B)**

I developed a business plan using entrepreneurial resources. For example, I used information from the career center at school, community-based organizations, and financial institutions when planning my future. **(C)**

Lesson 28

POSTSECONDARY TRANSITIONS FOR STUDENTS WITH DISABILITIES

"Helping students reach their goals."

Real Life

Counselor-in-Training: "Emily (a student with learning disabilities) came to me in tears because she didn't do well on her ACTs and she is afraid no colleges will want her. I don't have a lot of experience working with learning disabilities and I wasn't sure about the best way to go about helping her. I told her about study materials out there and asked her about an ACT tutor but I feel I could have done more. How you would have gone about helping this student?"

Site Supervisor: "Postsecondary transition for students with disabilities is a team effort. If possible, let's get her IEP team, along with her parents and teachers, involved to make sure she has the best resources available to her before she retakes the test. We will come up with a comprehensive plan and I will show you the postsecondary transition plans required for students with disabilities."

Lesson Twenty-Eight

Postsecondary Transitions for Students With Disabilities

"Helping students reach their goals."

Essential Question: How do I competently meet the postsecondary transitioning needs of students with disabilities? What are the legal and ethical requirements of this transition?

Objectives

Students will

- demonstrate an understanding of the multiple career and college options available to students with disabilities.
- demonstrate knowledge of career, college, and educational paths.
- demonstrate knowledge about resources available to students with disabilities.
- demonstrate knowledge about the legal requirements for postsecondary transitions for students with disabilities.
- demonstrate knowledge about the developmental process of students with disabilities and the role of an individual's disability in his or her life.
- understand career development and related life factors.
- understand career, avocational, educational, occupational, and labor market information resources and career information systems.
- understand interrelationships among and between work, family, and other life roles and factors, including the role of multicultural issues in career development.
- demonstrate knowledge of career and educational planning, placement, follow-up, and evaluation specific to students with disabilities.

CACREP 2016 Standards

- Implement interventions used to promote college and career readiness. (5.G.3.j)
- Demonstrate knowledge of assessments specific to P–12 education. (5.G.1.c)
- Implement strategies to promote equity in student achievement and college access. (5.G.3.k)
- Demonstrate knowledge of school counselors' role in relation to college and career readiness. (5.G.2.c)
- Implement interventions to promote academic development. (5.G.3.d)
- Use developmentally appropriate career counseling interventions and assessments. (5.G.3.e)
- Implement approaches to increase promotion and graduation rates. (5.G.3.i)

MPCAC Standards

- Ecological, contextual, multicultural, social-justice foundations of human development
- Career and life development
- Neuroscientific, physical, and biological foundations of human development and wellness.

Video Spark

http://www.thinkcollege.net/who-is-thinking-college

Who Is Thinking College?

http://www.going-to-college.org/myplace/index.html

Going to College videos

● INTRODUCTION

The postsecondary transition options presented in the previous chapter all apply to students with disabilities dependent on the individual's needs. These options include the work force, career and technical education, certification programs, community college, four-year college, military service, and the gap year. However, students with disabilities have many and additional variables to consider when making this choice. Students with special needs and/or with physical, sensory, developmental, cognitive, and neurological disabilities make up an incredibly diverse group of students. Hence, the postsecondary transition process requires time, reflection, and, if possible, a team approach. In addition to the student, this team may include the student's parents, IEP team, the school counselor, possibly the school social worker, and other professionals involved in this student's life. Building on the previous chapter's information, this chapter will address students with disabilities transitioning to postsecondary education.

Although always present on college campuses, students with disabilities are becoming an identified part of college and university communities at a rapidly increasing rate. Current statistics report that 15.5% of enrolled college students nationwide have a disability (National Institute on Disability and Rehabilitative Research, 2011). Students with disabilities are in 99% of public two-year and four-year postsecondary institutions, 88% of private four-year institutions, and 76% of private two-year institutions (Raue & Lewis, 2011). Due to the increased number of students with disabilities on higher education campuses, culturally competent services for these students continue to be needed. Further, the mandate to provide accommodations to students with disabilities challenges student services professionals on higher education campuses to generate a continually increasing range of services.

When addressing different types of institutional support for this growing population, the need for competent services is imperative when considering the career and employment implications of attaining a college degree. Although earning a college degree improves the employment outcome of individuals with disabilities, when compared with peers graduating from institutions of higher learning, college graduates with disabilities have less positive career and income outcomes (American Institutes for Research, 2015). In order to achieve academically and vocationally, Natalie Stipanovic (2016) wrote that students with disabilities must acquire skills that would facilitate success. Such skills include self-confidence, self-identity, educational and social skills, and career maturity. One reason these skills are essential to the success of students with disabilities is the shift in legal protection between high school and college (see Table 1).

The laws are Section 504 of the Rehabilitation Act (1973), the Individuals with Disabilities Education Act (IDEA, 1975, 2004), and Americans with Disabilities Act (ADA, 1990). IDEA is about success. ADA and Section are about access.

Research has further noted that acquisition of these skills is a developmental process. Career counselors cannot assume that students entering higher education arrive proficient in these skills; rather, effective career counseling with the students with disabilities begins by focusing on the skill level of the individual student and applying traditional theories of career development using a culturally competent lens. Using such a lens, scholars have written best practice guidelines that recommend focusing on the individual, using a collaborative approach to the postsecondary or high school-to-college transition, continuing the transition process through the integration of student support services on the college campus, and culminating in the transition from higher education to the work place. These guidelines highlight the importance of career counseling in higher education having a comprehensive, collaborative approach with an awareness of the academic, cultural, social, and psychological factors impacting the development of students with disabilities.

Table 1 Differences in Legal Protection Between High School and College

High School	*College*
Education is a RIGHT and must be accessible to you.	Education is NOT a right. Students must apply to attend.
Core modifications of classes and materials are required.	NO modifications are required—only accommodations.
School district develops Individual Education Plans (IEPs) and must follow this document in the provision of educational services.	Student must identify needs and ask for legal services. NO IEP exists and is not considered legal documentation.

Source: Think College, a project of the Institute for Community Inclusion at the University of Massachusetts Boston, 2010. The Think College initiatives are funded by grants from the National Institute on Disability and Rehabilitation Research, the Administration on Developmental Disabilities, and the Office of Special Education Programs.

Using a social-cognitive career framework, culturally competent counselors assist students in identifying how their self-efficacy may be impacting their career development (Brown & Lentz, 1996). For example, are there occupations the student has eliminated due to faulty self-efficacy and outcome expectation beliefs? What support systems are in the student's life? What barriers does the student see to potential careers? If students perceive significant barriers, they are less likely to pursue careers that may be of interest to them. Modifying faulty self-efficacy and outcome expectations can expand career options, improve the career decision-making process, and identify the complexities of the career process. As counselors work with students on the previously noted issues, facilitating skills development in the areas of self-determination and self-advocacy is also critical to successful transitions.

Table 2 Differences in Advocacy and Access Between High School and College

High School	*College*
Student is helped by parents and teachers, even without asking directly.	Students must request accommodations from Disability Services Office.
School is responsible for arranging for accommodations and modifications.	Student must self-advocate and arrange for accommodations.
Parent has access to student records.	Parent has no access to student records without student's written consent.
Parent advocates for student.	Student advocates for self.
Teachers meet regularly with parents to discuss their child's educational progress.	College faculty members seldom, if ever, interact with parents and expect the students to address issues with them directly.
Students need parent's permission to participate in most activities.	Student is adult and gives own permission.

Source: Think College, a project of the Institute for Community Inclusion at the University of Massachusetts Boston, 2010. The Think College initiatives are funded by grants from the National Institute on Disability and Rehabilitation Research, the Administration on Developmental Disabilities, and the Office of Special Education Programs.

"Another initiative to bridge the transition process from high school to college has focused on the documentation process in order to improve students' access to disability services in higher education" (Madaus & Shaw, 2006). This initiative has focused on using the current IDEA 2004 mandated documentation system, the Summary of Performance, and developing uniformity in the information provided in order to meet the needs of students in both high school and college. Joseph W. Madaus and Stan F. Shaw (2006) state that "representatives from key national organizations involved in the education of students with disabilities worked collaboratively to develop an SOP that would bridge the gap between IDEA and 504/ADA" (p. 16). The National Transition Documentation Summit (2005) developed a template for the SOP transition plan (Hamlet & Burnes, 2011).

The Summary of Performance (SOP) model is a holistic approach that includes relevant information from the secondary school and the student. This model addresses the unique developmental needs of the student by inquiring about his or her perspective on the impact or role the disability has had on their life. The SOP model facilitates the use of self-determination and self-advocacy skills through the collaborative and self-reflective nature of this approach. It provides objective data from the secondary school on the services or accommodations provided, and it encourages the student to connect postsecondary education with their future goals. Once the document is complete, a SOP meeting, similar to an IEP meeting, takes place. The meeting includes the student, the student's parents, the special education teacher, regular education teacher, and other service providers.

The Summary of Performance document then is shared with the postsecondary site. Consent to release information or consent to collaborate with postsecondary institutions is required. Students and their parents often chose to share this information directly with the postsecondary institution. Using a systemic approach, discussion of the format of the SOP without student information presents an opportunity to collaborate with the postsecondary site and support students through this transition. The SOP model is adaptable and can be altered to meet the specific needs of the student and the educational system.

The following case illustration provides an example of a postsecondary transition for a student with a disability and the Summary of Performance form used as the communication bridge. Note that Sections 1, 2, and 3 provides specific information, much of it with direct practical application to a new setting.

• CASE ILLUSTRATION OF POSTSECONDARY PLANNING AND TRANSITION

Maria

Maria is a student preparing to leave secondary school and transition to university. In fourth grade, she was identified as having dysgraphia (specific disability with writing), and showing indications of falling within the autism spectrum. However, she has no cognitive (intellectual) disabilities or delays.

With accommodations within the classroom, school, family, and community-based supports, Maria progressed satisfactorily through elementary and into secondary school. The accommodations focused on supporting Maria's writing difficulty (e.g., use of the computer for classroom assignments and testing) and support for the behavioral and social aspects of her mild form of autism.

Her strengths are exceptional organizational skills, ability to categorize facts, and a special talent for playing the piano. Maria would like to go to a large university to study public administration with a minor in music performance.

• SUMMARY OF PERFORMANCE

A model template has been formally ratified by the Council for Exceptional Children's Division on Career Development and Transition (DCDT), Division on Learning Disabilities (DLD), and Council on

Educational Diagnostic Services (CEDS), Learning Disability Association (LDA), the Higher Education Consortium for Special Education (HECSE), and the Council for Learning Disabilities (CLD). Many states have adapted or modified the SOP to meet their specific school district's needs. The following sample was adapted (Kansas State Department of Education, 2009).

Section 1. My Postschool Goals for ONE YEAR AFTER HIGH SCHOOL	
Living	**My Goal:** Complete one year of postsecondary education/training
	School's Recommendation To Achieve Goal: To successfully use self-determination/initiation and self-advocacy skills To collaborate with parents, school counselors, Office of Disability Services, residence hall personnel, and other student services personnel To use identified coping mechanism for dealing with transitions and other stressors
	Accommodations and/or Supports That May Assist in Achieving Goal: Structured schedule with tasks (e.g., laundry) broken down into concrete steps A list of conversation prompts to use in various social settings Planned schedule of social contacts including calls to parents Meeting weekly with student affairs personnel to learn about social events Meeting weekly with a counselor at the university counseling center
Learning	**My Goal:** Complete one year of postsecondary education/training
	School's Recommendation to Achieve Goal: To successfully use self-initiation/determination and self-advocacy in academics To collaborate with Office of Disability Services, faculty, faculty advisor To participate in formal and informal study groups
	Accommodations and/or Supports That May Assist in Achieving Goal Testing environment (quiet room due to sensory sensitivity) Computer for testing Support from the professor in clarifying assignment steps and due dates Note-taking on computer (due to fine motor coordination deficit) Seating in the front of the class (to reduce sensory distractions) A list of conversation prompts to use in various academic situations (e.g., group work) Academic planner with pictorial prompts
Working	**My Goal:** Will not work during the first year of postsecondary education/training
	School's Recommendation to Achieve Goal: Seek financial aid from multiple sources.
	Accommodations and/or Supports That May Assist in Achieving Goal: School counselor can provide information to the parents on the financial aid process.

● SUMMARY OF PERFORMANCE

Section 2 *My Perceptions of My Disability*	
Describing My Challenges	**My disability is:** Autism. In schoolwork, I am as smart as everybody else. I just have trouble with making friends, talking to people, knowing when other people are joking. Sometimes I have trouble being interested in other people's stuff. I don't like when things change too fast.
My Disability's Impact	**On my school work such as assignments, projects, time on tests, grades:** Even though I get As and Bs, I often get overwhelmed when I see an assignment and have to have it broken down into concrete steps. I don't need extra time on tests, but I do need a quiet space without those lights that hum. I also use a computer to take notes in class and to take tests because of my problem with writing.
	On school activities: Sometimes I had trouble fitting in with the other kids, but otherwise I was okay.
	On my mobility: I have trouble writing fast enough to keep up—so I use a computer.
	On extracurricular activities: I don't always know how to start talking or join into a group of people. So sometimes I just stay home. So I am not involved in a lot of extracurricular activities, but they do make me take gym. Sometimes I don't think the kids really like me.
Supports	**What works best, such as aids, adaptive equipment, or other services:** Computer for taking notes and tests My planner Breaking big assignments into smaller steps My smart phone—I use it for cues on what to say and do in different situations
	What does not work best: Going to the resource room Sitting in the back of the room When the teacher brings too much attention to me
Accommodations That Worked for Me in High School	**Setting: (distraction free, special lighting, adaptive furniture, etc.)** A quiet room to take tests; sitting in the front of the room during class; no lights that buzz (fluorescent lights in schools often make a buzzing sound)
	Timing/Scheduling: (flexible schedule, several sessions, frequent breaks, etc.) Structured schedule for the day
	Response: (assistive technology, mark in booklet, Brailler, colored overlays, dictate words to scribe, word processor, tape responses, etc.) Computer for note-taking
	Presentation: (large print, Braille, assistive devices, magnifier, read or sign items, calculator, re-read directions, etc.) None

<table>
<tr><th colspan="3">Section 3
The School's Perspective of My Disability</th></tr>
<tr><td rowspan="10">Educator Provided Disability Impact Summary on Academic Achievement and Functional Performance (e.g., general ability and problem-solving, attention and organization, communication, social skills, behavior, independent living, self-advocacy, learning style, vocational, employment)</td><td>Area of Functioning</td><td>Disability Impact</td></tr>
<tr><td>General Ability and Problem Solving</td><td>Does not impact overall academic ability; however, there is a tendency to lock into a rigid thought process.</td></tr>
<tr><td>Academics</td><td>No impact on ability to earn A grades.</td></tr>
<tr><td>Learning Skills</td><td>Attention and concentration can be compromised by peripheral distractions. Structure is essential to Maria's success.</td></tr>
<tr><td>Communications</td><td>Overall inability to recognize nonverbal cues. Difficulty with staying on topic when responding in the classroom. Tends to perseverate on areas of interest</td></tr>
<tr><td>Social Skills and Behavior</td><td>Difficulty initiating or joining social conversations. Difficulty with reciprocal social skills. Tends to isolate or keep to herself instead of interacting with peers.</td></tr>
<tr><td>Mobility</td><td>Disability impairs note-taking by hand.</td></tr>
<tr><td>Independent Living Skills</td><td>Need structured routines; at times daily tasks, such as hygiene, are overlooked.</td></tr>
<tr><td>Self-Determination Skills</td><td>Independent self-determination skills are developing, but currently she relies on adult support to believe in her skills and abilities.</td></tr>
<tr><td>Career/Vocational Preparation</td><td>Disability does not impact her career preparation at this time. Maria is academically prepared to move on to a postsecondary educational institution.</td></tr>
<tr><td rowspan="6">Educator Provided Summary of Successful Accommodations and Supports used in High School</td><td>Accommodation Type</td><td>Description of Support</td></tr>
<tr><td>Environmental</td><td>Testing environment (quiet room due to sensory sensitivity)
Seating in the front of the room (to reduce sensory distractions)</td></tr>
<tr><td>Technology</td><td>Computer for note-taking and testing (due to fine motor coordination deficit)</td></tr>
<tr><td>Academic</td><td>Support from professor in clarifying assignment steps and due dates
A list of conversation prompts to use in various academic situations (e.g., group work)
Academic planner with pictorial prompts</td></tr>
<tr><td>Social</td><td>Counseling</td></tr>
<tr><td></td><td></td></tr>
</table>

Section 4

School Produced Summary of My Academic Achievement and Functional Performance

Attach written copy of most recent assessment reports. A report does not have to be provided for each area. Only attach those reports used to document disability. NOTE: Postsecondary education programs rely upon assessments based on adult norms.

TESTING INFORMATION IS DEPENDENT ON THE COUNTRY'S EDUCATIONAL ASSESSMENT PROCESS

Documentation of My Disability:	**Type of Documentation**	**Assessment Name**	**Dates Administered**
	Psychological/Cognitive		
	Neuropsychological		
	Medical/Physical		
	Communication		
Other Assessments	**Type of Documentation**	**Assessment Name**	**Dates Administered**
	Achievement/Academic		
	Adaptive Behavior		
	Social/Interpersonal		
	Communication/Speech/ Language		
	Response to Intervention		
	Career/Vocational/ Transition		
	Community-Based Assessments		
	Self-Determination Assessment		
	Assistive Technology		
	Classroom Observations		
	Independent Living		
	Other:		

Team Participant Signatures			
Name	**Title**	**Name**	**Title**
	Student		Parent(s)
	Special Education Teacher		Administrative Representative
	Regular Classroom Teacher		Other Service Provider

Activity: Using a case study from your field experience site, complete the SOP form (Appendix A) and discuss with your site supervisor.

• REFERENCES

American Institutes for Research. (2015). *AIR Index: The pay gap for workers with disabilities*. Retrieved from http://www.air.org/resource/air-index-pay-gap-workers-disabilities

Brown, S. D., & Lentz, R. W. (1996). A social cognitive framework for career choice counseling. *The Career Development Quarterly, 44*, 355–367.

Council for Accreditation for Counseling and Related Program. (2014). *2016 standards*. Retrieved from http://www.cacrep.org

Hamlet, H. S., & Burnes, T. (2011). Career counseling: Students with special needs in higher education. In J. Samide, G. Eliason, & J. Patrick (Eds.), *Career development in higher education*. Charlotte, NC: Information Age.

Kansas State Department of Education. (2009). *Summary of Performance*. Retrieved from http://www.ksde.org/Portals/0/SES/forms/SOPExample.pdf

Madaus, J. W., & Shaw, S. F. (2006). The impact of the IDEA 2004 on transition to college for students with learning disabilities. *Learning Disabilities Research & Practice, 21*(4), 273–281.

Masters in Psychology and Counseling Accreditation Council. (2015). *Accreditation manual*. Retrieved from http://www.mpcacaccreditation.org/about/accreditation-manual

National Institute on Disability and Rehabilitative Research. (2011). *Annual disability statistics compendium*. Retrieved from http://www.aapd.com/resources/publications/disability-compendium-2011.pdf

Raue, K., & Lewis, L. (2011). *Students with disabilities at degree-granting postsecondary institutions* (NCES 2011-018). Washington, DC: U.S. Government Printing Office.

Stipanovic, N. (2016). Metacognitive strategies in the career development of individual with learning disabilities. *Career Planning and Adult Development Journal, 31*(4), 120–130

University of Massachusetts Boston. (2010). *Think college*. Retrieved from http://www.thinkcollege.net/

• APPENDIX A

Summary of Performance

This template was developed by the National Transition Documentation Summit 2005 based on the initial work of Stan Shaw, Carol Kochhar-Bryant, Margo Izzo, Ken Benedict, and David Parker. It reflects the contributions and suggestions of numerous stakeholders in professional organizations, school districts, and universities, particularly the Connecticut Interagency Transition Task Force. It is available to be freely copied or adapted for educational purposes. The model template has been formally ratified by the Council for Exceptional Children's Division on Career Development and Transition (DCDT), Division on Learning Disabilities (DLD), and Council on Educational Diagnostic Services (CEDS), Learning Disability

Association (LDA), the Higher Education Consortium for Special Education (HECSE), and the Council for Learning Disabilities (CLD). Many states have adapted or modified the SOP to meet their specific school district's needs.

Examples of completed SOPs are available at http://www.ksde.org/Portals/0/SES/forms/SOPExample.pdf

• NATIONALLY RATIFIED SUMMARY OF PERFORMANCE

Model Template

Part 1: Background Information

This form was completed by

Title

Student Name

Date of Birth

Year of Graduation/Exit

Address (Street)

Town

State

Zip Code

Telephone Number

Primary Language

Current School

City

Student's Primary Disability (diagnosis):

Student's Secondary Disability (if applicable):

When was the student's disability (or disabilities) formally diagnosed?

If English is not the student's primary language, what services were provided for this student as an English language learner?

Date of Most Recent IEP or Most Recent 504 Plan:

Date this summary was completed:

Please check below and attach to this form the most recent copy of assessment reports that diagnose and clearly identify the student's disability or functional limitations or that will otherwise assist in postsecondary planning:

	Psychological/Cognitive
	Response to Intervention (RTI)
	Neuropsychological
	Language proficiency assessments
	Medical/physical
	Reading assessments
	Achievement/academics
	Communication
	Adaptive behavior
	Behavioral analysis
	Social/interpersonal skills
	Classroom observations (or in other settings)
	Community-based assessment
	Career/vocational or transition assessment
	Self-determination
	Assistive technology
	Informal assessment:
	Informal assessment:
	Other:

Part 2: Student's Postsecondary Goal(s)

N.

O.

P.

Part 3: Summary of Performance

(Complete all that are relevant to the student.)

Academic Content Area	*Present level of performance (grade level, standard scores, strengths, needs)*	*Essential accommodations, modifications, and/or assistive technology utilized in high school and why needed*
Reading (basic reading/ decoding, reading comprehension, reading speed)		
Math (calculation skills, algebraic problem-solving, quantitative reasoning)		
Language (written expression, speaking, spelling)		
Learning skills (class participation, note-taking, keyboarding, organization, homework management, time management, study skills, test-taking skills)		

Cognitive Areas	*Present level of performance (grade level, standard scores, strengths, needs)*	*Essential accommodations, modifications, and/or assistive technology utilized in high school and why needed*
General ability and problem-solving (reasoning/processing)		
Attention and executive functioning (energy level, sustained attention, memory functions, processing speed, impulse control, activity level)		
Communication (speech/ language, assisted communication)		

Functional Areas	*Present level of performance (strengths and needs)*	*Essential accommodations, modifications, and/or assistive technology utilized in high school and why needed*
Social skills and behavior (interactions with teachers/peers, level of initiation in asking for assistance, responsiveness to services and accommodations, degree of involvement in extracurricular activities, confidence and persistence as a learner)		
Independent living skills (self-care, leisure skills, personal safety, transportation, banking)		
Environmental access/ mobility (assistive technology, mobility, transportation)		
Self-determination/self-advocacy skills (ability to identify and articulate postsecondary goals, learning strengths and needs)		
Career-vocational/ transition/employment (career interests, career exploration, job training, employment experiences and supports)		
Additional important considerations that can assist in making decisions about disability determination and needed accommodations (e.g., medical problems, family concerns, sleep disturbances)		

Part 4: Recommendations to assist the student in meeting postsecondary goals

Suggestions for accommodations, adaptive devices, assistive services, compensatory strategies, and/or collateral support services to enhance access in the following post-high school environments (only complete those relevant to the student's postsecondary goals).

Higher education or career technical education

Employment

Independent living

Community participation

Part 5: Student Input (Highly Recommended)

Summary of Performance: Student Perspective

A. How does your disability affect your schoolwork and school activities (such as grades, relationships, assignments, projects, communication, time on tests, mobility, extracurricular activities)?

B. In the past, what supports have been tried by teachers or by you to help you succeed in school (aids, adaptive equipment, physical accommodations, and other services)?

C. Which of these accommodations and supports has worked best for you?

D. Which of these accommodations and supports have not worked?

E. What strengths and needs should professionals know about you as you enter the postsecondary education or work environment?

I have reviewed and agree with the content of this Summary of Performance.

Student signature:

Date:

LESSON 29

HOW TO WRITE LETTERS OF RECOMMENDATION LEGALLY AND ETHICALLY

"Letters of recommendation—I'm writing how many?"

Counselor-in-Training: "How do you write letters of recommendation for students that you don't know that well? I'm really surprised at how many letters of recommendation school counselors write!"

Counselor: "I know! There really are a great many to write. We have forms for the students to complete to make it easier. Also, we can meet with the student if needed. Letters of recommendation are such an important part of our job. For example, students need a letter of recommendation to get their first job. It's challenging for the students. Without a letter, the student can't get a job and many of them don't have other people to write one for them."

Lesson Twenty-Nine

How to Write Letters of Recommendation Legally and Ethically

"Letters of recommendation—I'm writing how many?"

Essential Question: How do I write a letter of recommendation for my students?

Objectives: Student will be able to write letters of recommendation with knowledge of the legal and ethical concerns involved in this process.

CACREP 2016 Standards

Students will

- demonstrate understanding of the school counselor's role in relation to college and career readiness. (G.5.2.c)
- demonstrate an understanding of the school counselor's role in consultation with families, P–12 and postsecondary school personnel, and community agencies. (G.5.2.b)
- demonstrate use of strategies to facilitate school and postsecondary transitions. (G.5.3.g)
- demonstrate use of approaches to increase promotion and graduation rates. (G.5.3.i)
- demonstrate use of interventions to promote college and career readiness. (G.5.3.j)
- demonstrate use of strategies to promote equity in student achievement and college access. (G.5.3.k)

MPCAC Standards

- Professional counselor identity, ethical behavior, and social-justice practices
- Human development and wellness across the life span
- Career and life development

Video Spark

https://www.youtube.com/watch?v=B1tOqZUNebs&feature=em-share_video_user Word Choice—*Friends*—Adoption Letter

● INTRODUCTION

When talking about writing letters of recommendation, many immediately think of the college application process. This immediate thought makes sense because of the quantity of letters of recommendation written for students heading to college. However, students also need letters of recommendation for alternate paths, such as tech school, employment, or gap year experiences. With that in mind, the school counselor should craft letters of recommendation for the specific path the student hopes to pursue. While school counselors expect to write letter for college-bound students, it is essential that students who are not entering college or a school be given the same opportunity to receive a letter. Students entering the workforce directly after high school often lack work experience thus lack the resources to receive a letter of recommendation. Fortunately, the college or educational postsecondary path provides a structure for students. Unfortunately, the students entering the world of employment do not have that structure and can be overlooked. This is an opportunity for school counselors to advocate and provide resources to these students. Letters of recommendation can be an additional way to support these students. The guidelines for writing letters of recommendation can be applied to all student letters.

Why do many immediately think of college when the topic of letters of recommendation is brought up? This is because many colleges require students to submit a letter of recommendation from their school counselor with the application (bigfuture.collegeboard.org). With the mandate of required letters from school counselors and in light of the student-to-counselor ratio in most schools, writing letters of recommendation can be a significant part of the school counselor's role. As with any task done in large quantities, maintaining a standard of quality requires the school counselor to be vigilant and mindful. Facilitating and supporting postsecondary transition is essential to student success, and writing letters of recommendation should be done with purpose and in a legal and ethical manner.

Legal? Do school counselors or school districts get sued over college letters of recommendation? The answer is yes. Not often—but it does happen. Carolyn Stone (2015) reported that although the case did not go to court, a lawsuit was filed against a district for defamation of a student's character and emotional stress due to loss of a scholarship. The counselor who wrote the letter in question had no personal interactions with the student and only one brief conversation with a teacher. The college did reinstate the scholarship. Stone (2014) writes that "The McCoy court case informs the profession that if for some reason a school counselor feels compelled to include negative comments in a letter of recommendation, then it is imperative that personal knowledge and, ideally, more than one reliable source is needed to substantiate negative remarks" (p. 2).

How are counselors in the field proceeding when writing letters of recommendation? An American School Counselor Association (ASCA) 2013 survey of 558 ASCA members indicates that while some counselors (6%) will include negative comments in letters of recommendation, a larger percentage of counselors were not comfortable with this practice. Stone (2015) reported that the survey's results indicate that school counselors are gathering information from multiple sources in order to write an accurate and ethical letter. As you will see in your field experience site, counselors have developed "brag sheets" (see Appendix A) and request for information from teachers for letters of recommendation, and use multiple other methods to gather information. Additionally, many counselors place the responsibility for this data collection on the student in order to facilitate their full participation in the college application process.

Ethical? In keeping with the ethical standards listed below, writing a negative letter of recommendation is not consistent with the ASCA ethical standards. If a school counselor does not feel that he or she can write a letter recommending a student, then they should address their concerns with the student and refer the student to another counselor. In plain language—a letter of recommendation is just that—a letter that recommends. *Recommendation,* as defined by *Merriam-Webster's Dictionary* (http://www.merriam-webster.com/dictionary/recommendation), is "the act of saying that someone or something is good and deserves to be chosen" or "a formal letter that explains why a person is appropriate or qualified for a particular job, school, etc."

• AMERICAN SCHOOL COUNSELOR ASSOCIATION (ASCA, 2010)

A.1. Responsibilities to Students

Professional school counselors:

a. Have a primary obligation to the students, who are to be treated with dignity and respect as unique individuals.

b. Are concerned with the educational, academic, career, personal, and social needs and encourage the maximum development of every student.

c. Respect students' values, beliefs and cultural background and do not impose the school counselor's personal values on students or their families.

d. Are knowledgeable of laws, regulations, and policies relating to students and strive to protect and inform students regarding their rights.

e. Promote the welfare of individual students and collaborate with them to develop an action plan for success.

f. Consider the involvement of support networks valued by the individual students.

The purpose of a letter of recommendation is to advocate for the student.

● HOW TO WRITE A LETTER OF RECOMMENDATION

1. **Brag/Information Sheet** (Appendix A): Have the student complete the Brag/Information Sheet. The student will gather information from multiple sources (teachers, administrators, etc.) with signatures to complete the form. This information will be used to facilitate the school counselor's letter-writing by providing support for what is written. A sample of this form is provided.
2. Review the data gathered from multiple sources.
3. There are four parts to the letter:
    a. **Spark**: If possible, start with something that the student has done that will catch the reader's attention (e.g., the real life situations at the beginning of each lesson in this book). For example, many school counselors are active in community service and in other school-related activities. This provides opportunities to interact with students in other settings and may result in additional insight into who the student is and possible information on a student's interests.
    b. **Introduction:** Introduce the writer and your role in the student's context (e.g., who are you, how long you have known the student, etc.).
    c. **Presentation of the student:** Provide information on the student's context, accomplishments, and, if possible, identify qualities that will indicate the student's potential to be successful in college. If possible, provide information on how the student has impacted the school and community.
    d. **Summary:** End with a powerful summary (e.g., as illustrated by Megan's participation and involvement, etc.).

Letter of Recommendation Template is provided in Appendix B.

● SAMPLE LETTERS OF RECOMMENDATION

School Counselor Recommendation for Mark as he enters the workforce

Mark is a leader. One of his strengths is his ability to quietly and positively set the pace for a group or community service project. His natural enthusiasm is contagious.

It is my pleasure to recommend Mark for a position with your organization. I have known Mark for four years and am his school counselor. Mark is one of the hardest working young men that I have met in my

20 years as a school counselor. Combine his work ethic with his enthusiasm and you have a recipe for success and for an extremely valuable employee.

Mark coordinates a community service initiative that works with youth from other schools who are in need of tutoring and mentoring. Mark does all the scheduling for both the tutors and the students. In addition to that, he coordinates parent volunteers who chaperone and bring snacks. And, in true Mark-style, he has collaborated with the art department to develop and provide supplies for a brief art project for each meeting. This program is a huge success and is growing.

I recommend Mark without reservation. He will be a true asset to your organization. If can be of further assistance, please call or email me at ______________________.

Sincerely,

AN EXAMPLE OF A LETTER OF RECOMMENDATION FOR COLLEGE AND A CRITIQUE

Source: MIT Admissions, http://mitadmissions.org/apply/prepare/writingrecs

School Counselor Recommendation for Mary:

Mary has contributed to the school community in a variety of ways, most notably through her participation on the newspaper and yearbook staffs. Frankly, I am impressed with her aggressiveness, creativity, determination and ability to schedule extracurricular activities around a full academic workload. I have never heard Mary complain about her workload or refuse any assignment that she has been given. It is not adequate to say that she accepts responsibility readily. She seeks responsibility. Oh, for more such students!

As business manager for the paper and coeditor of the yearbook the past two years, Mary has done an outstanding job. She personally brought the town's business community from the view that the school newspaper was a charitable organization to the realization that the paper is a direct pipeline through which advertisers can reach students. She also took the initiative to set up the advertising rate schedule for the paper that produced enough revenue to expand coverage from a four-page paper, so that it is an eight-page and often 12-page paper. Her work as photographer for both publications has been equally outstanding.

Her motivation is not forced upon her, nor does she wear it like a badge. She has tremendous self-discipline. Mary is also a dedicated, versatile and talented student who will be an asset to your undergraduate community. She has my respect and my highest recommendation.

Critique: Good. Lots of specifics here give us a very clear impression and help us to know why that impression is held. We have evidence of her newspaper directives and overall character.

REFERENCES

American School Counselor Association. (2010). *Ethical standards for school counselors.* Retrieved from https://www.schoolcounselor.org/asca/media/asca/Resource%20Center/Legal%20and%20Ethical%20Issues/Sample%20Documents/EthicalStandards2010.pdf

Council for Accreditation for Counseling and Related Program. (2014). *2016 standards*. Retrieved from http://www.cacrep.org

Massachusetts Institute of Technology. (2015). *MIT admissions: Writing recommendations*. Retrieved from http://mitadmissions.org/apply/prepare/writingrecs

Masters in Psychology and Counseling Accreditation Council. (2015). *Accreditation manual*. Retrieved from http://www.mpcacaccreditation.org/about/accreditation-manual

Stone, C. (2014). *Negligence in writing letters of recommendation*. Retrieved from https://www.schoolcounselor.org/magazine/blogs/march-april-2014/negligence-in-writing-letters-of-recommendation

Stone, C. (2015). *Legal and ethical issues in writing recommendation letters*. Retrieved from https://www.schoolcounselor.org/magazine/blogs/march-april-2015/legal-and-ethical-issues-in-writing-recommendation

Webster-Merriam Dictionary. (2015). *Recommendation*. Retrieved from http://www.merriam-webster.com/dictionary/recommendation

● APPENDIX A

Letter of Recommendation Brag Sheet

Student Name: ______________________ **Date:** ______________

List any careers and/or college majors that you are considering and why.

What is your proudest accomplishment?

Are there any personal circumstances that have impacted your academic performance in high school? Please note, anything you share can be mentioned in your counselor's letter.

What career or academic skills have you demonstrated in high school that provide evidence that you will be successful in the workplace or in college (e.g., self-advocacy, note-taking, public speaking). Be specific and please provide a concrete example.

List any school activities you participated in. Please include years involved, positions held, and/or significant contributions. Activities can include clubs, sports, jobs, internships, and community service. Which activity was most important to you?

What do you consider your most important activities outside of school? List jobs, volunteering, music, travel, art, for example. Please write about creative work, hobbies, interests, or anything else not listed above to which you have devoted substantial time.

What would you like your future employer or educational institution to know about you?

● APPENDIX B

Date:

Employer

100 Main Street

City, State (Zip Code)

Dear ***(Mr., Mrs., Ms., Dr. Smith; if a name is not available, address to: To Whom It May Concern),***

It is my great pleasure to write this letter of recommendation. I highly recommend ***student name*** for employment with your organization. ***(If you have the name of the position and organization, include those. Specific is always better, however, students often need a general letter of recommendation to take with them on a job search—so a general one is also beneficial.)*** As the school counselor at ***name of school***, I have known ________________ for the past four years as ***(include what role(s) you have had with this students—e.g., his advisor, teacher, and as the community service faculty supervisor.)*** During those four years, ***student name*** has demonstrated a high degree of integrity, an exceptional level of motivation, and kindness to others.

Add information specific to the student and highlighting his or her strengths. Student name is a leader among his peers. He has rallied a strong group of students to participate in community service activities that were not necessarily the most sought after opportunities. During these community service activities, I have observed ________'s strong communication skills and strong social skills. Also, I have had the opportunity to observe his problem-solving skills—which were exceptional. When challenges arose, rather than standing by with the other students, he would begin to problem solve and positively generate solutions. For example, when volunteering at a kitchen in a homeless shelter, we ran out of a food item and _____ generated multiple food substitutions. In addition to all of these strengths, ________ is a pleasant, kind young man.

Student name is a ready for the challenges of the work place. He will be an asset to your organization and will bring a strong positive energy to the work place. I recommend ***student name*** without reservation. If you have any questions, please do not hesitate to contact me.

Sincerely,

Ms./Mr./Dr. Counselor

Professional School Counselor

School Name

Contact Information

PART VII

TRANSITION FROM GRADUATE SCHOOL TO A LEADERSHIP ROLE IN SCHOOL COUNSELING

Lesson 30

SCHOOL COUNSELORS AS LEADERS

Patricia A. Brenner
Kutztown University of Pennsylvania

"If your actions inspire others to dream more, learn more, do more and become more, you are a leader."

—John Quincy Adams

Listen empathetically

Educate to promote personal growth

Advocate for all students

Deliver a comprehensive guidance program

Excel in flexibility and multi-tasking

Respond to student needs

Support students, staff, and administration

—Amy Paton

MSCA Lake Area Division President

Lesson Thirty

School Counselors as Leaders

Patricia A. Brenner
Kutztown University of Pennsylvania

"If your actions inspire others to dream more, learn more, do more and become more, you are a leader."

—John Quincy Adams

Essential Questions: What is school counselor leadership? How do I become a school counselor leader?

Objectives

Students will

- demonstrate an understanding of the history and development of school counseling leadership.
- demonstrate an understanding of the ASCA National Model's mission and vision statement.
- demonstrate knowledge of transformational leadership theories and models.
- demonstrate an understanding of leadership competencies based on Daniel Goleman's concept of emotional intelligence.
- demonstrate an understanding of how the Five C's are incorporated into ASCA's School Counselor Leadership Model.

CACREP 2016 Standards

- Knowledge of the foundation history and development of school counseling and the history of leadership in the field (5.G.1.a)
- Knowledge of school counselor roles as leaders, advocates, and systems change agents in P–12 schools (5.G.2.a)
- Knowledge of competencies to advocate for school counseling roles (5.G.2.f)
- Knowledge of qualities and styles of effective leadership in schools (5.G.2.j)
- Knowledge of models of school-based collaboration and consultation (5.G.1.d)

MPCAC Standards

- Professional counselor identity, ethical behavior, and social-justice practices
- Human development and wellness across the life span
- Counseling, consultation, and social-justice-advocacy theories and skills
- Group theory, practice, and social-justice advocacy

Video Spark

https://www.ted.com/talks/linda_hill_how_to_manage_for_collective_creativity

Linda Hill: How to Manage for Collective Creativity

INTRODUCTION

The goals for this chapter will be to explain how the Five C's of Counselor Leadership are integrated within the four framework leadership approach contained in the American School Counselor Association's (ASCA) National Model (2012, pp. 2–3). This will enable students to explore the concept of transformational leadership and leadership theories that have evolved from this theory and their impact within the school environment, to describe the leadership competencies contained within Daniel Goleman's model of emotional intelligence and apply it to ASCA's counselor leadership model, and to provide learning exercises for future school counselors to expand their knowledge of current leadership styles and theories while examining their areas of strengths and need in the area of school counselor leadership.

Inclusivity is an important concept in the field of leadership. Many great leaders have opened our eyes to the realities and possibilities of transformational change that can occur when all parties involved are a part of the process. The benefits of inclusivity within the field of education have paved the way for desegregation along with equal opportunity for the disabled, migrant students and more recently the GLBTQ population to name a few. Yet this is a concept that continues to challenge not only educators, but our nation and global society as well.

When I think of a good example of an educational leader who has embraced this concept wholeheartedly, the person that first comes to mind is William Purkey. I was very fortunate early in my educational career to hear him speak at our local Intermediate Unit. His concept of invitational education contains important aspects of the leadership necessary for change in our ever-emerging technological and global world. When teaching about the concept of invitational education, he describes the Five P's that are most important for educators to focus on within a school environment: people, places, programs, policies, and processes (Purkey & Siegel, 2013).

People should be the primary focus in an educational environment. Purkey and Betty Siegel explain, "To think invitationally is to give major attention to the people in the process. At the same time, the Invitational Leader looks beyond people to take into account places, policies, programs and processes" (Purkey & Siegel, 2013, p. 105). Aspiring school counselors must recognize that all relationships with individuals within the school environment and community are central to fostering positive change.

A school counselor leader will begin establishing relationships from day one within the school environment. They will continue to grow and expand the initiatives and goals of the school community by establishing relationships with teachers, parents, administrators, school board members, community partnerships, local business partners, and local politicians.

School counselor leaders must first understand the Five P's within their own school environment before they can make transformational changes that will impact the entire school community. School counselor leaders need to embrace what I will call the Five C's of school counselor leadership. These are concepts and skills that are essential for a school counselor leader to display within the school community. These elements are collaboration, creativity, communication, commitment, and continual learning.

DEVELOPMENT OF SCHOOL COUNSELOR LEADERSHIP: VISION AND MISSION STATEMENTS

A Brief History of School Counseling

The job of school counseling emerged from historical, economic, and sociocultural factors at the dawn of the 20th century. The National Association of Manufacturers was created at that time by leaders in industry and entrepreneurs who saw the need for education to improve and enhance trade skills. Industrialists and trade unions supported a movement for high schools to have many tracks rather than just preparing a limited number of students for college. The Smith-Hughes National Vocational Educational Act of 1917 served as the catalyst for the concept of the job of school counselor as it provided federal funding for vocational programs. This early school counseling model is best understood as the services model in that the counselor's role could best be described by the services that were provided. These included orientation, assessment, counseling, placement, and follow-ups.

These programs, however, while embraced within the educational system were often delivered by administrators, teachers, parents, and community members who taught students vocational and life skills. When school counseling became a position, the model expanded to contain educational and psychological components. In addition to promoting vocations, counselors were responsible for character development and teaching socially acceptable behaviors. Essentially, these initial functions have not changed but rather increased, diversified, and evolved from a "position to a service, to a program" (Gysbers, 2010) into the organizational concept embedded in the ASCA National Model, which was first published in 2003.

In 1953, the fifth division of the American Personnel and Guidance Association was formed (Schimmel, 2008). This organization, along with the passage of the National Defense Education Act, for the first time in history provided funding to train and place school counselors whose sole purpose was to counsel youth. This organization today known as the American School Counselors Organization was very influential in the development of school counseling as a profession.

• SCHOOL COUNSELOR LEADERSHIP

In the professional arena of school counseling, the concept of leadership naturally wove its way into the framework of the American School Counselor Association's National Model (2003). This was a necessary integration as the new emerging role of the school counselor is multifaceted and calls for a new vision. This new vision incorporates leadership not only as a skill but a "mindset" (Stone & Dahir, 2006). School counselors become leaders not only in their individual schools among their colleagues but also within their communities. The school counselor National Model Framework (2012) includes the four themes—foundation, management, delivery, and accountability—which in business as well as educational realms are connected to leadership. In the fourth edition of *The Bass Handbook of Leadership* (Bass & Bass, 2008) the authors express that "leadership can be conceived as directing the attention of other members to goals and the paths to achieve them" (p. 25). The ASCA National Model framework has given the school counseling profession a road map.

In the article "School Counselor Educators as Educational Leaders Promoting Systemic Change" (McMahon, Mason, & Paisley, 2009), the authors explain how leadership experiences and concepts have navigated their way into current counselor education literature and practice. Accountability is a critical factor for the school counselor leader as described in Chapter 5 of *School Counselor Leadership: The Essential Practice* (Young & Miller-Kneale, 2013). Understanding the data cycle (pp. 46–47) will enable school counselors to be cognizant of how to plan school counseling programs whose goals align with a school counseling program mission, vision, and school goals. First Lady Michelle Obama recently highlighted the critical role that school counselors have by the creation of her Reach Higher Initiatives (Reach Higher, 2016). These reach higher goals are a direct parallel to accountability and equity for all students including those traditionally not targeted for education beyond high school.

• SCHOOL COUNSELOR LEADERSHIP RESEARCH

The need for data, hence accountability, has created an emphasis on using research to help shape and mold the processes involved in educating future and current school counselor leaders. I will highlight here one of many recent studies that are helping to provide change with regard to the great divide between what is taught in theory and the actual practice of being a school counselor leader. In an attempt to understand the process of leadership identity in counseling (Meany-Walen, Carnes-Holt, Minton, Purswell, & Pronchenko-Jain, 2013) conducted a quantitative descriptive statistical and qualitative analysis of 58 elected and appointed leaders from the American Counseling Association (ACA) and Chi Sigma Iota. One of their research questions addressed advice that they would give to counseling students and programs. The themes that emerged with regard to this question included take initiative, be selective, take professional responsibility, and participate in self-care.

The first theme, take initiative, referred to students' participation in professional organizations such as the American Counseling Association or local affiliates. Another important factor included securing mentors. The second theme, be selective, referred to designing their interests, skills, abilities, and passions to leadership opportunities. In finding an organization whose mission or philosophy aligned with theirs, they could find opportunities to volunteer or be a reference source. The third theme of taking professional responsibility referred to a counselors' overall professional identity as per their ability to be proactive and responsive to student needs and to initiate programs and services. The final theme of self-care was described as the ability to balance all of the demands of the field with having an outside life and identity.

Similar to the Five P's, all of these initiatives involve relationship-building, where the initial focus is on people. As a counseling practicum or intern student, your affiliation with ASCA shows your commitment toward becoming a professional school counselor in addition to the continual professional learning opportunities it provides. Your practicum and internship supervisors will be your initial mentors, but collaboration with the other school counselors in your school, district, or community can be advantageous as well. Anita Young and Marcy Miller-Kneale (2013) identify five characteristics that are associated with building school counselor leadership capacity (pp. 21–22). The characteristic of systematic collaboration enables a school counselor to accomplish goals and have a clear vision through communicating innovative ideas with building, administrative, and community leaders.

Collaboration usually leads to enhanced learning and finding one's passion in the counseling field. Being selective in this capacity refers to knowing your personal strengths and weaknesses. While one cannot be creative in all aspects of counseling, perhaps you have a specific skill and interest in technology. In this case, you may want to volunteer to help set up or revise a website for your school or district. In my personal observations as a school counselor, I have found that being proactive and responsive to students needs while putting out the fires of the day can be exhausting. This is where the Five C's of school counselor leadership are most necessary.

Responsiveness requires constant communication and collaboration on a daily basis about individual student cases, scheduling, lesson plans, IEPs, truancy plans, group-counseling sessions, or planning for yearly events such as a career or multicultural fair. The capacity to be proactive and initiate programs and services will require a school counselor leader to reflect at the end of each day, week, and school quarter or semester. The daily reflections of school counselors can be noted on to-do lists, school calendar planners, department meeting agendas, group plans, or lesson plans and assessments. These are our formative assessments in a sense to show our commitment to improve our services to students. These formative assessments can and should be shared with other school leaders who are responsible for being responsive to student needs. This collaboration often leads to future planning for professional development training.

Responsiveness has motivated me toward continual learning especially when it involves a new process, policy, or procedure. When my day as a middle school counselor became a continual cycle of crisis response and I learned that my peers in the district were experiencing similar results, I sought, through the assistance of mentors, a possible solution to this dilemma. After conferring with all of the district counselors that site-based school therapy presented itself as a viable option, I began the data cycle process for school counseling programs as identified by Jack Fraenkel, Norman Whallen, and Helen Hyun (2011) and Carol Kaffenberger and Anita Young (2013) (Young & Miller-Kneale, 2013, p. 46). My baseline data reflected building and district figures on the increase in our student assistance referrals over the past 3 years, the increase in those students who received free and reduced lunch, the increase in our transient student population, as well as participation results from a time study of counselor activities.

This process, which was set in motion out of responsiveness, has expanded from initial pilot programs having part-time school-based therapists at the middle and high school level to full-time therapists at the elementary, middle, and high school buildings. The data cycle for this program continues yearly as the outcome data are used for setting future program goals.

The researchers' final recommendation concerning this study was to find time for self-care. How does one balance career and work? My suggestion once again lies with implementation of the Five C's, but in this instance, using each skill to assist you in identifying how to maintain a life separate from being "the school counselor." Collaborate with school counselors who are new to the field and ask how they survived their first year or two. Join a local professional school counselor organization. Communicate with your administration and fellow counselors your needs and concerns about time management. Make a commitment to yourself to discover a new source of stress management or participate weekly in an exercise or health regiment. Sleep. And finally, each day continually learn to practice one small act of kindness toward yourself as in a typical day you will assist and advocate for many students.

Reflection Activity: Please take a few minutes to answer the questions individually and then share in small groups during your field experience course.

1. What was the emphasis on concerning school counseling when you went to elementary school, middle school, and high school?

   ____

   ____

   ____

   ____

2. What social, economic, political, or other factors affected the role of the school counselor at that time?

   ____

   ____

   ____

   ____

3. In your opinion, were school counselors considered leaders at that time? Please explain your answer and provide some concrete examples to support your opinion.

   ____

   ____

   ____

   ____

4. Did your school district have a mission and vision statement? Did your school counseling department have a school mission and vision statement? (Yes, I encourage you to google your former schools to locate a current mission and vision statements!)

   ____

   ____

   ____

   ____

• TRANSFORMATIONAL LEADERSHIP

What Is a Transformational Leader?

Transformational leadership theories can be conceptualized within recent school counseling reform initiatives. In these models, the vision is shared and emerges from the collective interests of those in the organization. According to Peter G. Northouse (2013),

> Transformational leaders are recognized as change agents who are good role models, who empower followers to achieve a higher standard, who act in ways that make others want to trust them, who encourage others and celebrate their accomplishments, and who give meaning to organizational life. (p. 200)

Transformational counselors in effect create change through relationships built on trust, collaboration, clearly defined goals and outcomes, and personal and professional integrity.

Collaboration and consultation are essential elements that can enable school counselors to become change agents even in difficult circumstances. A good example of this kind of leadership in school counselor literature is documented in the article "Handling PBIS with Care: Scaling up to School-wide Implementation" (Cressey, Whitcomb, McGilvray-Rivet, Morrison, & Shander-Reynolds, 2015). Fraught with challenges, which included limited financing, a diverse school population, and few external supports, the authors describe the data process and fidelity employed to expand what was essentially a pilot grade-level-only initiative which blossomed into a schoolwide program. Before you begin Activity 1 read this article and list how this counselor showed leadership behaviors in each of the four frames of leadership contained within ASCA's framework: structural, human resource, political, and symbolic.

Reflect

How has learning about this theory increased your knowledge on how to become a professional school counselor?

Activity: What makes school counselors transformational leaders?

Video Clip

http://www.ted.com/talks/stanley_mcchrystal

Listen, learn . . . then lead (Four Star General Stanley McChrystal shares what he has learned about leadership over his military career, which spanned decades.)

• DISCUSSION QUESTIONS

1. What transformational characteristics were described by Stanley in this presentation?

____

____

____

____

2. What reasons did he provide for changing his mindset and worldview on his former definition of *leadership*?

____

____

____

____

3. In your opinion, was he a leader or a follower? Please provide specific statements or evidence from his talk to support your opinion.

____

____

____

____

4. What aspects of systematic collaboration were identifiable when he described the Iraq War?

____

____

____

____

5. How did Stanley display the Five C's of counselor leadership? Are these skills useful in crisis situations such as Stanley described? How might they be useful in a school crisis?

____

____

____

____

In their 2013 book, *School Counselor Leadership: The Essential Practice*, Young and Miller-Kneale present an educational model of influence described for school counselor leaders titled the shared leadership framework (see also Lambert, 1998, p. 41). This approach is constructivist in nature. All members of the school leadership team reflect on their own actions and practices in order to create new and improved ways to perform their tasks in order to accomplish goals more effectively and efficiently.

Lambert's five key assumptions for increasing leadership capacity are explained succinctly by Stanley in the TED Talk that we just viewed. Her assumptions include that leadership is broad, leadership is connected to learning, everyone has the potential to lead, leadership is a shared endeavor, and power and authority are redistributed (p. 43). Since you now have a more firm grasp on the actions, behaviors, and traits of transformational leader you are ready for the case study.

Activity: Case Study—The Overwhelmed Staff

Shortly after graduating with your master of arts in school counseling, you secure a position at Mehoma Elementary School. The school has a population of approximately 350 students in Grades K–4. Last year, the school district hired a new principal, Mr. Smalls, to replace the male administrator who had been at the building for over 25 years. Mr. Smalls came to the district after having served as a teacher for 7 years in an elementary building and 4 years as the principal of that same school.

Upon his arrival, he was charged with getting the curriculum aligned with current standards, bringing new technology into the classroom, as well as getting a new reading curriculum in place for the current school year that would help students earn better benchmark scores each quarter to eventually take the building off of the "warning" list for the percentage of students who were below basic on PSSAs in the past 2 years of testing. Mr. Smalls is excited to have you in his building since you are familiar with the ASCA National Model. The counselor in his prior elementary school was working on the process of getting their RAMP application together. He is very encouraging. His mission and vision seem to be in alignment with your own.

Mr. Smalls has charged you with reinstating lessons in all classrooms using a curriculum that was recommended to him but not reviewed by the administrative team. He would like you to review the curriculum, present it to the faculty, and set up a schedule with the faculty for when you could teach the lessons. Mr. Smalls seems sincere and certainly has more experience than you. You are excited to get started on your first project. You eagerly prepare for the presentation and are anxious for the first in-service day. While the curriculum seems appropriate and will align with the district standards, you believe that the lessons are too long and that you may have to modify some lessons. You plan to share this insight with the faculty.

Your presentation at the faculty meeting is the last item on the agenda before the break for lunch. Mr. Smalls spent the morning describing the necessary training that would be required for the new reading program. In addition, most of the faculty members still had to align their current curriculum. He then presented the model for the new evaluation tool that the faculty would be using this school year, which he forgot to mention to you. During the morning break, you overhear many faculty members complaining in the hallway that they are tired of all of the changes since Mr. Smalls came. When you get up to begin your presentation, you look around the room and can sense the tensions and frustration of the faculty.

As a transformational counselor you

- Use the Five C's of counselor leadership to describe what you would do next.
    - Collaboration, creativity, communication, commitment, and continual learning
- Use the Five C's of counselor leadership to describe how you could have been more proactive about giving this presentation.
- Use Lambert's assumptions for shared leadership to describe what you would do next.
    - Leadership is broad; leadership is connected to learning. Everyone has the potential to lead; leadership is a shared endeavor, and power and authority are redistributed.
- Use Lambert's assumptions for shared leadership to describe how you could have been more proactive about giving this presentation.

LEADERSHIP COMPETENCIES AND EMOTIONAL INTELLIGENCE

In his article, "Emotional Intelligence and Research Development" Golnaz Sadri (2012) notes that primary and secondary research which examines the emotional intelligence of leaders is on the rise. He discusses several studies that link the competencies of emotional intelligence with the characteristics of transformational leadership. Sadri also noted a study by David Rosete and Joseph Ciarrochi which examined the link between emotional intelligence, personality, cognitive intelligence, and leadership effectiveness. The findings of this study revealed that emotional intelligence was directly related to higher levels of leadership effectiveness that were not correlated with personality or intelligence. He declares that overall higher levels of emotional intelligence lead to higher levels of leader effectiveness. In addition, studies have confirmed that one can be trained to be emotionally competent. How does this apply to school counselor leaders?

In their book, *Primal Leadership*, Daniel Goleman, Richard E. Boyatzis, and Annie McKee (2013) describe leadership competencies based on Goleman's model of emotional intelligence. This model presents leadership competencies in the areas of self-awareness, self-management, social awareness, and relationship management. I find that Goleman's competencies are fused with and embodied by the five characteristics noted in *School Counselor Leadership: The Essential Practice* (Young & Miller-Kneale, 2013), which include resourceful problem-solving, systemic collaboration, interpersonal influence, social-justice advocacy, and professional efficacy.

Goleman's model describes the areas of self-awareness and self-management which relates to personal competence. The first element of the self-awareness sector is emotional awareness. This is considered the ability to recognize how feelings can affect work performance and guide one to seek out core values in dealing with difficult situations. A second element in this sector is accurate self-assessment, which encompasses knowing personal values and strengths and the ability to deal effectively with constructive criticism. The third element in this sector is self-confidence, which consists of being able to admit to mistakes and failures without placing blame or criticism on a person or event.

In this model, there are also two areas that relate specifically to social competence. These areas are defined as social awareness and relationship management. The three elements included in the social awareness sector are empathy, organizational awareness, and service. The definition of *empathy* is extended to include displaying this characteristic on a consistent basis within all environments including work, home, and community. Organizational awareness is the ability for leaders to understand and manage system and political dynamics, which again use their values as a guiding force. The final element in this sector is service. This concept extends beyond the work environment or organization.

Relationship management includes six elements: inspiration, influence, developing others, change catalyst, conflict management, and teamwork and collaboration. Inspiration in this model is defined as motivating others to believe in their vision through modeling where values are shown to others. Influence accounts for the ability to be compelling and engaging to a wide variety of audiences. Developing others pertains to a leader's ability to be a coach and mentor while continually challenging himself or herself to learn and grow in his or her chosen field. Change catalyst implies that one recognizes the need for change and seeks ways to overcome barriers to attain change. As conflict managers, leaders are said to be able to understand differing points of view and seek to compromise. In the final element of teamwork and collaboration, leaders continually build cooperation and commitment within their organization. They seek to achieve goals collectively. These four domains combined have a specific relevancy to the leadership competencies necessary for school counselors. In the article, "The Leader Within," Kwok-Sze R. Wong (2014) connects the ASCA four framework model (structural, political, human resource, and symbolic) to Goleman's emotional intelligence competencies. He provides examples of these integrations in each area.

Activity: Reflect & Analyze Use Appendix A to conduct a personal reflection on which competencies you believe are your strengths and weaknesses by placing a plus sign (+) next to those competencies you feel are your strengths and a minus sign (–) next to those competencies that you believe still need to be more fully developed. Next, take the following online assessment on emotional intelligence provided by the Global Leadership Foundation (www.globalleadershipfoundation.com/geit/eitest.html).

Then compare and contrast your findings from your informal assessment and this assessment tool.

Final Activity: In this short chapter on leadership, we have examined through discussion, observation, research, and assessments important concepts of leadership that are relevant to future school counselor leaders. In her TED Talk on leadership, *How to Manage for Collective Creativity,* Linda Hill (2014) discusses the aspect of conflict within the business world that can either stifle or sustain a productive environment. Her revelations are very applicable to the school environments and communities.

Reflect

1. View the TED Talk, *How to Manage for Collective Creativity* at

   https://www.ted.com/talks/linda_hill_how_to_manage_for_collective_creativity.

2. Please reflect on the following:

   - Hill names leaders as "social architects." When describing the companies that were able to be collectively creative, what aspect of the Five C's of counselor leadership could be noted in her talk?
   - What characteristics of transformational leaders were mentioned specifically or alluded to during her talk?
   - What aspects of the four competency areas of emotional intelligence that we studied were described specifically or alluded to during her talk?
   - What aspects of her talk suggested that the environment was inclusive and inviting?
   - While counselor leaders can be found within our own borders and associations, we as a profession need to continue to broaden our relationships along with business and political affiliations to encompass a more global view of school counselors as leaders. Discuss some ways in which you, as future school counselor leaders, might be "stage setters" for national and international discussions and practices.

● REFERENCES

American School Counselor Association. (2005). *The ASCA National Model: A framework for school counseling programs* (2nd ed.). Alexandria, VA: Author.

Bass, B. M., & Bass, R. (2008). *The Bass handbook of leadership: Theory, research & managerial applications* (4th ed.). New York, NY: Free Press.

Cressey, J., Whitcomb, S., McGilvray-Rivet, S., Morrison, R., & Shander-Reynolds, K. (2014). Handling PBIS with care: Scaling up to school-wide implementation. *Professional School Counseling, 18*(1), 90–99.

Goleman, D., Boyatzis, R., & McKee, A. (2013). *Primal leadership.* Boston, MA: Harvard Business Review Press.

Gysbers, N. C. (2010). *Remembering the past, shaping the future: A history of school counseling.* Alexandria, VA: American School Counselor Association.

Hill, L. (2014, September). Linda Hill: How to manage for collective creativity [Video file]. Retrieved from https://www.ted.com/talks/linda_hill_how_to_manage_for_collective_creativity.html

Kaffenberger, C., & Young, A. (2013). *Making DATA work: A process for conducting action research* (3rd ed.). Alexandria, VA: American School Counselor Association.

Lambert, L. (1998). *Building leadership capacity in schools.* Alexandria VA: Association for Supervision & Curriculum Development.

McMahon, H. G., Mason, E. C. M., & Paisley, P. O. (2009). School counselor educators as educational leaders promoting systemic change. *Professional School Counseling, 13*(2), 116–120.

McChrystal, S. (2011, March). *Stanley McChrystal: Listen, learn . . . then lead.* [Video file]. Retrieved from http://www.ted.com/talks/stanley_mcchrystal.html

Meany-Walen, K. K., Carnes-Holt, K., Minton, C. A. B., Purswell, K., & Pronchenko-Jain, Y. (2013). An exploration of counselors' professional leadership development. *Journal of Counseling and Development, 91*(2), 206–215.

Northouse, P. G. (2013). *Leadership: Theory and practice* (6th ed.). Thousand Oaks, CA: Sage.

Paton, A. (2009). *Counselors as leaders* (Michigan State Counseling Association Guidelines). Retrieved from http://www.mnschoolcounselors.org/Downloads/Guidelines_2-09.pdf

Purkey, W., & Siegel, B. (2013). *Becoming an invitational leader: A new approach to professional and personal success.* Atlanta, GA: Brumby Holdings.

Reach Higher: Complete your education, claim your future. Retrieved from https://www.whitehouse.gov/reach-higher

Sadri, G. (2012). Emotional intelligence and leadership development. *Public Personnel Management, 41*(3), 535–548.

Schimmel, C. (2008). *School counseling: A brief historical overview*. Retrieved from http://www.wvde.state.wv.us/counselors/history/html

Stone, C. B., & Dahir, C. A. (2006). *The transformed school counselor.* New York, NY: Lahaska.

Wong, K.-S. R. (2014). *The leader within*. Alexandria, VA: American School Counselor Association.

Young, A., & Miller-Kneale, M. (2013). *School counselor leadership: The essential practice*. Alexandria, VA: American School Counselor Association.

• APPENDIX A

Leadership Competencies

Source: *Primal Leadership* by Daniel Goleman, Richard E. Boyatzis, & Annie McKee (2013)

http://www.thinkingpartners.com/wp-content/uploads/2014/02/Leadership_Competencies.pdf

Self-awareness

Emotional self-awareness: Leaders know their emotions so they can recognize how their feelings affect them and their job performance. They also know their core values, which can guide them to the best course of action, even in complex situations.

Accurate self-awareness: In addition to knowing their values, leaders know their strengths and limitations. They are open to suggestion for improvement and welcome constructive criticism and feedback without being defensive.

Self-confidence: Leaders know their abilities accurately and are self-assured without overstating their abilities. They also openly admit their mistakes or faults without avoiding them or blaming others.

Self-management

Self-control: Leaders who manage their emotions and impulses do not act inappropriately or allow their emotions to affect their performance negatively. Instead, they can redirect their emotions in positive ways. In addition, people respect leaders who don't panic in stressful situations.

Transparency: Leaders who live their values build trust because others know the reasons and beliefs behind their actions. They embody what they expect from others, so they cannot be accused of saying one thing and doing another.

Adaptability: Organizations are often ambiguous and ever changing, so leaders are flexible in their actions or judgments without losing their focus or energy.

Achievement: Leaders have high personal standards that drive them to high performance both for themselves and for their organizations. They set challenging but attainable goals and are never satisfied with mediocrity.

Initiative: Leaders are self-driven and constantly think of new ways to improve the organization. More importantly, they act on their ideas and inspire others to help carry out their plans.

Optimism: Leaders who expect the best inspire others to be the best. Leaders who fixate on problems and expect the worst do not inspire hope.

Social awareness

Empathy: Leaders who truly care about others, both inside and outside of the organization, establish bonds that help build trust and confidence. They also work more effectively with others because they can sense and understand others' points of view.

Organizational awareness: Leaders understand organizational and interpersonal dynamics. They not only navigate the political forces, they guide the values contributing to the political forces.

Service: Leaders seek to serve others, not to be served. They must ensure the organization meets the needs of the people within the organization as well as the people the organization serves.

Relationship management

Inspiration: Leaders inspire others to believe in their vision through both their words and actions. They do not force others to believe in their values but show why their values are worth believing.

Influence: Leaders are compelling and engaging. They know how to modify their message depending on the audience and know how to gain support from diverse groups.

Developing others: Leaders cultivate people's abilities and are natural coaches and mentors. They help others grow as they help the organization grow. Leaders are continually learning and teaching.

Change catalyst: Leaders are strong advocates for change, even in the faces of opposition. They recognize the need for change, challenge existing beliefs, and find ways to overcome barriers to change.

Conflict management: Leaders are able to manage conflicts by understanding different perspectives, acknowledging different points of view, and finding common areas of agreement.

Teamwork and collaboration: Leaders build collegiality, cooperation, commitment, and a spirit of group identity. They understand accomplishments are only achieved through collective, not individual, efforts.

Lesson 31

PORTFOLIO, DISTINGUISHING CAPSTONE PROJECT, JOB SEARCH, AND INTERVIEWS

"I just want a job . . ."

Essential Question: How do I increase my chances of getting a job?

Objectives: Student will demonstrate knowledge about the importance of professional portfolios and preparation in the job search process.

CACREP Standards

Student will

- demonstrate knowledge about the professional organizations, preparation standards, and credentials relevant to the practice of school counseling. (G.5.2.l)

MPCAC Standards

- Professional counselor identity, ethical behavior, and social-justice practices
- Human development and wellness across the life span
- Ecological, contextual, and social-justice foundations of human development
- Counseling, consultation, and social-justice-advocacy theories and skills
- Career and life development

Video Spark

https://www.ted.com/talks/angela_lee_duckworth_the_key_to_success_grit

Angela Lee Duckworth: Grit: The Power of Passion and Perseverance

INTRODUCTION: EMPLOYMENT OUTLOOK

The Bureau of Labor Statistics (2015) reports that employment projections for professional school counselors are positive with a projected growth 12% from 2012 to 2022. This statistic is based on the projected increase in enrollment in schools and higher education. State and local funding, however, can influence the number of available school counseling positions. School counselors as advocates and leaders can work to influence local and state funding by being proactive and communicating the need for school counselors through data, accountability, and identification of student needs. So—how do you get the job? Professional school counselors can prepare for the job search through development of a portfolio, preparing for the interview, and reflection on the process. As you reflect on this process, realize that a job search can be a stressful process. Stress is normal and to be expected. Seek support in your colleagues, supervisor, and university faculty.

PORTFOLIO

A professional portfolio is a collection of selected materials that represent the school counselor's experience, competencies, areas of interest, training, and philosophy of professional school counseling. Using this book as a structure for the portfolio, the school counselor will have developed materials such as developmental standards-based curricula, assessment of the curricula, a needs assessment, materials to run small groups, and a capstone project. As students develop these materials, they may ask me about a grade for one of the assignments (e.g., classroom lessons). My response to them is always—"At this point, the question is not about a grade, but about how you want to present yourself professionally in your portfolio. Each assignment is designed to become part of your professional portfolio." A level of excellence and professionalism should be the standard.

Portfolios may be hard copies of materials in a binder, but educators are also using e-folios. An e-folio is an electronic portfolio. There are many Web-based platforms for e-folio development. Your university may already be associated with one of these platforms. If not, a simple Web search will provide you with many options.

What to Put in the Portfolio

The materials in your professional portfolio are determined solely by you. The materials should be presented in a clear and concise format. You or the interviewer should be able to easily access each item in your portfolio. The following checklist identifies items that can be included in a portfolio.

INTERNSHIP PORTFOLIO CHECKLIST

Recommended Materials:

_____ Binder (Remember—this is how you are representing your professional work)

_____ Clear plastic sheet protectors

_____ Section dividers

Professional Experience:

_____ Resume*

_____ Letter of interest/Cover letter*

_____ Letters of recommendation

School Counselor Requirements:

_____ Clearances

_____ Certificates

_____ Liability insurance

Philosophies

_____ Philosophy of counseling

_____ Philosophy of education

Responsive Services:

_____ Curriculum sample (lesson planning)

_____ Group counseling outline

_____ Letter of recommendation example

_____ Postsecondary planning

Distinguishing Capstone Project

_____ Summary or materials of your capstone project

Scholarly Accomplishments (e.g., publications or presentations)

_____

_____

Professional Development

Certifications, trainings at your workplace or that you have done for professional development.

*Activity

Visit the university career center and work with them to develop your resume.

****

Activity

Print out the portfolio checklist and keep track of what you have accomplished as you progress through practicum and internship.

****

Activity

Reflect on how you are progressing and the materials you would like to include in your portfolio and/or identify materials that you would like to revise and then include in your portfolio.

____

____

____

____

____

____

Capstone Project

What is a capstone project? Capstone projects vary from university to university. Some universities focus the capstone project on a comprehensive case study paper and/or presentation. Others universities assign a career portfolio for their capstone project featuring the intern's work. The focus of the capstone project for the purposes of this book is on "***Making a Difference in the School Community***."

Let's walk through the steps taken to develop a Making a Difference in the School Community capstone project.

<u>Step One</u>: The counselor-in-training views the school from a systemic perspective. Taking on this perspective will give the counselor in training a comprehensive view of the needs and strengths of the school community. In addition, taking on a systemic perspective can provide counselors insight into the worldview of administrators.

Step Two: Develop a list of areas you think might benefit from some attention. Make an appointment with your site supervisor to present your list. Collaborate with your site supervisor on what area(s) might be feasible to target for your capstone project. At this point, you and your supervisor will identify one or two areas that would benefit from improvement or change (e.g., a program for students academically at risk; a newsletter for the counseling department).

Step Three: Now that the general areas are identified, develop options for a capstone project that would improve these areas. You will present these options to your site supervisor. Have the project ideas well developed and researched before the meeting with your supervisor.

Step Four: Present your project ideas to your site supervisor. During this meeting, brainstorm the positives and potential challenges to implementing the projects. Once you and your supervisor have agreed on a project, put together a presentation on your idea with concrete, specific plans and all related information. With your supervisor, present this information to the administration and other stakeholders for approval.

Step Five: After the presentation, get approval from the stakeholder to move forward with your capstone project.

Step Six: Identify the resources you will need to implement your project and begin!

Make a difference in the school community projects vary greatly depending on the needs of the school. Below are capstone projects implemented by my wonderful counselors-in-training!

- Established a peer tutoring program for academically at-risk students
- Prom Dress Event—Donated prom dresses provided to students for free; day of prom—community hair salons did hair and makeup free of charge for students who signed up
- Updated (a very outdated and weary) the school counseling department's website
- Developed a scholarship database
- Held a community Thanksgiving dinner for the students and families at an alternative setting
- Developed an NCAA workshop in collaboration with the PE department and coaches for parents and students. (Excellent turn out!)

Another benefit from doing a Make a Difference in the School Community capstone project is that it is memorable! A project like this is memorable to your site supervisor, the principal in the school, and to your faculty supervisor. The benefit can be seen when the school district has an opening (whether it be a substitute or a full time position) and the principal remembers you and your positive impact on the school. Additionally (and of specific interest to your faculty supervisor) one of the most consistently recurring questions asked during reference phone calls is "What has the student done to distinguish himself or herself from the other candidates?" As a faculty supervisor, I receive calls at all times of the day and the year. School districts often hire during the summer and need to reach your references.

My favorite way to emphasize the multiple benefits of this project is evidenced in the short story that follows. During the last two summers I have been shopping (one in the grocery and once in Target), my cell phone rang and I answered it. The callers were principals seeking a midsummer reference for one of the recent graduates of the school counseling program. I asked the principals to hold on for a moment until I could get to a quiet place (my car). The principals noted that they were hoping to "wrap up" this search as soon as possible and greatly appreciated that I took their call. Why am I telling you this? I tell you this because the distinguishing/capstone project is a memorable assignment that sets the student apart and gives the professor material to share in a reference phone call (in Target's parking lot). This project sets you apart as an exceptional candidate. Now you know why it is important—let's look at ideas you may have for a project at your school!

Ideas for Your Distinguishing/Capstone Project

____

____

____

____

____

The Job Search (written by Matthew Hamlet)

The old adage "getting a job is a full time job" is spot on. Matthew Hamlet, director of organizational development for an international financial services company, recommends approaching a job search as you would going to work. It is critical to have a plan on how you will approach the job market. You need to understand the market through research and target those potential employers that hire people with your skills and experiences. It is critical to be organized with a task list and timeline.

Think of the first stage of the job search process as a means of marketing yourself to a very diverse and complex employment market. You need to differentiate yourself within that competitive employment market and ensure that your personal brand comes across in your outreach. Your resume is the full-page ad that needs to attract an employer to want to hear more from you. And so, clearly define the highlights of your work and academic experiences and provide the employer with a reason for wanting to meet you and hear more. Focus your resume and cover letter on those skills and assets that are most marketable within your targeted employment market. You will want to research those employers who typically hire employees like you and use key words that are most associated with the type of role and career that you want.

You should approach all of your interactions and meetings with potential employers as an opportunity to articulate why you would be a great fit for their company and for the role. And so, you need to be prepared for those interactions—research the company and the role and be able to share with the people that you meet as to why they would want to hire you. The research and preparation will enable you to be targeted and succinct in your discussions and will show to the employer that you are interested in their company and the opportunity. Every interaction is a way for you to tell your professional story; have both an elevator (short) pitch and an introductory pitch that encapsulates who you are and what it is that you want to do. Your elevator pitch will be handy when you receive an initial phone call from an employer and your introductory speech will be a great way to kick off a face-to-face interview. Once again, it's about being prepared and focused.

The job search process is a very iterative process that can have its frustrations. Yet, by having a daily to-do list, you will remain energized around the process. Give yourself some daily targets on how many resumes that you will send to potential employers and how many networking calls that you will make. A good job-search project plan tracks the progress that you've made and the work that you've done. There are many tools and resources that are available to help support you through your search. There isn't a single tool that I would consider best for this process, but there are many tools that collectively will enable you to be successful in your search. I recommend that you leverage all of the tools that you can find.

There are many career sites and social networking sites that are specific to your profession. Ask your former colleagues and teachers about sites that they have used in their own searches. Your personal and professional network is as important as any online tool. You must let your network know that you are looking for a new role and ask them to share with you any relevant openings that they know. Share your resume with your network and give them permission to share it with folks within their networks. In most of the companies that I've worked with, one of the greatest sources of new hires was from their existing employees. Make as many connections as possible with employees that work for the organizations that you would like to work for. I am a firm believer in a revised version of an old adage—I believe that it is both what you know and who you know!

The key points are to stay focused, have an organized project plan, research, and be prepared. With every interaction that you have, you are one step closer to that dream role.

TIMELINE FOR THE JOB SEARCH

Timeline Prior to Employment	*Tasks*	✓
10–12 months	Networking	
	Identify grade level and type of schools of interest	
	Identify geographic locations of interest	
8–10 months	Networking	
	Resume and cover letter writing (Use university career center)	
	Request letters of recommendation	
6–8 months	Networking	
	Complete any testing required for certification	
	Identify employment websites for educators/school counselors	
	Identify websites for school districts of interest	
	Write application essay/educational or school counseling philosophy	
4–6 months	Networking	
	Create profiles on the online job search websites	
	Submit applications for all jobs of interest (paper and/or electronic)	
	Attend job fairs	
1–4 months	More assertive networking (since you will be available very soon!)	
	Monitor job listings, listserv, etc.	
	Monitor employment webpage of individual school district of interest	
	Consider other opportunities in school districts (e.g., substitute teaching)	

ELECTRONIC COMMUNICATION

All communication with a potential employer is an interview. Keep it professional and use appropriate vocabulary. Some recommendations are

- Your e-mail account address—is your address professional?
  - Not professional—hellokitty@hotmail.com; funlovinfrank@gmail.com
- Do include information in the subject line (e.g., Helen Hamlet School Counseling Application).

- Address the contact person by their proper professional name (e.g., Dr., Mr., Mrs., Ms.).
- Always check your spelling and grammar. (Helpful hint: Read the e-mail aloud. Mistakes are often easily identified when verbalized.)
- Use a professional tone to your communication. This is a professional communication.
- Do NOT use emoticons or abbreviations.
- Use an e-mail signature (e.g., full name, e-mail address, mailing address).

Networking

Networking opportunities occur daily. Make sure you are open to others about your job search. One young man got a job interview with a very prestigious firm because he was discussing his job search with his wife in the grocery line. Network with friends, colleagues, and other people in your world.

Excellent vehicles for networking are professional counseling organizations. Join blogs, attend conferences, volunteer, participate, and introduce yourself to others. Counselors will know about job openings in their school before the position is advertised. Network, network, network!

INTERVIEW

An interview is an opportunity to present the "best you" to potential employers. Seize the opportunity by making the most of the time you have with these influential individuals. Be prepared. Be yourself. Be professional.

- **Dress for success.** Wear clothing that is appropriate for the position you are interviewing and is appropriate for the school district and its culture (e.g., business suit, minimal jewelry, no perfume).
- **Research the school district.** For example, how many students are in the district? How many students attend the school? What community do they serve and what are the strengths and needs of that community? What initiatives are currently in progress?

Review possible interview questions. Rehearse your answers. ASCA provides a comprehensive list of possible interview questions, which are provided for you at the end of the chapter.

STAY CALM AND FOCUSED.

Turn Your Cell Phone Off!

Make a good first impression. Your interview began the moment you left your home. It's a small world—you may be sitting on the bus next to the superintendent.

Arrive on time. (I prefer to arrive 10 minutes early. Doing that reduces my stress.)

Be yourself. Smile. Be confident. Be concise. Focus—answer the question that is asked.

Remember body language. Sit up straight and be attentive. Be aware of any distracting habits you may have and try to avoid doing them during an interview (e.g., hair twirling, slouching).

Prepare questions about the school and/or school district. Most interviewers ask if you have any questions. Be prepared with great insightful questions.

Say "Thank You."

Follow up with a thank-you note.

Activity: ASCA provides possible interview questions for school counselors. Answer each one of these questions and discuss your answer with your colleagues and your supervisors.

Activity: Participate in mock interviews. Site supervisors may be available to do mock interviews, or the university's career center.

● INFORMATION FROM EXPERTS IN THE FIELD OF CAREER SERVICES

St. Xavier University

Career Services

3700 W. 103rd Street, Chicago, IL 60655

http://www.sxu.edu/student-life/career/interviewquestions_schoolcounseling.pdf

Questions Employers Might Ask at a School Counseling Interview

1. How do you see the word "leader" fitting in to your role as a counselor?
2. What is the role of the school counselor in relation to teachers, parents, administrators, and other counselors?
3. What do you see as the main role of a school counselor?
4. What influenced you to be a school counselor?
5. What is the counseling theory or approach that you most closely follow?
6. What is the most creative and innovative counseling technique you have used?
7. What innovative and new ideas would you like to employ as a school counselor?
8. How would you divide your time between meeting the immediate needs of students and keeping up with paperwork?
9. How are school personnel affected by working in a rural county vs. urban city (where there are more or less resources)? Describe your personal experience?
10. How will you evaluate your programs to meet (a) current state standards; (b) standards of best practice for a comprehensive guidance and counseling program; and (c) the ASCA National Model for School Counseling Programs?
11. How would you handle an irate parent?
12. How would you handle a passive (perhaps irresponsible) parent?
13. How would you handle a large group of students having attendance problems?

14. How do you see yourself fitting in with counselors who have many years of experience as veteran teachers?
15. How would you fit in with a large staff?
16. What is your strongest asset?
17. What do you think is the most important characteristic of a counselor?
18. What do you see as the role of a counselor in a school this large?
19. What do you know about our school that you would consider a strength? A weakness?
20. What makes you want to work at ______ School?
21. What is it that you like about working with (grade level) school students?
22. What is something new you could bring to our program?
23. How do you handle criticism?
24. How do you handle stress?
25. Are you opposed to working above and beyond school hours to get the job done?
26. Are you opposed to working at night for functions such as college night, senior night, etc.?
27. What is your experience with 504 accommodation plans?
28. What experiences have you had with transition plans?
29. How would you deal with cultural differences in a school setting?
30. Does your principal know you're applying for this job and how does he/she feel about it?
31. What technology applications do you see being useful in your work?
32. What might your professional development plan look like?
33. What do you think the role of the counselor is in preventing school violence?
34. What practical experiences have you had that make you feel capable of being a counselor?
35. What experiences have you had in working with special education students?
36. What can you provide that is different from a social worker, school psychologist, or mental health counselor?
37. When considering ethical standards and school policies, how would you handle a conflict between the two?
38. What do the most recent state standardized test results indicate about this school district and this school; and what is your role regarding standardized testing?
39. How does a school counselor assist with the implementation of ESL in building programming?
40. Describe how you would implement small-group counseling/guidance lessons?
41. Because time is a scarce resource in schools these days and because of a strong push for improved standardized test scores, best educational practices suggest that in-class guidance lessons not take away from classroom instructional minutes. How will you address this issue as a school counselor?
42. What has your experience been in working with students of color and GLBT students?

43. What is the difference between a therapist and a school counselor?
44. What is your view on collaborative consultation in the schools?
45. Tell us about a successful (satisfying) case that you have handled? And, one that was not so successful; what would you have done differently?
46. What is your experience with parenting programs?
47. Describe past interactions with parents in home visits.
48. What does your future comprehensive program look like? What is your plan for achieving this?
49. How do you handle conflict with a colleague? parent? administrator?
50. How do feel about writing letters of recommendation (HS)?
51. How do you keep yourself organized? Discuss how you multitask.
52. Where do you see yourself in the next five years?
53. Can we ask you a question in Spanish, and can you respond likewise?
54. Would you be interested in heading any extracurricular activities (i.e., club advisor)?
55. What does counseling mean to you?

What would you do if . . .

1. One of your students told you she was pregnant?
2. You suspected one of your students is being abused?
3. One of your students tells you they are being abused?
4. A student requests a teacher change because he/she doesn't like them?
5. A parent requests you to switch their child's teacher?
6. A student requests to be in the same lunch period as their friend?
7. You suspect one of your students is abusing drugs/alcohol?
8. One of your students admits to being sexually active?
9. One of your student's parents is terminally ill?
10. Your student does not get into her or his number one college choice?
11. One of your students wants to drop out of high school?
12. You overhear the makings of a fight that is about to happen?
13. One of your seniors is not going to graduate?
14. A parent asks to meet with you at 5:00 because that is the only time they can get off of work?
15. You see one of your students (or parents) in town?
16. One of your students continues to fail math (or any subject) each quarter?
17. You have a faculty member's child in your caseload?
18. One of your students talks to you about wanting to kill himself/herself?
19. One of your students told you he/she is gay?

Questions to Ask an Employer at a School Counseling Interview

1. What qualities or skills do you feel are most important for a counselor to possess?
2. What are some things that you would like to see the person in this role accomplish?
3. What would faculty, students, and parents say are the strengths of this district?
4. What type of in-service training does your district provide to counselors?
5. What are the greatest challenges that this district is currently facing?
6. What are the prospects for future growth in this community and its schools?
7. What committee work or extracurricular advising opportunities might be available?
8. Do parents and the community actively support the schools in the district?
9. What do you like best about your job?
10. What do you like best about working for this district?

***Sources:* American School Counselor Association, Illinois School Counselor Association, and American Association for Employment in Education.**

Skills/Qualities Employers Seek in School Counselors

- Adaptability/Flexibility
- Analytical Skills
- Communication Skills
- Creativity Skills
- Critical Thinking Skills
- Enthusiastic/Energetic
- Interpersonal Skills
- Listening Skills
- Organizational Skills
- Presentation Skills
- Problem-Solving Skills
- Service Oriented
- Social Perceptiveness
- Teamwork Skills

***Sources:* American School Counselor Association, Illinois School Counselor Association, and American Association for Employment in Education.**

SAMPLE THANK-YOU LETTER

10325 S. State Street

Orland Park, IL 60462

708-555-1111

kdoe@mailbox.com

March 10, 20xx

Kimberly Smith

Assistant Superintendent

Fairview School District 123

123 S. Main Street

Fairview, IL 60404

Dear Ms. Smith:

Thank you very much for interviewing me for the Guidance Counselor position with your district today. You and your colleagues provided me with a very warm reception and informative discussion.

As mentioned during our conversation, my two years as a part-time intake specialist at a runaway youth shelter has helped me develop sound counseling abilities. In addition, my school counseling internship allowed me to work with a wide array of cultural backgrounds and ability levels, and it required me to present to students and parents on key current issues such as bullying, smoking, and applying for college. All of this experience has enhanced my communication, interpersonal, organizational, and problem-solving skills, all of which would enable me to make a positive impact as a guidance counselor.

Once again, I wish to reiterate my genuine interest in the position and enthusiasm in working for the district. If you have any questions, please feel free to contact me at 708-555-1111 or at kdoe@mailbox.com. Thank you very much for your valuable time and consideration.

Sincerely,

Kerry J. Doe

INDEX